In 1850 St. Louis was the commercial capital of the West. By 1860, however, Chicago had supplanted St. Louis and become the great metropolis of the region. This book explains the rapid ascent and the abrupt collapse of the Missouri city. It devotes particular attention to the ways in which northeastern merchants fueled the rise of St. Louis. But unlike most studies of nineteenth-century cities, the book analyzes the influence of national politics on urbanization. It examines the process through which the sectional crisis transformed the role of Yankee merchants in St. Louis's development and thus triggered the fall of the first great city of the trans-Mississippi West.

Interdisciplinary Perspectives on Modern History

Editors
Robert Fogel and Stephan Thernstrom

Yankee Merchants and the Making of the Urban West

Other books in this series

Eric H. Monkkonen: *Police in urban America, 1860–1920*

Mary P. Ryan: *Cradle of the middle class: the family in Oneida County, New York, 1790–1865*

Ann Kussmaul: *Servants in husbandry in early modern England*

Tamara K. Hareven: *Family time and industrial time: the relationship between the family and work in a New England industrial community*

David Rosner: *A once charitable enterprise: hospitals and health care in Brooklyn and New York, 1885–1915*

Arnold R. Hirsch: *Making the second ghetto: race and housing in Chicago, 1940–1960*

Roy Rosenzweig: *Eight hours for what we will: workers and leisure in an industrial city, 1870–1920*

Hal S. Barron: *Those who stayed behind: rural society in nineteenth-century New England*

Jon Gjerde: *From peasants to farmers: the migration from Balestrand, Norway, to the Upper Middle West*

Ewa Morawska: *For bread with butter: the life-worlds of East Central Europeans in Johnstown, Pennsylvania, 1890–1940*

Alexander Keyssar: *Out of work: the first century of unemployment in Massachusetts*

Lance E. Davis and Robert A. Huttenback: *Mammon and the pursuit of Empire: the political economy of British imperialism, 1860–1912* (abridged edition also published)

Reed Ueda: *Avenues to adulthood: the origins of the high school and social mobility in an American suburb*

Allan G. Bogue: *The congressman's Civil War*

Joel Perlmann: *Ethnic differences: schooling and social structure among the Irish, Italians, Jews, and blacks in an American city, 1880–1935*

Stuart Blumin: *The emergence of the middle class: social experience in the American city, 1760–1900*

J. Matthew Gallman: *Mastering wartime: a social history of Philadelphia during the Civil War*

Yankee merchants and the making of the urban West
The rise and fall of antebellum St. Louis

JEFFREY S. ADLER

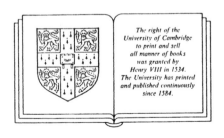

The right of the
University of Cambridge
to print and sell
all manner of books
was granted by
Henry VIII in 1534.
The University has printed
and published continuously
since 1584.

CAMBRIDGE UNIVERSITY PRESS

Cambridge
New York   Port Chester   Melbourne   Sydney

PUBLISHED BY THE PRESS SYNDICATE OF THE UNIVERSITY OF CAMBRIDGE
The Pitt Building, Trumpington Street, Cambridge, United Kingdom

CAMBRIDGE UNIVERSITY PRESS
The Edinburgh Building, Cambridge CB2 2RU, UK
40 West 20th Street, New York NY 10011–4211, USA
477 Williamstown Road, Port Melbourne, VIC 3207, Australia
Ruiz de Alarcón 13, 28014 Madrid, Spain
Dock House, The Waterfront, Cape Town 8001, South Africa

http://www.cambridge.org

First published 1991
First paperback edition 2002

A catalogue record for this book is available from the British Library

Library of Congress Cataloguing in Publication data
Adler, Jeffrey S.
Yankee merchants and the making of the urban West: the rise and
fall of Antebellum St. Louis / Jeffrey S. Adler.
          p.   cm. – (Interdisciplinary perspectives on modern history)
Includes bibliographical references.
ISBN 0 521 41284 6 (hardback)
1. St. Louis (Mo.) – Economic conditions.   2. St. Louis (Mo.) –
Commerce – History.   3. Sectionalism (United States) – History.
I. Title.   II. Series.
HC108.S2A64   1991
381′.09778′66–dc20   91-9106   CIP

ISBN 0 521 41284 6 hardback
ISBN 0 521 52235 8 paperback

Contents

Acknowledgments

Although writing history is, for the most part, a solitary exercise, many friends, colleagues, and institutions have contributed to this study. Librarians and archivists were of enormous assistance, and I am particularly indebted to Barbara Dames and Ruth Hoppe of the Inter-Library Loan Office at Harvard University's Widener Library, Florence Lathrop of Baker Library, Beverly Bishop and Stephanie Klein of the Missouri Historical Society, Mark Corriston of the Federal Archives and Records Center in Kansas City, and the staff of the Inter-Library Loan Office at the University of Florida. The project received generous support from the American Council of Learned Societies, the National Endowment for the Humanities, an Albert J. Beveridge Grant from the American Historical Association, the Division of Sponsored Research of the University of Florida, the Charles Warren Center for Studies in American History, and the Department of History of Harvard University. Carl Hindy and E. Michael Green provided crucial technical assistance for this project.

Friends and colleagues have been remarkably generous with their support and encouragement. David Colburn and Charles Thomas arranged for me to have uninterrupted research and writing time, and Kathleen Perucci served as my research assistant. I also benefited from the suggestions of Morton Keller, William Cronon, Thomas Gallant, David Colburn, Kermit Hall, Ken Winn, Patricia Limerick, Alexander von Hoffman, and especially Mark Hirsch. Diane Lindstrom and Glen Holt provided thoughtful comments on a conference paper that formed the core of Chapter Four. David Johnson, Alan Brinkley, George Pozzetta, and Jon Roberts read an early draft of the manuscript, and their suggestions improved it immeasurably. Don Doyle read two drafts and proved to be an extraordinarily helpful critic. Stephan Thernstrom directed the dissertation on which this book was based, and my debt to him is enormous. He was unfailingly generous and supportive, and he provided perceptive guidance.

My greatest debts, however, are to my wife, Donna, and to my

vi

parents. Donna spent two weeks in Missouri and read seven chapters, dozens of drafts, and too many awkward sentences. More important, her companionship has sustained me through every phase of the project. Finally, my parents, Marshall and Selma Adler, have helped me and guided me in every imaginable way.

1 Introduction

This study examines the forces that shaped the growth of western cities in antebellum America. The focus of the book is the rise and fall of St. Louis, the first major urban center of the trans-Mississippi region. During the mid-1840s St. Louis blossomed into a commercial giant and dominated the economic development of the Far West. Capital and migrants poured into the city, and it became a boomtown. Denied economic sustenance, rival trading centers withered and faded into obscurity. Cahokia, Kaskaskia, and Alton, for example, remained insignificant towns lost in a region controlled by the leading city of the Mississippi valley.[1] Moreover, the growth of St. Louis shaped the economic development of the West, determining the flow of eastern capital and migrants to the area, the vitality of its trading partners, and the role of the region in the national economy.

The sources of St. Louis's vitality, however, have remained unknown. Scholars have not explained why St. Louis outdistanced its rivals and became the dominant city in the West. Nor have historians explained why the city failed to maintain its position as the commercial capital of the West.[2] During the late 1850s Chicago supplanted St. Louis and became the leading city of the region, abruptly transforming the economic development of the region. This study analyzes the forces that sparked the rise and triggered the fall of St. Louis.[3] It also considers the ways in which those forces spurred the development of Chicago, the greatest boomtown in nineteenth-century America.

In the early competition for regional dominance, St. Louis was an unlikely winner. Cities grew at their fastest pace in American history during the antebellum period, and St. Louis was among the fastest-growing major cities for much of the era. Although contemporaries insisted that St. Louis had been "blessed" by nature, formidable obstacles disrupted the city's development.[4] Most nineteenth-century boomtowns experienced long periods of uninterrupted growth. For St. Louis, however, short bursts of economic development punctuated prolonged stagnation and frequent crises.

1

If nature "elevated" the city to greatness, it also contributed to the bumpy and uneven ascent of the city. To be sure, geography stimulated the growth of St. Louis. Located at the confluence of the Mississippi and Missouri rivers and just north of the junction of the Ohio and the Mississippi, the city seemed to be ideally situated for commerce. St. Louis became the jumping-off point for settlers migrating to the frontier and the principal trading post on the river system of the Far West.[5] But this location created problems as well.

Nature discouraged some migrants from settling in St. Louis and insured that others would never leave the city. The "miasmic" winds of the Mississippi valley, residents and visitors believed, descended upon the city and introduced disease and plague to St. Louis. Each summer these breezes blanketed the area and brought yellow fever, which killed large numbers of residents, particularly children. According to one editor, July and August were "very unfavorable to children."[6] Cholera epidemics, which struck the city in 1832 and 1849, also claimed large numbers of residents and blackened the city's reputation. The 1849 epidemic, for example, killed over 10 percent of the population of St. Louis, and an additional third of the city's inhabitants fled into the countryside, literally hoping to outrun the disease.[7] Smallpox, intermittent fever, and malaria decimated the local population as well.[8] One experienced traveler likened summer in St. Louis to the "Black Hole of Calcutta."[9] Charles Dickens, however, tried to be restrained in his description of the city. St. Louis, he noted in 1842, was as healthy as any territory with "vast tracts of undrained swampy land around it."[10]

Other obstacles flowed directly from the natural blessings of the great river of the West. Changes in the channel of the Mississippi River, for example, threatened to make St. Louis a landlocked river town. An enormous sandbar, called Bloody Island, emerged near the wharf area and redirected the flow of the river away from St. Louis and toward the Illinois shore.[11] On other occasions, the problem was just the opposite, and the Mississippi flowed too close to the city, flooding the levee and submerging the local business district in the muddy water of the river.[12] The transportation system spawned by the Mississippi also posed certain dangers. In 1849, at the height of the cholera epidemic, a fire spread from the steamer *White Cloud* to the levee area and consumed much of the business district of the city.[13] The editor of the *Missouri Republican*, perhaps with a touch of irony, boasted that "were it not for the broken walls, choked up streets, and smoldering ruins, no one would ever discover that a fire, and particularly one of such magnitude, had taken place in our midst."[14] The natural advantages of the city brought disease, flood, and fire.

Nor was the man-made atmosphere well suited to city building. In an age in which aggressive legislators used the legal system to spur urban growth, the state assembly of Missouri repeatedly dedicated itself to creating a legal and institutional environment that would prevent the growth of St. Louis.[15] Missouri legislators rejected the banking and corporate reforms that stimulated economic development in cities such as New York and Boston; St. Louis had no commercial banking facilities until the late 1850s.[16]

Internal improvements, another well-established source of urban prosperity, also contributed little to the city's growth. In the era of the steamboat and the canal, the city was served by no canals. Moreover, St. Louis residents contracted "railroad fever" during the antebellum period and invested more in railroad development than their Chicago counterparts, though local construction seemed doomed to failure.[17] Institutional and financial problems slowed progress. Bad luck plagued Missouri railroad builders as well. For example, one of the first major achievements for the city's railroad men, the much-publicized opening of a section of the Pacific Railroad, ended in tragedy when the train, filled with local dignitaries and politicians, crashed through a new wooden bridge and plunged into the river below. Thirty-one passengers died in the wreck, including the chief construction engineer of the railroad.[18] Although boosters tried desperately to manufacture growth, they enjoyed little success.

The economy of St. Louis was unusually fragile as well. Business cycles repeatedly and profoundly disrupted the local marketplace. The financial downturns that slowed the growth of other cities nearly arrested the growth of St. Louis. For example, the Panic of 1819 interrupted the city's development for almost a decade, and the effects of the depressions of the late 1830s and the late 1850s lingered almost as long.[19] Every national or regional disruption undermined the city's economic vitality.

Yet St. Louis mushroomed. In spite of disease, sandbars, a hostile legal and institutional atmosphere, the absence of banks, canals, and railroads, and a frail economy, the city blossomed and dominated its rivals. John Kasson, who later moved to Iowa and served in Congress, suggested that disasters "spent themselves vainly against the prosperity of this city, like waves at the foot of an eternal sea-rock."[20] At midcentury, St. Louis was the eighth largest city in the nation, and its trading hinterland stretched from the upper Midwest deep into the lower Mississippi valley and from the lower Ohio valley far into the western frontier.

Moreover, in antebellum America growth generated growth. As St. Louis became a cog in the national economy, eastern businessmen relocated to the city to take advantage of its new role in the commerce of the West. Thus, St. Louis emerged as the last major supply center before the frontier, and westward settlers increasingly chose to buy their supplies in the city. Commercial profits soared; more business-men migrated to the city; and growing numbers of settlers opted to purchase provisions in the bustling marketplace. Investment and migration patterns became well established; the advantages enjoyed by a leading city, geographers have noted, are cumulative and self-perpetuating.[21] Investors and migrants chose St. Louis during the 1840s because it was the major urban center of the region, and St. Louis remained the major urban center of the region because inves-tors and migrants chose it over smaller cities in the Mississippi valley.

If St. Louis was an unlikely winner in the battle for regional supremacy during the 1840s, the city was also an unlikely loser in the same contest a decade later. At the height of its prosperity, after having weathered epidemics, riots, fires, floods, railroad disasters, and economic downturns, St. Louis collapsed.[22] Although settlers and businessmen preferred to invest in established markets, migrants and capitalists abandoned St. Louis during the late 1850s and directed their attention and their resources to a smaller and less-developed city – Chicago. Despite its considerable headstart over Chicago, its celebrated advantages, and the inertia generated by regional supre-macy, St. Louis lost its leading position. Only one city could domi-nate the West, and at the start of Chicago's challenge, St. Louis's advantages seemed insurmountable.[23] But by 1860 Chicago had sup-planted St. Louis. Although the Missouri city did not wither like its old rival Alton, St. Louis was a declining city with a shrinking hinterland by the beginning of the Civil War.

Neither contemporary observers nor modern analysts have ex-plained the rise – or the fall – of the first major urban center of the antebellum West. Furthermore, historians have seldom explained the process through which a city dominated its region or the forces that shaped the rise and fall of western boomtowns.[24] Instead, writers and scholars have usually offered deterministic or teleological answers.

Many antebellum observers believed that nature ordained the growth of cities. The "natural laws of commerce," they argued, elevated St. Louis to greatness.[25] According to popular economic theory, commerce followed meridians.[26] Cities situated on rivers running from north to south would become trading centers where the products of northern regions would be exchanged for those of south-ern regions. St. Louis's location, at the break-point of the major river in the West, insured that the city would dominate its rivals. Amateur geographers and travel writers also predicted that the Mississippi valley would form the heart of the national economy. They noted that the "Father of the Waters" divided the United States into two roughly equal parts. Because natural currents of commerce focused the interior trade at St. Louis, the city was destined, they said, to become the largest trading center of the great valley and the next major emporium of the western world. According to Robert Sears, the author of *A Pictorial Description of the United States*, "nature never formed a plateau of ground more admirably adapted to the site of an immense city."[27]

Some contemporary thinkers formulated complex theories to predict urban growth. William Gilpin, for example, expanded and embellished the ideas of Alexander von Humboldt to explain the rise of cities and of civilizations. Gilpin reported that the "Isothermal Zodiac," the great natural band of human progress, determined the course of urban development. St. Louis, he noted, lay along the "Axis of Intensity" and therefore in the path of the natural current of civilization. Thus, it would ultimately assume great prominence, as had Rome, London, and New York before it.[28]

Like many urban theorists of the period, Gilpin developed ideas that reflected the imagination of a visionary and the heart of a land speculator. He announced the destiny of St. Louis, for example, shortly after settling in Missouri. Gilpin also purchased a parcel of land near Independence and predicted greatness for the future metropolis called "Gilpintown." When none of these sites fulfilled his expectations (and his political career stalled), Gilpin left Missouri. After moving to Colorado, reworking his calculations, and investing in a number of business ventures in the state, William Gilpin concluded that the true heir apparent to Athens, Rome, and London, the city situated at the center of the swath covered by the Isothermal Zodiac, was Denver.[29] Other theorists lacked Gilpin's creativity, though they shared his promotional zeal.[30]

More conventional writers substituted description for theory. The ascent of the leading city of the Far West always seemed to have been inevitable. Visitors to St. Louis during the height of its prosperity concluded that the Missouri city had been destined to dominate the West.[31] Nature had blessed it, they blithely explained, and no rival would challenge its supremacy. The city's advantages were incomparable; its economic empire was unparalleled; and its future was glorious. A decade later, however, Chicago dominated the commerce of the West, and travel writers and financial reporters argued that nature had chosen the Illinois city.[32] Its growth, they agreed, had been inevitable. In short, most observers used the conditions of the present to gauge the course of destiny. Successful cities must have been blessed by nature. Their growth had been inevitable.

Modern scholars sometimes rely on similar arguments. The ascent of Chicago, for example, is often assumed to have been inevitable. Some writers have traced the rise and fall of regional entrepôts to shifts in trade currents. Commercial traffic ran from north to south during the Jacksonian era, and thus, according to this theory, St. Louis enjoyed prosperity during the age of the steamboat. But the course of trade changed during the 1850s, and, as a consequence, Chicago became the leading city of the region. Shifting currents of commerce, therefore, triggered the rise and fall of St. Louis and the inevitable ascent of Chicago.[33]

Other scholars link the development of the leading cities of the Far West to railroad construction. Chicago, according to this view, was destined to become a railroad capital, and, therefore, the city ultimately dominated its rivals. One leading historian of Chicago noted that the city "found itself" at the center of an enormous railroad network.[34] The process was somehow inevitable; natural and undeniable forces directed railroad capital to Chicago and thus fueled the city's growth.[35] This argument, a reviewer observed, assumes that "railroad construction is an independent variable."[36]

But railroad construction was not an independent variable, and the rise of Chicago, like the fall of St. Louis, was no more inevitable than any other historical development. Destiny did not dictate the course of railroad construction; rather, builders and investors determined the course of railroad construction. Too often, historians have concluded that Chicago was destined to become the heart of the western rail system. As a result, scholars have seldom asked why railroad builders and investors chose to build lines centered in Chicago.

Until the early 1850s railroad financiers did not believe that Chicago constituted the obvious western rail hub. Many railroad investors during this period considered St. Louis a more promising site for railroad construction.[37] They hoped to build commercial empires around well-established cities that offered both rail and river transportation. Some influential commercial writers and promoters also argued that overland transportation would complement river traffic.[38] William Gilpin predicted that rail lines would be constructed along the "Axis of Intensity," enhancing the supremacy of river towns.[39] In the early 1850s railroad builders agreed that the new mode of transportation should serve older forms of transportation. For example, numerous roads served Cairo, Illinois, the town located at the confluence of the Ohio and the Mississippi rivers, and St. Louis lines attracted considerable interest from early investors.[40] Moreover, many contemporaries believed that St. Louis was likely to become the heart of the nation's rail system.[41] Modern scholars have also noted that nineteenth-century railroads most often reinforced the initial advantages enjoyed by existing commercial centers. "New transportation systems," according to Diane Lindstrom and John Sharpless, tended to "recapitulate the old," and construction supported and enhanced established trading patterns more often than it revolutionized economic development.[42]

Thus, the development of Chicago's railroad network was far from inevitable. Instead, it was one part of a larger change in migration and investment patterns during the 1850s. Financing ventures that centered in Chicago, a small, underdeveloped city until the 1850s, represented a new strategy for eastern capitalists and reflected a sharp break in economic thinking.[43] Powerful political and economic forces encouraged investors to shift their entrepreneurial efforts away from St. Louis and toward Chicago businesses. The pressures and processes that generated this shift accelerated the ascent of Chicago. Eastern investment strategies, acting in combination with locational forces, determined the course of railroad construction; the decisions of railroad builders were an effect – not a cause – of larger changes in the development of the urban West.

Some historians have traced Chicago's railroad network and its supremacy to the energy of local boosters.[44] They have argued that the aggressive promoters of Chicago enabled that city to defeat St. Louis and to control the commerce of the West. This view, most forcefully articulated by Wyatt Winton Belcher in 1947, holds that St. Louis boosters remained committed to the steamboat in the age of the railroad. Such a decision, Belcher insisted, reflected the southern backgrounds of local leaders and the "innate conservatism" that their roots generated.[45] According to Belcher's thesis, the complacent and shortsighted boosters of St. Louis doomed their city to defeat, while the "more astute business leadership" of Chicago, possessing knowledge that eluded the bumbling merchants of Missouri, embraced transportation improvements and led their city to victory and to regional supremacy.[46] Belcher's argument has been widely accepted.[47]

This interpretation, however, is flawed. St. Louis boosters did not reject the railroad in favor of the steamboat, and they were neither complacent nor blind to the benefits of overland transportation. Even before midcentury, for example, St. Louis editors concluded that the railroad "would be of incaluable [sic] advantage to the mercantile interest of our city."[48] During the height of the competition between the cities, St. Louis residents embraced the railroad as energetically as did their Chicago counterparts.[49] Again and again, local leaders and politicians insisted that the city "must have Railroads."[50] By some measures, St. Louis boosters made greater efforts to build railroads than did Chicago leaders. Merchants in the Missouri city pledged their own capital to hasten construction, and residents taxed themselves to support local railroads, a measure that Chicago residents avoided.[51] In short, St. Louis railroads did not lag behind Chicago lines for want of local support or because the city's leaders lacked foresight.

Belcher's thesis assumes that boosterism, like railroad construction, was an independent variable. He noted that during the late 1850s and the 1860s St. Louis boosters often rejected the aggressive growth schemes that enjoyed immense popularity in Chicago. The business leaders of St. Louis, Belcher concluded, seemed overly cautious and even ambivalent about their war with Chicago. But, as Don Doyle demonstrated in his study of Jacksonville, Illinois, the tone of boosterism is often more an effect than a cause of urban development.[52] Doyle explained that Jacksonville leaders redefined their aspirations when it became apparent that the town would never become the "Athens of the West." Boosters then embraced values that reflected local conditions and attempted to make a virtue out of necessity by celebrating the advantages of small-town life.[53] Doyle discovered that local leaders tried to project these new goals backward in time, insisting that they had always wanted Jacksonville to be a quiet, harmonious, small town.[54] Similarly, after Chicago's ascendance became undeniable, St. Louis boosters seemed conservative and complacent. They denigrated the promotional efforts of Chicago merchants and questioned the moral content of city dwellers who cherished only economic development.[55] A decade earlier, when the battle for regional supremacy was undecided, St. Louis boosters had espoused very different goals for themselves and very different aspirations for their city.[56]

Both the deterministic explanation and the booster thesis argued by Belcher obscure the process through which St. Louis – and then Chicago – blossomed. These analyses often assume that internal forces fueled the growth of major western cities. Moreover, scholars who have linked urban development in the region to the infusion of eastern capital have emphasized local promotional efforts rather than the eastern response to these efforts, the influence of outside investors, or the role that such investment played in the growth of western cities. By concentrating on local factors and internal sources of growth, these historians divorce urban development from the broader social, political, and economic currents of antebellum America. As a result, they overlook the larger processes and pressures that affected the growth of cities in the Far West during this period.[57]

External forces shaped the rise and fall of western cities. Young, growing trading posts relied on outside sources of sustenance.[58] The demographic development of western boomtowns, for example, depended on long-distance migration; western cities grew by attracting outsiders.[59] Similarly, newcomers established institutions and marshaled their growth in undeveloped trading centers such as St. Louis. They influenced the character of local associations and the goals of local clubs and charitable organizations. Even the legal system had external roots. For example, in 1821, when Missouri joined the Union, a new legal system was born. Newcomers to the state brought strong ideas about the role of government, and they translated their convictions into law; the state constitution as well as the legislation enacted by the new assembly reflected the migration routes that peopled Missouri.[60] The ideological traditions and the legal conventions of older states shaped the character of the legal system of Missouri and its principal city.

The economic building blocks of urban growth flowed principally from external sources as well. Unlike older, well established eastern cities, for which growth often emanated from subregional sources, frontier trading centers lacked capital markets, credit networks, and financial institutions.[61] Outside investors and newcomers supplied these resources and stimulated commercial development.[62] Moreover, for western boomtowns, venture capital flowed not from local or hinterland sources but from the cities along the Atlantic seaboard, and without the financial nourishment provided by distant entrepreneurs, frontier towns withered and died. With such eastern assistance, they could flourish.[63] Although regional and subregional conditions influenced this process, outsiders directed the rise and fall of transmontane trading centers.

Eastern interest in western cities such as St. Louis often began as a part of the ideological debates that raged in the older states. Many mid-nineteenth-century easterners, particularly members of the urban middle class, believed that western society was unmolded. Just as the maturation of St. Louis or Chicago could be shaped, the development of the Far West could be tailored.[64] A few Americans argued that the region needed to be reclaimed, either from Germans or from Catholics.[65] Others insisted that the savagery and the barbarism of the frontier needed to be conquered.[66] In addition, some Americans believed that the West held the future of America. The trans-Mississippi region, they suggested, represented the destiny of the nation. In the Far West the American character could be "regenerated" or perfected, and the nation's mission could be realized.[67] According to the historian Rush Welter, "the West served as a means of dramatizing fundamental conservative convictions."[68] Thus, prominent ministers announced their "claims" on the region, and migrants crossed the great river in order to remake the West in the image of a rarefied East.[69] "The effect," Welter argued, "was to define the West in the light of eastern needs; to shape its image according to eastern concerns."[70] For both ideological and logistical reasons, the major cities of the West figured prominently in plans to improve the nation by colonizing the frontier.

While thinkers such as Lyman Beecher and Edward Everett viewed the Far West in ideological terms, more practical-minded writers often subscribed to similar theories. Molding the development of the West could not only buttress the political institutions of the older states but also promise to sustain the economic and social development of established areas. If properly nurtured, the Far West, through its leading trading centers, could become an important outpost or colony, insuring the economic well-being of the older states. Markets would expand; profits would soar; upward mobility would continue; individual economic and political independence would be protected; and the "destiny" of the nation would be assured.

If relatively few migrants or investors viewed the region in such grandiose terms, many settlers and capitalists measured the attractions of the West in terms of the needs of the East.[71] Merchants, for example, poured capital into trans-Mississippi commercial ventures to serve the needs of their eastern businesses. Similarly, many Atlantic coast manufacturers established western outlets when factory production exceeded eastern demand. These New Yorkers and New Englanders – termed "Yankees" by St. Louis observers – directed surplus goods, extra capital, and ambitious clerks to the western city that seemed most responsive to their needs.[72] As a result, the perceptions and the interests of the residents of older states shaped the development of the leading cities of the Far West. Moreover, the forces that changed those perceptions transformed the urban West.

The rise and fall of St. Louis and the city's rivalry with Chicago, however, also occurred in an age of sectional expansion. Like other national issues, the debate over the future of slavery influenced the currents that fueled the growth of western cities. Just as the Panic of 1837 and the collapse of the China trade affected the flow of settlers and capital to the urban West, the tensions between the North and the South altered the development of young cities. But because sectionalism unleashed such powerful passions, its effects proved to be particularly dramatic; the sectional crisis abruptly transformed the urban West. In political and economic terms, Northerners and Southerners battled to control the cities of the region in order to protect their own institutions. Historians have long recognized that the sectional crisis influenced perceptions of the West and that the contest over the future of slavery transcended the bounds of formal politics. Few scholars, however, have considered the ways in which this controversy reshaped the development of western cities such as St. Louis and Chicago.[73]

The leading cities of the Far West assumed a special role in discussions of sectional expansion. Some contemporary observers believed that the principal trading centers of the region represented potential beachheads in the crusade to determine the character of the new western territories. Much as settlers during the 1840s had viewed frontier cities as jumping-off points for the wilderness, ideologues during the 1850s considered the cities of the Far West to be possible staging points for efforts to spread sectional culture.[74]

These assumptions proved to be both prescriptive and proscriptive. Radicals tried to control the political climate of western trading centers in order to make them suitable colonies or outposts for the migrants and for the institutions of a particular section.[75] The perception that a city had been conquered by the enemy, however, transformed the relationship between a section and its lost outpost. Extremists urged their followers to shun the city, and migrants avoided it as well, fearing a hostile reception from local residents.[76]

This debate also colored discussions of the economic attractions of the leading cities of the Far West. Many financial writers insisted that the economic systems of the North and the South were incompatible. Slavery, according to Northern observers, undermined the free-labor system.[77] The economic system of the North, commercial writers in the South warned, endangered the slave economy. As a consequence, during the 1850s northern entrepreneurs who looked to western markets in order to expand their businesses avoided trading centers identified with the South.[78] Their counterparts to the south demonstrated similar caution, reflecting economic considerations rather than political passions.[79] Thus, at the same time that the North and the South were competing to define the character of western cities, perceptions of this struggle determined the flow of people and resources to the major trading centers of the region.

In the West, where cities relied on external sources to sustain growth, sectionalism represented the ultimate external force. During the 1850s – the decisive period in the development of St. Louis – legal developments, migration decisions, investment strategies, and railroad construction plans were formulated within the context of the crisis between the North and the South. As a result, the debate over the future of slavery profoundly altered the development of St. Louis and that of its principal rival.

In sum, national and regional forces fueled the rise and triggered the fall of the first major city west of the Mississippi River. Shortsighted local business leaders did not stunt the development of St. Louis, and farsighted boosters did not ignite the growth of Chicago. Nor was either process inevitable. Rather, sectionalism, financial crises, and cultural movements shaped the growth of western cities and the outcome of the battle between St. Louis and Chicago.

2 *"These Yankee notions will not suit Missouri"*

Although newcomers, nonresidents, and external forces influenced the development of all western urban centers, the growth of antebellum St. Louis was unusually dependent on outsiders and unusually susceptible to outside pressures. Every frontier town faced capital shortages, trading obstacles, and institutional barriers, and the merchants and boosters of every young trading center looked to outside investors and migrants during times of crisis. Furthermore, towns that secured external assistance often flourished and defeated their regional rivals.[1] But for most western cities, growth and institutional development reduced this dependence. Merchants and bankers in well-established urban centers relied on local sources of economic sustenance, and large cities usually weathered crises without outside assistance. St. Louis, however, remained dependent on outsiders long after the city had become a major entrepôt.

Unlike other western commercial centers, St. Louis blossomed without shedding the "colonial" condition of urban youth. Rather, easterners supplied capital, manufactured goods, entrepreneurial talent, and cultural leadership; profits and raw materials flowed to the Atlantic coast as well.[2] Although the city commanded the commerce of the Far West at midcentury, external forces controlled its economy and its future. In addition, distant observers continued to believe that the character of the city could be molded from afar, and thus outsiders continued to intervene in local affairs. Even boosters in Missouri's largest urban center recognized St. Louis's unusual dependence on outside influence. For example, in the mid-1850s, when the population of the city exceeded one hundred thousand, local writers credited Yankee newcomers with the rise of St. Louis.[3]

Political and cultural battles within the state prevented St. Louis from outgrowing its colonial status. During the eighteenth century the area around St. Louis was largely unsettled. After the Louisiana Purchase, however, migrants poured into the trans-Mississippi West, generating important changes in the region. As St. Louis grew, the

13

character of the town and the interests of the local population began to diverge from those of rural Missourians.[4] Distinct settlement patterns reinforced these differences and sparked increasing hostility between the trading post and the farmers of the region.[5] The ideological debates that raged during the age of Jackson intensified this conflict and shaped the institutional development of Missouri in ways that distorted the growth of St. Louis.

In short, the political contest that erupted during the early years of statehood affected St. Louis for decades. The tensions between rural Missourians and the inhabitants of the state's principal commercial center exaggerated the city's long-term dependence on outsiders. Thus, the early history of the city, the period before St. Louis became a major urban center, defined the character of subsequent economic growth, contributing dramatically to the rise and fall of antebellum St. Louis and to the remaking of the urban West that resulted.

As Richard Wade noted, cities spearheaded the settlement of the frontier.[6] French merchants, for example, established a settlement at St. Louis decades before sizable numbers of farmers migrated to the area – and clashed with urban residents. It was the commercial potential of the frontier that attracted the first Europeans to St. Louis. In the aftermath of the Seven Years War, the French governor of Louisiana, hoping to bolster the colony's war-depleted treasuries, attempted to restore prosperity by granting trading monopolies to New Orleans merchants.[7] Gilbert Maxtent, a recipient of one such exclusive privilege, formed a partnership with Jean Francois Le Dée and Pierre de Laclède and agreed to establish a trading post in "the upper Louisiana."[8] In 1763 Laclède first observed the site of St. Louis – in his account of the founding, Laclède claimed to have prophesied that this position "might become, hereafter, one of the finest cities in America."[9] A year later, in 1764, Laclède and his party settled in the area. Despite their efforts, however, St. Louis remained little more than an obscure outpost in the wilderness for the next four decades.[10]

The structure of the early fur trade hardly lent itself to city building. Rather, the St. Louis fur trade, which consisted of a series of loose alliances with the Indians of the region, owed its success to the isolation of the town. Located far from the line of agricultural settlement and thus deep in the wilderness and close to rich trapping grounds, St. Louis was an ideal outpost for the industry. But because most of the surrounding Indian nations were under British influence, the fur traders of St. Louis remained close to the protective confines of the town and relied on the Indians to deliver the pelts.[11] Moreover, the early fur trade generated scant economic growth in the region. It required neither capital nor commercial connections. Instead, local traders sustained and strengthened their businesses by establishing personal relationships with the Indians and with other traders. Manual Lisa, for example, accelerated his rise to the top of the industry when he married into a prominent Omaha family and thus cemented an alliance with the nation.[12]

The town experienced little growth during the eighteenth century. St. Louis remained an isolated trading post with a small, tightly clustered population. Between the arrival of the original settlement party in 1764 and the end of the century, the population of St. Louis grew by only 425.[13] In 1800 fewer than 950 people lived in the town, and more than three-fourths of its inhabitants were involved in the fur trade, many of whom were part-time residents.[14] French rivermen, or "voyageurs," left St. Louis and worked the lower Mississippi during the winter months.[15]

The tiny permanent population of traders and rivermen provided a poor foundation for urban growth. Few of the town's fur traders possessed any wealth.[16] Moreover, the small, impoverished, and insecure population of early St. Louis barely altered the physical environment of the area, according to the western lawyer and traveler Henry Brackenridge.[17] Beyond the stone walls and towers that protected the inhabitants from the Indians of the region, Brackenridge saw only "a vast waste."[18]

The transfer of the Louisiana Territory to the United States triggered the first signs of vitality in St. Louis. The arrival of troops to the frontier safeguarded the area and provided a small market for goods. But the major turning point in the early history of St. Louis came when the western explorer Meriwether Lewis reported that the new territory was "richer in beaver and otter than any country on earth."[19] His description of the area, combined with the presence of American troops on the frontier, stimulated the fur trade and the growth of St. Louis.

Awakened to the extraordinary resources just beyond their reach, St. Louis fur traders reorganized their industry. Increasingly they relied on white trappers for their supplies of pelts, reducing their dependence on the surrounding Indian nations.[20] The scale of the fur industry exploded during this period; the riches of the upper Missouri, for example, attracted better-organized and better-financed merchants, many of whom competed with the old French families of St. Louis. The leading traders of St. Louis began to establish supply posts deeper in the wilderness. In 1808 local traders formed the Missouri Fur Company, joining forces and pooling their limited capital in order to compete with John Jacob Astor's powerful New

York-based American Fur Company.[21] During the next four decades, the export trade in pelts averaged $250,000 per year.[22]

The expansion of the fur trade created commercial opportunities for St. Louis residents, and the town became more than simply the collection point for pelts. Rather, St. Louis emerged as the jumping-off point for long expeditions into the wilderness. Moreover, St. Louis fur traders became merchants in this process, providing supplies or "fixens" for the trappers and mountain men working out of the town.[23] Even Astor relied on local traders to supply his trappers.[24] As a result, the marketplace of the town expanded, and the economy began to develop.[25]

The new government of the territory, centered in St. Louis, provided additional impetus for growth. Civil officials and army officers, for example, added to the floating population of the town and increased the number of permanent residents.[26] The War of 1812 brought more troops to the area and generated greater prosperity. The soldiers stationed in the region were also paid in St. Louis, adding $60,000 annually to the local economy and expanding the size of the domestic market.[27] Moreover, the army purchased large quantities of provisions for the troops in the region, including 643 barrels of whiskey in 1818.[28] Supplying goods for the army in the Mississippi valley, the soldiers stationed around St. Louis, and the permanent residents of the town constituted a growing and lucrative market that hastened the transformation of fur traders into merchants.[29]

The presence of troops also opened new areas for immigration, and settlers exploded into the region.[30] Increasing numbers of farmers migrated to the trans-Mississippi West during this period. In October of 1819, for example, thousands of settlers passed through St. Louis on their way to Boone's Lick in the central portion of Missouri.[31] Most of the newcomers to rural Missouri migrated from Kentucky, Tennessee, and Virginia; virtually all hailed from agricultural regions; and some owned slaves.[32] "A stranger to witness this scene," a St. Louis resident recorded in his journal in 1816, "would imagine that Kentucky, Virginia, Tennessee and the Carolinas had made an agreement to introduce us as soon as possible to the bosom of the American family."[33] Both the flow of settlers to the frontier and the settlement of the region contributed to St. Louis's new prosperity.

After more than half a century of stagnation and isolation, St. Louis burst forth as a rapidly growing town during the second decade of the century. Migrants poured into the trading center, and St. Louis experienced its first economic and demographic boom. By 1820 the population of the town exceeded forty-five hundred, having increased by 228 percent between 1810 and 1820; four-fifths of the newcomers arrived late in the decade.[34] "Some families came in the spring of 1815," one resident noted, "but in the winter, summer and autumn of 1816, they came like an avalanche."[35]

Early urban growth also transformed the character of local society. While yeoman farmers from the upper South settled in the rural parts of Missouri, land speculators, merchants, and lawyers migrated to St. Louis.[36] According to one observer, the town "witnessed the arrival of a legion of judges, lawyers, notaries, collectors of taxes, etc., etc., and, above all, a flock of vampires in the shape of land speculators."[37] Aggressive young entrepreneurs, such as Thomas Hart Benton, Missouri's first major political figure, and Peter Lindell, later the wealthiest resident of the city, headed west in search of adventure and fortune and settled in St. Louis because they believed that the town offered a promising site for enterprising newcomers.[38]

The growing population of St. Louis attracted entrepreneurs and accelerated commercial development in the town. The merchant class, for example, ballooned, and the number of stores increased more than four-fold between 1807 and 1817.[39] As a result of the expanding domestic market and the commercial and speculative efforts of the newcomers, the characteristic features of urban growth became visible. General stores began to line the principal streets, rents soared, and wages rose.[40] Moreover, the attitudes and the needs of the residents changed. Local businessmen, for example, began to demand improved streets and better market and wharf facilities.[41] In the mid-1810s St. Louis started to emerge as an important supply station for trans-Mississippi settlers, and gradually the town became a commercial center.[42]

St. Louis's newest residents also challenged the old elite of the town and the society that they had created. Lawyers, real estate speculators, and "men of business" competed with French fur traders for cultural and economic control of the town.[43] American "vampires" quickly outnumbered Europeans, and the French character of early St. Louis began to fade.[44] The most successful fur traders, however, changed with the town and retained considerable wealth and power. For example, the Chouteaus, the leading fur trading family, expanded their business empire, investing in commercial ventures and local real estate.[45] Moreover, rather than opposing the transformation occurring in the trading center, they began to join forces with many of the adventurers and to support efforts at local improvements.[46] Thus, the arrival of the newcomers stimulated changes that began to redefine the character of St. Louis from a frontier outpost to a commercial center.

This transformation, however, proceeded unevenly. In some ways, the migrants were scarcely better suited for city building than their fur-trading predecessors. Although many of them hailed from urban backgrounds, such as Joseph Charless, who printed the first newspaper west of the Mississippi and had spent time in New York, Philadelphia, Lexington, and Louisville before settling in St. Louis, few of the newcomers possessed business experience and still fewer arrived with capital; wealthier migrants opted for more-established cities, such as Cincinnati.[47] St. Louis merchants and lawyers sought stronger ties with eastern commercial centers, but they lacked the resources, the experience, and the political influence to marshal the town's development.

Structural factors slowed the development of St. Louis as well. Increasing waves of settlers crossed the Mississippi River during this period, though the region remained sparsely settled, limiting the scale of local commerce. Furthermore, because neither the new merchants of the town nor the old fur traders had access to large quantities of capital, commercial expansion was sharply constrained, and transactions with eastern merchants and capitalists remained cumbersome. Equally important, the local economy expanded without an adequate circulating medium – a problem that was legion for western cities.[48] Well after the War of 1812, for example, the barter system persisted; pelts, lead, and whiskey constituted the town's principal exchange media.[49]

During the height of the postwar boom, local merchants established two banks in St. Louis. Backed by the town's wealthiest men, the banks represented an effort to expand local commerce beyond the limitations imposed by a barter economy.[50] The transition to a money economy, however, was far from complete when the banks opened their doors; pelts and lead, for example, continued to be accepted as collateral for loans.[51] Moreover, pioneer banking, frontier commerce, and land speculation proved to be a dangerous combination in the late 1810s.

External forces arrested the growth of St. Louis before the end of the decade. In 1819 a financial panic seized the West and hit St. Louis with devastating force. Within months a decade of institutional and economic development began to fade. "Land fever," as contemporaries termed it, had been greater in Missouri and Illinois than in any other region.[52] When the financial pressure reduced the flow of westward migrants to a trickle, the Missouri speculative balloon was punctured. Suddenly deprived of the revenue from land sales and the trade generated by the flow of settlers, local merchants and speculators turned to the town's fledgling banks. The strain, however, was too great for the young banks to bear. Badly overextended and plagued by mismanagement, both banks failed.[53]

The Panic of 1819 halted the growth of St. Louis. According to Timothy Flint, the missionary and author who traveled throughout the region during this period, "the town was then stationary or perhaps retrograde."[54] Few newcomers arrived in St. Louis for nearly a decade; more than half of St. Louis's businesses failed; most of the town's stores closed; and a large proportion of the nascent merchant class fled.[55] "Destruction is hurrying upon the people in all directions," a resident observed.[56] Moreover, property values fell by over 33 percent, and rents plummeted.[57] "There is not half enough money in the country to pay laborers for digging the graves of the inhabitants," a newcomer recorded.[58] For land speculators, the fall was particularly swift. Justus Post despondently predicted that "we shall all be in jail. I believe on my soul, half of us are there already."[59]

In addition, the depression exposed ideological and cultural tensions that had been festering for nearly two decades. As St. Louis grew, the differences between the residents of the town and the inhabitants of the region became more pronounced. The agricultural areas to the west of St. Louis continued to attract settlers from Kentucky, Tennessee, the Carolinas, and Virginia. Most of the newcomers, however, possessed no bondsmen; slaves comprised only 15 percent of the population of Missouri in 1820, a smaller proportion than in the slave states of the region.[60] Rather, the migrants were yeomen farmers who crossed the Mississippi River at least in part to escape the commercial and economic changes that seemed to threaten their independence.[61]

At the same time that rural sections of the state were becoming a haven for yeomen trying to avoid the evils of commercial development, St. Louis was evolving into a small but growing commercial center.[62] Merchants and lawyers increasingly replaced the French residents of the town, assumed the reins of local government, and dominated public life in the town. Because St. Louis was the center of land exchange in the region, the town also became a small magnet for the real estate speculators and the peddlers who preyed on the westward settlers. The rise of frontier banking in St. Louis symbolized the commercial orientation of the town. Moreover, the sudden demise of the local banks confirmed the worst fears held by rural Missourians during the early 1820s.

Farmers in the interior of the state blamed St. Louis and its merchants for the Panic of 1819 and for the economic disruption that ensued.[63] Rural residents believed that banks threatened their independence.[64] According to local farmers, St. Louis speculators had introduced such institutions to the region and entangled Missouri in the financial crisis. Published reports estimating the severity of the panic and the losses incurred as a result of the bank failures reinforced these concerns. Bank customers lost $150,000 when the institutions closed; property values plunged; and farmers who lacked the currency to pay their taxes lost their land.[65]

Rural Missourians insisted that the dangerous commercial activities of St. Louis had to be stopped. The *Missouri Gazette*, for example, reported that farmers believed that St. Louis "was obnoxious to our Legislature – that its growth and influence were looked on with a jealous eye, and its pretensions such as ought to be discouraged."[66] As the economic crisis worsened, hostility toward St. Louis mushroomed and assumed an increasingly political form.

Evidence of the tensions surfaced almost immediately, and the newly formed state legislature became the forum for these grievances. Dominated by rural elements, the assembly demonstrated little sympathy – and often open disdain – for urban problems or for commercial concerns. The growing friction between St. Louis interests and those of the remainder of the state transcended party lines; the St. Louis delegation voted as a bloc – the opposing bloc consisted of the remainder of the state legislature.[67] As time passed, the battle lines sharpened and the tensions increased. Two increasingly divergent and internecine cultures took root during the early days of statehood.

The constitution of the state of Missouri, framed during the depths of the depression, reflected the anger of the rural spokesmen who controlled the legislature and thus the welling antipathy toward urban and commercial concerns.[68] Lawmakers devoted special attention to potential sources of "foreign" influence, most notably corporations and banks. For example, they rejected the legal devices that attracted outside investment and generated economic growth in the eastern states.[69] Instead, stockholders in Missouri manufactories, according to the constitution, would face personal liability for the debts of the corporation.[70] Although the lawmakers consulted the constitutions of many of the surrounding states, they relied most heavily on those of Alabama and Kentucky.[71] From the Alabama State Constitution, for example, the Missouri framers borrowed a provision that prohibited the incorporation of more than a single bank in the state.[72] Such restrictive clauses were intended to limit the influence of merchants and protect the state from eastern capitalists.

These impulses also shaped the first legislative program enacted by the new assembly. The Missouri lawmakers immediately turned their attention to the economic crisis that wracked the state. Under pressure from farmers, the legislature adopted a stay law, designed to postpone debt payment, and a state loan office. Lawmakers patterned this program after the relief efforts undertaken by a number of southern and western states.[73] The loan office and the stay law represented an attempt to provide relief during the economic crisis. But they also represented a crusade to free the yeomen of Missouri from the influence of St. Louis and its merchants. Moreover, rural spokesmen argued that the two goals were inseparable. The residents of Franklin, Missouri, for example, held a banquet to honor the legislators who voted for the relief bill. After "a splendid and elegant dinner," they thanked the lawmakers and offered toasts to "the farmers ... [who] understand their interests too well to be governed by a mercantile faction."[74] One Franklin resident hoisted his glass in the air and offered "9 cheers" to the merchants of the state. "When they have drained us of our specie," Thomas Alsop rejoiced, "we shall be drained of them."[75]

St. Louis merchants, however, objected to the relief program. The emergency legislation authorized the loan office to lend notes that would serve as a circulating medium. But this solution posed special problems for St. Louis businessmen. Because the paper issued by the state loan office could not be remitted to eastern creditors, merchants were reluctant to accept these notes.[76] Caught between legislation intended to relieve rural hardship and the demands of eastern suppliers, St. Louis entrepreneurs failed in increasing numbers.[77] The tensions between urban entrepreneurs and rural residents of the state exploded when St. Louis representatives initiated a successful legal challenge to the relief program.[78] In the eyes of Missouri farmers, urban vampires had introduced the Panic of 1819, profited from the turmoil it sparked, and undermined the relief effort. The state legislature became openly hostile to St. Louis interests – and would remain so through the antebellum period.[79]

The conservative influence was felt for decades. Missouri legislators did not incorporate a single bank for seventeen years; they failed to adopt corporate reforms until the late 1840s; manufacturing remained in its infancy through the antebellum period; and capital-scarce merchants were denied locally controlled financial institutions.[80] The legislation, however, hit St. Louis entrepreneurs hardest. It became extremely difficult for Missouri merchants to establish businesses, to pool their capital, or to expand their enterprises. In its attempt to protect the state from "foreign" interests, the legislature impeded the commercial development of St. Louis. Ironically, the program outlawed local institutions in order to repel outside speculators.

These institutional pressures hastened the decline of the Missouri fur trade, long the linchpin of the local economy. Even before the new legislation, the St. Louis fur industry had been in disarray.[81] Decades of trapping had dramatically reduced the beaver and otter populations in familiar trapping grounds, and fur traders were forced to venture deeper into the wilderness. Longer expeditions, however, required better planning and greater financial resources, and St. Louis fur traders lacked the capital to expand their ventures. The old French fur families of the town had never cultivated close connections with outside capitalists; the early structure of the fur trade had not required heavy financing or capital reserves. At the same time that the closing of local financial institutions and the harsh response of the state legislature were weakening St. Louis traders, New York- and Boston-backed competitors were entering the field.[82]

During the 1820s the fur trade began to pass into the hands of easterners.[83] Led by John Jacob Astor, who had waited until 1822 before engaging in direct competition with St. Louis traders, eastern capitalists wrested the profits from the old French families of St. Louis.[84] Boston and New York entrepreneurs increasingly financed Rocky Mountain expeditions. As trappers invaded this region, profits migrated to the East.[85] The fur industry remained an important part of the economy of St. Louis, though the town's role changed dramatically.[86] St. Louis became a supply depot; New York became the headquarters.

Capital shortages and weak ties to eastern markets limited the growth of St. Louis in other ways as well. The institutional responses to the Panic of 1819 retarded economic recovery and discouraged commercial ventures. Local businessmen lacked both capital and access to banks, forcing St. Louis merchants to search for alternate sources of capital. Some entrepreneurs, such as the real estate speculator Justus Post, looked to informal mechanisms and to outside sources of financing. Post tried to weather the financial crisis by borrowing from family and friends. Rebuffed by relatives in Vermont, he visited New York, Philadelphia, and Washington in an unsuccessful quest for funds.[87] St. Louis, however, hardly offered an attractive market for eastern investment during this period. The panic had crippled the local economy; the town's principal industry was in decay; and state lawmakers actively discouraged outside investment. The effects of the Panic of 1819 lingered for nearly a decade, and St. Louis remained geographically and economically isolated from the East.[88]

Not surprisingly, recovery proceeded slowly in St. Louis. The value of assessed real estate, for example, did not surpass its 1818 level for a decade.[89] Moreover, between 1820 and 1828 the population of St.

Louis increased by only 402 inhabitants – or 8.7 percent. By comparison, western rivals Cincinnati and Louisville grew nearly six times as fast as St. Louis during the 1820s. Even in Pittsburgh, a city crushed by the depression, the population increased almost three times faster than that of St. Louis.[90]

During the mid-1820s external forces stimulated the first signs of prosperity. Improvements in steamboat technology and in the economic development of the West sparked the town's rebirth. "All the commerce of the West," the French traveler Michel Chevalier noted, "was carried on by the Ohio and the Mississippi."[91] St. Louis commanded both rivers. Because the town was located at a "break in the waters," all cargo crossing its path needed to be reloaded in St. Louis. The shallow upper Mississippi demanded boats of light draught, better suited to the riverbed above the city. Conversely, the lower river, the portion between St. Louis and New Orleans, required vessels adapted to deeper waters. It was unsafe for larger boats to operate above St. Louis, and it was unprofitable for smaller steamers to work the river below the town. As a result, St. Louis became a reloading – or "transshipping" – point, the northern terminus for one fleet of steamboats and the southern terminus for another fleet. Furthermore, St. Louis was located at the confluence of the Mississippi and Missouri rivers and close to the confluence of the Mississippi and the Ohio rivers. The increasing flow of traffic on the rivers brought prosperity to St. Louis.[92]

During the late 1820s the steamboat transformed the West and St. Louis with it. The first steamboat to dock in the town arrived in 1817.[93] By 1826, as the effects of the Panic began to wane, at least one steamboat docked at St. Louis each day during the warmer months.[94] In 1830 278 steam-powered vessels arrived in the harbor; the next year 432 steamboats docked in St. Louis; in 1833 573 steam-driven vessels arrived; and by 1840 over two thousand steamboats docked annually in the city.[95] Following in the wake of the steamboat, St. Louis assumed the status of a regional trading center – and a growing city – by 1830.

With St. Louis at the heart of its network, the steamboat drew new areas into the national economy, creating markets for western crops and eastern manufactured goods. The shift from keelboat to steamboat made long-distance interregional trade both feasible and profitable. Downstream time dropped by two-thirds, and upstream transit fell by fully 700 percent.[96] Moreover, transportation costs fell by as much as 80 percent.[97] If the steamboat linked East, West, and South into a commercial network, then St. Louis emerged as the point where the regions met.

Local merchants and speculators profited handsomely from these changes. The cargo bays of steamboats carried passengers as well as goods. Early on, the steamboat captured the passenger trade.[98] Falling fares democratized westward migration; by the late 1830s deck passage from New Orleans to St. Louis cost as little as five dollars, about one week's pay for an unskilled worker.[99] The luxury and elegance of cabin passage required an investment of only twenty dollars.[100] More important, passage from Pittsburgh to St. Louis was just twenty-five dollars, opening the trans-Mississippi West to migrants from the Northeast and the Ohio valley.[101] Regular service at modest costs brought thousands of settlers to the West, and many of them changed vessels in St. Louis and bought provisions in the rapidly developing business district that spanned the levee. Steamboats also directed farmers to St. Louis, where they purchased land. During the 1820s the city became a major center for land exchange – Missouri ranked fourth among all states in federal land sales.[102]

During the warmer months, the waves of westward settlers reached tidal proportions. St. Louis residents watched with astonishment as each day and each steamboat brought more migrants, generating a new feeling of density and a frenetic spirit in the area. By the mid-1830s local newspapers had transformed steamboat watching into a kind of spectator sport, each day announcing the level of the flow of newcomers. "It is a fair computation to say, that within a week past," the *Missouri Republican* reported in 1835, "fifteen hundred persons have landed on our shores."[103] A short time later, the newspaper boasted that in one thirty-six hour period "between seven and eight hundred strangers arrived in the city."[104] Nor was this pastime confined to the local press. Drawing national attention to the commercial potential of St. Louis, the *Niles Register* reported on April 11, 1836, that "in the course of the preceding week upwards of five thousand emigrants and strangers landed in that city."[105] Frances Fackler urged her sister in Virginia to hurry to the region. "If you intend to move to this country," Fackler warned, "the sooner you come the better, as the country is filling up very fast; every steamboat that lands at St. Louis is loaded with emigrants to this country."[106]

The colonization of the West – with St. Louis as the gateway – generated prosperity and linked the city to the evolving national economy. Even though deck passage was relatively inexpensive, few settlers carried their supplies and farm equipment over long distances. Instead, most migrants purchased their provisions in St. Louis, the last commercial center before the frontier; settlers comprised a captive market for agricultural implements and for manufactured goods.

Although business expanded in St. Louis during this period, the scale of commercial development remained modest. Capital and specie shortages imposed sharp limitations on commercial expansion, and St. Louis merchants operated at an enormous disadvantage in eastern markets.[107] They lacked credit standing and possessed little acceptable currency. Denied access to financial institutions, St. Louis merchants often relied on forwarding houses for banking services. The firm of Keen and Page, for example, advertised their banking services in St. Louis newspapers and promised to make "liberal advances" on shipments.[108] This system, however, was cumbersome, expensive, and inefficient.[109]

Capital shortages and the absence of an adequate circulating medium left St. Louis only loosely connected to the burgeoning national economy. Moreover, balance of trade deficits dramatically reduced the purchasing power of St. Louis merchants in eastern markets. Specie was scarce in the region; western notes were heavily discounted; and eastern notes were extremely expensive in western markets. Although business was plentiful and trade with eastern commercial centers was growing, currency "derangements" prevented St. Louis merchants from establishing regular interregional trade or from maintaining formal ties with eastern markets. As a result, most St. Louis merchants purchased their supplies in Louisville or Pittsburgh, rather than operating under disadvantageous terms with Boston, New York, or Philadelphia merchants and manufacturers.[110] Beer, for example, was generally imported from Pittsburgh during this era – one astute visitor suggested that "beer brewers would soon become rich" in St. Louis.[111] The growth of the provisions trade in St. Louis produced windfall business for commission merchants in the cities along the Ohio River; St. Louis entrepreneurs profited only indirectly from their own prosperity.[112] Local merchants were unable to expand. The economy remained truncated and distorted by institutional pressures.

Nonetheless, St. Louis grew during this period. Eastern merchants were not the only source of money. The Santa Fe trade, which brought sizable sums of Mexican silver to Missouri, and the eastern notes left by westward settlers provided some specie and thus sustained business.[113] Moreover, the Galena lead trade stimulated economic vitality.[114] In short, the institutional climate retarded the development of the marketplace but did not arrest growth, and during the late 1820s St. Louis crossed the threshold that separates towns from cities.[115] By 1830 the local population approached six thousand, and the value of taxable property exceeded one $1 million.[116]

Nowhere was the transformation more apparent than in municipal government. Beginning in the 1820s an active and aggressive style of governance replaced the deferential style of leadership that had predominated earlier in the century.[117] Many of the most powerful fur traders, the men who had comprised the old elite and a decade before had opposed government by elected officials, joined with the merchants, lawyers, and speculators who arrived during the late 1810s to form a new elite. Although friction between the groups persisted, both supported institutional reforms that would enhance the city's economic environment.[118] The scope of municipal government expanded dramatically during this period. The city leveled, straightened, and paved streets; it regulated markets; and local leaders tried to improve law enforcement and health conditions in order to bolster the city's reputation.[119]

William Carr Lane, the first mayor of St. Louis and, in fact, the mayor during most of this period, spearheaded the municipal revolution.[120] Born in western Pennsylvania and trained as a doctor, Lane settled in St. Louis shortly before the depression and served as the "post surgeon" at an area military installation.[121] More important, he brought a decidedly urban perspective to local government. Lane had received his medical training in Philadelphia, and there he had been exposed to big-city government.[122] Not surprisingly, Lane introduced Philadelphia-type institutions and prescriptions to local problems.[123] With the aid of other transplanted Pennsylvanians, he even persuaded local officials to copy Philadelphia's convention of naming streets for trees.[124]

Under Lane's leadership, municipal officials began patterning St. Louis after eastern models. In 1825, for example, the mayor urged the board of aldermen to examine the character of municipal government in other cities.[125] As a result of Lane's ties to Philadelphia and the city's early economic connections to the Pennsylvania metropolis, St. Louis officials looked first to Philadelphia. In 1828 Lane asked a local resident who planned to visit the Quaker City to purchase a copy of Philadelphia's laws, so that St. Louis lawmakers could borrow from them.[126] Similarly, the following year, St. Louis officials instructed the local water works committee to "procure from the Cities [sic] of Philadelphia and New Orleans such information as can be obtained on the subject of conveying water."[127] So began a system of self-conscious patterning.

The flow of goods from eastern cities to St. Louis produced greater contact with urban centers and greater awareness of urban institutions. Lane's successor, Daniel Page, brought a similar perspective to the office and reinforced the urban character of the city. A merchant who had worked in business ventures in Boston and New Orleans, Page, like Lane, arrived in St. Louis during the pre-panic boom and bolstered the commercial orientation of the city.[128] Merchants and lawyers, most of whom hailed from urban backgrounds, dominated municipal government during this period and strengthened the institutional foundation forged by Lane.[129] To the horror of rural Missourians, St. Louis officials began to imitate their New York, Boston, and Philadelphia counterparts.

As a result of the larger economic changes occurring in the region and buttressed by the new "urban" spirit, St. Louis matured as a city during this period. To be sure, not all residents coveted growth, and many feared its disruptive effects. Moreover, while municipal leaders struggled to convince inhabitants of the benefits of development, local boosters labored to convince outsiders that St. Louis would be the nation's great metropolis.[130] The signs of growth, however, abounded. Land owners subdivided vast tracts near the outskirts of the city; residents established fire companies, newspapers, and a local theater; and by 1840 St. Louis possessed two colleges, fourteen churches, six grist mills, and two breweries.[131] The commercial advantages that flowed from the steamboat and from the increasing settlement of the West generated a kind of critical mass. Growth became a self-perpetuating process. Prosperity attracted newcomers, and newcomers sustained the prosperity.

Economic development reinforced these impulses in other ways as well. St. Louis, for example, began to attract increasing numbers of migrants from northeastern urban centers during this period. One visitor to the city was shocked to find St. Louis "overrun by the speculative New Englanders."[132] The geologist George Featherstonhaugh was equally disappointed. In St. Louis he had hoped to find "the romance of Canadian cottages, old French physiognomies, and crowds of Indians walking about." Instead, he was greeted by the "avaricious looks of the numerous Yankee storekeepers. . . . I saw at a glance," Featherstonhaugh complained, "that everlasting Jonathan had struck his roots deep into the ground, and that the LaSales [sic] had given way to Doolittle & Company."[133] Yankee newcomers contributed to the commercial orientation of St. Louis and helped to transform the city into a stronghold for the newly established Whig Party.[134]

The economic forces that stimulated the growth of St. Louis also exaggerated the southern character of Missouri. Migrants poured into rural sections of the state during this period. The vast majority of the newcomers – as before – hailed from Tennessee, Kentucky, and Virginia.[135] Farmers from Tennessee, for example, established settlements in the Ozarks and in southern Missouri.[136] Kentuckians dominated the western edge of the Ozarks and the Osage and Springfield plateaus.[137] Similarly, migrants from Kentucky, Tennessee, and Virginia settled the Missouri Valley; the counties to the north of the river came to be known as "Little Dixie."[138] According to one estimate, over 90 percent of native-born rural Missourians came from agricultural and southern backgrounds.[139]

Thus, the economic, social, and cultural differences between St. Louis and rural Missouri increased. The merchant population of St. Louis as well as the white southern and the slave populations of rural Missouri rose. During the 1820s the number of bondsmen in the state increased by 145 percent.[140] During the following decade the number of slaves increased by an additional 132 percent.[141] Moreover, the flow of settlers to the Missouri frontier reinforced the rural character of the state just as St. Louis was becoming more urban. Even at midcentury, Missouri remained extraordinarily rural; excluding the population of St. Louis, nearly 95 percent of the state's residents lived in settlements with fewer than 250 inhabitants.[142]

The demographic contrast between the city and the country reflected economic differences. According to the 1840 census, agriculture occupied more than 84 percent of the work force in Missouri, though less than one-half of 1 percent of St. Louis workers were tied to the land.[143] Similarly, St. Louis constituted only 4 percent of the population of the state, but it accounted for over one-third of those employed in commerce.[144] St. Louis County, which comprised less than 9 percent of Missouri's population in 1840, accounted for 52 percent of the state's investment in commerce and 53 percent of the value of buildings within the state.[145] Expanding markets and increasing migration simultaneously widened the gap separating the two factions and increased the contact between them.

Settlement patterns also exacerbated political differences in the state. Migrants to rural Missouri disproportionately joined the Democratic Party, and by the early 1830s, Jackson's party claimed nearly 70 percent of Missouri voters.[146] Moreover, the Democracy suffered very few setbacks in the state; it "carried every major election" until the Civil War.[147] According to one historian, Missouri "ranked second only to New Hampshire in producing consistently large majorities for the party after 1832."[148]

Nor did the formation of the Whig Party in the state alter the political balance in Missouri. In 1837 St. Louis residents took the first steps toward organizing an opposition party, and two years later the Whig Party of Missouri held its first convention.[149] St. Louis proved to be the principal Whig stronghold in the state, though the party had some support in rural areas, particularly in older sections of the state where the market economy had matured.[150] Like their brethren elsewhere, Missouri Whigs favored a program that emphasized government support for economic development, a position that had considerable appeal in St. Louis.[151] Even after 1840, however, Missouri Whigs rarely challenged the Democrats; the party of Andrew Jackson and his former colonel, Thomas Hart Benton, usually carried at least 55 percent of the votes in the state.[152]

If St. Louis residents established the Whig Party in opposition to the Democratic Party, in Missouri the Democratic Party gained much of its support by standing in opposition to St. Louis. Anti–St. Louis rhetoric meshed nicely with the ideology of the Democratic Party, blending frontier assumptions with rural and southern views and integrating newcomers into the political culture of the state. Long-time residents of Missouri backed the Democratic Party for many reasons. Despite internal divisions in the party, it provided the principal political organization in the state, and its members included Missouri's most powerful figures, such as Benton. Moreover, the Democratic Party had championed the relief efforts during the early 1820s; it had led the fight to outlaw banks; it had challenged the "pretensions" of St. Louis merchants; and it had defended the frontier areas of the state from the policies of the older sections. In short, the Party had supported Missouri farmers since the day the state joined the Union.[153]

The Democratic Party appealed to newcomers to rural Missouri as well. Although the lion's share of these settlers hailed from slave-holding states, relatively few owned bondsmen. Missouri had always had a smaller percentage of slaves than surrounding slave states, and the proportion of slaves in the population began to fall during the 1830s.[154] Missouri attracted relatively poor farmers, most of whom had probably lived far from cities and at the fringes of the market economy in the upper South.[155] These migrants avoided the well-developed, commercial-farming areas of the state. Instead, they settled in the frontier sections of Missouri, such as the Ozark Mountain region.[156] To the newcomers, the Missouri Democratic Party offered protection from encroaching markets and from the foreign institutions that threatened their political and economic independence. Not surprisingly, legislators representing the frontier sections of Missouri led the crusade against St. Louis, internal improvements, corporations, and other forces associated with the market economy.[157] Thus, the well-established program of the state's Democratic Party found considerable support among the newest residents of rural Missouri.

In short, hostility toward St. Louis generated unity between the newcomers who feared outside forces and commercial interests and the more established residents of the state who remembered the Panic of 1819. The ideology of the Democratic Party, with its discussion of class conflict and its defense of local and individual autonomy, appealed to southern, rural, yeomen, and frontier voters. In Jacksonian Missouri, political, cultural, ideological, regional, and economic affiliations overlapped and reinforced one another. St. Louis became a target – and a rallying point – for rural enmity toward urban interests, for agrarian enmity toward commercial interests, for Democratic enmity toward Whig interests, and for Southern enmity toward Yankee interests.

Andrew Jackson's decision not to renew the charter of the Second Bank provided the issue and the battleground for the warfare between St. Louis and rural interests. Banking remained an intensely emotional topic in Missouri. Moreover, rural legislators continued to hold St. Louis merchants and "their" banks responsible for the Panic of 1819. For Missouri farmers, the lessons of the pressure were clear and powerful. Banks were a curse perpetrated by the wealthy urban manipulators to defraud the poor.

These sentiments resurfaced during the early 1830s. Missourians seeking statewide office borrowed the theme repeatedly and vowed to protect the honest yeomen of the state from the speculators and bankers of St. Louis.[158] Newspaper editors in rural sections of Missouri relied on similar rhetoric to stir partisan passions before every election.[159] According to a St. Louis editor, rural editors taught the "country people" to believe that the city's merchants conspired to steal from interior farmers and that commercial banks "are aristocratical [sic] contrivances to make the rich richer and the poor poorer."[160]

The expiration of the United States Bank, however, posed an immediate threat to St. Louis. Severe capital and specie shortages already constrained local merchants. Because country storekeepers lacked currency, they were unable to settle their accounts with St. Louis merchants. In turn, St. Louis businessmen, denied local financial institutions, had difficulty settling their accounts with eastern suppliers and creditors. Without any banking facilities, commerce would be impossible.[161] St. Louis entrepreneurs looked to the hostile state legislature for help. Softening their demands, they implored the state legislature to incorporate a "judiciously organized" bank for the good of all Missourians.[162]

Although antibank sentiment remained popular in rural parts of the state, many legislators recognized the utility of banks and the utility of banking regulation.[163] The prosperity of the early 1830s had increased the tensions between urban interests and rural concerns, but it had also taught some rural legislators the importance of markets and financial institutions. Furthermore, most lawmakers acknowledged that the Branch Bank had provided important services.[164] For some, however, the threat of foreign invaders, operating through the "tentacles" of bank influence, loomed larger than ever.

Thomas Hart Benton, a St. Louis resident, joined forces with rural spokesmen and championed the "hard money" position. Benton had been born in North Carolina and raised in Tennessee. After serving in the army during the War of 1812 under the command of Andrew Jackson, he had headed west to start a new life.[165] Like hundreds of other speculators and entrepreneurs, Benton moved to St. Louis in 1815 and established a law practice. Moreover, like many ambitious newcomers, Benton lost a considerable sum of money when the local banks failed, and this experience had a dramatic effect on the young lawyer.[166] Benton passionately supported and even led the crusade to redeem Missouri from the influence of outside speculators and bankers.[167] "Old Bullion" Benton believed that Missouri could be protected by imposing state controls over banking.[168] His rural allies, however, sought a more extensive system of safeguards to repel the alien vampires.

Antibank sentiment increasingly manifested itself in demands for a tightly controlled and locally owned financial institution.[169] A state bank seemed to offer the best of both worlds – a carefully regulated stimulus to trade and a weapon against St. Louis and outside interests. Many antibank spokesmen believed that a state-controlled institution could regulate the economy and prevent explosive, destabilizing commercial expansion.[170] Thus, a state bank in Missouri – as in South Carolina, Georgia, and many other southern States – represented a kind of antibank – or at least anti-commercial – prescription.[171] By controlling currency, the state could exercise control over the economy and over St. Louis merchants. In announcing his candidacy for governor in 1836, Lilburn Boggs acknowledged that banks were unrepublican, though he added that they had become "mingled in so great a degree with the business of the people of the other states" that it was nearly impossible to eliminate them. Boggs proposed that Missourians had two choices. The state could establish a "monied institution" and a circulating medium that was regulated by the legislature. Alternatively, it could do nothing, continue to rely on the banks and the currency of other states, and "have all the evils of Banking without any of its advantages."[172] Boggs won the election and delivered essentially the same address to the legislature, as his "first biennial message" – in fact, it seemed to have been such an effective address that the following year, Alexander McNutt, the newly elected governor of Mississippi delivered virtually the same speech to his constituents.[173]

Missourians supported the notion that a state-controlled bank could protect residents from the dangers of unsound currency and speculators. Regulation and reform, they concluded, offered greater safeguards than prohibition. A state committee agreed and recommended the incorporation of a specie-paying state institution. Safe banking, the committee's report suggested, was feasible in Missouri because there was so little capital in the state that a run on the institution was impossible.[174] To St. Louis merchants, this admission demonstrated the constraints under which they struggled. To rural Missourians, however, this represented the formula for safe banking.

The charter of the state bank reflected the southern backgrounds of most of the state's residents and the political culture born of those backgrounds. While eastern and most midwestern states were moving toward open, decentralized banking and the excessive issue of credit, Missouri lawmakers copied the conservative institutions of the South.[175] Indiana and Illinois borrowed banking principles from New York; Missouri framers, on the other hand, looked to South Carolina, Kentucky, and Tennessee banks for models.[176] Safeguards abounded. The directors of the state bank, for example, were made personally liable if the bank failed as a result of an excessive issue of currency.[177] Furthermore, the interest rates on commercial loans were strictly regulated; notes of twenty dollars or less were not issued by the bank; the issue of larger notes was sharply limited; and at least half of the institution's capital was to be reserved for the use of the state.[178]

The Bank of the State of Missouri represented a bulwark against the outside forces, unstable currencies, and alien banks, and as soon as the charter of the state bank became effective, the legislature expelled "foreign" banks. The secretary of the treasury had authorized the Commercial Bank of Cincinnati to become the depository of all public funds in Illinois and Missouri and to perform all government financial business for the region after the Branch Bank closed.[179] The charter of the State Bank of Missouri, however, stipulated that only the state institution could perform banking services.[180] Moreover, lawmakers levied draconian penalties against violators. A fine of one thousand dollars for each offense and every day of operation was invoked; half of the penalty was to be remitted to the informer. Furthermore, any money carried into the state by outside corporations in order to evade the law was to be confiscated.[181]

The limited impact of the Panic of 1837 seemed to vindicate these policies. According to both contemporaries and subsequent observers, Missouri was spared the immediate effects of the financial crisis.[182] Thomas Hart Benton credited the conservative program, proclaiming that it "has given us solid, permanent, and diffused wealth, with happiness and tranquillity."[183] Although the depression struck soon after the state bank opened its doors, the panic had scant influence on the institution during 1837, and its specie remained strong.[184] State legislators, proud of their apparent achievement, vowed to continue the conservative program that had "saved Missouri."[185] More important, the depression of the late 1830s convinced rural Missourians that only outside influence could draw the state into the financial quagmire that crippled eastern and other midwestern states.[186] In short, the anti-urban reforms received renewed support in the aftermath of the depression, and a kind of financial and institutional xenophobia swept Missouri.

Conservative sentiment in Missouri extended beyond the banking issue during the 1830s. Eschewing both expensive state commitments and economic ties to dreaded eastern markets, Missourians chose to avoid internal improvement efforts.[187] Just as it had been the only state in the nation without banks, Missouri stood alone in its transportation policies.[188] "Nearly allied to banking," one writer complained, "is that system of internal improvements that has been adopted in every state, and among all civilized people, except those of Missouri."[189] The financial problems of Illinois during this period – annual interest payments on the Illinois state debt exceeded the principal of the Missouri debt – hardened the resolve of state legislators and reinforced their hostility toward costly internal improvements.[190] Other spending programs received similar treatment. Lawmakers, for example, rejected a measure designed to generate revenue for education. "These Yankee notions will not suit Missouri," one legislator explained.[191] Nor did the legislature stray from its course, a St. Louis-based newspaper complained. "Missouri has not one single mile of railroad, turnpike or canal, not a single bridge, lock or dam, not a single improved road or river, not a single school, academy or college, built or endowed by the State."[192] Moreover, Missouri legislators remained committed to this agenda through the 1840s – a policy that proved to be disastrous in the long run.

As the effects of the Panic of 1837 spread across the nation, however, Missouri lawmakers redoubled their efforts to insulate the state from external shocks. First, they ordered the State Bank to reduce its circulation of notes.[193] The supply of Missouri notes, therefore, fell. In order to maintain commerce, St. Louis merchants relied on Illinois notes, a currency deemed acceptable by the state bank. Fearful of outside influences, the board of directors of the state institution resolved to refuse the notes of all nonspecie paying banks.[194] Illinois currency, the approved mainstay of commerce, became virtually worthless within Missouri. The economy of St. Louis was left without enough currency to transact business, and the merchants of the city were left with considerable reserves of now-unacceptable paper. Businessmen complained loudly but to no avail.[195] Enraged by the policy, many of the leading businessmen of St. Louis withdrew their funds from the state bank.[196] Thus, the initial response to the Panic of 1837 worsened the plight of St. Louis merchants and heightened rural antipathies toward both urban interests and outside influences.

If the legislative prescription spared rural Missouri from much of the immediate devastation of the panic, the cure nearly killed St. Louis. The conservative program triggered bewildering financial problems in the city; customers abounded, goods were available, and yet commerce languished.[197] St. Louis merchants found themselves caught in the crossfire between the "hard money" policies of the state bank of Missouri and the "soft money" policies of eastern and midwestern banks and suppliers. Westward settlers, most of whom planned to purchase their provisions in St. Louis, continued to pour into the city. The state bank, however, refused to accept the scrip that these settlers remitted to local merchants. Unwilling to accept foreign paper, the bank also continued to restrict the issue of its own notes. In 1841 its circulation was only $257,000; local newspapers insisted that daily transactions in St. Louis alone required more than $500,000.[198] An 1843 survey of thirteen state banks, conducted by *Hunt's Merchants' Magazine*, revealed that the Bank of the State of Missouri ranked last in the issue of loans, last in the value of circulation, and twelfth in the issue of specie.[199] "There is no such thing as a circulating medium," the *Missouri Republican* complained.[200] One St. Louis merchant discovered the extent of the "monetary derangement" when he attempted to collect the ten thousand dollars owed to him by his country customers. He returned from his "collecting tour" with $181.[201] Moreover, businessmen "who have merchandise or property to sell," a local editor lamented, "refuse to trade because they do not know what kind of money to take."[202]

While the local economy was faltering, banking problems depressed long-distance commerce. Without specie or eastern credit, St. Louis merchants were unable to purchase eastern goods. "Eastern funds are scarce beyond any former precedent," a local newspaper noted.[203] When eastern currency was available, it was prohibitively expensive. "Our merchants," complained the *Missouri Republican*, "cannot afford to pay 12% for their eastern bills – and the evil does not end here – exchange is rising every day."[204] Local businessmen found themselves unable to pay their suppliers, and the already tenuous ties to eastern markets deteriorated.[205] While the market for provisions burgeoned, the local economy spiraled downward.

The effects of the pressure were severe and prolonged. "One-third of the inhabitants," a longtime St. Louis resident reported, "are ruined."[206] "Many of our best business men [sic]," according to the *Missouri Republican*, "found themselves, after years of toil, left without a dollar."[207] Nearly crippled by the pressure, the *Missouri Argus* implored its customers "to immediately pay their little debts due to this establishment."[208] Even a local racetrack felt the effects of the depression. According to observers, "the hardness of the times" probably accounted for the reduced attendance and betting that track officials reported.[209] The downturn lasted for nearly eight years in St. Louis.

As the depression lingered, local businessmen searched for alternate forms of economic relief. After a series of unsuccessful attempts to negotiate loans from "prominent men" in New York, Boston, and Philadelphia, city officials and merchants turned to extralegal banking practices to mitigate the crippling effects of the financial pressures.[210] In spite of state prohibitions, St. Louis officials issued city warrants in small denominations in 1841.[211] At the same time, a number of local corporations began to offer banking services. By 1841 nine insurance companies and the St. Louis Gas Light Company engaged in the largely illegal private banking business.[212] Although these corporations could not issue notes, they received money on deposit and made loans. The insurance companies circulated foreign notes and thereby provided local merchants with a medium for commercial transactions. City officials and local newspapers applauded such practices. "These companies," the *Missouri Republican* noted, "in fact are the main stay [sic] of the whole commercial business of the city."[213] It is "the duty of every man," the newspaper added, to deposit his money in the "incorporated institutions."[214]

But private banks provided only limited relief. Many were unsound, and most had limited capital.[215] Although widely acknowledged to be "great auxiliaries," the insurance companies were "not able to add any thing [sic] to the amount of circulating medium."[216] Punitive legislation undermined other efforts to ease the city's shortage of capital and currency. For example, the state-imposed license fee of two thousand dollars largely prevented money brokers from easing the currency shortage.[217]

Nonetheless, private banks kept the local economy afloat. According to the *Missouri Republican*, these institutions provided currency "for local purposes, that is, for the payment of debts between persons resident here. . . . If the credit and availability of this [local currency] is maintained," the newspaper noted, "there need not be any pressure among ourselves."[218] A growing domestic market, fueled by discounted city scrip and "shaky" Illinois shinplasters, gave life to the economy of St. Louis during the depths of the depression. Remote areas of Missouri, however, had no such hedge against the increasing hardness of the times.

During the early 1840s the depression reached rural Missouri. Farmers were hit particularly hard. Land sales fell, and prices plummeted.[219] For the first time in decades, notices of bankruptcies, sheriff's sales, and land forfeitures filled rural newspapers.[220] According to the Reverend F. R. Gray, a Protestant missionary living in a farming section, the people "have no money, [sic] and can get none."[221] Mortgages went unpaid; land was sold for back taxes; and desperate farmers began paying taxes in produce. In 1842 Boone County taxes could be paid at the rate of fifty cents per barrel of corn.[222] Similarly, the *Jefferson Inquirer* announced that "all kinds of country produce [would be] taken for subscription."[223] Although Missouri was spared the immediate effects of the Panic of 1837, the depression soon arrived and brought economic devastation to the countryside.

Rural Missourians, as in 1819, blamed St. Louis merchants for the depression. Country people had long believed that St. Louis represented the gateway through which outside evils entered Missouri.[224] This time, however, they possessed direct evidence that St. Louis merchants had introduced the depression. The extralegal private banks of the city, according to rural spokesmen, had tied the state to the yoke of unsound foreign banking.[225] Conservative state policy, they argued, had protected Missouri until St. Louis insurance companies flooded the state with heavily discounted "paper trash."[226]

Indeed the depression and the unsound currency had entered the state through its principal trading center. Moreover, the private banks had introduced thousands of dollars of unstable Illinois paper into rural areas, and farmers had come to rely on this currency.[227] Thus, the suspension of the Bank of Illinois triggered the economic crisis in Missouri, rendering these notes virtually worthless, ruining thousands of Missourians, and dragging the state into the national financial abyss. Although state banking policy had forced St. Louis merchants to look outside of Missouri for currency, rural spokesmen held the city and its businessmen responsible for the depression.[228]

Political leaders and newspaper editors from farming areas cast the depression in conspiratorial terms. They explained that the Panic of 1837 represented a struggle between the honest people of the state and the wealthy manipulators of St. Louis. The crisis fit perfectly with well-established Jacksonian rhetoric about the clash between producers and speculators. "It is a contest between the many and the few, the privileged orders, the incorporated wealth, the aristocracy of St. Louis, and the unbought democracy of Missouri," one editor reported.[229] The monied interests of the East had conspired with the merchants of St. Louis to defraud "the people" of the state.[230]

Moreover, they noted that the aristocrats of the city had used the banking system to accomplish their evil program. According to Robert Wells, a lawmaker representing a rural section of the state, the "effects" of the currency fluctuations transferred "the hard earnings of hundreds of thousands from themselves and families to the wily speculator, who lies like a spider in his den, waiting for the fly to become entangled." The result of the crisis, Wells concluded, was "poverty, ruin and distress to the many who labor – enormous and overgrown fortunes to the few."[231] Rural editors provided similar explanations. The *Jefferson Inquirer*, which led the crusade against St. Louis interests with daily reports entitled "war items," announced that agents had been hired to circulate the shinplasters of "foreign" banks, "much as counterfeiters pass their base coins." City merchants then tricked the "ignorant country folk" into exchanging their hard-earned specie for Illinois paper trash. "This specie," the newspaper continued, was "packed off to St. Louis and shipped East. When the countryman comes to St. Louis with his shinplasters . . . the farmer must pay fifty per cent more for his goods than they are worth in the specie he has been gulled out of by the shinplaster peddlers."[232] Although the commercial ties between St. Louis merchants and eastern suppliers remained weak, rural spokesmen traced the wrongdoers to St. Louis, insisting that the flow of goods from the Northeast to the city confirmed the existence of a Yankee conspiracy against the people of Missouri.

The strongest anticommercial and anticorporation sentiment came from the most remote, rural areas of the state. Demands for tight restrictions of corporations, according to the historian James Primm, were greatest in areas "where there was little likelihood that aggregations of private capital would be attracted to form corporations in the interests of the community."[233] Voters in remote parts of Missouri, therefore, tended to resist internal improvements and other measures that would integrate them into commercial networks. Only economic development could attune these Missourians to the advantages of economic growth. Rural isolation translated into a self-perpetuating force. The inhabitants of isolated areas were hostile to economic development as long as they remained isolated, and they remained isolated as long as they were hostile to economic development. The virtual absence of railroads and canals in antebellum Missouri can be ascribed to the force and the persistence of these feelings.

The electoral strength of the anti-commercial, Democratic, frontier voters even exceeded their numerical superiority. Missouri's apportionment system inflated the power of the anti-urban elements. In 1841 the legislature increased the number of counties in the state from sixty to seventy-seven. Because the general assembly already included ninety-eight members and the state constitution limited the number of representatives to one hundred, lawmakers could only add two new seats. Nonetheless, the constitution required every county to have at least one representative. Thus, the formation of the new counties transformed the apportionment system in the state and gave disproportionate strength to frontier areas.[234] Just as the Panic of 1837 reached rural Missouri, farming areas gained political strength at the expense of St. Louis and urban interests. The assembly became more anti-commercial and more Democratic during the early 1840s, insuring the passage of and the continued support for the punitive legislation.

State lawmakers responded quickly to the depression and to the demands of frontier voters. They vowed to control banking practices, to resist the encroachment of commerce, to reduce foreign influence in the state, and, finally, to punish the merchants of St. Louis.[235] During the 1840–41 legislative session the assembly tightened the legal restrictions on corporations, and during the 1842–43 session the legislature passed two sweeping bank reform measures, popularly known as the "bills of pains and penalties."[236] Only the state bank, the laws stipulated, could exercise banking privileges. Enraged legislators also forbade all other corporations from issuing notes, receiving money on deposit, or discounting notes. Furthermore, the new legislation barred exchange brokers from dealing in notes smaller than ten dollars.[237]

The heart of the "bills of pains and penalties," however, was corporate reform. In addition to the new banking regulations, the legislation increased the assembly's control over corporations. First, the new laws repealed acts providing charters for the corporations that had engaged in unlawful practices. Moreover, the assembly granted charters less readily than it had in the past.[238] Between 1840 and 1845 the legislature granted only twenty-four insurance and transportation charters; by contrast, in the 1836–37 session alone it had granted forty-four charters.[239] Furthermore, during the early 1840s lawmakers often denied corporate status to transportation companies such as the St. Louis and River Des Peres Turnpike Company.[240] Rural spokesmen occasionally urged the assembly to deny charters to charitable or public institutions, particularly if the requests came from St. Louis. The *Jefferson Inquirer*, for example, sarcastically encouraged the legislature to reject such a request from the St. Louis Rural Cemetery Association. "After fangling all the living," the newspaper asked, "can they not spare the dead?"[241] Nor was the impulse short-lived; only during the final legislative session of the decade did the number of charters reach the levels established during the 1830s.[242] The assembly also chose to maintain unlimited liability for stockholders in corporations.[243] These restrictive policies discouraged manufacturers from locating in the state, discouraged capitalists from investing in Missouri, and probably discouraged local entrepreneurs from establishing businesses.[244]

The "bills of pains and penalties" immediately affected St. Louis. Although the suspension of the Bank of Illinois had compelled many of the city's insurance companies to close their doors, the legislative sanctions forced the remaining firms to concentrate on the insurance business.[245] As a result, the supply of circulating currency plunged. When the value of city warrants fell, St. Louis was left "with almost no currency at all; and laborers, mechanics and merchants are all reduced to the last extremity of distress."[246] The legislation, therefore, exacerbated the financial crisis in the city.

For some, the pressure was too much to bear. Samuel Faggery, anxious about the future of his deposits, demanded his share of the gold and silver housed in the Bank of Missouri. In the summer of 1843 Faggery declared that "the money should be divided and the bank shut up." Rebuffed by bank clerks, Faggery attempted to set fire to the institution. The *Missouri Republican* casually reported the incident under the headline, "One of the Hards."[247] Most residents of the city chose more cautious strategies. According to local observers, laborers avoided unnecessary expenses, and merchants tightened their belts and limited their risks, eschewing all but the safest business ventures.[248] Thus, the scale of commerce remained small.

The financial storms of the late 1830s and the early 1840s, however, did not destroy the economy of St. Louis. Although the institutional pressures imposed by the state legislature depressed trade and deepened the downward spiral, commerce never ceased. Even during the worst months of the panic, the river trade provided commercial sustenance.[249] The vitality of the New Orleans produce market, for example, generated business for St. Louis industries, keeping steamboat owners, rivermen, and forwarding merchants active; the number of steamboats that docked in the wharf rose steadily during this period.[250] Furthermore, westward settlers continued to leave some specie in the market of St. Louis. The "progress" of the city, the *Niles Register* reported, "has been mainly accelerated by the hundreds of thousands of emigrants who have overspread the prairies."[251] Finally, Mexican silver and Galena lead continued to pass through St. Louis on their way to the east.[252] These sources of income and business mitigated the worst shocks of the depression.

But legislative responses to the crisis distorted the growth of St. Louis, and the cumulative force of rural injunctions launched in response to the depressions of the 1810s and the 1830s shaped the development of the city in important ways. Currency problems and increasing capital shortages made St. Louis an unattractive site for many migrants. "Business conditions," Gustavus Wulfing wrote to his mother in 1843, "are still very bad, and I thought best to advise Fritz [a relative] not to come to St. Louis."[253] During the first half of the century, travel accounts and guidebooks warned migrants to avoid St. Louis unless they brought large sums of capital. One widely circulated German guidebook simply stated, "bring some capital with you." "With a small capital," Gottfried Duden concluded, "very little can be done."[254] Other warnings were more emphatic. Frederick Graff, for example, observed in 1838 that "men without capital can do nothing at anything."[255] Doubtless, large numbers of migrants avoided St. Louis for this reason. Travel writers advised ambitious men of modest means to look elsewhere; the state's legislative policies created an environment that directed migrants to Cairo, Quincy, Chicago, and other rivals. Stephen Douglas, for example, chose to establish his career in Illinois after finding that St. Louis was a difficult place in which to begin on a "small pittance."[256]

Equally important, institutional forces exerted a selective pressure on the economic development of St. Louis. While state policies disrupted the domestic marketplace, the legislative sanctions virtually precluded long-distance commerce.[257] In the early 1840s the city was frozen in the midst of a transition. St. Louis foundered on the threshold of becoming a major commercial center and a cog in the national economy. The river trade, the Santa Fe trade, and the settlement of the trans-Mississippi frontier made St. Louis the gateway to the West and created potentially enormous markets for eastern manufactures. The pressures exerted by the state legislature, however, prevented St. Louis from establishing stronger links to the national economy.

Local merchants lacked the capital, the credit, and the currency to maintain long-distance commerce. Without access to financial institutions, St. Louis businessmen traded under enormous disadvantages in eastern markets. Unfavorable exchange levels and the high interest rates charged on short-term loans eroded profit margins and reduced the scale of their operations, forcing St. Louis merchants to buy goods in small – and more expensive – lots. Moreover, without the legal safeguards that stimulated capital accumulation, even wealthy businessmen were reluctant to engage in long-distance commerce.[258] At the western end of the commercial network, eastern currency was extremely expensive, and specie was scarce in St. Louis, making it difficult for local merchants to meet their obligations to suppliers.[259] Well into the 1840s, St. Louis businessmen found direct trade with eastern merchants difficult. Rather than purchasing goods from the manufacturers and distributors of the Northeast, local entrepreneurs remained dependent on the commission merchants of the Ohio River cities.[260] As a result, eastern goods were expensive and in short supply. Although the steamboat made St. Louis the gateway to the West, Ohio merchants continued to control the commerce of the region, and Cincinnati remained the "Queen City" of the West.

The long-term implications of rural influence on St. Louis were ironic. The state legislature forbade indigenous financial institutions and discouraged internal improvements, corporations, and capital accumulation in order to reduce foreign influence. To a considerable extent, this policy succeeded; it deprived St. Louis merchants of the "proper facilities" for economic growth. At the same time, however, the legislation convinced St. Louis merchants that the "remedy" would "be supplied from another quarter."[261] The xenophobic program, which was designed to insulate Missouri from outside influences, forced St. Louis merchants to look beyond the borders of the state and to become dependent upon outside capital and foreign investors.

The political climate of the state exaggerated and prolonged St. Louis's colonial status. Businessmen in other western and southern commercial centers faced capital shortages and battled against Democratic and rural-dominated state legislatures.[262] But in Missouri, rural, anti-commercial, Democratic, yeoman, frontier, and southern political passions overlapped, and thus political power was unusually concentrated. As a result, St. Louis voters failed to blunt the strength of their opponents and failed to dilute the legislative program that prolonged the city's financial problems. In short, the political and cultural climate of Jacksonian Missouri, transplanted from the South and nourished by conditions within the state, produced an institutional environment that retarded the development of St. Louis. The city grew; its marketplace expanded; land speculators flourished; and migrants poured into the growing population center during this period. Nonetheless, the local economy remained loosely connected to the national economy, and St. Louis remained unusually dependent on outside sources of economic sustenance.

Despite the city's economic problems – no banks, no railroads, no canals, an inadequate circulating currency, and a hostile legal setting for investors – the commercial potential of St. Louis became widely known during the 1830s and the 1840s.[263] Steamboat routes and other sources exposed thousands of travelers and businessmen to the economic potential of the city. "The time is not far off," one visitor noted, "when St. Louis will rank amoung [sic] the commercial cities of the new world."[264] Similarly, the influential western writer James Hall predicted that "the commerce of St. Louis" would "soon be of the first class."[265] In 1843 *Hunt's Merchants' Magazine* reported that the local economy "has hardly begun to develop itself."[266] The economic future of the city was unparalleled, the magazine explained, unless "she be crushed by the jealousy of the legislators from the interior of the state."[267] If rural jealousy threatened the city's glorious future, it also ensured that outsiders would shape the development of St. Louis.

3 Savagedom, destiny, and the isothermal zodiac

For western cities, growth began in the East. Migrants and capital from the eastern states generated urban development in the antebellum West and transformed frontier towns into major commercial centers. The great urban rivalries of the nineteenth century, therefore, were often decided hundreds of miles from the cities that were involved. Moreover, frontier boosters recognized this fact and waged their literary wars in New York, Boston, Philadelphia, and other large population centers. Victory did not depend on the quantity of the promotional literature that energetic editors manufactured. Instead, eastern perceptions of western cities – and the responses that those perceptions triggered – determined the winner. St. Louis crushed Quincy, for example, because easterners knew more about St. Louis and because they responded favorably to what they had read and heard about St. Louis. The city that attracted migrants and investors denied such resources to its rivals.[1] As a result, St. Louis triumphed.

But because victory began in the East rather than in the West, success reflected what easterners read – not what westerners wrote. Thus, the body of information available to easterners shaped the course of urban development. Potential settlers and investors, however, knew far more about western cities than what local boosters manufactured. Many other – and more compelling – sources provided information about St. Louis, Quincy, Alton, and Chicago during the antebellum period, when these cities battled for supremacy.

Both personal and published material contributed to the public images that easterners formed and that distinguished one western city from the next. Private letters, for example, probably generated more interest in western cities than the best efforts of trans-Mississippi editors and speculators. Soldiers who had visited the region and merchants who had traveled near the frontier recorded their observations in personal correspondence that was often widely circulated and even printed in local newspapers. Published sources contributed to eastern perceptions of western cities as well. Religious

43

magazines, guidebooks, literary magazines such as the *North American Review*, and commercial journals such as *Hunt's Merchants' Magazine*, devoted considerable attention to the West and its leading cities.

These sources, produced by eastern travelers, shaped the public image of St. Louis. In fact, local boosters assumed a small role in the formation of the city's public image. Furthermore, not only did boosters fail to distinguish the city from its rivals, but most of the writers who directed attention to St. Louis cared little about the city. The editors and travel writers who forged St. Louis's reputation in the East were concerned with the *West* – not with a particular city or state. They were interested in the frontier, either its scenery or its political, spiritual, or economic development.

St. Louis received particular attention from these writers because the city was located at the major break in the western transportation system. Thus, frontier travelers spent time in St. Louis, and their travel accounts typically devoted a chapter to the city "at the edge of civilization," "at the great break in the waters," or "at the extreme western point" of the journey.[2] Moreover, travel accounts were formulaic. Readers expected their guides to visit the principal sites of the West, and travel itineraries – or at least published accounts – assumed a self-perpetuating form. Just as travelers had read about cities such as New Orleans and St. Louis, they anticipated visiting those cities and writing about them – in order to fulfill the expectations of their readers. In short, attention begot attention.

By comparison, St. Louis's competitors received scant attention during the 1830s and 1840s. Because wagons and steamboats failed to stop in Kaskaskia, Cape Girardeau, or Vincennes for extended periods, these towns commanded only a line or two in most travel accounts. On his way to St. Louis in 1842, for example, J. S. Buckingham noted that Passage des Sioux, Kaskaskia, and Vincennes had "declined."[3] Similarly, Harriet Martineau dismissed Memphis as "bare and hot."[4] More damaging to these trading centers, such brief descriptions served to underscore St. Louis's distinctive qualities, thereby justifying the attention devoted to the Missouri city. If the western traveler Patrick Shirreff concluded in 1835 that Chicago's "situation is not so favourable to growth as many other places in the Union," he also argued that St. Louis "may justly be called the metropolis of the valley of the Mississippi."[5] More often, however, travel writers devoted all of their attention to a single city. During their journeys on the Ohio River, they discussed only Cincinnati, and during their voyages on the Mississippi River, they discussed only St. Louis. As a result, these authors usually neglected to mention St. Louis's rivals in the Mississippi valley.

The crusades and the quests that inspired travelers to visit St. Louis also shaped descriptions of the city. The imagery created by reformers who were concerned with the spiritual destiny of the Far West, for example, spilled over onto descriptions of St. Louis and gave the city a reputation that extended far beyond endless predictions of profitable factories, the staple of the booster literature. Moreover, the specific character of the writers who visited the city and the focus of the publications that printed their travel accounts distorted assessments of the city in important ways, placing local economic problems in a perspective that enhanced the appeal of St. Louis. These literary descriptions of the city generated eastern interest and enabled St. Louis to surpass its rivals. Deprived of adequate and positive attention along the Atlantic coast, many competing trading centers withered and faded into regional obscurity. For example, according to *De Bow's Review*, Cahokia, an old rival, had become, by the 1850s, a "fifth-rate village" whose residents were "cankered by spite, bile, revenge and unavailing despondency and gloom, at the growth and success of its former feeble protege and bantling, St. Louis."[6]

The geography of the West and the lore of the frontier dominated eastern perceptions of St. Louis. One traveler, for example, described St. Louis as the place where "we unshipped the western horses."[7] The trans-Mississippi region was sparsely settled during this period, and as soon as travelers crossed the "Father of the Waters," they described the world around them in the terminology that they had reserved for the wild West. Eastern writers warned that two vastly different worlds met and clashed in St. Louis, and the raw passion of the "West" triumphed.

According to many travel accounts, the frontier began at St. Louis. Narcissa Whitman, a missionary who traveled through the city on her way to Oregon, described St. Louis as "the very border of civilization."[8] The geologist George Featherstonhaugh concurred, terming the city "the terminus of civilisation [sic]."[9] Similarly, in 1833 the Congregationalist minister Truman Post called St. Louis the "end of the world – the jumping off place."[10] Turning westward from the middle of the city, Post saw "a new, virgin, and for the most part wild and solitary world, a dark continent of wandering savages and the wild creatures of nature."[11] Eastern travelers reported that trappers and "adventurers" gathered in St. Louis before disappearing into the wilderness.[12] In 1846, for example, the historian and writer Francis Parkman found the city crowded with Indian guides, "mountain men, and passengers on their way to the frontier."[13] Long after the Mississippi valley was settled, this image persisted. According to an

1857 gazetteer, "St. Louis is the starting point for savagedom."[14]

Even the journey to St. Louis, eastern writers reported, was fraught with the dangers and the adventure of the Far West. Guides warned travelers that they were leaving the safety of civilization. Transportation, according to popular guidebooks, became treacherous as travelers approached St. Louis.[15] Steamboat disasters were particularly common between the mouth of the Ohio River and St. Louis; the portion of the Mississippi River directly below the city was widely known as "the graveyard."[16] John Audubon's arrival in St. Louis in 1843 was neither unusual nor disappointing. "She [the steamboat] struck a sawyer [fallen tree] . . . the ladies screamed, the babies squalled, the dogs yelled, the steam roared, the captain swore – not like an angel, but like the very devil – and all was confusion and uproar."[17] Between sandbars, crazed steamboat captains, and the oppressive, fever-plagued atmosphere of the valley, many tourists reported that they merely hoped to survive St. Louis.[18] The English traveler Frederick Marryat, for example, ended his description of the city by tersely noting, "thank heaven I have escaped St. Louis."[19]

Between 1830 and 1850 travel writers reported that St. Louis was the "ultima thule of western adventure."[20] Soon after departing from Cincinnati, for example, one Oregon pioneer was cautioned that "guides could not take women through [St. Louis]."[21] Travelers warned that both wild men and wild beasts stalked the city. The Swedish writer Frederika Bremer observed that "bowie-knives and pistols belong to the wardrobe of a man" in St. Louis.[22] Eastern writers gleefully reported that brawling and dueling were so common in St. Louis that local residents used a sandbar in the harbor – known as "Bloody Island" – exclusively for such primitive displays.[23] Other observers urged visitors to exercise extreme caution within the city. An agent for the Home Missionary warned that "this place is a noted and favorite resort for the drunkard, gambler, and other like characters."[24] Travelers reported that the primitive state of the West permeated local culture and social life.

Many travel writers emphasized the "characteristic" features of western society, such as Indians. Accounts of visits to the city, for example, often told of savage Indians "strid[ing] through the streets."[25] According to one eastern writer, the rugged men of St. Louis "think as much of an Indian encounter as a New York blood does of a spree with a watchman."[26] Similarly, in 1840 the Niles Register explained that St. Louis residents "are accustomed to seeing many red gentlemen."[27] Other eastern visitors and writers reported Indian encounters as well.[28]

More important, such reports shaped perceptions of the city. Georg

Engelmann, for example, relied on travel accounts to plan his journey from Germany to St. Louis. After reading that the city was located at the edge of the frontier, he withdrew his son from school in Germany and had him trained as a tanner. Engelmann noted in his diary that he wanted to be prepared for the buffalo and deer that he anticipated killing in the area.[29]

While travel accounts and guidebooks exaggerated the "western" character of St. Louis, they also enhanced the city's appeal with distant readers. Romantic and exciting images of urban life in the rough-hewn West captured eastern notice.[30] Readers contrasted the staid "civilization" of the East with the adventure of life in St. Louis.[31] Warnings about the degeneracy of the "western character" merely whetted eastern appetites for excitement.

If the city seemed exciting, it did not appear dangerous. Although readers on the Atlantic coast associated St. Louis with the rugged frontier, the city represented only the gateway to an uncivilized world. It remained protected from the greatest dangers of the region. According to one travel writer, St. Louis seemed "only one stage from where we should find Nature [sic] in a perfect stage of undress."[32] Guidebooks warned that the river around St. Louis posed a threat to travelers, and wild animals grazed close to the city. Moreover, the residents appeared coarse, drunkards abounded, brawling was common, and Indians strolled through the streets, though travel writers did not report riots, murders, or Indian attacks in St. Louis. To those frustrated with the conventions of polite Yankee society, St. Louis presented a sharp contrast. The not-so-wild West offered excitement and the veneer of danger within a relatively safe urban setting.

But St. Louis's reputation as a rugged outpost implied that the city offered something far more important. To many readers, this image suggested extraordinary potential. Because the area was untamed, because local culture was unformed, and because the city's residents were primitive, St. Louis seemed malleable. Its character and indeed its future, eastern writers implied and eastern readers inferred, could be molded. Newcomers could shape the development of the city to meet the needs of the region or even needs of the nation.[33] Determined settlers might transplant eastern religion to the West, reinvigorate conservative politics, or introduce moral reform in a strategically located western site such as St. Louis. More important, a moral wellspring in the West might inspire reform along the Atlantic coast.[34] The problems of the East could be solved in the West; St. Louis represented a staging point for a larger crusade. The city seemed particularly promising and interesting to eastern reformers because it appeared to be coarse and primitive. Thus, the Missouri metropolis enjoyed prominence in eastern population centers, an ironic by-product of its image in the travel literature of the period.

Between 1830 and 1850 religious and nationalist spokesmen discussed the potential of an unmolded trading center close to the frontier. They viewed the city as a possible stronghold in a larger, spiritual battle to claim the West. The influential Baptist minister John Mason Peck, for example, expressed a widely held belief when he noted that in the struggle for the destiny of the West "St. Louis is the most important point."[35] Peck's *New Guide for Emigrants to the West* emphasized the spiritual possibilities of the untamed city.[36] Other writers echoed Peck's message and discussed the strategic importance of establishing a colony in the city.[37] For thousands of eastern readers, information about St. Louis came as a part of political, religious, and nationalistic crusades. The city became associated with a grand mission in the wilderness.[38]

Nor was St. Louis's plastic reputation confined to the United States. The city attracted considerable attention in Germany during the 1830s and 1840s. In fact, German writers, many of whom were disturbed by political instability and mounting population pressures in their homeland, were among the first observers to consider the potential of the West and the strategic importance of St. Louis.[39]

Gottfried Duden stimulated much of this attention. A civil servant from the Rhineland, Duden visited the Mississippi valley during the late 1820s and published a widely circulated account of his travels in the region. Duden believed that a colony in the American West could relieve the demographic and political pressures that plagued his homeland and reinvigorate German life. Thus, he proposed the formation of an embryonic state, a "rejuvenated Germania," in the Mississippi valley.[40] Duden's immensely popular writings – the most important pieces of literature in the history of German immigration according to Marcus Hansen – directed widespread attention to the region and made a generation of German readers familiar with Missouri.[41]

St. Louis occupied a prominent place in Duden's American colony. The city would form the heart of the new German state in the American West. Duden's earliest travel reports from the United States had suggested that "if a little city were founded with the intention of serving the American Germans as a center of culture, one would soon see a rejuvenated Germania arise and the European Germans would then have a second country here."[42] Few German readers doubted that St. Louis was Duden's "little city," and many emigration societies launched efforts to establish the "rejuvenated Germania" in St. Louis.[43] According to an 1838 traveler, "since the distribution of Duden's book St. Louis has become the main goal and gathering place of German immigrants."[44] Dozens of emigration societies responded to Duden's plan, and within Germany St. Louis became associated with the proposed *Vaterland* in the American wilderness. For example, in 1834 the Giessen Gesellschaft sent its colonists to the city to establish a German state in the Midwest.[45] Five years later a group of Saxons, the founders of the Missouri Synod, tried to establish an orthodox Lutheran state in the region.[46] "The immediate goal of the journey," the group's "emigration code" noted, "shall be St. Louis."[47] The German St. Louis described in this travel literature would form the cornerstone of a nationalist mission on the frontier.

Thus, nationalist causes colored German literary descriptions of Missouri during the 1830s and 1840s. In their zeal to promote a viable colonization plan, Duden and his followers portrayed the region and the city in pristine terms. These writers treated their readers to wildly embellished images of a trans-Mississippi paradise. The location, topography, and natural resources of St. Louis and the surrounding territory, these writers announced, were deemed "ideal for Germans."[48] The climate, Duden noted, resembled his native Remscheid, though – predictably – a bit milder.[49] He even praised Missouri's violent thundershowers. Such driving rains, Duden concluded, maintained "natural drainage basins."[50] The soil of the region was rich beyond description. Duden reported that cornstalks extended eighteen feet into the air and grapevines reached a foot around and stretched a hundred feet into the sky.[51] St. Louis, Duden and other writers explained, formed the heart of a "fairytaled" [sic] land, ideally situated to become the gathering point for German colonists and the commercial capital for their colony.[52]

As Germans consumed this literature, St. Louis obtained a growing reputation in Europe as a stronghold for German culture. Moreover, this reputation became self-perpetuating. German immigrants settled in or near the city because of its German character, and that character increased as Germans relocated to St. Louis. Frederick Gustorf, for example, traveled to the area "because I wanted to see with my own eyes this place, which is highly praised by Frankfurters and Rhinelanders on account of its German settlement."[53] Similarly, the western traveler Moritz Busch told his German readers that "if in any one of the large cities of America there is reason for Germans to console themselves about the distance from home, it is in St. Louis – where our countrymen are numerous and highly regarded."[54] Other writers noted that the German population of St. Louis was comprised of "learned men," many of them classically educated.[55] "Latin farmers," a group of German professionals who had turned to agriculture in America, cultivated the land surrounding St. Louis, according to these reports.[56] One immigrant, Gustavus Wulfing, became interested in St. Louis after reading of the "German style" of the city, the "educated Germans in St. Louis" with whom he could associate, and the "very fine German school" in the city.[57] In short, German travel writers viewed untamed St. Louis in terms of its potential and described migration to the urban center in terms of a nationalist or religious mission.[58]

Many Americans shared Duden's vision of the importance of the city. They, too, believed that the West was a land of destiny and that St. Louis occupied a strategic position in the future of the region. The eastern vision of St. Louis and the trans-Mississippi frontier, however, was less sanguine than the German perception. Rather, American writers – particularly religious spokesmen – approached the destiny of the West and the future of St. Louis in combative terms. The Presbyterian clergyman Albert Barnes, for example, explained in 1849 that "the Mississippi valley [is] the great battle field of the world – the place where probably more than anywhere else the destinies of the world are to be decided."[59] The *Home Missionary* also predicted "a great battle" in the West.[60] Observers warned that the period between 1830 and 1850 marked a crucial juncture in the history of the nation. The West, according to many American religious and nationalist writers, had to be reclaimed from heathens and infidels, and, like German observers, many Americans believed that the future of the region would be decided in St. Louis.[61]

This religious literature portrayed the city as a decisive battleground in the earthly struggle between good and evil.[62] Eastern religious magazines maintained a constant vigil on St. Louis and issued battle reports that provided a steady source of information about the city. Congregationalist, Unitarian, Baptist, Presbyterian, and Methodist spokesmen focused much of their western campaigns on a crusade to reclaim St. Louis from barbarism and to make the city a beacon in a dark land.[63] St. Louis, the Baptist missionary John Mason Peck observed, could be a "New Jerusalem" in the West.[64] Just as German writers linked the future of St. Louis to a nationalist crusade, many American writers linked the city to a religious mission, and for thousands of American readers, migration to St. Louis was described as a rare opportunity to serve Christ and to safeguard Christianity.[65] This religious appeal, however, unwittingly enhanced the reputation of St. Louis.

According to many American writers, the barbarism and savagery of the West constituted the principal enemy. Drawing on popular literary images of rough-hewn St. Louis, religious writers warned that the degenerating effects of western life demanded immediate attention. The clergyman John Clark, for example, noted in 1842 that the "institutions of God are trampled in the dust" in St. Louis.[66] Two years later the *Home Missionary* reported "wickedness so great that a Methodist minister who was asked to preach in the place replied: It is too wicked."[67] In short, the city desperately needed to be claimed from the barbarism of the region.

Eastern missionaries, religious writers suggested, could transform the development of St. Louis and the region. For example, William Greenleaf Eliot, a Harvard-trained Unitarian minister, concluded in 1837 that the unrestrained character of local culture could "be checked by strong counteracting influences."[68] The Presbyterian minister George Lewis, writing during the 1840s, concurred. According to Lewis, the "precarious" religious climate of St. Louis "loudly calls for the wise and good."[69] A unique opportunity – a rare moment in history – was at hand.[70] "The field is ripe for the harvest," the clergyman T. R. Durfee noted in the *Home Missionary*, "and the sickle must be thrust in now, or the precious grain will be lost."[71]

The crusade to reclaim St. Louis from the wilderness presented important opportunities for the crusaders. Writing in Yankee religious magazines, observers emphasized that sturdy New Englanders and New Yorkers could shape the future by bringing religion and moral education to the city. The *Home Missionary*, for example, assured moral New Englanders and New Yorkers that they would "exert amazing influence" in St. Louis.[72] This literature promised cultural prominence, social standing, and a mission in the name of Christ to the "noble" young men involved in the crusade to save the city from barbarism.[73] American society would be uplifted, the West would be claimed from heathenism, and missionaries would reap personal rewards.

Other American religious writers sought foot soldiers in a war to wrest St. Louis from papist invaders. During the 1830s and 1840s nativist literature directed attention to the city.[74] Many writers, including Lyman Beecher, believed that St. Louis and the West had to be reclaimed from Catholic agents – not western barbarism.[75] In *A Plea for the West*, Beecher likened Catholicism in the region to the "locusts of Egypt."[76] Popery, he proclaimed, had grand designs on the West; the threat was both immediate and dire.[77] Religious writers warned New England and New York readers that the papist presence in the West posed a direct challenge to the destiny of America.[78] Moreover, the battle over the future of the region and the nation would be fought in St. Louis.

Eastern readers were told that St. Louis was the Catholic strong-hold in the West. In 1833, for example, the *Home Missionary* con-cluded that "St. Louis is the seat of Romanism in the West."[79] "The most energetic of the agents of Rome," a Presbyterian minister observed in 1848, "have chosen St. Louis as their centre of operations in the valley of the Mississippi."[80] Some writers viewed German settlement plans as open and direct evidence of popish aggression. To these observers, the increasing German population of St. Louis signaled the start of a Romanist invasion.[81] Nativists also noted that French Catholics had founded St. Louis; the name of the city pro-vided a constant reminder of the Catholic presence in the region.[82] Moreover, evidence of their designs abounded. In 1835 Lyman Beecher charged that Catholics had already gained control of local institutions.[83] A Presbyterian official reached a similar conclusion, explaining that Rome had successfully "destroyed" the common school system and reduced the local press to a state of "bondage."[84] With its fortified position in St. Louis, popery had begun to "compen-sate herself for her losses in the old world," another religious spokes-man warned.[85] More important, from their base in St. Louis the agents of Rome planned to lay siege to the region and to the nation.[86]

Nativist literature increased eastern interest in St. Louis. The tone of Beecher's message was one of moral crusade, not resignation. Like other religious writers, he called for a vigorous campaign to reclaim the city and the region. Thus, this literature complemented the more sanguine appeals to save the West from savagery, and the two movements overlapped, issuing a broad-based call to arms to "noble Christians" in the Northeast.[87] The American Home Missionary Soci-ety was established with both crusades firmly in mind.[88] Spearhead-ing the campaign for the promotion of "moral advancement and political stability in the United States," this organization generated interest in the Christian mission in the region.[89] Other groups, such as the American Sunday-School Union, echoed the message of an apocalyptic struggle to reclaim the city.[90]

This crusade to save the West from Romanism enhanced the reputation of the city. Along with other religious writers, Beecher indirectly but unmistakably emphasized the less spiritual advantages of St. Louis. As the principal battleground in this decisive struggle, St. Louis was deemed the "place of destiny" by religious and nativist writers.[91] The Pope had chosen the city, the *Home Missionary* ob-served, because it commanded the West. "Where is the centre that is to have the greatest influence?" the magazine inquired. "Let our enemies instruct us. The Bishop of St. Louis has more ecclesiastics under his control than any other in the country."[92] All of St. Louis's advantages are appreciated "in the conclaves of Rome and Vienna," the *Home Missionary* noted in 1842, "and an army of ecclesiastics is poured in to gain and to hold this fair position for Antichrist."[93] The clergyman W. W. Whipple, writing in 1847, was hardly surprised that popery had expended "all this effort" on St. Louis. "The importance of Missouri . . . is beyond our conception," he concluded.[94] Unintentionally drawing attention to the more worldly advantages of the city, the *Home Missionary* observed in 1842 that "St. Louis enjoys the preeminent advantage of a position in the centre of the great valley of the West . . . this is a commanding point."[95] Eastern readers recognized that the potential of such a "commanding point" extended far beyond the spiritual realm.[96]

In their zeal to reclaim the West from savagery and Romanism, religious and nativist writers elevated St. Louis to hitherto unknown prominence. Discussions of the strategic importance of St. Louis appeared again and again in eastern magazines during this period, and battle tales and missionary reports announced the extraordinary geographical advantages of the city. If the "combined forces of Infidelity and Popery" conquer St. Louis, nativists warned, the battle will be lost.[97] On the other hand, Beecher, the *Home Missionary*, the American Sunday-School Union, and a host of other influential sources concluded that a successful campaign would establish St. Louis as the centerpiece of a flourishing Christian republic. The forecast was conditional, though the advantages of St. Louis were obvious. St. Louis would become the commercial and cultural capital of the West for the same reasons that it would become the religious cornerstone of the region. Worldly missions and spiritual crusades were easily blurred by eastern readers; doubtless religious leaders were not unaware of the utility of a broad appeal and of confused goals.

Travel writers and religious crusaders distorted the reputation of St. Louis. They were more concerned with the literary purposes or the moral crusades that inspired western visits than with accuracy. Adventure writers, for example, exaggerated the rugged character of St. Louis in order to lend excitement to their western narratives, and eastern migrants, desperately searching for the St. Louis of popular literature, often expressed disappointment with the city.[98] The Vermont-native Goodell Bancroft, feeling misled by the "eastern views of the western country," complained that "as to the inhabitants of St. Louis and the western country being a set of gamblers, cutthroats, murderers and robbers it is all humbug. I cannot hardly realize that I am in the far west."[99] The images that attracted Bancroft were both seductive and overdrawn.

Religious and nativist writers were equally guilty of generating embellished images to suit their crusades.[100] Despite the extraordinary attention that the *Home Missionary* devoted to the Catholic threat in St. Louis, agents for the American Home Missionary Society consistently reported that the Catholic presence in the region was weak.[101] Such correspondence, however, never appeared in the magazine. One St. Louis resident warned that the nativist crusaders posed a greater threat than the "popish invaders." "We are told, indeed, by sectarists, that the Catholics have evil designs," William Greenleaf Eliot noted in 1837. "Perhaps it is so; but, until they exhibit such designs by other modes than doing good, we do not feel authorized to join in preaching a crusade against them."[102] Eliot found the specter of "a thousand preachers raising the war-cry against the Pope" misguided and dangerous.[103]

Similarly, reports of heathens and outlaws ravaging the city were borrowed from western adventure stories. Literary accounts, it seems, drew heavily from one another. In 1828, for example, Timothy Flint, the missionary who traveled throughout the Mississippi valley, reported that "miners, trappers, adventurers, immigrants, and people of all characters" gathered in St. Louis. Moreover, he warned that the city, because it was located at the very edge of civilized society, "still furnishes a temporary home to desperate and abandoned characters, who hope, in crossing the Mississippi, to fly beyond law and conscience."[104] Two decades later, Carter A. Goodrich, the author of *The Family Tourist*, described St. Louis with exactly the same words – without attribution.[105] Nine years later, Charles Dana borrowed part of this quotation in his description of St. Louis – also without attribution.[106] If the city had changed during the three decades after Flint's visit, travel accounts often recorded literally no flux – either in the city or in the words chosen to describe it.

These exaggerated images, however, shaped eastern perceptions of St. Louis between 1830 and 1850. They sharpened the apparent contrast between staid eastern life and exciting western life. Although few migrants traveled to St. Louis specifically to save the West from Catholic invaders, to bring civilization to a land of savagery, or to fight Indians in the streets, such images directed attention to St. Louis. But more important, this publicity broadened the appeal of the city. Religious and nationalist crusades, like western adventure, provided additional justifications for migrating to St. Louis. These images lent a cloak of respectability to more worldly pursuits in the area. Popular literary descriptions of a moral crusade and a religious mission in St. Louis simultaneously reinforced and veiled the lure of western riches.

Most discussions of the city included implicit or explicit allusions to the extraordinary economic potential of St. Louis. Even religious spokesmen tried to mold their crusades and battle cries to dovetail with the powerful economic appeal of the city. Ministers blended and confused the unstated worldly advantages of St. Louis with a much-discussed spiritual mission in the Far West.

In their desire to demonstrate the malleability of the city, eastern writers emphasized the vitality and the promise of St. Louis. Even observers who visited during the depths of the financial panic of the late 1830s and the early 1840s, for example, discussed the vigor of the city. Some of these writers simply pandered to their audiences. They described the West of legend rather than the West of reality. Daniel Webster saw only growth and progress when he visited the city in 1837. "All this," Webster wrote, "from the wilderness which but a few short years since, was howling here."[107] Other visitors, no doubt, failed to appreciate the nature of local problems. St. Louis continued to grow, even during the most depressed years of the period – often at a faster rate than older and much larger urban centers. But some writers, particularly religious and nationalist crusaders, needed to affirm the vitality of St. Louis; images of flux reinforced the potential of the city and underscored the urgency of their campaigns. Regardless of their motivations, however, eastern writers reported that St. Louis was mushrooming. Its growth exceeded "the anticipations of futurity."[108]

Far from considering the institutional obstacles that strained the local economy, they told their readers that St. Louis was a city of "astonishing progress."[109] Its development, De Bow's Review concluded, "has had no parallel in any country."[110] Western gazetteer Charles Dana reported that its growth "outrivals the most astonishing performances of the genii of the Lamp of Alladin."[111] So rapid was the city's ascent that one British traveler insisted the "gigantically-growing-up dwellings seemed every morning to be about a story higher than we left them on the preceding night."[112] Somewhat less enchanting was Lady Emmeline Stuart-Wortley's explanation for such unbridled growth: It was "as if they [local buildings] slept during the night on guano."[113]

Eastern observers assured their readers that St. Louis was a city of "destiny." Moreover, according to travel writers, the economic destiny of St. Louis matched the spiritual destiny of the city. If the small trading post inevitably would become the religious capital of the West, its commercial future appeared equally certain. One travel account, for example, insisted that St. Louis was "destined in time to become the GREAT CITY OF THE WEST [sic]."[114] The North American Review reported that St. Louis "is destined to become . . . the metropolis of a widespread and fertile region."[115] According to other writers, St. Louis would become the "New York of the interior," "one of the largest cities of the world," the "London of the New World," and even the "next Rome."[116] Such predictions were commonplace. In 1842, J. S. Buckingham, the author of *The Eastern and Western States of America*, conceded that "it requires no gift of prophecy, therefore, to predict that it will ultimately become the largest city in the Western World."[117] These reports, which emphasized the economic potential of the city, blended nicely with the religious and nativist literature that discussed the spiritual and political destiny of the trading center.

Many writers insisted that natural forces would elevate St. Louis to preeminence. The western editor, promoter, and politician William Gilpin announced that St. Louis possessed a hinterland roughly the same size as the Mediterranean basin.[118] More important, Gilpin noted that St. Louis was squarely situated on the "Isothermal Zodiac," the latitudinal band upon which the great civilizations of mankind and the principal commercial centers have been located.[119] Borrowing freely from the German geographer Alexander von Humboldt, Gilpin traced fifty centuries of the "divine instinct of progress."[120] The great natural "axis of intensity," "the immortal fire of civilization," he noted, would soon reach St. Louis. Independence and St. Louis, according to Gilpin, would ultimately "stand out upon the face of the continent like eyes in the human head. The peculiar configuration of the continent, and its rivers and plains," Gilpin concluded, "make these two natural focal points."[121]

Many more conventional thinkers also believed that nature had blessed St. Louis. In 1839 the conservative *North American Review* reported that St. Louis "is one of those points which seemed formed by nature for the sites of large cities."[122] Travel writers announced that St. Louis "commanded" the Mississippi valley, and its domain extended from the Ohio valley to the farthest reaches of settlement.[123] "Physical law," *De Bow's Review* maintained, must make St. Louis a "great distributing center."[124]

Some travel writers compared the city to New York. Not only was St. Louis following in the footsteps of the great eastern metropolis, but the character of the Missouri trading post reminded many visitors of the nation's commercial capital. St. Louis, wrote one observer in 1841, "has a lofty air . . . and its business exhibits an activity and animation like New York."[125] Elizabeth Ellet, the author of *Summer Rambles in the West*, reported that the "forest-girdled mart" of St. Louis was "the New York of the West."[126] The "apparently inextricable confusion and bustle, noise and animation of the levee" confirmed such observations, and explicit comparisons between New York and St. Louis framed many assessments of the commercial potential of the city.[127]

Unlike New York, however, St. Louis was a young city. Although New York had few commercial rivals, St. Louis, travel writers insisted, would be the city of the future. Ubiquitous references to youth and growth highlighted the economic promise of the western entrepôt. "The city of St. Louis," *De Bow's Review* noted in 1846, "is yet in its infancy."[128] A western gazetteer insisted that St. Louis was still in the "morning of life."[129] With such a "childhood," a German visitor wrote in 1851, "what a manhood this suggests."[130] Other observers noted that "this incipient city" was "just of age."[131] Such allusions to youth reinforced the view that St. Louis's development could be shaped.

Opportunity appeared unparalleled in St. Louis precisely because the economy of the city was just beginning to blossom. Writers noted that newcomers could occupy commanding positions in the burgeoning economy. Not only was local commerce unfettered by the flabby offspring of an established elite, but the marketplace was expanding with astonishing speed. "The pulsations of a mighty commercial youth," according to one writer, "offered a wide and rapidly expanding field."[132] Although Cincinnati remained larger through the 1840s, travel writers argued that St. Louis would soon "outstrip" its rival. Charles Mackay, a British traveler, concluded that "St. Louis contains greater elements of prosperity and increase than its sister on the Ohio."[133] Travel writers, like religious spokesmen, were quick to note that the harvest of opportunity could soon be reaped in St. Louis; the future beckoned.

Ironically, according to some eastern visitors, the economic problems that beset St. Louis underscored the city's rich future. Only the problems of commercial youth limited local development. Many writers predicted that, with proper cultivation, the city would simply outgrow its structural defects. These observers, for example, explained that the fixtures of economic growth were not yet in place in youthful St. Louis; manufacturing and banking remained in their infancies. The economy was pregnant with opportunity, though easterners concluded that local residents lacked the resources and the skills to develop such raw potential. The marketplace needed to be nurtured and shaped by more experienced and capable hands. Like the moral climate of the city, the economy demanded eastern guidance.[134]

More important, travel writers told their Atlantic coast readers that for men of capital and talent – those able to marshal the unbridled character of the local economy – opportunity appeared limitless. Entrepreneurs who could establish new businesses in an uncharted marketplace would realize "profits equal to our hopes."[135] Opportunity dwarfed capital, and men with ample resources could forge their commercial empires in St. Louis. Only capital and experience were needed. "If persons have money to invest, here, is the place," a Philadelphia native noted in 1838.[136] St. Louis offered "wealth and prosperity," a British traveler concluded, to any stranger with "an active and zealous deportment."[137]

But travel writers did not encourage all of their eastern readers to migrate to St. Louis. Just as religious spokesmen sought only the strong and the righteous for the crusade in the city, travel writers cautioned men without resources, talent, or pluck to go elsewhere. St. Louis, most visitors agreed, lacked the "fixed institutions" that would provide steady work for men who depended on others for employment. Even the most optimistic observers cautioned that St. Louis was a dangerous place for those unable to forge their own opportunities. Gottfried Duden, the writer who discovered enormous virtue in Missouri's torrential thunderstorms, urged Germans who lacked resources and skills to avoid St. Louis. "Emigration without some capital," Duden warned, "is a risk which only the most dire necessity should impel one to undertake."[138] Another German writer warned "persons who cannot with absolute assurance count upon a definite amount of available capital . . . [to] positively desist from entertaining thoughts of emigration [to St. Louis]."[139] American writers concurred.[140]

These warnings reflected the hasty conclusions of travelers. Many eastern visitors attributed the rocky development of the depression-plagued city to the shortcomings of St. Louis residents. Just as they failed to conquer barbarism and proved unable to repel Catholic agents, the city's residents lacked the experience to harness the untamed economic potential of St. Louis. Commercial opportunities in the West required greater skill than that possessed by local traders. Some visitors overlooked the structural problems that St. Louis merchants confronted. Other writers, however, suggested that these difficulties provided additional evidence that St. Louis was the city of destiny.[141] The local economy, they concluded, simply lacked the maturity to provide for its own needs. In short, even the city's economic problems seemed to affirm the vigor of St. Louis.

The combination of an expanding marketplace, unbounded opportunity, and open institutions captured the attention of many distant readers. Literary sources are filled with references to the unique blend of youth and opportunity that travel writers toasted.[142] In 1844, for example, John Seaton explained to his father that he chose to migrate to St. Louis because he wanted "a small but growing place so that I could grow with it, and be looked upon, as you are in Greensburg [Kentucky], a firm and honest man."[143] Other migrants responded to the same attractions. John Kasson, frustrated that "hereditary tendencies" in the East "effectively shut out the younger men," migrated to St. Louis in 1850 because he believed that the city offered a "splendid" future for an enterprising stranger.[144] "Of all the cities or towns in the United States," according to Arthur Cunyghame's *A Glimpse at the Great Western Republic*, "St. Louis appeared to me to afford a good chance of success to a young and enterprising stranger."[145] In St. Louis, according to eastern writers, young men of talent and pluck could forge their own destinies.

In sum, the imagery of the West transformed every shortcoming into an asset. According to eastern writers, the plethora of local problems only confirmed the malleability and potential of St. Louis. The savagery of the residents called out to moral easterners, promising positions of influence to religious newcomers; the presence of Catholic invaders highlighted the strategic importance of the city; and the sluggish economic development of St. Louis bespoke the need for men of skill and experience. Thus, eastern writers insisted that talented and strong-willed Yankees could transform the city, making it a spiritual stronghold in an uncivilized land and a boomtown in a flourishing region.[146] The problems of the East and the problems of easterners could be solved on the banks of the Mississippi River. In the hands of writers who cared little about the city, St. Louis's image on the Atlantic coast distinguished it from its less celebrated rivals and exaggerated its attractions.

Many visitors reported that St. Louis was "primitive." The streets were rough; the residents were coarse; local institutions were immature; and the economy of St. Louis was undeveloped. Even steamboat travel became unsafe as visitors approached the city. Eastern writers, however, discovered that this image was uniquely malleable, and they tailored the city's reputation for specific purposes. Adventure writers found that St. Louis provided a splendid setting for tales of western excitement. Religious writers, building on the city's frontier reputation, shaped their descriptions of St. Louis to meet the larger spiritual crusades of the period. They argued that the city could become a Christian fortress in a crude land. To other observers, the primitive state of society implied a youthfulness and vigor that emphasized the growth that would inevitably accompany maturation. More important, the ease with which these cultural and economic attractions overlapped during the 1830s and 1840s gave the city an unusual reputation and set St. Louis apart from towns that relied exclusively upon locally manufactured images.

During the early 1840s the economy of St. Louis was in disarray. The effects of the Panic of 1837 had lingered well into the next decade, and the xenophobic state legislative program seemed to render recovery all but impossible. Local merchants saw little cause for optimism. Easterners, however, perceived another St. Louis. Unaware of the precise nature of the city's economic problems, distant readers associated St. Louis with the travel accounts of Timothy Flint and Carter Goodrich, the religious crusades of John Mason Peck and the *Home Missionary*, and the economic forecasts of James Hall and Freeman Hunt. Moreover, these images overlapped, forming a coherent and enticing picture.

The travel writers of the 1830s and 1840s reshaped the future of St. Louis. Their descriptions of the city blended the ideological, cultural, and religious concerns of the East with the spiritual attractions of the West and the economic attractions of the Missouri trading center. St. Louis appeared to be a kind of mirror image of eastern society, substituting the passion, the fluidity, and the promise of the West for the complacence, the rigidity, and the stagnation of the East. During the mid-1840s Yankees poured into St. Louis in search of economic and spiritual rewards. These newcomers were drawn to the St. Louis they had discovered in popular literature – a city of destiny in a land of unbounded opportunity.

4 *Yankee newcomers and prosperity*

Eastern attention did not, by itself, stimulate the development of western cities. Travel writers, religious spokesmen, and newspaper editors could present alluring portraits of bustling cities at the edge of civilization, but unless capitalists and potential migrants responded to these images, they had little effect. The dissemination of information about the urban West was only a catalyst for growth if it triggered investment and migration.[1] Many easterners, for example, had read about Alton, Illinois. Newspapers and western travelers often described the Mississippi river town where Elijah Lovejoy, the abolitionist editor, had been murdered. This information, however, directed few settlers to Alton, and thus it failed to influence the growth of the Illinois town. Descriptions of St. Louis, by comparison, not only captured the attention of Yankee readers but also produced an eastern response that transformed the development of the Missouri city and the urban West.

Accounts of life in St. Louis attracted investors and migrants, accelerating the pace of economic growth. During the mid-1840s many eastern entrepreneurs became convinced that the undeveloped river town would become the "New York of the West," and they directed their surplus capital to the city and lifted the local economy from the doldrums of the depression years. Moreover, descriptions in newspapers, personal correspondence, and popular literature persuaded eastern merchants and workers to "remove" to St. Louis, spurring local construction, inflating real estate values, and providing consumers for the increasingly busy shops that lined the levee. This influx of settlers and investment capital from the Atlantic coast enabled the economy to expand beyond the limitations imposed by the institutional "reforms" of the era and thus provided an ironic solution to the city's financial problems. After nearly a decade of relative stagnation, the local economy burgeoned, and the Missouri city mushroomed. During the late 1840s the population grew by more than 120 percent, increasing from 35,930 in 1845 to nearly eighty

61

thousand by the end of the decade; at midcentury St. Louis was the largest city west of Cincinnati and the eighth largest city in the nation. Eastern responses to literary descriptions sparked the boom.

Travel accounts and similar sources shaped the character of the migrants and capitalists who directed the city's ascent. Not all potential migrants and entrepreneurs knew about St. Louis. Many easterners were not exposed to the books and periodicals that celebrated the advantages of the Missouri trading center. Equally important, the images portrayed in tourist's journals and religious magazines did not appeal to most easterners. Relatively few Yankees wanted to travel half way across the continent and reestablish themselves in the urban West. Others were deterred by descriptions of local conditions, such as the frequent "visitations" of cholera, the presence of large numbers of Catholic and German settlers, and the primitive state of the city's economy. For a small group of easterners, however, St. Louis seemed ideal. To them, the combination of religious, cultural, and commercial attractions made the city especially appealing. Moreover, their backgrounds gave them special advantages in the urban West and enabled them to transform the city.

In short, eastern perceptions of the city exerted an enduring influence on the development of St. Louis. As a result of the reports and forecasts that they had read, Yankees arrived in St. Louis with specific business plans, investment strategies, and goals. These decisions – and the activities based upon them – triggered the midcentury boom and established St. Louis as the commercial capital of the West. But they also distorted the city's development in important ways.

By the late 1840s St. Louis was a population magnet. Newcomers flooded the city, filling its hotels and boarding houses beyond capacity. "The current," according to one migrant, was "ceaseless and unbroken."[2] During 1849 more than sixty thousand "strangers" passed through St. Louis, pouring in "literally from the four corners of the globe."[3] Over one-third of these travelers remained in the city; many chose to settle in St. Louis, while others were trapped in the city by disease and misfortune. Although the newcomers contributed handsomely to St. Louis's new prosperity, an earlier and much smaller wave of migrants had forged the foundation of this midcentury boom.

To the horror of rural Missourians, Yankees dominated the wave of migrants that settled in St. Louis during the mid-1840s. Nearly half of the native-born non-Missourians in the city in 1850 had traveled from the New England and mid-Atlantic states, and Pennsylvania and New York supplied more migrants than any other states in the

Union.[4] Unlike German and Irish newcomers, most of whom arrived at the height of the boom, these Yankees began migrating to St. Louis during the mid-1840s.[5] According to local observers, "go-ahead young New Englanders" and New Yorkers disembarked from their steamers and promptly transformed the city and its economy.[6]

The rebirth of St. Louis began on the fashionable streets of Boston and New York. During the 1840s social and economic changes weakened the bonds that tied many young Yankees to the Northeast. At the same time, these changes increased eastern interest in the Far West and dramatically enhanced the appeal of St. Louis. The antebellum period was a frustrating era for many well-bred Yankees. New England society no longer seemed to offer the challenges or the opportunities upon which earlier generations of hard-driving Yankees had flourished.[7] To many ambitious young men, the economy of the region appeared stale and overcrowded. Family businesses had few openings for enterprising young sons, and perhaps equally important, few trails seemed left to be blazed. After two generations of dramatic economic change and exciting entrepreneurial frontiers, including the rise of manufacturing, the early canal and railroad booms, and the China trade, the economy of the region appeared to offer little room for expansion – or excitement. The demise of the New Bedford whaling industry and the larger decline of the local economy, for example, convinced at least one New Englander, John Kasson, to leave the region, believing that young men faced bleak futures in the Northeast.[8] Increasingly, investors also looked beyond the Northeast for new ventures and challenges.[9]

But economic obstacles merely exaggerated other frustrations. New England and New York appeared socially stagnant. The vigor and spirit of the revolutionary generation haunted the sons of the men who had, according to local folklore, shaped their world. Polite rhythms of convention and order seemed to replace the challenges and opportunities of the past. One observer reported that aggressive young easterners "go into the wilderness" because they "feel themselves curbed in their outward and upward careers."[10] According to a New Englander, a "well-entrenched" elite prevented young men from succeeding in the region.[11] Distant struggles, however, attracted considerable attention. While northeastern society seemed staid and suffocating, the Far West was being wrested from "savagedom."[12]

Some young easterners turned to adventure-seeking and charged headlong into the wilderness. Men like Francis Parkman, searching for the excitement and challenges that had inspired earlier generations, looked far beyond the borders of their well-ordered world for spiritual fulfillment.[13] Somewhat later, Oliver Wendell Holmes, Jr., would look to the Civil War to escape the psychological burdens imposed by having been born a generation after the struggles of legend.[14]

Although neither Parkman nor Holmes was a typical New Englander, large numbers of young Yankees expressed the same kinds of frustrations.[15] The "settled institutions of old eastern society," for example, disillusioned John Kasson, driving the young attorney from the region.[16] Similarly, recent Williams College graduate Josiah McClellan found that the Atlantic coast offered neither fulfillment nor opportunity to an enterprising young man during the 1840s.[17] Both men, like Parkman and Holmes, felt that the Northeast held little for its ambitious and restless sons.

At the same time that frustrated easterners such as Kasson searched for new opportunities, the reputation of St. Louis became widely known. The city seemed to offer the kind of vigor and mission that northeastern society lacked. Travel writers insisted that St. Louis was young, dynamic, and a bit untamed.[18] Equally important, the character of the city, according to eastern visitors, remained unmolded; institutions were both open and growing. "Our standard of morality [in St. Louis] is not established," an influential minister warned. "It is chiefly for the young men of this city to say what it shall hereafter be. . . . The character of our young men is the character of our city."[19] The apparent "immaturity" and instability of St. Louis appeared especially alluring in comparison with the stodgy character of old New England. "Look particularly at the position which [St. Louis] occupies, and see if a young man could reasonably ask a nobler sphere of action or better opportunities," one writer noted. "Society places no obstacles in the way of his advancement."[20]

But St. Louis did not draw randomly from the pool of disaffected Yankee sons. Rather, newcomers came from a narrow band of eastern society. Economic factors discouraged poor men from undertaking the long trek from the Atlantic coast to the banks of the Mississippi. Steamboat fare to St. Louis often exceeded forty dollars during this period – more than a month's earnings for a worker – and few personal possessions could be transported.[21] Moreover, descriptions of the city often noted that St. Louis offered few opportunities for newcomers without considerable means.[22] Many knowledgeable observers recommended that unskilled workers avoid St. Louis. For men with "small capital," Gardner Folsome warned, "there is not much prospect for making anything."[23] Until the late 1840s, the economy of the city foundered; commerce languished, and manufacturing was virtually nonexistent. Writers urged men without resources to migrate elsewhere, though many reports indicated that "it is different for men of capital."[24]

The uneven circulation of information in antebellum America also exerted a selective influence on the flow of Yankees to St. Louis. Wealthy easterners, for example, had greater access to information about St. Louis than their working-class counterparts.[25] The religious journals that devoted attention to the city enjoyed larger followings in Beacon Hill parlors than in the saloons of the North End of Boston. More important, commercial networks comprised the principal conduits for detailed information about the western cities at this time. Business communications even dominated private correspondence during this period.[26] Commercial journals were leading sources of information about St. Louis. *Hunt's Merchants' Magazine*, for example, provided a wealth of data about the city and predicted that St. Louis would soon become an "emporium" of unrivaled dimension.[27] Thus, members of the middle class possessed the greatest knowledge of distant cities, and clerks, merchants, and shippers were most familiar with St. Louis and best able to evaluate its offerings. As a result of the flow of information, migrants were overwhelmingly drawn from major urban centers. Bostonians comprised over 90 percent of the New Englanders in St. Louis during this period, and migrants from New York City dominated the current of travelers from the mid-Atlantic region.[28]

Finally, cultural factors shaped the character of the migrants who traveled to St. Louis during the mid-1840s. Religious and literary descriptions of the city promised social standing and public influence to the hardy souls who dared to tame rough-hewn St. Louis.[29] Such descriptions, like the economic attractions of the city, held a special resonance for the frustrated well-bred young men of the antebellum Northeast. Henry Adams, a man uniquely tormented by the social changes that denied prominence to the young patriciate, contemplated migrating to St. Louis in order to find fulfillment. Writing during the 1850s, Adams noted that St. Louis, unlike his native Boston, was a place where "an educated and reasonably able man can make his mark."[30] Similarly, newcomer James Cowan assured an eastern friend that "there is every advantage here to bring a man of your turn and genius into notice."[31] On the banks of the great river educated and well-bred Yankees expected to enjoy the prominence, to find the independence, and to encounter the sense of mission that had eluded them in the East. Moreover, the West seemed to hold the prescriptions for eastern ills.[32] Thus, the interaction between cultural and economic forces defined the pool of Yankees to whom St. Louis would be attractive.

Until the boom of the late 1840s, few easterners found the long and difficult journey to St. Louis worth undertaking. Most potential migrants were relatively unfamiliar with the attractions of the region.

Others, discouraged by economic factors, knew enough to avoid St. Louis. For wealthier Yankees, however, St. Louis represented an attractive site, one worthy of additional investigation.

But migration required careful consideration and planning. Easterners weighed the attractions of the urban West and studied conditions in St. Louis. John Lane, for example, solicited the advice of many relatives. After much thought, he concluded that because "necessity compels me to seek employment, and preferring to engage in business in a city, I have chosen St. Louis."[33] Similarly, before choosing to migrate to the Missouri trading center, Jonathan Clark traveled throughout the West and visited most of the major cities in the region.[34] Few working-class easterners could undertake so thorough and costly a search. Wealthy and middle-class Yankees possessed the greatest familiarity with St. Louis, the resources to undertake the journey, and the capital that was necessary to speculate in a wide-open market. Moreover, many middle-class easterners possessed the chauvinism to migrate to the West in order to recreate eastern society. In short, St. Louis appealed to wealthy Yankees, the majority of whom chose their western destinations long before they left the Northeast.

Most Yankee newcomers migrated directly to the city. If population movements within the Northeast were swirling and chaotic, the flow of newcomers to St. Louis during the mid-1840s was the opposite.[35] This migration was well organized and carefully planned.[36] Some Yankees had jobs awaiting them in the West. William Crowell, for example, left Boston with plans to edit a Baptist newspaper – the *Western Watchman* – in St. Louis, and William Babcock moved from Massachusetts in order to become the St. Louis agent for the Boston Belting Company.[37] Still more typical was Albert Pierce, who left New York City with plans to operate the western branch of his father-in-law's dry goods house.[38] Other Yankees emigrated from the Northeast with only general plans. William Young had five hundred dollars and a business venture in mind when he left his father's home in Vermont.[39] The overwhelming majority of the city's Yankees migrated to the West specifically to pursue opportunities in St. Louis.

The socio-economic status of the migrants varied directly with distance to the city.[40] As distance from St. Louis increased, economic and logistic factors made migration more difficult. In 1850 90 percent of adult males from New England and 53 percent of adult males from the mid-Atlantic region worked in commercial or professional positions in St. Louis. Young attorneys, such as John Kasson, and businessmen, such as Jonathan Clark, were typical of this group. Poorer Yankees, unable to investigate distant sites or to justify difficult journeys, more often traveled to regional entrepôts, thereby adding to the wave of short-distance migrants that peopled eastern cities.[41] By comparison, newcomers from the Midwest and the Mississippi valley clustered in manual callings. For example, more than three-fourths of the midwestern-born migrants to St. Louis during this period worked on the levee, in the craftsman's shop, or in other manual positions. For these travelers, the trip to St. Louis required little planning and scant expense. The economy of the city, however, held few attractions for midwesterners during this period, and most of these migrants were temporary residents such as John Phillips, a twenty-eight-year-old deckhand from Ohio. Phillips, who resided on board the steamboat *Iroquois*, was a part of the floating population of rivermen who regularly moved in and out of the city.[42] Until the economic explosion of the late 1840s, most native-born newcomers to St. Louis were wealthy young Yankees.

Once the flow of migrants from a particular region was established, friends, relatives, and business associates invariably followed.[43] A transplanted Newport merchant, for example, convinced the Unitarian minister William Greenleaf Eliot, a recent Harvard graduate, to migrate to St. Louis in 1836. During the next two decades Eliot made frequent trips to Boston, often returning to St. Louis with small groups of young Bostonians, including his brother-in-law John Kasson and his family. Nearly three-fourths of Eliot's St. Louis congregation had New England roots; the majority came from Boston and many had been friends before departing for St. Louis.[44] Similarly, during the mid-1830s Giles Filley migrated from New Haven to St. Louis, hoping to establish a stove manufactory in the Far West. Oliver Filley, later the mayor of St. Louis, followed his brother and assisted in the operation of the Excelsior Stove Works. The Filleys recruited their molders and factory workers from the New York area as well – all men of "considerable experience and respectably connected." Chauncy Filley, a native of New York City, also accompanied his cousins to the West and later established a china shop in the city. In all, dozens of relatives, workers, and their families followed Giles Filley from New Haven to St. Louis, contributing to the success of the stove works and the peopling of the urban West.[45] "Respectably connected" Yankees from urban backgrounds, traveling along well-established networks, migrated to St. Louis in increasing numbers during the mid-1840s and shaped the growth of the city.

Young doctors, lawyers, and ministers comprised nearly 10 percent of these northeastern migrants.[46] St. Louis offered special attractions to such young men, particularly the promise of status and independence. According to one young physician from Philadelphia, in St.

Louis "I could get into [a medical] practice sooner than at home." "In the East," John Seaton explained, "they are too cruel in keeping a man reading his eyes out for two or three years."[47] Similarly, a young Boston attorney explained that the "law business is very good here – much more than at the East . . . you can attain a livelihood easier than in N. England [sic]."[48] Another newcomer agreed, concluding in 1847 that "there is very little [legal] Talent [sic] here compared with the importance of the place."[49] Nathaniel Holmes traveled to the city shortly after graduating from Harvard College and being admitted to the Massachusetts Bar.[50] Harvard and Yale men migrated to St. Louis and assumed prominent positions in the bulging middle class of the city.[51]

A reputation for disease, rumors about protracted court battles involving old Spanish land titles, a general reputation for godlessness, and the potential for instant status made St. Louis a magnet for Yankee doctors, lawyers, and clergymen during this period. Unfortunately, the arrival of these young easterners preceded the long-expected boom, and doctors and lawyers abounded. "There are too many physicians here," a doctor complained.[52] Newspapers overflowed with advertisements for newly arrived doctors and lawyers from the East, and local law enforcers felt compelled to arrest dozens of "lawyers without licenses."[53] One newcomer discovered that "the name of dentist, like that of attorney, is to be seen on every other door in the principal streets."[54] "Every third or fourth house," another observer noted, "had its inscription of physician."[55] The impact of this wave of Yankees was immediate and ironic; young doctors and lawyers affected one another more than they changed the city. According to Frederick Graff, "they undermine and abuse each other."[56] "It is ludicrous in the extreme," John Seaton wrote to his father in 1844.[57] Local conditions "disheartened and disgusted" many of the newcomers.[58]

For other well-bred young easterners, however, St. Louis fulfilled every expectation, and their impact was dramatic. The potential of the city's marketplace attracted a small army of Yankee merchants to Missouri. "The counting-rooms, the stores, the mills and the machine-shops [sic]," an eastern newspaper correspondent reported, were ". . . filled by New Englanders and New Yorkers."[59] These newcomers started nearly three-fourths of the businesses that opened their doors in the city between 1845 and 1847.[60] In 1850 over 70 percent of the Massachusetts men in St. Louis were merchants, and over one-third of New York and Pennsylvania men engaged in commercial pursuits. "Unprincipled fortune hunters," one unimpressed observer complained, "hasten from Europe and the Eastern States to the West [in order] to find a freer scope for their savage passions."[61] But more important, Yankee merchants transformed the local economy and the development of antebellum St. Louis.

Structural changes in the economy of the Northeast directed young businessmen to the urban West. Cultural forces, such as dreams of power, status, and mission, may have pulled these men to St. Louis, though broader economic forces pushed them from the Atlantic coast. International events, for example, contributed to this migration, forcing the leading commercial houses of New York and Boston to search for new markets. Just as eastern investors sought new outlets, the maturing West became a fertile field for investment.

Nearly 40 percent of the merchants who migrated to St. Louis during the mid-1840s came from New York. These businessmen responded to the changing structure of the economy of the Northeast. After nearly five years of stagnation, the economy of New York recovered from the depression of the previous decade during the early 1840s and blossomed during the mid-1840s. The repeal of the English Corn Laws and repeated European crop failures created booming markets for American agricultural goods.[62] Millions of tons of western produce passed through New York on its way to Europe, bringing new wealth to New York shippers and commission merchants and making the city a major international port. In return for cotton and for foodstuffs, English, French, and German merchants transported European manufactures to New York and flooded the city with ready-made clothing and other goods; New York was deluged by a sea of cheap clothes.[63] The increasing bounty of western agriculture exacerbated this balance-of-trade problem and contributed to the glut of manufactures in New York. Local merchants were left with far more imports than they could sell within the region. Searching for new markets for surplus clothing and textile goods, New York commission merchants looked outside the region and often turned to the West, a rapidly expanding market for manufactures. Many of these businessmen settled in St. Louis in order to tap the western market.

By comparison, Philadelphia sent relatively few merchants to St. Louis. Although the economy of Philadelphia, like that of New York, burgeoned during the 1840s, merchants from the Pennsylvania city established fewer than 9 percent of the businesses that opened during this period. Instead, the Philadelphia market captured the fruits of local prosperity.[64] The city's hinterland became a major manufacturing center and the driving force in the economic development of the region. Moreover, this growing manufacturing sector absorbed both surplus capital and entrepreneurial energy, reducing the flow of merchants or venture capital outside the region.[65] In fact, local producers lacked the resources and the expertise to distribute their goods, and Philadelphia manufacturers relied on New York merchants to market their manufactures. As a consequence, the expanding production of Philadelphia factories added to the overstocked New York market and reinforced the tendency of New York merchants to consider distant markets and long-distance trade.[66]

Many Boston merchants migrated to St. Louis during the mid-1840s. These newcomers quickly established themselves in the local marketplace, directing nearly one-fifth of the commercial ventures in St. Louis during the late 1840s. Like New Yorkers, Bostonians were directed to the Far West by changes in the economy of the Northeast. In part, Boston manufacturers simply produced more goods than the local market could absorb. Shoe production, for example, far exceeded regional consumption, and manufacturers from Lynn, Hopkington, and other surrounding towns had long looked outside of the region to market surplus goods. As early as the 1830s Lynn manufacturers had employed traveling agents to sell their shoes in the South and the West.[67] Because the output of Massachusetts factories grew much faster than the local market, the sale of surplus goods outside New England increased dramatically during the antebellum period.

Moreover, many wealthy Boston merchants were familiar with long-distance commerce. Although the great manufactories of Waltham, Lynn, and Lowell had absorbed vast pools of capital earlier in the century, by the 1830s the economy of the region offered fewer attractive outlets for investment.[68] Instead, Boston capitalists often looked outside the region. Some entrepreneurs had already been active in the China trade, which educated a generation of merchants, including John Murray Forbes and William Sturgis, in the complexities and the rewards of far-flung investments and commerce.[69] During the mid-1840s, however, changing political conditions in the Far East disrupted the China trade, robbing Boston merchants of their profitable and glamorous distant enterprises.[70] Yankee investors searched for new investments between 1845 and 1850, when, according to Forbes, the city overflowed with surplus capital.[71] Unsatisfied with local investments, Boston capitalists once again looked beyond the region. At the same time, the West offered attractive returns and excitement. During the mid-1840s Boston capital flowed into a variety of new and distant ventures, including St. Louis commission houses, Illinois railroads, Michigan copper mines, and California wholesale firms.[72]

At a time when structural changes in the economy of New York and Boston directed the attention of Yankee merchants and capitalists to the West, improvements in transportation technology focused much of that attention on St. Louis. Until the early 1840s most eastern manufactures and imported goods reached southern and western destinations via New Orleans. Steamers carried these articles up the Mississippi to smaller distribution centers along the river, comprising the "up trade" of the antebellum period. Thus, New York commission merchants maintained close ties with southern traders. The construction of northern canals, however, gradually redirected the flow of goods, and Yankee merchants increasingly relied on canals and the northern river system to carry manufactures to distant markets.[73]

This route generated enormous prosperity for St. Louis. Located at the western tip of the northern river network, the city became the principal distribution point for both western and southern markets. Ohio River steamboats, for example, brought increasing cargoes of New York goods to St. Louis for distribution in the West. Furthermore, a growing proportion of manufactured goods traveling down the Mississippi passed through the city before reaching southern markets. By the late 1840s this "down trade" far exceeded the flow of goods up the Mississippi, and St. Louis surpassed New Orleans as a steamboat port. For example, in 1851 – still before railroads altered the rhythms of western commerce – the "down trade" was worth nearly three times the value of goods carried up the river.[74] St. Louis captured the lion's share of this trade. But more important, eastern entrepreneurs believed that the city would "command" the western economy, and during the mid-1840s St. Louis became a magnet for eastern merchants, who expected to make 10 percent to 15 percent on their Missouri investments.[75]

Market forces shaped Yankee involvement in the western marketplace during this period, discouraging all but the largest northeastern firms from engaging in long-distance commerce. The western trade was an expensive and hazardous undertaking during the 1840s. Long-distance commerce required considerable capital. Eastern suppliers had to advance large amounts of capital to their distributors, often for the entire course of the selling season. In addition, remittances included heavily discounted – and sometimes worthless – local scrip. Purchasing stock and transporting it to the West was costly as well. Western commission houses or manufactories frequently required initial investments of tens of thousands of dollars. The shortcomings of the antebellum banking system magnified these demands; venture capital was expensive and in relatively short supply.[76] Even small operations required sizable investments. In 1846 Samuel Troth, a Philadelphia drug manufacturer, estimated that establishing a "respectable" drugstore in St. Louis would require at least one thousand dollars of working capital.[77] Few eastern entrepreneurs could afford such outlays.

Other obstacles contributed to the hazards of long-distance trade as well. Western markets were notoriously unstable during this period, and smaller houses could seldom withstand the financial storms that rocked commerce in the region; fires, bankruptcies, and other mishaps were legion. Bernard Manheimer, for example, reported to his creditors that a bizarre string of bad luck left him unable to settle his account. After closing his country store, Manheimer resolved to visit New Orleans in order to repay his debts. Along the way, he explained, tragedy struck. "With $1500 and $900 which I borrowed I went to settle up with my creditors and was attacked by Indians and White men and robbed of all this money." Manheimer's anxious creditors received nothing.[78] More conventional problems also haunted Yankee capitalists. Steamboat explosions, for example, destroyed tons of eastern manufactures long before they arrived in distant markets. In 1849 eighty-three vessels "sunk, burned . . . or were otherwise destroyed on the Western waters." Losses exceeded $1.5 million, giving pause to suppliers, backers, and insurers.[79] Only the largest and strongest eastern houses could purchase surplus manufactured goods in the East, transport them to the Far West, and speculate in the St. Louis provisions market. Although the western trade offered handsome profits, it entailed considerable risks as well.

These obstacles influenced the character and the structure of Yankee ventures in the West. Northeasterners came from wealthy families and established large-scale and well-financed enterprises during the mid-1840s.[80] Nearly half the firms operated by Boston and New York entrepreneurs began with capital investments in excess of ten thousand dollars.[81] The cultural attractions of the city appealed especially to middle-class Yankees; the logistical difficulties of migration reinforced this selective migration; and the financial requirements of merchandising narrowed the socio-economic character of the newcomers still more.

Yankee entrepreneurs organized their St. Louis business ventures in ways that facilitated the flow of goods, capital, and personnel over great distances and minimized the problems that disrupted such commerce.[82] Some newcomers formed partnerships with local merchants. The eastern partner usually provided the capital and procured the manufactured goods. The western partner in such arrangements drew upon his knowledge of the local marketplace and managed the store or dealt with the country merchants who pur-

chased their supplies in the city. Other Yankees used their northeastern connections to become agents for Atlantic coast firms. A. M.
Farley, for example, migrated from Boston, where he had worked for
a rubber company, to St. Louis and established himself as the local
agent for a number of Boston and New York businesses, including
U.S. Rubber, Novelty Rubber, Congress Rubber, American Rubber,
and Boston Rubber.[83] These arrangements enabled northeastern entrepreneurs to enter the western market without having to rely on
strangers, and they allowed migrants to obtain capital and goods and
to establish businesses very quickly.

More often, however, formal ties linked Yankee newcomers to their
suppliers and financial backers. Many migrants formed independent
firms in St. Louis that shared partners with independent firms in
Boston or New York. For example, John J. Manny settled in St. Louis
in 1848 and established Manny & Weld, a business that sold shoes for
Bennett & Weld of Boston. Aaron Weld oversaw both ventures, and
in Manny, his former bookkeeper, he had a trustworthy, experienced
manager for the western outlet.[84] Other Yankees established formal
branches of northeastern businesses. The distinction between a formal branch and a set of ventures with overlapping partners was often
minimal, and financial writers frequently used the term "branch"
when discussing either arrangement.

Most Yankee newcomers established branches of large northeastern firms. Nearly 80 percent of the businesses begun by Massachusetts natives and 66 percent of those initiated by New York
migrants operated as outlets for eastern firms – fewer than one-third
of the firms started by midwesterners during the mid-1840s operated
as branches. Many of these businesses distributed the surplus manufactures of the leading houses in the Northeast. Harris Breed, for
example, managed the St. Louis outlet of the Breed Shoe and Boot
Company, the largest shoe manufacturer in Lynn, Massachusetts.[85]
The greater the distance the entrepreneur traveled, the greater the
likelihood that his firm had formal ties to northeastern backers and
suppliers and the larger the scale of the enterprise.

As a consequence of these business arrangements, a steady stream
of well-bred young Yankees migrated to St. Louis during the 1840s.
The majority of the largest commercial houses in the antebellum
period were family concerns, and the sons and nephews of prominent eastern merchants poured into the city.[86] William Claflin, for
example, arrived in St. Louis during the early 1840s in order to
manage the western outlet of his father's shoe manufactory. The son
of a wealthy Hopkington, Massachusetts factory owner and banker,
Claflin had attended Brown University and spent three years learning

the family business before he relocated to St. Louis. The elder Claflin, however, maintained a close eye on the branch, sending a steady stream of stock, capital, and experienced clerks to his western outlet.[87] Similarly, Robert Henning, a partner in one of New York City's largest clothing houses, sent his son-in-law to establish Woodruff and Henning, a St. Louis branch of the New York firm.[88] Other eastern merchants expanded their houses to accommodate maturing sons. Benjamin Fenton, the founding partner of a New York commission house, had three sons and established branches in Cincinnati, Memphis, and St. Louis during this period.[89] For Henry Simon, however, the problem was not as easily solved. The head of "one of the oldest retail dry goods houses in Baltimore," Simon had twelve children, seven of whom were "engaged in the business." Although three were sent to St. Louis, Simon's younger sons crowded into the Baltimore office.[90]

Operating a distant outlet often represented a kind of apprenticeship in a family firm.[91] Young merchants hoped to prove themselves in the urban West, and their fathers hoped to test their sons' business acumen and, at the same time, to tap profitable western markets. In 1842, for example, Luther Laflin became impressed with the commercial potential of St. Louis and sent his son Sylvester to the city to establish a "branch depot" of the family's Saugerties, New York, powder company. Sylvester Laflin was to "commence at the bottom and work up, and show by the business character he developed, whether he was capable of managing an important business interest." After seven years he received a partial interest in the St. Louis branch.[92] John Willard, the outlet manager for a New York commission house, received one-third of the profits of his branch.[93] Such arrangements were quite common, and resident partners received a portion – often half – of that outlet's profits. Former clerks who operated branches often got the same kind of limited partnerships.

Because they began as outlets for eastern commercial houses, Yankee ventures in St. Louis depended on home offices and fathers in Boston and New York. Personnel, capital, supplies, and every other form of corporate sustenance flowed to St. Louis from the Atlantic coast.[94] Without support from State Street and Wall Street headquarters, St. Louis branches could not survive. Like most large firms in the city, William Jennings's commission house depended on outside assistance. According to St. Louis credit investigators, "if not for this [rich father] do not think [the firm] would last long."[95] Western outlets, by design, relied on capital from eastern offices. Although independent concerns lacked formal ties to backers and suppliers, these firms also depended on premigration business net-

works, and pleas to relatives for financial assistance dominated business correspondence during this period.[96] Most transplanted
Yankees relied on northeastern backers during the 1840s, and New
York firms comprised the principal creditors in all but a few of the
deeds and debts of assignment filed in the Missouri Circuit Court
during this period.[97]

Thus, eastern investors controlled the fortunes of the largest
houses in St. Louis; or rather, eastern merchants kept tight reins on
their young sons in the West. When enthusiastic young merchants in
St. Louis overstepped their authority, New York fathers merely
tightened the commercial purse strings and constricted the flow of
resources. More important, the largest businesses in St. Louis were
vulnerable to financial problems in New York or Boston. The failure
of eastern offices, for example, invariably toppled western branches.
Despite a $100,000 investment and nearly four years of prosperity,
Theodore Simmons's St. Louis clothing house survived less than one
month after the failure of McKnight, Enders, and Simmons of
Boston.[98] Close ties to eastern markets translated into a peculiar
vulnerability for St. Louis firms. John J. Murdock's commission business, long considered "as safe as any house in St. Louis," collapsed
immediately after the failure of its Philadelphia backer.[99] When the
New York market sputtered, eastern ties became lethal bonds and
dragged even the strongest western firms into bankruptcy.[100]

The close relationship between eastern houses and St. Louis
branches manifested itself in other ways as well. Resident managers,
for example, seldom developed close ties to St. Louis. These migrants
served temporary terms in distant outlets. Eastern offices generally
shuttled young clerks to and from western branches, exposing young
managers to all sides of family operations while they served their
commercial apprenticeships. Archibald Young established a St. Louis
branch of his father's New York clothing firm in 1846. Two years later
Young was replaced by his brothers David and Thomas. By the
mid-1850s brothers Daniel and Alex were in charge of the St. Louis
branch.[101] Similarly, Aaron Weld served for four years in the St. Louis
branch of his father's boot and shoe firm. In 1852 Weld was "recalled"
to Boston, and William Downing, a young shoe merchant from Lynn,
filled his slot as branch manager.[102] For William Claflin, independence accompanied his return to Boston. After three years in his
father's Hopkington shoe factory and an additional three years as the
manager of his father's St. Louis outlet, Claflin's apprenticeship had
finally ended. In 1850 he returned to Massachusetts, having achieved
symbolic adulthood; a short time later, Claflin married and opened
his own factory.[103]

As a result of the flow of branch managers to and from St. Louis, many of the men who directed the largest commercial houses in the West considered themselves visitors in the city.[104] Ninety percent of St. Louis's Massachusetts-born businessmen and 87 percent of New York merchants were recent migrants to the city. More important, nearly half of these Yankee merchants lived in boardinghouses, and most remained unmarried during their terms in St. Louis. The operators of major commercial firms often occupied rooms in the city's more fashionable hotels; many lived in the opulent Planter's House, an inn patterned after the Tremont, an exclusive Boston hotel.[105] St. Louis's newest and wealthiest entrepreneurs maintained abiding ties to the Northeast.

Unlike eastern businessmen, the merchants of St. Louis rarely owned property in the city. Only 17 percent of local businessmen in 1850 possessed real estate in St. Louis.[106] Barely 11 percent of New York natives in the city owned property, and among transplanted New Englanders, most of whom were wealthy branch operators, only 5 percent invested in real estate. Credit investigators, unaccustomed to the peculiar status of St. Louis merchants, were puzzled by the financial position of local firms such as the Riggs and Levering Commission House. Although the venture's operators owned no real estate, a sure sign of standing and solidity in the East, Riggs and Levering possessed considerable wealth and directed a large and well-financed business.[107] In St. Louis during the 1840s there was no clear relationship among wealth, residential status, and real estate holdings.[108] The eastern ties that sustained western ventures discouraged Yankee merchants from establishing economic roots in St. Louis. Newcomers relocated in order to serve Yankee businesses and Yankee culture; St. Louis represented a temporary staging point – not a permanent home.

Changes in the economic fortunes of branches often prompted Yankees to return to the Northeast. Successful managers were recalled and rewarded with partnership in the main offices, and unsuccessful Yankee merchants were either replaced by their siblings or, more frequently, entrepreneurs abandoned their commercial efforts in the urban West. More than two-thirds of the eastern traders whose ventures failed during the late 1840s left the city; the majority returned to New York and Boston.[109] St. Louis held little for these men. W. L. Bigelow, for example, told credit reporters that he had not "succeeded as well as expected." Bigelow "transferred" his stock to New York and returned home.[110] Boothe, Drake, and Conn, the western branch of a New York commission house, conceded that they had "met with poor success here and have become discouraged."

Shortly thereafter, the resident partners departed for New York City.[111] Boston native Elizabeth Sargent begged her husband to "return home" before necessity compelled such a move. "A great many failures are expected this summer," she warned in 1846. "I tell Haven he must make a fortune quick and go east to settle."[112] Successful firms shuttled young partners back and forth from the East, and less successful merchants returned to New York and Boston at the first chance. Elizabeth Sargent explained that St. Louis "is a good place to make money . . . but I feel a drawing toward dear native New England."[113] For many Yankee merchants, economic ties to the Northeast reinforced emotional bonds; "home" remained on the Atlantic coast.

Maintaining close ties to eastern backers and suppliers proved to be a double-edged sword for Yankee migrants in St. Louis during the 1840s. Somewhat shielded from the vicissitudes of western commerce, young newcomers enjoyed much of the status that had eluded them in their father's counting rooms on Wall Street and State Street. In St. Louis, they received the respect accorded prominent merchants in a trading center, and local observers considered branch managers to be "men of means."[114] The thousand-mile journey to the Mississippi valley, however, provided only limited independence for Yankee merchants. Despite their new-found status, they remained largely agents for their fathers and uncles in the East. Even their wealth was more symbolic than real. Far from being men of means, Yankee newcomers were the sons of men of means and exercised little control over the businesses they managed. In fact, Yankee newcomers probably enjoyed greater independence after they returned from St. Louis than they had while operating a Missouri outlet.

But if branch arrangements forced migrants to remain dependent on their relatives in the Northeast, such arrangements also gave Boston and New York businessmen a dramatic advantage in the local marketplace. The economic ties that linked branches in the West to main offices in the East – and sons in St. Louis to their fathers in New York and Boston – provided the economic ingredients that contributed to commercial success in the Missouri trading center. As a result of their connections to eastern capital, credit, and distribution networks, Yankee merchants enjoyed tremendous prosperity in St. Louis.

Western capital shortages, for example, presented few problems for Yankee entrepreneurs. While St. Louis natives struggled to sustain their businesses in a city without banking facilities and without adequate capital or credit reserves, Yankee merchants relied on kinship networks and premigration sources for financial support.[115] Local credit investigators, for example, often reported that "very indulgent fathers" in the East poured capital into the businesses of young Yankee traders.[116] William Grier, who operated a grocery in the city, explained to credit investigators that his "relations are wealthy and he can get all the money he wants."[117] Eastern capital markets provided hundreds of Yankee migrants with large pools of venture capital. Nearly 90 percent of the firms begun by northeastern merchants received financial assistance from Yankee investors. By comparison, fewer than 9 percent of St. Louis entrepreneurs were backed by local capitalists. Indulgent and wealthy relatives living in areas with greater capital reserves sustained branch operations in St. Louis.

In short, because Yankee newcomers possessed direct ties to major eastern houses, their business enjoyed solid financial backing during this period. More than half these branches started with over ten thousand dollars of venture capital, while only one-third of independent firms were able to do so. Furthermore, the average western "depot" was launched with an initial investment five times greater than that of a nonbranch. Even independent Yankee commercial ventures, however, were relatively well backed during the late 1840s.

Businesses with strong backing enjoyed the greatest success in the capital-scarce St. Louis marketplace. "Money," the *Missouri Republican* conceded, "is the great desideratum in commercial operations."[118] Firms that began with more than ten thousand dollars, for example, remained in business for an average of nine years, surviving 83 percent longer than ventures that started with less than that amount. Moreover, well-backed firms, most of them branches of leading eastern houses, were three times more likely than poorer firms to remain in business for more than a decade. Abundant capital reserves enabled businessmen to operate more effectively in distant markets, to buy in larger quantities, and to survive the frequent financial storms that disrupted western markets. Adequate resources, therefore, provided a resilience that translated into longevity and commercial success. Local financial writers recognized that Yankee newcomers comprised a self-selected group. According to a business reporter for the *Missouri Democrat*, merchants understood that capital and credit were in short supply in the city. "St. Louis is not the place for men who trade on borrowed capital."[119] Thus, the "men who locate here," the reporter concluded, "know that they have no resources to depend on but their own."[120] Yankee merchants arrived with capital reserves or with access to capital, and for these men, the streets of St. Louis seemed to be lined with gold.

Wealthy eastern merchants enjoyed a cumulative advantage in the St. Louis marketplace. Family money followed migration routes, and well-born Yankee businessmen could rely upon financial support from eastern relations. In addition, these merchants possessed ready access to eastern credit. New York and Boston banks were only too willing to assist the sons of the leading merchants in the nation. Young Albert Pierce, for example, could borrow on the basis of his ties to his father-in-law's dry goods house, one of the largest firms in New York.[121]

Not only were entrepreneurs such as Pierce related to men of means, they were also well known to eastern bankers. Yankee merchants needed only the endorsement of their wealthy fathers or uncles in order to borrow from the largest lenders in the East. For example, Archibald S. Rutherford "lent . . . the power of his name" to two young New Yorkers, probably his nephews, in order "to gain credit in the East until the firm was established."[122] John Tevis, on the other hand, relied on his father for stock and backing. The death of Joshua Tevis, a leading Philadelphia dry goods merchant, destroyed the foundation of the firm and "induced the determination to wind up the concern." Philadelphia lenders, however, were well acquainted with the family business and, according to credit reporters, a number of "banks in Philadelphia offer to advance [Tevis and his brother] all the money they want."[123] Transplanted Yankees obtained credit on the basis of their eastern connections. Westerners, however, had no such ties to capital sources. In antebellum America wealth begot wealth, and men of means possessed both capital and easy access to credit.

Eastern ties and eastern backing permitted Yankee newcomers to transport large quantities of manufactured goods to the St. Louis marketplace. Thus, branches tended to be the largest firms in the city; according to credit investigators, 40 percent were considered large firms, compared to only 24 percent of nonbranches. Moreover, large-scale ventures enjoyed great success in St. Louis. In part, this merely reflected the advantages of strong financial backing. Nonetheless, larger firms grew faster than smaller businesses and enjoyed greater profit margins and longer lifespans. Among the largest commercial houses in the city (those termed "enormous" by credit investigators), the average life span was over eight and a half years, compared to less than three years for small firms. While nearly half of the city's largest-scale ventures survived for more than a decade, 90 percent of smaller ventures failed within ten years.

Strong financial backing provided Yankee newcomers with a hedge against shortages and pressures. Branch managers had access to large pools of credit, allowing them to endure short-term disruptions and to flourish when local firms faced their greatest difficulties. If business boomed and eastern manufactures became relatively scarce, transplanted Yankees possessed the resources and the connections to maintain full stockrooms and service the market. One transplanted easterner bragged that his New York buyers "enabled [him] to sell Goods cheap, as we can readily replenish."[124] Thus, during prosperous times branch coffers were fattened, while the cramped businesses established and sustained by local traders failed.

When the provisions trade languished or when market conditions worsened, men with ties to eastern backers more often remained solvent. For example, in 1845 James Woodruff, the St. Louis manager of a New York firm, made a sizable investment in wheat, anticipating an increased demand for foodstuffs in England. The price of wheat, however, fell sharply. Woodruff turned to his New York relatives for help. Although his father-in-law, the entrepreneur who owned the business, could have sustained the branch, on this occasion Woodruff received financial assistance from E. K. Collins, his brother-in-law, who operated a shipping line in New York.[125] Similarly, in 1846 one transplanted New Yorker informed his trading partner in Boston that, as a result of his eastern connections, the firm could "draw on New York for what funds we may want for any shipments to be made in time to meet said drafts."[126] According to a St. Louis newspaper reporter, because Yankee newcomers had access to external sources of capital, they survived fluctuations in prices and in market conditions. "Such men ought to break [i.e. fail]" during financial downturns, the writer explained, "but, in St. Louis, they as a general thing, don't break."[127] Thus, these entrepreneurs remained protected from short-term market disruptions, capital shortages, and other common problems; the absence of western banks had little direct effect on their businesses. Ironically, xenophobic Missouri banking policies hurt local men more than newcomers and provided Yankee entrepreneurs with an overwhelming competitive advantage in Missouri markets.

Branch arrangements provided other benefits as well. Boston and New York merchants, for example, took full advantage of glutted eastern markets and responded to fluctuations in eastern prices. Rather than undertaking costly and inefficient annual buying trips, Yankee branch managers relied on relatives in the commercial centers on the Atlantic coast. According to the *Missouri Republican*, "almost all wholesale houses have resident partners in the East."[128] Experienced buyers, most often in New York, purchased manufactured goods when eastern markets were particularly overstocked. According to one merchant, "our Staple Goods are purchased directly at Philadelphia and New York auctions, at prices considerably lower than when bought in the regular way."[129] Archibald Young, a Yankee branch manager, boasted that his "eastern connections" enabled him "to sell at New York prices."[130]

Nor did currency problems pose a great problem for transplanted Yankees. St. Louis-born merchants remained dependent upon heavily discounted Illinois scrip and paid 14 to 16 percent premiums on New York paper, though their counterparts from the Northeast purchased goods through New York offices and with currency that was scarcely discounted.[131] Money changing, discounting, and remitting advances occurred between relatives and assumed an informal quality. In 1848, for example, J. F. Franklin, a hardware dealer who had recently moved to St. Louis, instructed his trading partner to "remit the proceeds to Father [sic] in New York."[132] Such transactions proved to be simpler, but they also reduced the cost of long-distance commerce and increased the profit margins for Yankee merchants.

All of the ingredients for commercial success in the St. Louis marketplace overlapped. Size and backing, for example, reflected wealth and direct ties to distant suppliers and investors. Moreover, as a result of eastern economic conditions and cultural assumptions, Yankees established the largest and the best-financed businesses in St. Louis during the late 1840s. According to local credit investigators, more than three-fourths of the wealthy men engaged in business in St. Louis came from the Northeast, and Yankee merchants controlled over 90 percent of the largest firms in the city.[133] In short, wealthy Bostonians and New Yorkers brought sizable competitive advantages to the St. Louis marketplace and enjoyed considerable success.

These advantages, however, were not restricted to Yankee merchants. A small number of European immigrants possessed the same resources and enjoyed the same success as easterners. Ferdinand Fuchs, a German newcomer, experienced enormous prosperity in the St. Louis marketplace. Wealthy friends in Germany backed Fuchs's liquor importing business.[134] Like Yankee branch managers, he was well backed, well supplied, and operated a large-scale enterprise. Similarly, James Wheeler, a forty-year-old Englishman, received cheap manufactured goods and capital from his wealthy brother in England. The elder Wheeler, according to local credit reporters, "buys 2nd [sic] class goods in England which he [his brother in Missouri] sells as lrst class goods at profit."[135]

Scale and backing even enabled some entrepreneurs to overcome pervasive prejudice. Samuel Jacks, for example, was a Jewish merchant in an age when native businessmen were deeply suspicious of "Jew-traders." Jacks, however, enjoyed the backing of a wealthy New Yorker and operated a large store. Credit investigators noted that "like most Jews, we think he needs watching." Nonetheless, they reported that his business was likely to succeed, and they gave Jacks a strong credit rating.[136] Moreover, a few longtime residents of St. Louis possessed the capital and connections to enjoy the advantages of scale and backing.[137] Men such as Fuchs, Wheeler, and Jacks, however, were rare; the majority of the city's successful entrepreneurs were newcomers from New York and Boston.

Local conditions reinforced Yankee success in the region. If New Yorkers and Bostonians arrived with considerable advantages, their local counterparts offered scant competition. Rather, institutional obstacles and the cumulative effects of prolonged depression combined to weaken the competitive positions of the city's merchants. Unlike newcomers from the Northeast, these businessmen lacked capital and credit, access to eastern markets and distribution networks, and the advantages generated by such connections. As a result, the merchants who were best acquainted with the St. Louis marketplace experienced little success, while the young newcomers who migrated from New York and Boston enjoyed enormous success.[138] The Missouri native Julia Dent, who later married Ulysses Grant, recalled that her father eschewed commerce in St. Louis, complaining that "the Yankees that come west have reduced business to a system."[139] This system, predicated on eastern commercial networks, excluded local traders.

The institutional environment created by Missouri legislators and reinforced by the lingering effects of the Panic of 1837 prevented St. Louis residents from taking advantage of the maturation of the regional economy or the growth of the provisions trade. "Why cannot we engage in this business, so immensely profitable?" asked one resident. The answer, according to John Hogan, was quite simple: "want of capital."[140] The city ranked last among the nation's twenty-five largest urban centers in banking capital during this period, and state policy deprived local entrepreneurs of credit sources, exacerbating the city's financial problems.[141] Moreover, a decade of stagnation cut deeply into many old fortunes, leaving the economy of St. Louis with little surplus capital. Long-distance commerce, however, was a capital-intensive enterprise. Securing manufactures from eastern suppliers, transporting bulky cargoes more than a thousand miles, and withstanding the disruptions that plagued commercial enterprises demanded considerable capital reserves or access to credit. Most St. Louis businessmen possessed neither. "Our merchants," one observer noted, "are perpetually more or less cramped."[142]

According to Lewis Tappan's credit investigators, nearly half the local men engaged in commerce were "poor." Because they had little capital, their businesses failed – and failed quickly. Greater knowledge of the city's marketplace and greater business experience proved to be no substitute for the financial resources and the eastern connections that Yankee newcomers possessed. Nearly a quarter of the firms that began with an investment of less than five hundred dollars failed within one year, and 60 percent of these businesses closed their doors within four years. Success was rare for entrepreneurs who lacked capital, and the merchants of St. Louis possessed little capital.

Furthermore, men of modest means faced self-perpetuating obstacles and suffered at every stage of the commercial process. For example, because they lacked the financial resources to have permanent buyers in northeastern markets, most St. Louis businessmen were unable to take full advantage of the benefits of the New York marketplace. Long the "dumping ground" for European manufactures, the market of New York fluctuated from month to month, depending on European harvests, southern cotton production, and American business cycles.[143] St. Louis merchants, however, made only brief buying trips. For a week or two, western businessmen scoured eastern trading centers. These visits were geared to the St. Louis selling season; local merchants most often bought their stocks during the closing weeks of the winter, in preparation for the spring provisions market.[144] But European manufactured goods were relatively expensive during this season. Late summer and early fall markets, buoyed by manufactured remittances for American foodstuffs, were fuller and richer.[145] The expenses and constraints of annual buying trips rendered manufactured goods particularly expensive for visiting St. Louis traders, further eroding the purchasing power of western merchants.

St. Louis merchants also experienced difficulty obtaining credit in eastern markets. The capital shortages and currency problems that undermined St. Louis ventures made these firms poor risks for New York or Boston capitalists. Furthermore, western merchants were unfamiliar to eastern investors, and thus unlikely to receive advances. Some western houses, however, obtained short-term loans, and many St. Louis merchants relied on the sixty- and ninety-day notes floated by New York commission houses. These loans drew 10 percent interest, payable in New York paper, for which local merchant remitted their heavily discounted Illinois scrip; premiums, interest charges, and currency depreciation often exceeded 25 percent of the principal of the note.[146] Such problems cut deeply into the competitive position of St. Louis entrepreneurs and, according to the *Missouri Republican*, "crushed the hopes of those engaged in business."[147]

Some Missouri men eschewed eastern markets entirely. Instead, they relied on eastern jobbers who operated in the St. Louis market-place. But Yankee jobbers, one trader estimated, "generally [charge] fifteen to twenty percent higher" than New York prices, and they guaranteed supplies only to larger customers.[148] These terms crippled poorer merchants and reinforced the credit, seasonal, and currency problems that St. Louis entrepreneurs endured.

Financial problems dramatically reduced the scale of local commercial ventures. Capital shortages and exchange rates, for example, increased the costs of eastern goods for western traders. These expenses diminished the purchasing power of Missouri capital and forced St. Louis merchants to buy in small lots, adding to the price of manufactures and the relative cost of transportation to the trans-Mississippi market. Thus, the financial demands of long-distance commerce often exceeded the limited resources of most St. Louis merchants. Ill-equipped to compete in distant markets, western commercial ventures remained overwhelmingly small, and small firms failed with extraordinary speed and frequency in antebellum St. Louis. The average life span for smaller firms was less than three years – nearly one-third closed within a year. As a result of xeno-phobic state banking policies, local merchants were unable to compete in the St. Louis marketplace, and local firms failed 30 percent faster than businesses with outside sources of goods and capital.

Not all local merchants failed in business, however. The growing population of the city created opportunities for men of small means, and some St. Louis entrepreneurs enjoyed modest success in neigh-borhood shops, such as small groceries, or in semi-artisanal trades, such as custom tailoring.[149] Because these ventures catered to small sectors of the market, they remained somewhat protected from the economic forces that made more dynamic sectors, such as the provisions trade, risky but profitable. Although many St. Louis residents established small businesses during this period, few became wealthy from neighborhood shops. According to local observers, men from modest circumstances seldom experienced greater success than Charles Abramson, a chemist who stayed in business for six years and earned a "living and not much more."[150]

Nor were all longtime residents poor. A small, well-established elite, which included the Chouteau family, Bernard Pratte, and others with ties to the early fur trade, flourished in the city during this period. Some of these men engaged in entrepreneurial pursuits, occasionally forming partnerships with eastern merchants. For exam-ple, James Lucas, who was reported to have been the wealthiest man in the city, established a business with New York merchants.[151] More often, however, members of the old elite focused their energies on the law, on real estate, or on established industries, such as the lead trade and the steamboat business. In 1851 *Hunt's Merchants' Magazine* reported that sixty-two residents of the city possessed real and personal estates worth more than fifty thousand dollars. Fewer than half these people owned or operated commercial houses, shops, factories, or other businesses.[152] Longtime residents either lacked the resources to tap the burgeoning provisions trade or preferred other investments.

The combination of Yankee success and local failure enabled outsiders to dominate the fastest-growing sectors of the St. Louis economy. Reflecting market forces in the Northeast and the conditions that encouraged New York and Boston merchants to send their sons to St. Louis, Yankees clustered in the commission, transshipping, and wholesale dry goods businesses at a time when those sectors boomed and when local merchants chose – or were compelled to choose – other investments.[153] Improvements in transportation, the increasing flow of migrants to the Far West, the settlement of the Mississippi valley, the expansion of commercial agriculture in the region, the development of national and hinterland marketing networks, and the growth of manufacturing in the Northeast created opportunities for merchants able to transport capital and factory goods to the West and farm produce to the East. Drawing on eastern capital, credit, buyers, and their relations on the Atlantic coast, New Yorkers and Bostonians tapped this trade and directed the largest and most successful businesses in antebellum St. Louis. If northeasterners stimulated the economic rebirth of St. Louis, they also reaped the greatest rewards from the recovery.

But more important, during the late 1840s New York and Boston merchants molded the economy of St Louis in a way that linked the western city to the flourishing commercial and manufacturing centers of the Northeast. According to one recent study, by midcentury St. Louis possessed stronger ties to the northeastern economy than any city outside the Northeast.[154] In fact, only New York City had deeper ties to major commercial centers.[155] Yankee branch managers brought goods, capital, and entrepreneurial energy to the sagging St. Louis marketplace. As a result, these newcomers forged bonds between East and West, fueling the expansion of the local economy and triggering the boom of the late 1840s. By 1857 the president of the city's Chamber of Commerce was able to report that "St. Louis has long been married to New York and Boston."[156]

The commercial ventures – and the success – of Yankee migrants integrated St. Louis into the national economy. Increasingly, the levee of the city became the point at which eastern, western, and southern goods were exchanged. Through branch outlets and other business arrangements that linked the Missouri trading center to markets on the Atlantic coast, the St. Louis market was finally stocked. For the first time in the history of the city, eastern goods became plentiful in local shops. Supplies "have gone beyond the actual consumption of trade," the *Missouri Republican* triumphantly announced in 1845.[157] "Eastern operators render the market buoyant and firm."[158] After eight years of stagnation, the economy of St. Louis blossomed. "Business," a commercial reporter observed in 1849, was "increasing beyond a precedent in the history of this country."[159] Trade flourished, profits soared, and the city finally fulfilled its destiny.[160]

During the late 1840s St. Louis became a major commercial center and the leading metropolis of the region. The population of the city surged during this period, increasing at more than double the rate of the surrounding territory.[161] Although a major fire destroyed much of the business district in 1849, merchants and workers continued to settle in the city.[162] More impressive, not even the cholera epidemic of 1849 slowed the city's growth. The "visitation" of the disease hit St. Louis harder than any other city in the nation, claiming more than one-tenth of the city's residents. An additional thirty thousand residents fled from the city during the summer of 1849.[163] Nonetheless, the population increased by over 23 percent during the final year of the decade.

The growth of commerce was still more impressive. Receipts at the St. Louis Customs House rose by over 1200 percent during the late 1840s.[164] The dry goods trade increased more than sixfold during the 1840s, while capital investment in industry grew by 550 percent during the same period – virtually all of this increase occurred during the second half of the decade.[165] A survey of commercial houses, conducted between 1845 and 1853, also revealed the magnitude of the boom. According to hardware dealers, business increased by more than 220 percent during this period, while local grocery operators reported that their trade more than quadrupled.[166] "The hum of business has revived," a local observer noted, "and population and capital are pouring in upon us like a flood."[167]

The economic ties between St. Louis and eastern commercial centers accelerated the city's transformation to a major agricultural market as well. The availability of inexpensive New York clothes, Pittsburgh iron goods, and European textiles combined with the maturation of the regional economy to draw increasing numbers of Illinois and Missouri farmers into the local market, extending the economic sphere of St. Louis deep into the surrounding countryside.[168] As a result, more and more western agricultural produce passed through the levee of St. Louis before arriving in distant markets, and the Illinois and Missouri rivers became important shipping channels. Steamboat arrivals from the city's agricultural hinterland more than doubled between 1845 and 1850, and agricultural receipts skyrocketed.[169] Barley and malt imports grew tenfold during this period, while oats receipts increased by more than 730 percent.[170] Thus, the eastern links that revived the local economy generated a second range of economic connections, tying St. Louis to a growing agricultural hinterland, as well as to the burgeoning national economy.[171] The expanding provisions trade triggered a commercial revolution in St. Louis during the late 1840s.

Prosperity begot prosperity in antebellum America. Once St. Louis emerged as a major commercial entrepôt, once the marketplace was stocked with eastern manufactures, thousands of settlers visited the levee to purchase provisions for the westward trek.[172] Migrants followed trade routes, taking advantage of the lower fares on larger vessels.[173] As a consequence, more and more settlers passed through St. Louis and bolstered its provisions market. "Owing to the rapid advancement of the city," for example, Mormon elders chose St. Louis as their "most important" transit point on the journey to Zion.[174] Each spring thousands of Latter Day Saints gathered in the city in preparation for the long migration across the Great Plains.[175]

The expansion of the St. Louis marketplace dovetailed with the larger political and demographic changes of the late 1840s and generated extraordinary prosperity for the invigorated Missouri trading center. For example, St. Louis became the principal troop-staging point during the Mexican War, bringing tens of thousands of soldiers to the city and millions of dollars to local traders.[176] Army supply agents remitted enormous sums of Mexican silver, as much as fifty thousand dollars a year, to the city's merchants, and government contracts added to the prosperity of St. Louis during the late 1840s.[177] Demand for eastern manufactures reached new heights; profits kept pace; and the boom spiraled upward.

The California gold rush brought still greater prosperity to St. Louis. The city "came of age" just as the current of trans-Mississippi settlers reached flood proportions. St. Louis was the last major commercial center on the overland route to the Pacific Coast and "the most convenient point for reshipping and obtaining outfits."[178] "Our hotels, boarding houses and steamboats are filled," the *Missouri Republican* reported in 1849. "Camps are formed in the neighborhood. The rush is tremendous. Persons on their way to California are flocking to our city from every quarter."[179] Every steamboat brought three or four hundred "California emigrants" to the city, most in need of provisions and all in need of lodging.[180] According to one local editor, "it is not extravagant to say that thirty thousand persons will leave for California, by this route, in the next three months."[181] Others estimated that as many as fifty thousand gold-crazed adventurers passed through the city during the spring of 1849.[182] Demand for side arms, wagons, and leather goods hit unimagined levels. "California has given a wonderful impetus to business," one newcomer noted.[183] "The demand for all descriptions of stock," the *Missouri Democrat* predicted, "is likely to force prices up to an extraordinary extent, and to insure still greater profits."[184] Merchants with well-stocked supply rooms "realized handsome fortunes."[185] Thomas Albright's gun shop, for example, became a gold mine in 1849. Local credit investigators reported that Albright "has had almost a monopoly of trade among the California emigrants. . . . He is [now] wealthy."[186] "California fever," extended beyond the rush of 1849 and buoyed the local provisions market well into the next decade.

Virtually every western event redounded to the benefit of St. Louis traders during this period, and the economy of the city continued to expand. Plains Indians, for example, attracted troops and government contracts to St. Louis, while western canal construction increased the flow of produce through the city on its journey to eastern markets. St. Louis faced few competitors in the western trade during this period (Chicago presented little challenge until the early 1850s), and the city reaped a disproportionate share of western commercial prosperity.[187] Each year brought greater prosperity, greater optimism; and the problems of the past were at least temporarily buried in a mountain of profit. According to *Hunt's Merchants' Magazine*, the spiral had no end in sight. "Business has never been more flourishing. . . . Stocks were never better, hotels never more crowded."[188] During the second half of the 1840s a commercial giant was born.

The relationship between the needs of eastern businesses and the peculiarities of the local marketplace shaped the economic development of antebellum St. Louis. During the early 1840s the Missouri legislature had framed a series of codes that were designed to forestall the commercial ascent of St. Louis. These statutes weakened the economic foundation of the city and the competitive positions of local merchants. At the same time, eastern business and cultural forces encouraged hundreds of young, middle-class Yankees to look to the Far West. Facing little competition from local traders, New York and Boston merchants dominated important sectors of western commerce. "Young emigrants from New England," one easterner observed, "build up great commercial interests in the West."[189] Although these Yankee newcomers triggered the boom of the late 1840s, their commanding role in the western marketplace distorted the economy of St. Louis in important ways.

The economic revival of the city was constructed on a Yankee foundation. Prosperity depended on Yankee capital, Yankee entrepreneurs, and Yankee commercial networks. This connection enabled the city's economy to blossom in spite of severe structural weaknesses; local institutions played a limited role in the economic rebirth of St. Louis. At the height of the boom, for example, the city had virtually no banking facilities, and it grew without local banks.[190] Instead, eastern dollars followed Boston and New York merchants to St. Louis, filling the financial void and buoying the local economy.

But eastern involvement in the St. Louis marketplace indirectly undermined the formation of local financial institutions. Merchants controlled the vast majority of capital in antebellum America.[191] In fact, most bankers were successful merchants, men who expanded their commercial empires to include moneylending.[192] Many invested in financial institutions and became bank officers during this period. The most successful businessmen in antebellum St. Louis, however, were branch managers; they were agents, not capitalists. The city's commercial pioneers lived in Boston and New York, and the venture capital that spearheaded the economic rebirth of St. Louis remained in the hands – and vaults – of eastern entrepreneurs. St. Louis had neither capital, bankers, nor a natural breeding ground for bankers or capitalists. State Street and Wall Street controlled the financial lifeblood of the "lion of the valley."

Eastern dominance shaped other sectors of the western economy as well. Although stores lined the levee and business boomed during the late 1840s, manufacturing remained in its infancy in the city. Early on, municipal officials and boosters had recognized that "manufactures have not assumed that relative importance which they have attained in some of our sister cities."[193] According to the *Missouri Republican*, factories "struggled for being" in St. Louis. Most were fragile concerns, undertaken "on a small scale."[194] Without "greater encouragement" for local manufactories, the newspaper concluded, "there must be a pause in the progress of St. Louis."[195]

Antebellum municipal leaders believed that manufacturing generated an "independent" internal momentum for the city, and thus St. Louis needed "manufactories of all descriptions, large and small. Her commerce, great and extended as it is," a local editor predicted, "will be found unavailing . . . unless manufactures take broad and deep root within her limits."[196] City fathers turned to the legal system to destroy "impediments in the way of manufactures."[197] Municipal officials even persuaded the governor to propose a general incorporation law "to encourage domestic manufactures."[198] These efforts, however, failed, and manufacturing remained underdeveloped in antebellum St. Louis.

In eastern cities, the mercantile sector supported the manufacturing sector. Successful merchants established, backed, and owned the largest factories in the Northeast.[199] But the leading investors in St. Louis businesses lived a thousand miles to the east, and their agents in the city lacked the authority to invest in local manufactories. Ironically, the handsome fortunes that Yankee branch managers reaped in the St. Louis provisions trade financed the construction and expansion of Boston and New York factories. William Claflin, for example, used the profits drawn from his St. Louis venture to construct his own shoe factory, though he built the facility in Milford, Massachusetts.[200] Yankee capital invariably returned to the Northeast, and St. Louis matured without banks, without factories, and without a rising commercial elite.

In short, the great prosperity of the late 1840s rested on a flawed foundation. St. Louis was not married to Boston and New York, but rather the city was a colony of eastern commercial centers.[201] The "great trade emporium of the West" remained dependent on Yankee support and vulnerable to Yankee whims. Although the long-term effects of this dependence were disastrous, for the short-term St. Louis was a boomtown.

5   "The offspring of the East"

A cultural revolution accompanied the economic transformation of the late 1840s. No longer a small frontier trading post, St. Louis became, almost overnight, a major urban center with big-city problems. The population surged; housing and municipal institutions became inadequate; criminals flocked to St. Louis to tap its wealthy newcomers; disease decimated the residents; and the extraordinary pace of growth created a political and cultural vacuum in the city.[1] Like San Francisco and other western boomtowns, St. Louis was in flux, and residents struggled to stabilize society and to shape its development.[2] The architects of the city's economic rebirth, however, also stood at the center of the city's cultural rebirth.

Yankee influence in the urban West extended beyond the marketplace. As migrants left the Atlantic coast and moved westward, they introduced Yankee culture throughout the Ohio and the Mississippi valleys.[3] Newcomers from the the Northeast brought New York fashions, Boston cultural conventions, Philadelphia institutions, and Yankee "isms" to every city and town in the region. Migration entailed the self-conscious extension of culture as well as the extension of commercial networks, and eastern merchants attempted to mold western cities in the images of New York, Boston, and Philadelphia.[4]

Only a small group of Yankees settled in St. Louis during the late 1840s, though these newcomers assumed a particularly prominent role in the city's development. Visitors frequently reported that New Yorkers and Bostonians were "abundantly represented" in St. Louis, and migrants concluded that the city contained a remarkably "dense" population of Yankees who "regulate society around them."[5] In fact, newcomers from the Northeast were more conspicuous than they were numerous. They comprised only 10 percent of the local population in 1850. The economic boom that they helped to spark reinforced the flow of Yankee merchants to the Missouri metropolis, and each year hundreds of northeastern businessmen settled in the city, often

91

replacing their older brothers. At the same time, however, the recovery of the late 1840s attracted tens of thousands of German and Irish settlers to St. Louis, making it an immigrant city.[6] Nonetheless, Yankees shaped local development. Not only did they spur activity in the city's business district and integrate the local economy into the national economy, these migrants also transformed the character of St. Louis.

Young northeastern businessmen exerted disproportionate influence for many reasons. First, because the forces that stimulated Yankee migration to the urban West included a powerful cultural dimension, the newcomers sought to regulate the development of the city. According to many observers, the branch managers who settled in Missouri in order to strengthen the New York commercial houses owned by their fathers also migrated to the region to battle heathenism, to confront the soldiers of Rome, and to eliminate the taint of demon rum from the urban frontier.[7] Thus, they quickly became involved in reform movements and political crusades. Furthermore, Yankee newcomers were concentrated in occupations that gave them considerable standing in the community.[8] Antebellum Americans expected merchants, particularly wealthy and well-bred entrepreneurs, to be active in the community. In western cities, as in eastern urban centers, businessmen played important roles in municipal politics, voluntary associations, and civic affairs.

Local conditions, however, exaggerated Yankee influence in St. Louis. The changing composition of the population reinforced the missionary impulse that Yankees brought to the city. Moreover, the economic success enjoyed by the migrants, in combination with the financial problems experienced by local entrepreneurs, gave the newcomers unusual prominence in cultural affairs as well as in business matters. Even old residents of the city often deferred to the upstart newcomers. Finally, and ironically, the weakness of the ties that linked New Yorkers and Bostonians to St. Louis generated a peculiar cultural coherence in the city; transience, rather than persistence, sustained Yankee influence.

Throughout the antebellum period northeastern migrants attempted to transplant Yankee culture to the fertile ground of the West and to mold the character of western cities. In St. Louis, they experienced considerable success. Yankee "isms" enjoyed immense popularity on the banks of the Mississippi river, and northeastern traditions and innovations shaped the institutional development of the Missouri trading center. By midcentury, St. Louis had become a Yankee city.

The problems that plagued St. Louis simultaneously weakened the ties that bound Yankees to the city, reinforced their desire to be active in the community, and enabled the newcomers to shape the character of St. Louis. First, social instability created a need for "proper" men to step to the fore, exaggerating the sense of mission that colored Yankee migrations to the Far West.[9] Even if few young easterners shared the *New Englander's* dream of "a reorganization of [western] society after the New England model," many Yankees relished the chance to "regulate society around them."[10] Well-bred easterners recognized an opportunity to mold the character of the city. But perhaps more important, they saw a setting in which they could exert personal influence and enjoy the standing that their fathers exercised in the Northeast. Such an opportunity meshed nicely with the personal ambitions and the cultural chauvinism that lent respectability to gold-seeking in the region. Thus, the chaos that Yankee merchants discovered when they arrived in St. Louis presented a challenge.

The midcentury boom disrupted St. Louis society. Migrants poured into the city, and the once-quiet outpost became a beehive of activity. In 1851 one visitor concluded that "there is probably no busier scene in America."[11] Every steamboat brought hundreds of newcomers. "The emigration is very great," an observer reported, "some over a thousand a week."[12] In 1840 barely sixteen thousand people lived in St. Louis; by 1845 the local population had passed forty thousand, and St. Louis contained close to eighty thousand inhabitants by the end of the decade. Nearly as many people died in St. Louis in 1849 as had lived in the city at the start of the decade. "Everyone but the old French settler," one traveler bemused, "is comparatively a new comer [sic]."[13] The census of 1850 confirmed this conclusion. Over half the city's residents had been in St. Louis for less than two years; local enumerators recorded that forty thousand newcomers settled in the city between 1848 and 1850. "The man born in St. Louis," the *Missouri Republican* noted, "now finds himself in the midst of a great city, surrounded by thousands of strangers, and knows not whence they came, what their character may be, or whither they are going."[14]

The influx of migrants overwhelmed local institutions. For example, newcomers experienced enormous difficulties procuring lodging. "Hotels are so overthronged," a St. Louis editor reported, that "many applications are turned away daily."[15] Well-bred easterners often found that "respectable" accommodations were in short supply.[16] Municipal institutions, sometimes only a few years old, also fared badly under the weight of tens of thousands of newcomers. The city hospital, for example, overflowed with patients during the boom, and officials admitted being "at a loss to find sufficient room for the applicants."[17] Law enforcement and sewage mechanisms faltered, and the market, health, and building regulations enacted before the population surge became inadequate.[18] Although residents had been predicting the boom for decades, the scale of growth exceeded most forecasts.

The character of the migrants also exaggerated the shock of rapid population growth. Immigrants comprised two-thirds of the newcomers, and by 1850 the foreign-born outnumbered the native-born residents of the city. Germans came in particularly large numbers. From the publication of Gottfried Duden's first travel report in 1829, St. Louis had possessed a reputation throughout Europe as a German city, and the Missouri trading center became a magnet for German immigrants.[19] During the late 1840s more than ten thousand "Dutch" immigrants arrived in St. Louis each year. Over twenty thousand Germans landed in the city in 1852, and by 1854 the current exceeded twenty-five thousand newcomers.[20] Unlike their wealthy predecessors, the celebrated "Latin farmers," these immigrants were more often craftsmen and laborers, and most traveled to St. Louis for economic as well as cultural reasons.[21] In large part, they migrated in response to the boom, anticipating high wages and abundant work in the growing city. Nearly 90 percent of the midcentury German residents arrived in St. Louis after the start of the local boom. By 1850 nearly one resident in three hailed from Germany, an unsettling discovery for more than a few Yankee merchants.[22]

Irish immigrants added to the spiraling population of St. Louis. A tiny group of Irishmen, many of whom belonged to the middle class, had lived in the city for decades. Their boom-era countrymen, however, were drawn from a very different stratum. Thousands of relatively poor Irish immigrants migrated to St. Louis during the potato blights.[23] The cargo holds of cotton ships provided inexpensive passage to New Orleans, and railroad work and steamboat jobs attracted unskilled Irishmen to St. Louis. Many of these newcomers, like twenty-seven-year-old William Donahue, found employment as deckhands on riverboats. According to census enumerators, Donahue lived on board the steamer *Iroquois*.[24] In 1850 nearly 70 percent of the city's Irish residents were newcomers, and these immigrants comprised almost 16 percent of the local population and 44 percent of the unskilled ranks. Almost overnight, St. Louis possessed an industrial work force and the cultural tensions of an immigrant city.

The new prosperity attracted smaller groups of migrants as well. A sizable number of English immigrants, for example, visited the city during the late 1840s and the early 1850s. The majority of these settlers were Mormon pilgrims who stopped in St. Louis on their journey to Salt Lake City. They most often arrived in the early spring, and they remained "only long enough to recuperate from the fatigue of the sea voyage and then resume their journey to Salt Lake."[25] Moreover, the burgeoning economy of the city and the maturation of the region directed an increasing number of farm laborers to the city, where they sought employment on steamboats, the levee, or construction sites in St. Louis. According to one migrant, who visited the city on his way to the goldfields of California, St. Louis was a "modern Babel."[26]

Most newcomers migrated to St. Louis for economic reasons. Cultural factors enhanced the appeal of the city for some goups, such as the northeastern merchants or the German immigrants in search of a setting with a large German population, but high wages and the perception of opportunity in the urban West generated most of the interest in St. Louis and much of the migration. J. W. McClure, for example, settled in St. Louis because "I intend to make money."[27] Bostonian Elizabeth Sargent expressed a similarly instrumental view of the city in a series of letters to her friends and relatives in New England. To close friends, she wrote "I would rather live east, but I will be content awhile here, if Haven [her husband] can do well."[28] Sargent expressed the same sentiment to her family, explaining that "anybody may have the west – but I like [St. Louis] tolerable well as long as Haven is doing well and his prospects are very good."[29] According to another resident, "Easterners come out here to speculate because their money will yield at a greater per cent with less labor but when it comes to living good honest lives and where their families can enjoy the comforts of this world it is New England [that they prefer]."[30] In short, St. Louis was an attractive place to make money.

This perception shaped the migration process. Married men often left their wives and children "at home." As a result, sex ratios remained imbalanced during this period, and the urban center retained many of its "frontier" qualities. In 1850 St. Louis contained 185 adult men for every 100 adult women. According to one western merchant "the young men set out to seek their fortunes, leaving their sisters behind."[31] "In St. Louis," a Yankee newcomer added, "the streets are black with masculine broadcloth and cassimere – a more than Egyptian plague – of men."[32] The Missouri merchant Luke Shortfield, calculating the "scarcity of the commodity" in economic terms, determined that the region "affords any enterprising girl a capital opportunity of making an advantageous speculation in the matrimonial line."[33] Magdalena Korger was unable to resist such an opportunity. In 1853 she migrated to St. Louis, while her husband remained in Germany. During her brief stay in St. Louis Korger married two more men. She finally landed in the city jail after her second and third husbands met – and brawled.[34] The paucity of women made St. Louis an unattractive place to settle permanently and accelerated the pace of gold-seeking in the city.

The scramble for wealth on the urban frontier was also the province of the young. "A grey-haired man is but now and then seen among us," a local minister observed.[35] Nearly one-third of the city's residents were between twenty and thirty years of age, and among all inhabitants of St. Louis in 1850, the average age was twenty-one – immigrants were slightly older than their native-born counterparts, averaging almost twenty-five years of age.[36] Furthermore, only half the adults in the city were married, both a cause and an effect of the unbalanced sex ratios. Young, unattached men dominated every level of society. Fewer than one unskilled worker in four was married, and among clerks, only 19 percent were married. Even merchants, the guardians of communal values, proved to be youthful and unattached; most businessmen in the city were single newcomers in their twenties. The frailties of youth, according to local clergymen, threatened to run rampant in antebellum St. Louis.[37]

The instrumental needs of migrants influenced living conditions in the city. The newcomers crowded into boardinghouses, legendary caldrons of temptation and vice. Although housing shortages contributed to the popularity of such accommodations, "boarding" suited the needs of many migrants. Fewer than 7 percent of the city's immigrants owned land, and overall only 12 percent of St. Louis residents invested in real estate. In 1850 nearly one resident in three lived as a boarder, and almost half of the city's Irish population lodged in these "dens." Furthermore, 29 percent of St. Louis residents crowded into units containing more than ten people. Enormous boardinghouses, sometimes containing hundreds of newcomers, lined the streets of St. Louis. Irishmen often lived in these massive houses or in shanties on the outskirts of the city limits. Edward Fitzgerdon, a day laborer, lived in the Foundry Boarding House, along with fifty-six other foundry workers.[38] Henry Baum, a twenty-four-year-old German newcomer, was one of sixty-two guests at the Walton Hotel and Livery Stable.[39] Mrs. Blakeley's Boarding House advertised two "styles" of accommodation. Mrs. Blakeley herself promised to serve "boarders with board and lodging." In addition, she offered shelter to "transients" or "day boarders."[40]

Although class differences affected consumption patterns and lifestyles, wealthy newcomers eschewed permanent living arrangements and opted for boardinghouse life as well. Three-fourths of the city's rising young clerks lived as boarders during this period, and St.

Louis's lodger population included much of the city's merchant class. For well-bred newcomers, however, "hotels" rather than converted livery stables provided temporary shelter. Eliphalet Blatchford, a twenty-eight-year-old entrepreneur from Connecticut, stayed at the plush City Hotel, where German maids and Irish porters served wealthy Yankee guests.[41] Newcomers in search of quick fortunes chose to live in accommodations that reflected their weak, conditional ties to the city. At midcentury, "movers" and "floaters" filled St. Louis.

Most newcomers intended to make money in St. Louis and quickly leave the city. Moreover, they usually remained in the area for only a few years. Two-thirds of the residents listed in the census of 1850 had left St. Louis by 1854. Among clerks, skilled workers, and day laborers, only one resident in five remained in the city for more than four years. Church records reveal similar transience at the top of society, and prominent citizens proved to be nearly as mobile as day laborers.

Many nineteenth-century migrants carried "letters of transfer"or "letters of dismission." These documents provided a mechanism whereby newcomers could be admitted as members of churches in their adoptive cities. Ministers testified that the applicant had been a member in good standing of his old congregation and, therefore, should be admitted to the new church. Wealthy parishioners, those who had assumed prominent roles in the community, carried these documents more often than poorer, more transient migrants. According to the records of the Second Baptist Church of St. Louis, the average length of stay in the city during the boom period was less than two years, and 82 percent of "dismissed" parishioners returned to the Northeast.[42] Similarly, among members of the Bonhomme Presbyterian Church, the average stay in St. Louis was less than four years during this period. Prior to the boom, however, parishioners remained in the city for nearly eleven years on average.[43] Prosperity generated migration, not persistence.[44]

But most of these migrants were not rootless. Rather, their roots remained firmly planted elsewhere. Elizabeth Sargent considered herself a stranger throughout her stay in St. Louis; Boston, she frequently reminded her husband, was their home. "Not here I feel my place of residence will always be," Sargent explained. "I hope to return North ere many years and enjoy the sweets of life."[45] Branch managers expected to stay only three or four years, and independent entrepreneurs returned to safer commercial fields at the first sign of economic instability. Other migrants were "birds of passage," target earners who planned to return to the Northeast or Europe after they had accumulated a sufficient fortune.[46] Lucius Salisbury, for example, explained that "the reason of my coming here was to try to make some money and then in a few years go back to Old Vermont and purchase a home."[47]

Nor did immigrants or other residents establish strong ties to the city. They too often considered St. Louis attractive only as long as economic conditions remained favorable.[48] Thus, brighter lodestones prompted thousands of St. Louis residents to abandon their temporary homes and migrate yet again. The lure of California goldfields, for example, had a special resonance in a city of fortune hunters, and men with weak ties to St. Louis seemed only too willing to "fall victim to California fever." In 1848 the *Missouri Republican* reported that "the gold fever is raging with unusual violence in this community, and there are thousands seeking the means of flight to the new El Dorado of California."[49] "Are you for California?" William Kelly noted, "was the recurring question of the day." "One would almost imagine the whole city was on wheels bound for that attractive region."[50] Dozens of prominent and well-established merchants joined the "rush of movers" to the goldfields. In 1849 Albert Guild and David Dorvant abandoned their thriving dry goods business for the Pacific coast.[51] Daniel Garrison, one of the most successful manufacturers in St. Louis, also departed for San Francisco in 1849.[52] Before the rush abated, a local judge and two former governors left for western goldfields.[53]

"California fever" exaggerated both the attractions and the instability of antebellum St. Louis. Transience increased during the "hysteria" as newcomers and old residents alike hurried to gold country. According to some observers, the rush was so great that merchants "cannot collect their accounts." Customers invested "all their means" in provisions and migrated without settling their debts.[54] But the gold rush also increased the demand for manufactured goods, and well-backed merchants enjoyed wild prosperity. More than ever before, Yankees believed that St. Louis was an ideal setting in which to accumulate "quick wealth." Thus, gold fever induced fortune-hunting newcomers to migrate to the city, and it increased the rate of population turnover among residents.

The "rush of movers" affected every event in the city. Municipal officials, for example, discovered that the tide of mobility disrupted the operation of city courts. Local judges complained that because victims, witnesses, and criminals were transients, courtroom proceedings were often futile; only those locked in the calaboose remained in the city long enough for trials.[55] Similarly, public officials struggled to find public burial plots in which to inter the thousands of newcomers who died in the city.[56] Transience challenged stability in the workplace as well. Many businessmen, hoping to obtain steady, reliable workers, stipulated that "none need apply but a man with a family."[57] Family men, employers reasoned, would submit to immediate pressures and engage in regular work in order to feed their children. Many businessmen complained that fortune-hunting newcomers would rather starve than work for wages. On hot summer days potential laborers preferred to conserve their energies for "future speculations" rather than toil for wages under the intense Missouri sun.[58]

Health conditions in St. Louis reinforced the instrumental attitudes of the city's residents. Frequent epidemics claimed thousands of lives during this period. In 1849, for example, cholera ravaged the local population. City officials claimed that 10 percent of the city's residents died during the summer epidemic, and, over the course of the year, over 12 percent of the population died.[59] Some observers, however, charged that "the Board of Health doesn't report one half of the cases."[60] Yellow fever and other "warm-weather diseases" regularly visited the city as well, and St. Louis became widely known as one of the unhealthiest cities in the nation.[61]

If newcomers brought disease to the city, children disproportionately fell victim to the epidemics. Weekly mortality figures indicated that very young children accounted for over half the deaths in St. Louis during this period. In view of the high proportion of adults in the city, these statistics were staggering, and local editors implored parents to "carry their children out of the city" for the summer.[62] According to F. R. Roueché, "it is allmost [sic] impossible to raise children here."[63] Similarly, residents told an English clergyman who visited the city in 1848 that the area was better suited "for making money than raising a family. One-third of the children," a local doctor explained to the Reverend George Lewis, "die in infancy."[64] Such warnings helped to convince migrants to leave their families "at the East" and encouraged newcomers to "reap all he can" in St. Louis and then return home.[65]

The effects of these scourges permeated St. Louis. Cholera and yellow fever carried away hundreds of prominent citizens and thousands of newcomers, and the municipal "dead cart was continually engaged" during the boom years.[66] Residents prayed to survive the "miasmic" winds of Missouri summers and avoid the deadly poisons that they believed were introduced by infected immigrants. Municipal officials hardly weathered the "malignant storms" with grace; at the height of the 1849 cholera visitation, elected representatives "adjourned" city government and fled into the countryside, fearing for their health.[67] Survivors, however, pressed onward with new determination. According to local observers, the omnipresence of death increased the resolve of newcomers to "make a quick fortune" and resettle elsewhere.[68] "All I ask," James Cowan announced, "is health and ordinary degree of Luck [sic], to make money."[69]

Only the dead remained in St. Louis, and even they proved to be mobile. The influx of newcomers continued during epidemics, and population pressures forced municipal officials to relocate dozens of small burial grounds.[70] Death, riches, and transience coexisted and reinforced one another during this period. While the mean duration of life in St. Louis was under eighteen years, newcomers poured into the city, hoping to find wealth, to elude disease, and finally to escape from St. Louis.

Disease accelerated the race for quick wealth, though it also promoted "fast-living" and the accompanying problems, at least according middle-class residents. Without the safety net of "proper" influences, newcomers seemed to be dangerously vulnerable to worldly temptation. Most migrants, William Greenleaf Eliot complained, "think only of the fortune they have come to seek."[71] Well-bred young men often fell victim to the gold-chasing lust and the life-style that it spawned. "With money enough to expend, they have no maturity of character," Eliot complained. "Even those who have no fixed disposition to do evil, find themselves in bad company."[72] "Our city has taken him [the well-bred newcomer] into its bosom, and with its temples of folly and sloughs of vices," another minister conceded, it "has blotted out the purest instincts and aspirations of his heart."[73] Put somewhat differently, young men living far beyond the gaze of their elders engaged in activities in the urban West that they might have shunned in the East.[74]

The concentration of vulnerable young people attracted new evils to the city. "Resorts of pleasures," local leaders lamented, dotted the newly paved streets of the city. According to one traveler, "the numbers of gambling hells [sic] and disorderly houses is exceedingly large, and everywhere force and deception lie in wait for the unsuspecting."[75] In a city with thousands of newcomers and a spirit of worldly pursuit, wicked dens seemed to occupy every street corner. In 1852, for example, temperance reformers announced that St. Louis contained one "licensed" dramshop for every ninety residents in the city; the number of illegal tippling houses defied enumeration.[76] Brothels multiplied as well. "Madams" flocked to a city of fast-living, unattached, young men.[77] The absence of adult women in the city contributed to the appeal of midcentury St. Louis. "Dames du pave" migrated to the city, established brothels, and flourished.[78]

Pickpockets, thieves, and "pigeon-droppers" also settled in St. Louis – to mine the migrants. "The continued increase in our population," the *Missouri Republican* noted, "is a new inducement for their visits."[79] "Blacklegs, swindlers and pickpockets are as thick as the locusts of Egypt," Randall Hobart reported in 1849.[80] "Many a green'un," he added, "has been relieved of his tin by the time he has been in St. Louis three days and has had to forgo his golden dreams and return to the old diggings."[81] Land speculators with imaginary plots in storied valleys preyed on would-be yeomen, "induc[ing] those simple fools . . . [to] buy up largely."[82] One "housing agent," for example, established the St. Louis Emigrating Club to "furnish information and assistance" to newcomers.[83] "Sharpers" and swindlers invented new arts designed to separate newcomers from their savings. Bernard Reid fell victim to one such scheme. Reid paid a sizable fee to a man offering "lessons [to California emigrants] in the art of smelting gold and silver."[84] Each spring "upstart bugs and public sharpers" infested St. Louis "to win money from the emigrants," and every fall they departed for warmer climates, contributing to the baneful influences that haunted the city as well as the enormous flow of gold-seeking transients who passed through St. Louis.[85]

Evidence of the moral decline of the community seemed to abound. Paupers, drunkards, and wanderers "infested" every alley, and thousands of orphans – the children of transients who either died of disease or migrated to other flourishing towns – roamed the streets in search of food and shelter. In 1852 local editors admitted that the city contained ten thousand vagrant child thieves and three thousand "destitute little children."[86] Moreover, each day fortune hunters abandoned infants "at gentlemen's doors."[87] For many old residents, these "children of crime or of misery" symbolized the moral turpitude of antebellum St. Louis.[88]

The temptations of a boomtown, however, generated different problems for different groups. Among well-bred gold seekers, the unrestrained atmosphere of St. Louis may have contributed to drunkenness and whore-mongering. Among immigrants, however, local leaders feared that the absence of "proper influences" bred violence. Brawling immigrants, for example, terrorized native-born residents of the city during this period, providing a powerful reminder of the dangers of living in a city of newcomers.[89] Irish deckhands engaged in bloody "rows" nearly every day, often featuring battles between "Corkians" and "Fardowners."[90] These skirmishes frequently escalated into small wars involving hundreds of "boys from the green sod."[91] One local park, a favorite site for such clashes, was termed "battle row."[92] National antipathies between German and Irish immigrants

grants fueled dozens of quarrels as well.[93] In 1854 a "blow-up" between a knife-wielding Irishman and a city election judge exploded into a major riot. For three days gangs prowled the streets, attacking rival boardinghouses with rocks and bottles. By the time municipal officials restored order, the riot had claimed ten lives and damaged nearly one hundred buildings.[94] Yankee newcomers seldom found the rugged flavor of the West on the streets of the city; instead, they saw drunkards, abandoned children, prostitutes, "ruined" young fortune hunters, and mobs of immigrants "breaking each other's heads in a ginteel [sic] manner."[95]

In many ways, St. Louis fulfilled its reputation. For men of means, particularly those who brought their father's money, it offered opportunity. The city also contained elements of the excitement that travel writers promised. Although northeasterners did not engage in open warfare with Indians or Papist invaders, they confronted a good deal of immorality and even some rough-hewn conditions. Overcrowded boardinghouses, Catholic immigrants, German beerhalls, Mormon pilgrims, cholera, uneven sex ratios, brothels, and rowdy levee workers combined to produce contradictory impulses for Yankee newcomers. First, local conditions made northeasterners anxious to return to New York and Boston. If many Yankees reported that St. Louis was a good place to make money, few expressed any desire to settle in the city. Moreover, new outbreaks of yellow fever and cholera made northeastern society seem a bit less stodgy and a lot more appealing. One disappointed newcomer, for example, rushed "to get out of this city as soon as the steamer will carry us."[96]

But at the same time that the threat of disease, the flow of rum, and the arrival of large numbers of Irishmen hastened the return of Yankees to the Northeast, local conditions enticed some of the newcomers to become active in local affairs. Even though they did not purchase real estate in St. Louis and they longed to settle in the Northeast, these merchants joined voluntary associations and supported reform movements in the city. In cultural terms, they attempted to assume middle-class status. Men who migrated to the urban West in part to introduce eastern culture to the region could indeed battle Irish politicians, uplift fallen women, and bring Sunday schools to the edge of the frontier. With the exceptions of cholera and yellow fever, the problems that Yankees encountered seemed familiar and even manageable. Moreover, in confronting the evils posed by laggards and bawds, they could assume roles similar to those occupied by their fathers in New York and Boston. Thus, by joining the Know-Nothing Party, by signing a temperance pledge, by supporting prison reform and antislavery sentiments, and by introducing eastern literary standards to the urban West, they could satisfy the sense of mission that they had carried from the Northeast.

More important, the established leaders of the community embraced the newcomers and pushed – or pulled – the young merchants into prominent roles in local society. Local clergymen, many of whom had come from the Northeast, challenged the Yankee merchants to "come up" and assume "the place of their fathers."[97] First, local writers and religious spokesmen argued that newcomers would determine the character of the city. Moreover, clergymen, such as Eliot and T. M. Cunningham, and the editors of local journals such as *The Teacher and Western Educational Magazine, Presbyterian Casket*, and the *Western Journal and Civilian*, insisted that businessmen will "lay the foundations of those moral institutions, which are to exert a controlling influence in forming the character of the future population of St. Louis."[98] According to Eliot, "the merchant feels it to be his duty to introduce into the community where he lives, all the means of improvement which are found elsewhere."[99] Finally, influential local leaders directed their efforts toward Yankees. "The West is the offspring of the East: her runaway child, which left the parental roof, and went into the wilderness to set up for itself," *The Teacher and Western Educational Magazine* instructed its readers, and it was for the sons of the East to establish "such institutions as their ideas of perfect-ability [sic] suggest."[100]

The old economic and political elite of the city embraced the newcomers as well. For wealthy longtime residents, Yankee merchants were natural allies. Most of the migrants supported the Whig Party and the economic reforms that municipal leaders advocated. Yankees also sided with local political officials on ethno-cultural questions, fearing the surging electoral power and cultural influence of immigrants and Catholics.[101] Moreover, the newcomers proved to be malleable partners. They provided vocal support for reform, but their efforts assumed a largely symbolic form. Yankees signed pledges, established voluntary associations, and attended meetings in St. Louis, though they seldom sought political office. Instead, these businessmen, who probably eschewed officeholding because they did not intend to stay in the city, left real political power in the hands of longtime political leaders. Thus, the old elite deferred to the newcomers in the cultural arena; they urged the newcomers to be active in civic affairs; and they championed Yankee cultural and moral reform. In return, the old leaders retained political power in a city with an increasing population of foreign-born and Democratic voters.

Local efforts to strengthen the link between St. Louis and eastern

commercial centers added to the prominence of transplanted Yankees. Political leaders, for example, hoped to cultivate investment
networks by drawing on the relatives and associates of Yankee
migrants. Many residents believed that the economic future of the
city would be determined in New York and Boston. Local newspapers, for example, urged municipal leaders to advertise the advantages of St. Louis "in the papers of Boston, New York, and
Philadelphia. By paying a few dollars for advertising in these cities,"
the *Missouri Democrat* predicted, "the city will probably gain
thousands."[102] An 1848 pamphlet implored local officials to "push
railroads from Boston, New York, and Philadelphia . . . to this
point," in order to cement ties with Atlantic coast cities.[103] The future
of Missouri industry, the *Missouri Republican* counseled, depended
upon "capital from abroad." The newspaper suggested that "New
York and Boston money" is the solution "to the present scarcity of
capital in the West."[104] Efforts to stimulate the growth of the economy, therefore, strengthened the alliance between the old landed
elite and the new commercial elite.

Buoyed by this support, New York and Boston newcomers attempted to mold their western home after familiar eastern examples.
Some migrants self-consciously reproduced New York or Boston
conventions, adopting the dreams of Yankee missionaries. The Reverend Truman Post, for example, promised to sustain the "Puritan
clime" in the transmontane region. "We at the west," Post explained,
"are trying to be true to our motherhood."[105]

More often, however, Yankee newcomers simply borrowed well-
established eastern prescriptions for the problems of urban growth.
Erastus Wells reproduced the omnibus network that had impressed
him when he lived in New York and forged a transportation empire
in St. Louis.[106] Similarly, merchants urged city officials to "introduce
the New York plan of converting uncurrent money," and local editors
recommended the adoption of a community "complaint book" as was
the custom in New York.[107] In 1855 municipal officials recommended
the repeal of restrictions on huckstering because "all the Eastern cities
have thrown their markets open."[108] New York and Boston innovations also provided ready solutions to St. Louis's crime and sewage
problems, dirty streets, and nearly every other urban ill.[109] Local
nativists even borrowed eastern legislative models when they tried to
restrict Irish beer drinking on Sundays.[110]

Yankee newcomers and their local supporters measured the progress of St. Louis against eastern society, and every New York reform
or Boston institution inspired a local equivalent. St. Louis residents,
for example, invited Dorothea Dix to the city.[111] Local reformers

urged city officials to establish a public library similar to the institution that served Boston and a mercantile library patterned after those
in the Northeast.[112] When New York municipal officials established a
city flower market, the *Missouri Democrat* suggested that it would "be
advisable to establish a market of this kind in St. Louis."[113] The
Missouri Republican encouraged local ministers to visit the city's pris-
ons because "in New York the clergy regularly preach to the prison-
ers on Blackwell's Island and in the Tombs."[114] Community leaders
even copied local streets from familiar eastern thoroughfares. "Fourth
Street," a writer noted, "is, at present, the Broadway of St. Louis."
Local editors, however, complained that "it is not a likeness of the
great original in New York. It falls far short," they argued, "in one
respect which might be easily remedied": Fourth Street in St. Louis
was unpaved.[115] For advice on street paving, the mayor of St. Louis
consulted a New York official.[116] St. Louis lawyers demanded that
local courts rule on "the law of Boston," and St. Louis merchants,
apparently uninformed about the nature of Missouri politics, demanded that legislators copy the free banking legislation of New
York.[117] They noted that savings banks similar to those of New York
would serve a useful purpose in the city. "Will not the good people of
St. Louis," a local editor asked, "establish a similar and permanent
institution?"[118] Clergymen urged "the ladies of St. Louis" to establish
institutions to care for the children of working mothers because "New
York societies . . . proved most successful."[119] "Our city must not be
outstripped in benevolent enterprises."[120] Young newcomers from
the Northeast defined culture and reform in familiar terms, and St.
Louis bore a self-conscious, if somewhat superficial, resemblance to
Boston and New York.

Some institutions possessed a particularly strong Yankee cast. A
group of seventeen merchants and civic leaders, most of whom hailed
from Boston or New York and all of whom belonged to a single
Unitarian congregation, established Washington University in 1853
with Harvard firmly in mind.[121] William Greenleaf Eliot, himself a
Harvard graduate, belonged to the group, led the congregation of
Bostonians, and served as the president of the board of directors of
the institution.[122] Similarly, in 1853 northeasterners organized the
city's Young Men's Christian Association, drawing its constitution
and many of its members from "New York and Boston Associations."[123] Although the Atlantic coast chapters influenced the structure of the institution, the local institution also reflected the status of
the Yankee merchants in St. Louis. A young merchant from Connecticut served as the first president, and northeastern businessmen and
clergymen held many of the remaining offices in the organization.[124]

Designed to protect "the class devoted to mercantile pursuits" from "the temptations to which young men are exposed," the St. Louis Young Men's Christian Association assisted well-bred newcomers "in finding comfortable boarding houses, and respectable businesses."[125] The institution also attempted to educate its members; it sponsored lectures and subscribed to twenty-two periodicals – of which five were published locally and twelve of the remaining seventeen were published in New York, Boston, or Philadelphia.[126] Thus, it directed northeastern merchants to Yankee-dominated accommodations and businesses to provide them with a safe, proper, and exclusive setting, and it sustained the connection to northeastern culture and society.[127]

These institutions also enabled Yankees to consolidate their social and economic power. Northeasterners formed a small but homogeneous and remarkably cohesive community. Economic interests united the group, though religion also generated a powerful bond. For example, most transplanted eastern merchants belonged to a small number of Protestant congregations, such as Eliot's Church of the Messiah, which were led by Yankee clergymen.[128] Furthermore, many of these residents lived in the city's "proper" hotels, clustering into a small settlement in a city of newcomers and boardinghouses.[129] Class, religion, and residential patterns overlapped and enhanced Yankee influence in the city.

But if Yankees wanted to mold the development of St. Louis and the old elite encouraged them to do so, forces beyond the control of the newcomers contributed to their success. Divisions in local society, for example, enabled Yankees to exert disproportionate influence in a city in which they comprised less than one-tenth of the population. Cultural fissures reduced the political and social power of the numerically superior German population of St. Louis.[130] "Forty-Eighters," Lutherans, and Catholics battled with one another and undermined German power in the city. "Even where they [German immigrants] form the majority," one European visitor complained, "the helm is in the hands of the Yankees."[131] Bostonians and New Yorkers "hold the power in their hands in all important matters," the German writer Moritz Busch added.[132]

The entrepreneurial success of eastern businessmen reinforced their influence as well, generating social prestige for these strangers. Yankee connections became badges of respectability in local society and symbols of standing in the marketplace.[133] For example, newcomers, hoping to ride the crest of Yankee commercial prominence, literally advertised their eastern ties. Young migrants searched for employment by celebrating their "New York references." Local newspapers were filled with these notices during the late 1840s. One migrant, seeking a position in a dry goods house, noted that he "has twenty years experience in the business." More important, he announced, "five of them were spent in New York City in the dry goods jobbing trade."[134] References to employment in Massachusetts, New York, and Connecticut constituted strong credentials in an economy dependent on ties to eastern commercial centers, and letters from leading New York merchants provided an open door to the upper rungs of the burgeoning St. Louis merchant class.[135] Yankee culture and breeding became symbols of success and power in the city.

Similarly, eastern products became symbols of culture and refinement. Merchants, for example, boasted of their exclusive lines of "Lynn shoes," "New York Fancy Goods," and "Pennsylvania German Pills," and every entrepreneur seemed to claim Boston relations or New York backers.[136] The popularity of eastern products, a reflection both of cultural conventions and the dynamic role of Yankees in local society, heightened the commercial success of Boston and New York outlets and enhanced the standing of northeastern products and northeasterners.

Yankee influence also became self-perpetuating. Local newspapers, for example, recruited writers and editors from New York and Boston, believing that easterners possessed elevated standards of refinement.[137] As a result, St. Louis newspapers assumed an increasingly Yankee character. Pervasive assumptions about the influence of proper easterners shaped other institutions as well. In 1848 municipal officials instructed "Mr. E. Wyman, of this city, to proceed to Massachusetts, and select a sufficient number of competent teachers for the public schools in St. Louis."[138] Cultural chauvinism triggered recruitment efforts, increasing the flow of eastern migrants to the city and exaggerating Yankee influence in St. Louis.

Municipal ordinances, public institutions, voluntary associations, clothing styles, literary conventions, and even local streets resembled – and were intended to resemble – those in New York and Boston. Ambitious clerks in St. Louis sought references from northeastern merchants, admission to the churches established by Yankee clergymen, books written by eastern authors, membership in the local branches of northeastern associations, and rooms in the Tremont, the hotel patterned after The Tremont of Boston. To be sure, most members of the working class and many immigrants rejected such posturing; their counterparts in New York and Boston also rejected middle-class Yankee culture. More important, northeastern merchants struggled to control the character of St. Louis, and they largely succeeded, molding middle-class St. Louis in the image of middle-class New York and middle-class Boston. From the New

York–dominated business district and Washington University to the Boston-style prison reform and the New York–style police department, the city bore a distinct Yankee flavor.

Ironically, Yankee influence undermined the formation of a local, homegrown cultural elite. St. Louis merchants and professionals and city officials preferred to hire easterners. Moreover, community leaders opted to send their children to Boston and New York for "respectable" educations.[139] The prominent clergyman Truman Post, for example, celebrated the "glory" of Puritan New England from his St. Louis pulpit and sent his sons to Yale.[140] These practices preserved emotional and cultural bonds to "Yankeedom." Just as New York merchants depended on Wall Street investors for commercial sustenance, they remained loyal to eastern conventions. Thus, influential residents belittled local culture, deeming it primitive and unrefined; they preferred eastern literature and newspapers.[141] The economic status of branch managers preserved their ties to New York and Boston, and their cultural missions in the urban West performed the same function. Even as they tried to transplant Yankee culture to the streets of St. Louis, the effort reinforced their bonds with the Atlantic coast. Successful branch managers returned to the Northeast within a few years, as did successful missionaries. The new members of the economic and cultural elite remained visitors in the city that they dominated. Nonetheless, at midcentury, St. Louis was a Yankee city.

During the late 1840s St. Louis became a boomtown. Hundreds of thousands of migrants passed through the city, and shortsighted, fast-living newcomers dominated the city and shaped its development. Chaos reigned, and instability begot instability. Western towns like St. Louis grew so rapidly that newcomers, men without abiding ties to the community, predominated in the local population.[142] Thus, prosperity produced seemingly conflicting demographic patterns; while armies of "movers" flooded the booming city, rates of persistence plunged.[143] The top of society, St. Louis's commercial elite, proved to be nearly as transient as the bottom of society. Although the presence of "Romanism, sectarianism, and worldliness" provided both a challenge and an opportunity for Yankee migrants, the lure of other lodestones and the demands of fathers and employers sufficed to uproot potential community leaders. In some ways, however, this instability stabilized the social and institutional development of the city.

Most transplanted Yankees wanted to return to the Northeast as quickly as possible. Local conditions, particularly disease and social disorder, reminded the newcomers that the city was a convenient place to make a quick fortune, though a poor place to settle. Moreover, Yankee cultural dominance exacerbated the low persistence rate among St. Louis's social and economic leaders, bolstering ties to the Atlantic coast. As a result, the city's elite always included a very high proportion of newcomers from the East.

The constant influx of Yankee newcomers, however, insured cultural continuity in St. Louis. Migrants, fresh from Boston and New York, provided a continuous infusion of the latest eastern prescriptions and the most fashionable Yankee reforms. They also strengthened the city's dependence on northeastern urban centers and exaggerated St. Louis's colonial status. But as long as wealthy New York and Boston merchants remained active in the marketplace, the local economy would boom; and as long as well-bred easterners migrated to the city, Yankee culture would flourish in St. Louis. This process, however, placed the city in an increasingly anomalous position within Missouri. Always a commercial center in an agricultural region, St. Louis was becoming a Yankee outpost in a Southern province and a Northern city in a slave state.

6   A border city in an age of sectionalism

The midcentury boom – and the social changes that it generated – reinforced the Northeast's claim on St. Louis and St. Louis's dependence on the Northeast. Although geographical factors contributed significantly to the city's development, St. Louis continued to owe much of its prosperity to New York and Boston entrepreneurs. Well into the 1850s Yankee perceptions of the city – as a Yankee outpost in the West – sparked the investment and migration decisions that linked the western trading center to sources of capital, business expertise, and cultural institutions on the Atlantic coast. Ironically, the surge in the population, the expansion of the marketplace, and the maturation of local society exaggerated St. Louis's colonial relationship with the Northeast and exposed the city to the instability inherent in such a relationship. Any changes in northeastern perceptions of St. Louis threatened to upset the ties that fueled the city's economic ascent.

The extraordinary pace of growth masked important elements of continuity. During the late 1840s the local population increased by nearly 120 percent, and by 1852 the city held more than ninety thousand residents. The influx of newcomers, the subdivision of vacant tracts into bustling residential areas, the formation of cohesive neighborhoods, and the settlement of the Mississippi valley altered the local economy. Thus, internal and regional forces exerted increasing influence in the marketplace. Immigrant sections of the city, for example, began to support shops and businesses that catered to Old World tastes. Moreover, regional markets assumed a greater role in the St. Louis economy. These developments created new entrepreneurial opportunities in the city and brought new groups into the marketplace. Nonetheless, the overall character of the economy remained unchanged. The Missouri urban center flourished because it occupied an important role in the national economy, and Yankee businessmen defined that role. St. Louis, therefore, retained its colonial status, even as its markets burgeoned, its region matured, and its population approached one hundred thousand.

Although many local observers recognized the sources of the city's economic vitality, the pace of growth became intoxicating. In spite of three quarters of a century of halting, erratic development, St. Louis seemed to be fulfilling its destiny during the late 1840s and the early 1850s. It became the "lion of the valley" and the leading trading center of the West. The city had endured floods, fires, and disease. It had survived every challenge from the state legislature, outdistanced every rival, and blossomed without the aid of banks, canals, corporations, or harbor improvements. According to one financial writer, "none of the evils predicted have overtaken or checked our commercial prosperity."[1] The foundation of the city's prosperity, however, proved to be vulnerable to external pressures, particularly the kind of pressures that erupted during the 1850s.

Between 1854 and 1856 national political forces transformed Yankee perceptions of St. Louis and disrupted the relationship between the Northeast and its colony in the Mississippi valley. As a result, the local economy deteriorated. Commerce languished; capital sources withered; and migration to the city waned.[2] New Yorkers and Bostonians began to avoid St. Louis during this period, and investors withdrew their capital from the city. Eastern journals no longer toasted the city as the "New York of the West." Instead, according to a local editor, "St. Louis became the target for the journalism of every rival city. Ill-fame was heaped upon our head."[3] Worse still, Yankees compared St. Louis to Norfolk during this period. Both cities, according to observers, were "giants by nature," though their development remained "dwarfed" and paralyzed.[4]

The events of the mid-1850s remade the urban West. Political forces profoundly altered eastern economic strategies, redefining St. Louis's role in the national economy and accelerating the development of rival cities. For the Missouri trading center, the changes would be permanent; never again would St. Louis compete for regional dominance or for national economic power. In 1856 a prominent local editor and politician concluded that "St. Louis is a city smitten with the plague, a moral leper among the cities of the land."[5] If St. Louis was reborn during the late 1840s, the city was mortally wounded during the mid-1850s, a victim of the sectional crisis.

Large numbers of newcomers migrated to St. Louis during the early 1850s. Irish immigrants, for example, poured into the city. According to the *Missouri Republican*, over eight thousand settlers from Ireland "landed" in St. Louis in 1853.[6] German immigration surged as well, rising until 1854, when nearly twenty-nine thousand "Deutsch emigrants" arrived in the city.[7] Moreover, an increasing number of native-born settlers migrated to the Missouri urban center.

Many of these newcomers did not intend to remain in St. Louis. German officials in the city, for example, noted that nearly half the German immigrants who disembarked from steamboats in the harbor planned to stop in St. Louis only long enough to purchase land and provisions, before establishing farms in the upper Midwest.[8] Similarly, many Irish and native-born newcomers did not expect to settle in the city. Sickness, the death of a spouse, financial miscalculations, or other problems, however, trapped many travelers in St. Louis. The rising price of land posed particular difficulties for migrants. Thousands of German immigrants, a disgruntled migrant explained, "in vain looked for a piece of ground suitable to their means."[9] Natives faced similar difficulties. In 1854, for example, Anson Ashley migrated from central Ohio to St. Louis to buy farmland in northern Missouri or Iowa. A year later, however, he conceded that "the length of my purse . . . attached me" to the city. Month after month Ashley remained in St. Louis. "I intended to purchase land as soon as I was able," Ashley explained to his father, "but that I had not got enough money."[10]

These newcomers transformed the character of the city and the structure of the local economy. As immigrants settled in the city, started families, and established neighborhoods, small new niches in the marketplace emerged. The clustering of German immigrants in two of the city's six wards and the concentration of Irish newcomers in two sections of St. Louis, for example, created opportunities for men of small means, and entrepreneurs opened businesses that catered to specific neighborhoods.[11] Leopold Fischer established a small millinery shop in 1855. Begun with little capital, Fischer's business relied on a "steady" trade "in the German part of the city . . . with the German population" according to credit investigators.[12] Similarly, Otto Ernst, a school teacher, started a small German bookstore in St. Louis in 1856, and Frederick Rover's dry goods shop relied on a "safe German trade," with "German friends."[13] Although few of these ventures flourished, most survived for four or five years. Neighborhood patronage shielded them from many of the pressures that crippled other kinds of commercial ventures.

Growing neighborhoods also supported a wide range of small specialty shops. Many residents responded to this market as well and expanded their crafts into small business ventures.[14] Hundreds of tailors, furniture-makers, jewelers, and shoemakers opened small stores in St. Louis during this period. In 1857 Frederick Dieckroeger established a tailoring shop in the city. Dieckroeger manufactured for his "own sales and to order." In addition, he carried a small stock of ready-made "eastern" clothing.[15] Unable to compete with New York clothing merchants, men like Dieckroeger responded to the growing local market by combining custom work with a small retail stock. These artisanal or manufacturing ventures satisfied specialized local needs and dovetailed with the larger and more competitive retail market.[16]

Thus, the ballooning population of the city generated opportunities for local craftsmen and workers, and artisanal ventures comprised the fastest-growing sector of the local economy during this period.[17] Craftsmen operated more than one-fourth of the firms that opened their doors between 1850 and 1854 – compared to only 10 percent of the firms in business during the late 1840s. Moreover, such ventures attracted large numbers of immigrants, particularly German newcomers, into the local marketplace. These immigrants operated one-third of the businesses that opened in St. Louis between 1851 and 1856 – compared to one-fifth of the city's firms during the late 1840s. As St. Louis grew and the domestic market expanded, the economy became more broadly based and the commercial class became more diverse.

The settlement of the upper Mississippi valley also influenced the structure of the local economy. St. Louis served as a regional entrepôt during this period, and the hinterland market became an important sector of the city's economy.[18] Between 1840 and 1850 the population of the region more than doubled – most of this increase occurred during the late 1840s. Territories that were sparsely settled in 1845 constituted sizable markets for eastern goods five years later and enormous markets a decade later. For example, the population of Missouri increased nearly fivefold during the 1840s, and the population of Wisconsin increased ninefold.

Just as immigrants discovered new niches in the domestic economy, rural entrepreneurs found new opportunities in the regional economy.[19] Country merchants transported modest quantities of a broad range of goods to small – but growing – pockets of settlement scattered throughout the region.[20] Relying on the network of streams and rivers that served St. Louis, these men used the city's market in much the same way as St. Louis traders used the New York market. Each spring, they traveled to St. Louis and purchased their stock for an entire season.[21] The March migration of country buyers supplemented the larger spring provisions trade and contributed to local prosperity.

Ties to the hinterland reshaped the economy in surprising ways. First, migrants from the region and country traders assumed an increasing role in the local marketplace. Midwesterners established 41 percent of the businesses that opened during the early 1850s, compared to only one-fifth of new firms during the late 1840s. But these changes also introduced greater instability to the St. Louis marketplace. The hinterland trade remained erratic and fragmented, and most country traders possessed little capital and operated modest businesses. As a result, the proportion of small firms in the marketplace increased by nearly 20 percent, making the local economy less top-heavy. Moreover, because smaller firms, operated by poorer merchants, comprised a growing proportion of the market, the failure rate for all businesses in the city skyrocketed and the average life span for commercial ventures plummeted, falling by 22 percent during the early 1850s.[22] The maturation of the upper Mississippi valley expanded the weakest sector of the local economy.

The economic development of the Ohio valley reinforced this process. Cincinnati and Pittsburgh became major commercial and manufacturing centers during this period, and merchants from the river cities migrated to St. Louis during the early 1850s.[23] Some of these entrepreneurs tried to bring the Missouri market into their economic networks, buying goods in the Northeast and marketing these manufactures throughout the Midwest.[24] More often, however, Cincinnati and Pittsburgh merchants sold locally or regionally produced goods in the St. Louis marketplace.[25] River transportation, for example, gave Pittsburgh iron producers an enormous advantage over their English competitors, and thus intraregional interdependence increased as western cities grew and matured.[26] Some Cincinnati factory owners, such as John Bart, sent their sons and brothers to St. Louis to open trans-Mississippi outlets. In 1855 E. K. Bart established the Missouri branch of his brother's Cincinnati-based jewelry and Indian-rubber goods firm.[27]

Although few midwestern merchants possessed the resources or the economic ties to compete against powerful eastern branches during this period, low transportation costs and the increasing production of regional specialties enabled men of modest means from the region to establish commercial ventures in St. Louis. Most Cincinnati migrants operated small, fledgling businesses, and these ventures failed 75 percent faster than northeastern firms. But businesses owned by Cincinnatians also increased the regional orientation of the local economy, and the proportion of debts contracted in midwestern commercial centers grew during the early 1850s.[28] More important, the flow of entrepreneurs and goods from Ohio river cities to St. Louis added to the rapidly growing proportion of small and weak firms that operated in the local marketplace.

Changes in the Northeast contributed to this shift in the structure of the economy. While the regional economy was maturing, Yankee interest in the St. Louis market was waning slightly.[29] The settlement of the West should have enlarged the eastern wholesale trade in St. Louis and enhanced eastern interest in the Missouri city. After all, country customers needed Lynn shoes and Philadelphia textiles. The changing structure of the local economy should have expanded both the base and the apex of the marketplace, creating greater opportunities for small-scale traders and large eastern agents.

Instead, however, relatively fewer Yankee merchants migrated to St. Louis during the early 1850s. Northeastern involvement in the local economy peaked between 1845 and 1847. Boston and New York merchants continued to move to St. Louis, though eastern men started only one-third of the businesses established during the early 1850s, compared to more than one-half of the city's new firms during the late 1840s. Furthermore, the proportion of businesses controlled by Yankee migrants dropped between the late 1840s and the early 1850s. For example, the total number of businesses in operation in the city increased by 43 percent during the early 1850s. The number of northeastern firms in operation, however, rose by only 23 percent; thus, the proportion of businesses controlled by Yankee merchants dropped by 32 percent.[30]

The flow of newcomers from Boston began to decline during the late 1840s and fell more sharply during the early 1850s. Massachusetts migrants established over one-fifth of the businesses that opened their doors in the city during the late 1840s. During the early 1850s, however, Boston men started only one firm for every seven new businesses in St. Louis. New York involvement in the local marketplace dropped as well, though the decline was considerably more gradual. Moreover, fewer outlets were established in the city as branches failed, and the proportion of businesses operating as branch concerns fell by 28 percent during the early 1850s, adding to the regional orientation of the marketplace.

Shifts in the northeastern economy affected westward migration and investment. St. Louis had blossomed at the height of – and as a result of – an extraordinary surge of prosperity in Boston and New York. With capital markets full, outlets for investment scarce, and "western fever" raging, St. Louis had captured Yankee attention, capital, and migrants. For Boston, however, this boom was short-lived. Heavy investment in western ventures quickly absorbed surplus capital in the city. According to one recent study, "by 1848, Bostonians' commitments were widely-extended, and they were for the time being frozen in their existing investments."[31] Boston merchants embarked on fewer new western ventures after the late 1840s, and migration to St. Louis peaked before midcentury.[32] Nonetheless, early investments kept Bostonians deeply involved in the St. Louis marketplace during the early 1850s; the Missouri entrepôt remained the principal western distribution center for New England goods, such as shoes and boots.[33]

More than any other single cause, the burgeoning economy of New York had buoyed the western provisions trade and peopled St. Louis's commercial class. Although New York migration to and investment in St. Louis also peaked during the 1840s, New Yorkers remained active in the local marketplace long after their Boston counterparts.[34] These newcomers continued to migrate to St. Louis during the early 1850s, bringing Wall Street dollars and eastern entrepreneurial energy. The volume of both migration and investment, however, began to wane by 1854. The economy of New York, feeling the early tremors that culminated in the Panic of 1857, lurched during this period, encouraging cautious entrepreneurs to reduce the scale of their far-flung investments.[35] Migration did not stop, though changing financial conditions constricted the flood tide to a steady stream.

Despite shifts in the local and regional markets and a reduction in the flow of northeastern entrepreneurs to the city, Yankee merchants continued to dominate the St. Louis economy. They controlled the provisions trade and the wholesale market. Moreover, their commission and transshipping firms supplied goods to neighborhood shopkeepers and to country merchants.[36] Thus, Yankee branch managers assumed central, though somewhat indirect, roles in the expansion in the local economy. More important, they continued to operate the largest commercial houses in the city. Nearly three-fourths of the biggest businesses operating in St. Louis in 1855, for example, were established by eastern migrants during the late 1840s. Yankees started fewer new businesses after midcentury, though they controlled nearly half the firms in operation in St. Louis and the vast majority of the city's largest and strongest enterprises. Somewhat weakened, Yankee commercial dominance persisted.

But Yankee perceptions of St. Louis began to change during the first half of the 1850s. According to a writer in 1849, St. Louis was known as "the place where cash and lots can be made very fast."[37] Five years later, however, the city seemed overcrowded, and newcomers complained that fewer opportunities were available.[38] In part, St. Louis became a victim of its reputation. Boom-era visitors had reported that men of vision forged empires in the city, and rags-to-riches legends both attracted newcomers to the Missouri urban center and shaped eastern perceptions of St. Louis. The success of Yankee branches seemed to confirm these reports, and more migrants moved to the city. Waves of eastern newcomers, however, heightened competition in St. Louis. The once "open" city, according to many migrants, became increasingly "settled."[39] Even during the boom, some newcomers had expressed disappointment. One settler, lured to the West by "glowing accounts" of St. Louis, complained that "the place is getting over loaded and tremendously overrated."[40] The proliferation of small businesses during the early 1850s exacerbated this crowded feeling and influenced eastern perceptions of St. Louis.

Easterners also became increasingly bored with St. Louis during this period. The city's boom became familiar and timeworn in eastern commercial circles, and it no longer sparked great interest along the Atlantic coast.[41] Moreover, the settlement of the region rendered St. Louis less exciting, less savage, and somehow less "western." Just as Yankee readers had tired of reading about Cincinnati during the 1840s, visitors came to consider St. Louis "a mere common-place [sic] business city" during the 1850s.[42] As a result, Yankee journals devoted less attention to the "New York of the West"; potential migrants possessed less information about the city; and the magnetic quality of St. Louis gradually faded. Fickle eastern audiences demanded novel subjects, and the economy of St. Louis – like that of Cincinnati before it – suffered.[43]

At the same time, other western cities beckoned. Although St. Louis had faced little competition for Yankee sons during the mid-1840s, a decade later the city attracted a smaller share of restless easterners. St. Louis's luster, however, did not fade as much as the Missouri city was displaced in eastern journals and literature. Upstart rivals such as Chicago and San Francisco, younger and more exciting, increasingly captured eastern imaginations during this period. Suddenly, Yankee travelers flocked to these cities in their search for "western vigor," and eastern writers toasted the "inevitable greatness" of a new group of rising western towns.[44] One observer, for example, noted that St. Louis lacked the "charm of novelty such as we meet with in a perfectly new place, like Chicago."[45] Other writers predicted that the "final destiny" of San Francisco was to be the "great commercial city of the world."[46] During the first half of the 1850s rival trading centers gained national prominence. Although they failed to supplant St. Louis during this period, a new battle for eastern favor and Yankee investment loomed.

Descriptions of Chicago during the 1850s differed little from those that had attracted Yankee entrepreneurs to St. Louis during the mid-1840s. For example, an 1857 writer reported that Chicago "rapidly advances in manhood."[47] A Polish visitor announced that the city "rises like a mushroom out of the earth," while a prominent eastern financial journal suggested that Chicago "sprung forward as a racehorse from the stand."[48] To the chagrin of St. Louis residents, travelers insisted that Chicago embodied "western promise."[49] *Hunt's Merchants' Magazine*, for example, deemed the Illinois city the "star of empire."[50] Similarly, an English visitor reported that "Chicago tells more forcibly of the astonishing energy and progress of the Americans than anything."[51]

Even the cultural attractions of Chicago resembled those of the Missouri entrepôt. According to one Congregational minister, "Chicago is one of the most extensive and promising fields of evangelical labor in the world."[52] Another clergyman termed the city "a field of exalted moral influence."[53] Proper easterners, many writers concluded during the 1850s, could best serve the religious needs of the Far West by migrating to Chicago. A decade earlier religious writers had considered St. Louis the crucial battleground for the future of the West.[54] Similarly, just as well-bred eastern visitors to St. Louis stayed at the Tremont House, the hotel modeled after the Boston inn of the same name, wealthy travelers to Chicago during the 1850s stayed at a fashionable new facility in that city called the Tremont House.[55]

More damaging, many writers announced that the commercial future of Chicago "is absolutely without parallel."[56] The journals that had celebrated St. Louis's "unparalleled" position, now judged Chicago "the most promising" city in the nation. Its growth, *Hunt's Merchants' Magazine* reported in 1855, "has been truly astonishing, more rapid than any city in the world."[57] Much as in the case of St. Louis a decade earlier, travelers detected "a bustling go-ahead" spirit in Chicago during the early 1850s.[58]

During the 1850s the two cities competed for eastern favor.[59] Many New York entrepreneurs continued to believe that the better-established Missouri city, with a population more than twice that of its rival at midcentury, offered a safer and more profitable field for eastern investors, and Yankee traders remained active in the St. Louis marketplace. Other eastern merchants, however, insisted that Chicago would be the "great metropolis of the West." As a result, eastern interest in the Illinois city soared.[60] *Hunt's Merchants' Magazine*, long impressed by the commercial advantages of St. Louis, reported in 1853 that "there is great interest in Chicago. She is talked about, inquired about, and sought after by thousands at the East."[61] Visitors observed that hard-driving Yankees poured into Chicago during this period.[62] According to one traveler, "New Englanders of active enterprise and successful progress" were building the city.[63] Although the cities offered similar attractions, the competition broke St. Louis's stranglehold on the far western trade and reduced the flow of Yankee migrants and capital to the Missouri city.[64]

The fight for eastern dollars assumed greater importance during the mid-1850s. New York investors had long fueled the growth of western cities, though the railroad boom increased the capital requirements for economic development. Railroads linked producers to consumers and extended urban markets into the countryside, thereby enlarging the hinterland of the cities they served. But railroads possessed a symbolic meaning as well.[65] To many mid-nineteenth-century Americans, they represented progress, and cities served by such "iron fingers" seemed dynamic and vigorous.[66] Thus, for both real and symbolic reasons, the railroad became an important component of the battle for eastern interest. The expense of building a railroad network also made the fight for capital even more urgent.

The residents of both cities contracted "railroad mania" during this period, and St. Louis boosters exerted as much effort to stimulate internal improvements as did their Illinois counterparts.[67] Beginning in the mid-1830s, when businessmen planned a road from the banks of the Mississippi river to Boston, St. Louis residents undertook repeated and sustained attempts to secure a rail network for their city.[68] The prosperity of the late 1840s increased pressure for a rail system, and politicians and businessmen joined in a crusade to attract capital and to stimulate construction. Far from eschewing the railroad in favor of the steamboat, local leaders argued that St. Louis needed both mechanisms. During the late 1840s, for example, the editor of the *Missouri Republican* charged that St. Louis must have railroads if she is to "retain her present commercial position and superiority."[69] "She has more at stake, and her prosperity suffers more from the neglect of these improvements," an 1849 pamphlet explained, "than any other Western [sic] city."[70] By 1853 local boosters announced that the railroad had become more important to the city than the steamboat, arguing that it "will be more productive of good results than the commerce of the Mississippi."[71]

Nor was this empty rhetoric. Although Missouri did not have a single mile of track in operation until 1852, St. Louis residents hosted railroad conventions and made enormous financial commitments to rail construction. In 1849, for example, local businessmen convened a meeting at which they pledged to buy more than $150,000 worth of Missouri Pacific stock.[72] Another meeting, held only four months after the first, raised an additional $319,000.[73] Moreover, municipal government assumed an active role in the effort. In 1853 the city's charter was amended in order to permit the corporation to subscribe to railroad stock.[74] The following year, voters increased their taxes in order to raise $1.2 million to "aid this enterprise."[75] Local editors, however, demanded more. A financial writer for the *Missouri Democrat* implored "large merchants and manufacturers to give $10,000 each" to the county for railroad construction.[76] City officials and local entrepreneurs spearheaded numerous similar efforts during the early 1850s.[77] Despite decades of dependence on the river trade, St. Louis residents were hardly blind to the "incalculable benefit" of railroads.[78] But community leaders also recognized that local resources were inadequate for the task. The state would have to support rail construction, as state legislatures throughout the nation had done. In addition, capital would have to be "drawn from beyond the limits of the state."[79]

Missouri lawmakers began to express enthusiasm for internal improvements during this period. Interior farmers, having flourished during this period, increasingly sought "mechanisms for commercial exchange."[80] As early as 1848, for example, Governor John C. Edwards had announced that "the increasing wealth, population, agricultural products, and manufactures of Missouri justifies preparation for the prosecution of a system of internal improvements."[81] In the same legislative session, the assembly incorporated the Pacific Railroad, and construction began three years later.[82] Although rural lawmakers continued to be wary of St. Louis traders, their constituents demanded greater access to markets. "Railroads," Governor Austin A. King reported in 1852, "will greatly advance all that appertains to her [Missouri's] interests."[83]

But rural legislators remained suspicious of "foreign" schemes, St. Louis merchants, and state spending. The prosperity of the era, according to interior representatives, had confirmed the wisdom of the conservative legislative program of the early 1840s; Governor Sterling Price reminded voters that "indiscriminate and reckless" projects "entail widespread pecuniary embarrassment."[84] He also urged the assembly to "use great caution and discretion."[85] Other politicians charged that railroad construction must benefit Missouri farmers, not just St. Louis speculators. Lawmakers warned that "reforms" should not bring rural Missourians "into a commercial subjection."[86] Old Jacksonians celebrated the benefits of railroads, though they remained sensitive to state-sanctioned privilege, particularly expensive privileges that contributed to the commercial supremacy of St. Louis. Thus, the legislators chose not to fund internal improvements; Missouri railroads would be privately constructed. In a state with little surplus capital, the legislature declined to shoulder the burden of building a railroad system.[87]

At the same time that massive improvement projects were requiring extraordinary sums of capital, more and more Yankee investors were choosing to invest in Chicago ventures rather than in St. Louis businesses.[88] Regional competition exacerbated local capital shortages just when capital became the crucial resource in the war for commercial supremacy.[89] Missouri railroad builders complained that "industry is limited by capital," and construction lagged.[90] According to one local writer, capital shortages "leave our Railroad System [sic] like the roofless frame of an unfinished building."[91] In 1854 only fifty miles of track were in operation in Missouri; by contrast, nearly three hundred miles of railroad tracks crisscrossed the sparsely settled state of Wisconsin.[92] Moreover, political leaders recognized that "Missouri is falling behind her sister states" and began to wonder if "private enterprise can build the roads."[93]

State legislators, however, offered a solution. The Missouri assembly authorized state assistance to railroad companies. Lawmakers would issue twenty-year state bonds, to be sold in New York, in order to finance construction. The state's credit, therefore, would be summoned to the aid of Missouri railroads.[94]

This plan tied the pace of construction to eastern perceptions of the future of Missouri. New York and Boston capitalists believed that railroads brought prosperity. The sale of Missouri bonds, they reasoned, would initiate the railroad construction that, in turn, would sustain the economy of St. Louis. Thus, the potential of St. Louis businesses depended on the railroad construction financed by the sale of state bonds.[95] The Missouri railroad program had two important effects. First, it insured that the economic future of St. Louis would be determined in New York financial markets. And second, the plan formally and inextricably bound the economy of St. Louis to the reputation of Missouri, particularly its reputation in New York.

The results of this unlikely union between city and state proved to be disastrous. The events of the mid-1850s dramatically altered Yankee perceptions of Missouri, instantly sapping the commercial vitality of St. Louis. Within five years the lion of the valley languished, and Chicago commanded the Far West.

On May 30, 1854, Congress passed the Kansas-Nebraska Act and changed the history of St. Louis. Championed by Stephen Douglas, the bill divided the Kansas territory into two states and declared that Congress would not intervene in the settlement process.[96] Instead, the new regions would be organized according to the principle of "popular sovereignty." Thus, the Kansas-Nebraska Act repealed the Missouri Compromise and reopened the slavery question. Douglas believed that the territories would remain free-soil, while many Southern leaders predicted that each side would claim one of the new states.[97] St. Louis merchants anticipated new levels of prosperity from the settlement of the region, since thousands of migrants would pass through the city and buoy the local provisions market.[98] Responses to the bill, however, transformed the development of St. Louis and dramatically altered the character of the urban West.

A small group of Northern politicians and reformers shaped the settlement of the new territories and distorted Northern perceptions of the region. Even before the Kansas-Nebraska Act passed, these radicals declared war on Southern interests in the territories. William Seward, for example, vowed to challenge the efforts of proslavery migrants in the region.[99] Still more incendiary were the words and actions of Eli Thayer, an entrepreneur and schoolmaster from Worcester, Massachusetts. Backed by Horace Greeley, William Cullen Bryant, and some of the most influential merchants and lawyers in the Northeast, Thayer established a "plan of operation."[100] Under the auspices of the New England Emigrant Aid Company, he claimed to have raised $5 million from merchants in order to "convey" twenty thousand Massachusetts residents to Kansas.[101] The free-soil cause in the region, he promised, would thus triumph. According to some historians, economic motives spurred Thayer to action.[102] Regardless of his motives, however, Thayer loudly proclaimed his plan to invade and to "secure" the territory.

Thayer's scheme produced a powerful reaction in rural Missouri, reviving deep-seated fears of "foreign vampires" scourging the countryside. Local politicians had held Yankee speculators responsible for the panics of 1819 and 1837. Only the legislative shield directed at eastern capitalists and their St. Louis agents, rural spokesmen maintained, had protected Missourians from these manipulators during the 1840s.[103] To Missouri farmers, Thayer's plan to send twenty thousand Yankees to the region rekindled memories of earlier depressions and of social upheaval.[104]

Thayer's crusade also exaggerated cultural tensions in the state. As Bostonians and New Yorkers migrated to St. Louis and assumed prominent positions in local society, the river city became a Yankee trading center. During the same period, Virginians and Kentuckians settled in the remainder of Missouri. Over 90 percent of native-born Missourians hailed from Southern backgrounds; most had migrated from Virginia, Kentucky, and Tennessee.[105] Thus, settlement patterns reinforced the cultural and ideological chasm that separated the state's farmers from the city's merchants.

The political force of this migration swelled as the sectional controversy flared. Until the late 1840s rural Missourians focused their political strength on efforts to harness – and repel – northeasterners, particularly northeastern traders and speculators. Gradually, however, Northern culture and the Northern economic system became the rallying point for rural Missouri's increasingly Southern cultural climate, and political leaders began to argue that Missouri belonged to the South. In 1849, for example, Senator Claiborne Jackson publicly endorsed John C. Calhoun's combative stance, announcing that "Missouri will be found in hearty cooperation with the Slaveholding states . . . against the encroachments of Northern fanaticism."[106] But sectionalism provided a new context for the continuing battle between rural Missouri and commercial St. Louis. Although the political war changed little, rural lawmakers couched their rhetoric in increasingly sectional terms. As Southern issues infused Missouri politics, Thayer's invasion became a part of the long-standing St. Louis plan to control the state as well as a part of the Yankee plot to devour the South.[107]

A quirk of geography fanned the fires of sectionalism in antebellum Missouri and transformed the development of the state. Slavery barely took root in Missouri during this period. Most of the state's farmers migrated to the region without bondsmen, and the proportion of slaves in the Missouri population dropped by nearly 50 percent during the antebellum period.[108] The climate of the state, according to local observers, discouraged slaveholding.[109] In one section of Missouri, however, the slave economy flourished. Tobacco and hemp farms provided the principal crops in the counties near the Missouri River and along the western border of the state, and this area contained most of Missouri's bondsmen.[110] For example, fifty thousand slaves, worth over $25 million, worked at the western edge of the state.[111] David Atchison, Missouri's most powerful political figure, also hailed from the western part of the state, the region abutting the Kansas territory.

Missouri slaveholders felt particularly vulnerable during this period, and the rhetoric of Thayer stirred these anxieties to a fevered pitch. Free soil bordered Missouri on three sides, "exposing" slaves to constant temptation. The Mississippi River also provided a convenient channel for escape into free territories, and steamboats offered transportation beyond the pale of the peculiar institution. Contemporaries believed that the underground railroad flourished on the eastern shore of the great river, reinforcing the fears of Missouri slaveholders.[112] Eli Thayer's proclamations provided another reminder that Missouri formed "a slaveholding peninsula jutting up into a sea of free-soil."[113]

Led by the fiery Atchison, western Missourians accepted Eli Thayer's pronouncements: the New England Emigrant Aid Company planned to "abolitionize" the region.[114] Many Missourians believed that this crusade constituted more than just another Yankee "ism"; instead, they felt that Thayer's plan threatened the basis of their economy, the source of their independence, and the future of their state. "After making Kansas a free state," a Missouri newspaper editor explained, Thayer's soldiers intended "to come over into Missouri and interfere with slavery."[115] "The ultimate object," another resident concluded, "was to surround Missouri with free states, and eventually affect the institution of slavery in Missouri."[116] Seizing the moment, David Atchison, the champion of Southern rights, warned that the survival of Missouri and the future of the South hinged on repelling the "vermin of the North."[117] He promised to resist the invaders with the "last drop of his blood and his last breath."[118]

Believing that the settlement of the Kansas territory directly threatened their state, Missourians readied for a war, and farmers throughout the state formed secret societies, known as "Blue Lodges," "Friends' Societies," or "the Sons of the South," in order to defend themselves, their property, and their state.[119] A Gentry County group, for example, submitted resolutions to the House of Representatives declaring that "it is the duty of the State and her citizens . . . to prevent, if possible, that beautiful country [Kansas] from becoming an asylum for abolitionists and free-soilers, to harass and destroy our peace and safety."[120] Students at the University of Missouri announced a similar pledge, issued in the name of "the youth of the South."[121] Large numbers of Missouri farmers, excited by both Atchison and Thayer, became stridently Southern in their sympathies during the months following the passage of the Kansas bill. The residents of Boone, a rural county in the center of the state, resolved to speak "for Missouri, for the South, and for the North to hear."[122]

When government officials announced the date of the first election of a territorial delegate to Congress, the moment for action beckoned. "Nip the thing in the bud," the Liberty Weekly Tribune warned.[123] Arriving just in time for the autumn election, western Missourians flooded Kansas – and voted. The invaders cast nearly two thousand fraudulent ballots and carried the election. Equally important, Missourians made no apologies for their extralegal actions.[124]

The election of the territorial legislature in March of 1855 provided a more decisive contest for the future of the region and another opportunity for Missourians to protect their state from Yankee abolitionists and "nigger stealers."[125] Atchison publicly excused himself from the senate in order to spearhead the charge.[126] Leading with a barrage of threats and warnings, he announced yet another invasion of the Kansas territory. "There are 1,100 coming over from Platte County and if that ain't enough we can send you 5,000." For good measure and the public notice, Atchison added that "we came to vote, and we are going to vote, or kill every God-damned abolitionist in the district."[127] "We are going to have Kansas," another Missouri resident warned, "if we wade to the knees in blood to get it."[128] Brandishing sidearms and bowie knives, Atchison's band of five thousand controlled the territorial election, casting four fraudulent ballots for every legal vote.[129] The newly elected territorial legislature immediately adopted Missouri statutes, adding draconian codes to protect slaves in the region.[130]

Atchison's proclamations and the assault on Kansas received national attention and shaped popular perceptions of Missourians. The antislavery press provided the principal conduit of information about the Kansas elections, and radical editors caricatured the actions of Missourians to fuel the anti-Southern hysteria.[131] These editors devoted particular attention to Atchison, whose fiery rhetoric required little embellishment, and to his "border ruffians," most of whom were poor farmers.[132] Yankee spokesmen told the nation about "bands of whiskey-drinking, degraded, foul-mouthed marauders."[133] According to Sara Robinson, the wife of Thayer's agent in Kansas, Missourians were "ragged, ignorant, debauched, semi-savages, the very offshoot and growth of the peculiar institution."[134]

Northern writers issued sensational accounts of the March election. Border ruffians, these journalists wrote, planned to control Kansas by killing innocent Yankee settlers.[135] According to one observer, the Missourians ravaged women, beat children, and prowled the countryside "threatening to cut the throats" of free soilers "amid shouts of hurra for Missouri."[136] Calls of "kill the damned nigger-thieves," "rip his guts out," and "cut his throat," filled the air, according to Thayer's settlers and sympathetic newspapers.[137] Carefully tailored to fit the cause, the image of drunken, violent Missourians became fixed in Northern imaginations; the New York Times termed Missouri "the Border-Ruffian State."[138] During the mid-1850s the "barbaric" actions of "crazed" Missourians became an important symbol for the antislavery cause.[139]

Buoyed by free publicity for his venture and Northern reactions to border ruffianism, Thayer increased the stakes. The New England Emigrant Aid Company, he and his supporters vowed, would not sit idly by while Missouri savages "exterminated" "quiet, unoffending citizens."[140] Thayer announced plans to increase the flow of free-soil settlers to the region and to arm these "authentic" settlers. Prominent merchants, such as Amos Lawrence, began raising funds in order to purchase "Sharps rifles" for Massachusetts migrants.[141] Other Northerners joined the effort as well. For example, Henry Ward Beecher, no stranger to crusades to save the West, collected money from his congregation to procure guns – termed "Beecher's Bibles" – for the battle in Kansas.[142]

Widely circulated reports about the activities of Thayer's armed settlers wedded Southern radicals to the Missouri cause.[143] Missourians received increasingly generous support, Northern journalists reported, from their slaveholding brethren. According to the antislavery observers, armed contingents from Alabama, South Carolina, Georgia, and other Southern states hastened to the area "for the avowed and sole purpose of aiding Missouri in the conquest of Kansas."[144] The flag of South Carolina flew along side the Missouri banner, and the "motto of Southern rights" echoed throughout the region.[145] Fire-eaters embraced Missouri radicals, and Southern settlers, armed with "Mississippi rifles," prepared to do battle with free-soilers and their "Beecher's Bibles."[146]

On May 21, 1856, sectional tensions exploded on the Kansas border. An army of seven hundred fifty Missourians, reportedly chanting "wipe out the damned abolitionists," "sacked" Lawrence, Kansas.[147] Although only a single settler died in the assault, Northern newspapers announced that "war" had begun.[148] Within a week Preston Brooks bludgeoned Charles Sumner; John Brown attacked Pottawatomie, slaughtering five innocent settlers; and radicals blockaded the mouth of the Missouri River in a desperate effort to control the flow of firearms to the region.

These events and the ensuing political turmoil dramatically altered the history of St. Louis. Within Missouri, the border war revived and exaggerated long-standing hostilities between St. Louis merchants, with their Yankee ties, and interior farmers, with their growing Southern sympathies. In 1856 the *Missouri Republican* lamented that the city "is in an anomalous position – a position antagonistic to the prevailing sentiment of the whole State – a position which makes us the object of suspicion within all our broad boundary."[149] The controversy rapidly disrupted local society – it would also redefine St. Louis's role in the national economy.

Mounting sectional pressures transformed St. Louis politics during the mid-1850s. Local politicians initially tried to avoid the controversy. Thomas Hart Benton, for example, committed himself "to keeping the slavery agitation out of the state."[150] His lieutenants and closest allies followed suit.[151] Local Whigs also declared their neutrality, explaining that they rejected all forms of "fanaticism."[152] Some St. Louis radicals channeled their energies into the colonization movement, believing that the resettlement of blacks might dampen "the rage of a conflagration that threatens to sweep in a deluge of fire over the land."[153]

Local clergymen led a chorus of calls for restraint. The prominent Presbyterian minister Nathan L. Rice, for example, announced his "dread of both northern and southern agitators," and the Reverend Montgomery Schuyler warned his colleagues in the clergy to refrain from "intermeddling in the strife of party."[154] "Blessed are the peace makers," Schuyler reminded his followers.[155] William Greenleaf Eliot, perhaps the most influential minister in the city and a man with deep ties to Boston, also urged residents to avoid the fray. "I am a friend of the negro and a friend of freedom," Eliot declared, "and would hail with the utmost joy the day which makes Missouri a free State. But," he cautioned, "there is no course which hampers the actions of those who would work for this ultimate end, so much as the unwise interference of societies and individuals."[156] Eliot even tried block the efforts of the Western Unitarian Conference to condemn the institution of slavery. According to a local newspaper reporter, Eliot argued "that the conference had no right or authority to pass any resolutions on the subject."[157]

Similarly, local editors initially attempted to sidestep the issue. The editor of the *Missouri Democrat*, for example, explained that "St. Louis is a Western [sic] city and has nothing to do with the prejudices of either North or South."[158] The newspaper's principal rival, the *Missouri Republican*, urged newcomers to the city to "let slavery alone."[159] "Let us frown down and put flight from our borders the demon of discord and domestic strife," the *Missouri Democrat* added in 1856.[160] Restraint, however, failed to diffuse the tensions between city and state and between North and South in antebellum Missouri, and moderation rapidly gave way in a storm of sectional rage.

Ideological differences between antislavery spokesmen and local supporters of the peculiar institution polarized municipal politics. Unable to divert the slavery juggernaut any longer, Thomas Hart Benton lost his political empire, and long-standing alliances crumbled.[161] Between the passage of the Kansas-Nebraska bill and the sack of Lawrence, St. Louis politics degenerated and tensions flared.[162] In the ensuing political realignment the city's Whig journal – the *Missouri Republican* – became a Democratic organ, and the *Missouri Democrat* evolved into an increasingly radical Free Soil newspaper, uniting former Benton Democrats, Northern Whigs, many German immigrants, and most of the city's transplanted Yankees.[163] One local politician compared warring factions in St. Louis to "two sets of incendiaries . . . setting fire to the opposite sides of the same house at the same time."[164]

Antislavery forces in the city denounced "Atchison and his followers." "He must be destroyed," the *Missouri Democrat* warned.[165] B. Gratz Brown, the newspaper's editor and later a Republican candidate for vice president, warned that the ruffians threatened to disrupt the economic development of the city. "The border inroads are bringing disgrace upon our State and are doing incalculable injury to its commercial interests," he charged.[166] First, antislavery writers explained, the violent and unrestrained behavior of Atchison's "ruffians" imperiled property in St. Louis, no small concern for a commercial center.[167] Unless the proslavery radicals were stopped, Brown explained, "we will be swamped by slavery."[168] But Atchison also created immediate problems for the city. The Missouri senator, antislavery spokesmen noted, "degraded" white labor in St. Louis, attracting the "criminal offscourings of the slave markets of Virginia and Carolina."[169]

Proslavery forces within St. Louis, claiming growing support from the city's Irish population, employed a similar argument to defend their position.[170] "Abolitionists," the *Missouri Republican* charged, endangered the future of St. Louis. Northerners would "degrade" white labor by "inviting 60,000 free blacks to pour into St. Louis to loaf and steal."[171] More important, the newspaper reported that the "unwarrantable thefts of abolition societies and under ground [sic] railroads paralyze the grandest enterprises of commerce."[172] According to proslavery spokesmen, Thayer's "genuine settlers" consisted of "filthy convicts," some of whom "were caught in the act of pilfering on the levee."[173] Until Northern fanatics were controlled, the *Republican* warned, neither life nor property was secure in St. Louis.[174]

The rhetoric of the city's newspaper editors fed the national reaction to the Kansas crisis. Many New York and Massachusetts newspapers reprinted overblown editorials from St. Louis organs, exaggerating the combative tone of daily life in a border city.[175] This publicity made Yankee visitors to Missouri extremely sensitive to the slavery controversy and reminded Northern travelers that St. Louis was in a slave state.

Suddenly, the slaves who worked on the city's levee became conspicuous symbols of the peculiar institution. Isabella Trotter, for example, reported that "the institution was brought more prominently before us there [in St. Louis] than it has yet been."[176] Slave auctions, rare occurrences in the city, attracted widespread attention from curious visitors during this period.[177] Ironically, the proportion of slaves in the population of St. Louis plummeted during the antebellum years, falling by 85 percent between 1840 and 1860.[178] On the eve of the Civil War slaves accounted for only 2 percent of the city's residents. In part, Irish and German laborers provided cheaper alternatives to bondsmen.[179] Furthermore, easy access to free territory provided constant temptation for local slaves. Nonetheless, visitors began to see slaves everywhere in St. Louis.

If few travelers noticed the racial composition of levee workers before the Kansas war, every migrant commented on the "nigger teamsters" after the sack of Lawrence. "The crew and stockers [on steamboats]," Charles Mackay insisted, "were all negro slaves."[180] Another traveler most remembered St. Louis for the "nigger songs" she heard in the city.[181] At the same time, a celebrated legal controversy reinforced St. Louis's ties to the peculiar institution, as a local slave – named Dred Scott – sued his owners for his freedom.[182] Long the gateway to the West, St. Louis became the gateway to lawless Missouri and to the slaveholding South in the charged atmosphere of "bleeding Kansas."

While geography linked St. Louis to Atchison's Missouri in the minds of westward travelers, antislavery editors and propagandists sealed the association throughout the North.[183] Northern radicals argued that St. Louis residents, and particularly the merchants of the city, contributed to the Kansas bloodshed. Painting the border war with broad brush strokes, these writers and lecturers publicly and self-consciously tied St. Louis businessmen to the border difficulties.

Officials with Thayer's New Emigrant Aid Company intentionally exaggerated the relationship between the city and the crazed Southern Yankee killers skulking along the borders of the state. Searching for a way to control proslavery Missourians, Massachusetts antislavery crusaders proposed a "new mode of warfare."[184] They sought to sully the commercial reputation of St. Louis until the city's merchants restrained Atchison and his supporters. R. A. Chapman, a prominent lawyer, a director of the New England Emigrant Aid Company, and later Chief Justice of the Massachusetts Supreme Court, formulated the strategy. In October of 1855 he suggested that "the eastern people in that city [St. Louis]" could be instrumental in the Kansas campaign. But to that point, they had acted "meekly," preferring to avoid the fractious controversy. Chapman believed that "the only way to reach them is to excite fears for the prosperity of their city." He urged the company to use its influence to place negative articles about St. Louis in the leading newspapers of Massachusetts and New York. It "shall actually deter emigrants from going into the State," he noted, and "it does not take much effort to create a very general and decided public sentiment through the press." Most important, Chapman explained, "if we can thus get our battle fought by the St. Louis people, it will be a great gain." In short, Chapman argued that by exerting pressure on the economy of St. Louis, he could "compel" Yankee merchants in the city "to take sides against Stringfellow and his following."[185] Eli Thayer, Amos Lawrence, and other leaders of the New England Emigrant Aid Company supported the idea and initiated a crusade against St. Louis.

A tireless promoter, Thayer spearheaded the scheme to implicate St. Louis merchants in the "crime against Kansas."[186] He informed his supporters that slaveholding Missourians could be controlled "principally through the merchants of St. Louis," three-fourths of whom, he calculated, sympathized with his Kansas crusade.[187] In an attempt to spread the message (and to raise funds for his financially troubled emigration company), the Massachusetts reformer traveled throughout New York and New England delivering a series of lectures on the Kansas crisis.[188] Again and again, Thayer warned merchants of the dangers of Missouri investments.[189] Border ruffians, he explained, ruled St. Louis.[190]

But the foundation of the effort remained Chapman's newspaper campaign. Thayer persuaded William Cullen Bryant, the editor of the *New York Evening Post*, to promote the scheme, and the newspaper published a series of powerful editorials about slaveholding Missouri and the economic future of St. Louis.[191] After reiterating Thayer's threat that "it will be for them [the merchants of St. Louis] to devise the remedy," the editor took aim at the city.[192] Bryant emphasized two themes relating to the economic consequences of Missouri politics. First, he tried to discourage investment in St. Louis. And second, his editorials warned settlers to be wary of traveling in St. Louis and Missouri. In part, ideological concerns, Bryant noted, should influence investment and migration decisions. He also emphasized, however, that barbaric Missourians posed an enormous threat to life and to commerce in St. Louis. Property, he charged, was unsafe in the city. "Men who have no regard for the rights of others, cannot be expected to pay their debts. The rule of mob law [is] triumphant everywhere," the antislavery editor reported.[193] "The folly of the Missourians," William Cullen Bryant added, "has made a passage through their state as much dreaded as a passage through the country of the Pawnees."[194] "Emigrants to Kansas cannot safely ship from St. Louis. They are almost sure to fall among thieves."[195]

Other northeastern newspapers associated border ruffians with St.

Louis as well. The *New York Independent* linked Missouri business failures to border ruffianism.[196] "The unmitigated wrong" in western Missouri, the *Erie Constitution* speculated, directed "universal reprehension and indignation" at St. Louis.[197] Missouri became a convenient symbol for Southern savagery, and St. Louis was a casualty of the publicity. The *New York Times*, for example, interpreted all St. Louis news items in terms of border lawlessness. After a minor Know-Nothing brawl in 1855, the newspaper warned that "our neighbors in St. Louis should remember that capital and enterprise are timid, and seek the protection of law and order. Illegal violence," it added, must be "conquered" or St. Louis would inevitably suffer "from a great calamity."[198] The *New York Daily Tribune* advised settlers to "avoid St. Louis."[199]

This campaign transformed Northern perceptions of St. Louis. In 1856, for example, a St. Louis merchant returned from "a visit to the East" and reported that Yankees "have settled into the belief that we are a lawless people, indifferent to the rights of others, and determined to infringe those rights regardless of every consequence."[200] Other residents detected similar sentiments, explaining that Northerners believed that they would be unsafe in the city.[201] To Yankees, St. Louis increasingly appeared to be the commercial capital of a lawless, slaveholding state.

Northern religious writers, though not necessarily working in consort with Thayer and Chapman, reinforced the belief that bands of border ruffians roamed the streets of St. Louis and imperiled the safety of Yankees. The journals that had once encouraged easterners to fulfill their missions by migrating to St. Louis issued harsh warnings about the city during the mid-1850s. The *Home Missionary*, for example, recounted tales of violence and "suffering" in Missouri in the years following the Kansas war. Because the American Home Missionary Society's regional corresponding secretary lived in St. Louis, most reports from Missouri bore St. Louis labels, thus implicating the city in the problems of border missionaries.[202] "Distrust and suspicion," the journal's correspondent reported, "have been excited in reference to the missionaries, especially those who are natives of the Northern States."[203] Another minister admitted that "the state of anarchy in my field had become so extended, and personal security had become so impaired, that my friends urged me not to expose myself further. If I had remained ten days longer," the correspondent added, "there would have been insults, threats, and perhaps physical violence to myself."[204] Northern visitors also noted that Missourians had vowed to drive the "northern division of the Methodist Episcopal Church" from the state.[205]

According to many writers, the religious and cultural mission that had lent respectability to gold-seeking in St. Louis ended during this period. In 1856 the *Home Missionary's* Missouri secretary predicted "nothing but darkness for the cause of Christ here."[206] The cause of God in Missouri was hopeless.[207] "An Eastern man can labor here with little satisfaction," a writer for the magazine explained in 1857.[208] After nearly three decades in the state, with St. Louis as its regional headquarters, the American Home Missionary Society announced its readiness to abandon Missouri.[209] The clergyman W. W. Whipple, who had once celebrated Missouri's importance as a field of ministerial labor, warned that "Eastern men who will not swallow slavery, head and horns, had better not go into the slave states to preach. They can do more good elsewhere."[210]

Yankee religious writers, like antislavery editors, increasingly considered St. Louis a Southern outpost.[211] For example, the *Home Missionary*, a journal that had strongly encouraged hardy young Yankees to bring civilization to the West by migrating to St. Louis, urged young Yankees to "shun" the city along with the remainder of the South.[212] During this period the magazine defined the "West" as the states of Michigan, Indiana, Illinois, Iowa, Wisconsin, Kansas, Nebraska, California, and Oregon. Missouri, though surrounded by the "West" on three sides, was banished from the region.[213] Religious and economic writers argued that the West, *excluding* Missouri and its leading city, still beckoned to well-bred Yankees. St. Louis no longer represented an attractive destination for the restless sons of the Northeast.

If the cultural appeal of the city waned during the Kansas years, the economic attractions of St. Louis declined even more dramatically. During the Kansas war Wall Street traders and State Street entrepreneurs became uneasy about St. Louis investments. They began to question the wisdom of financing commercial enterprises in a slave state.

Practical considerations – rather than ideological concerns – forced Yankee merchants to reassess their St. Louis ties. Although many Boston and New York branch managers supported the antislavery cause, voted for local Free-Soil candidates, and subscribed to the city's abolitionist newspaper, Yankee traders struggled to avoid the political fray. Like local clergymen, they pleaded for restraint. "What the business men of St. Louis wish to see," a western traveler concluded, "is the territory prosperously settled, and provided it be attained they do not care what institutions prevail."[214] The transplanted Boston merchant Francis Hunt reiterated the neutral position of local traders. "We know no party or sect in connection with our business," Hunt announced. "Neither can we see why the merchants of St. Louis should be called into the controversy politically between slavery and freedom."[215]

Although the city's merchants proclaimed their neutrality, sectional pressures created enormous problems for Yankee entrepreneurs. Political tensions permeated every facet of life in antebellum Missouri, and businessmen quickly discovered that commerce could not be separated from politics. Proslavery spokesmen, for example, believed that New York capitalists ruled St. Louis and that through their agents, transplanted businessmen, Yankees attempted to dominate Missouri. So thorough was this control, according to radicals, that "when the New England fanatics took snuff, Missouri fanatics would sneeze."[216] Moreover, supporters of slavery insisted that the city's Yankee merchants had spearheaded the crusade to seize Kansas.[217] For example, Atchison and his followers believed that local commission merchants, such as Francis Hunt and Benjamin Slater, acted as Eli Thayer's agents and knowingly supplied Sharps rifles to Thayer's settlers.[218]

The proslavery radicals were correct. Hunt and Slater were indeed Thayer's agents.[219] In view of popular shipping channels to the region and the close economic relationship between St. Louis and Boston, the river city provided the logical western staging point for the New England Emigrant Aid Company.[220] Hunt and Slater also owed much of their business to their connections with Thayer and other Yankee radicals. Originally from Boston, Francis Hunt arrived in St. Louis in 1851 in order to establish a western outlet for a Connecticut dry goods merchant. The young manager, credit investigators reported, was a "smart energetic Yankee" – he also "pleases the ladies," they added.[221] Relying on his ties with the Kansas Emigration Aid Society, the New England Emigrant Aid Company, and premigration contacts, Hunt established his own commission house in 1855 and began handling shipments of "machinery."[222] The following year, Benjamin Slater joined the firm, and the two men specialized in transshipping cargo and passengers from Boston to Kansas. "Whatever boxes came, shipped to his care," Slater explained, "he sent forward."[223] Although "we have never knowingly made a shipment of Sharpe's [sic] rifles to Kansas," Hunt conceded that "it is possible that shipments may have been made by every boat."[224] Proslavery Missourians believed – correctly – that the merchants assumed a more conscious and deliberate role in the flow of arms to Kansas, and they vowed to punish them and the city for such treasonous behavior.[225]

Enraged by the relationship between Thayer and his St. Louis agents, local ruffians began to threaten and to harass the city's

merchants. At the height of the Kansas war, for example, an angry
Missourian provided Benjamin Slater with a rather forceful lesson on
Missouri politics, brusquely cornering the merchant and demanding
to know if Slater realized that "he had no right to send rifles to
Kansas."[226] Similarly, a manufacturer from Massachusetts complained to a local journalist that residents "denounced [him] as a
Yankee and abolitionist, threats were made to drive him from the
country, and influential men deliberately went to work to organize a
system to foment opposition to him."[227] Ordinary activities became
difficult and unpleasant for Yankee branch managers.

St. Louis shippers also faced direct threats to their livelihoods. In
1855 proslavery radicals, hoping to intercept shipments of rifles to the
Kansas border, began seizing packages bound for the western territories. Soon, local commission merchants complained that their business was in shambles.[228] Ruffians "molested" packages, confiscated
"contraband," and disposed of the remainder of the contents.[229]
According to St. Louis merchants, proslavery forces destroyed shipments of "steam-engines, mill machinery and household furniture"
in their hysterical hunt for Sharps rifles.[230] As a result of these
robberies, Northern merchants became reluctant to send goods to St.
Louis for transshipment to the Far West.[231] For example, Thayer's
New England Emigrant Aid Company, despite its campaign to divert
commerce from St. Louis, continued to use local merchants until
Missourians disrupted the flow of traffic. In 1856 an official of the
organization explained that "the dangers of encountering piratical
hordes" – not ideological concerns – compelled the company to sever
its commercial ties with St. Louis.[232]

Local businessmen begged proslavery radicals to stop interfering
with the commerce of the city. In 1856, for example, an outraged
commission agent published "a card to the public" in the *Missouri
Democrat*. "If their [Northern shippers] merchandise is spotted or
seized in transit, if our merchants are to be called Abolitionists and
negro stealers, who chance to do their business, their patronage to us
as merchants, and to the citizens of Missouri is at an end. It remains
for the citizens of St. Louis, and of Missouri," Francis Hunt warned,
"to say whether this source of their prosperity shall be cut off and
driven to a northern route." Such an alternative, he added, "is now
seriously contemplated."[233] Although Hunt's close relationship with
Thayer made him a particularly controversial figure, other shippers
endured similar problems. Within three months of his plea, Francis
Hunt left St. Louis.[234] Many of the city's commission merchants
shared Hunt's sentiments and followed his example.

St. Louis businessmen encountered increasing difficulties outside

the city as well. Not only did local proslavery men interrupt commerce, but shippers, commission merchants, and shopkeepers in
central and western parts of the state shunned St. Louis companies
during the mid-1850s. Feeling betrayed by the city's mercantile class,
businessmen and farmers in Liberty, Lexington, Brunswick, Independence, Platte City, and other towns pledged to refrain from trading
with St. Louis merchants, vowing to "render themselves independent of heartless speculators in St. Louis."[235] Some radicals, according to one of the city's businessmen, also circulated blacklists, "with
the cowardly intent of destroying or damaging the business of our
merchants."[236] Ironically, radicals from both camps blamed St. Louis
merchants, and both sides boycotted St. Louis businesses during the
mid-1850s. The situation of the city, the editor of the *Missouri Democrat* bemoaned, "is precarious. She has to shape her sails (and sales)
to meet two opposing breezes of public opinion."[237]

Some Yankee entrepreneurs simply returned to the Northeast.
Christopher Rhodes, for example, chose to retire from his commission business in 1856 and resettle in his native Rhode Island. Like
hundreds of Yankee merchants, Rhodes had arrived in St. Louis in
1845. During the next eleven years the transplanted Newport trader's
business had failed once and been reorganized twice, but by 1854 the
firm was flourishing. The "changes and vicissitudes" of the mid-
1850s, however, convinced Rhodes to leave St. Louis. At the height of
the Kansas turmoil the fifty-six-year-old merchant closed his firm,
took his hard-earned competency, and returned to New England.[238]
"The business men of St. Louis," the *Boston Journal* concluded in
1857, "have begun to feel that they will be swamped by slavery."[239]

Northern capitalists also became increasingly anxious about their
Missouri investments. Businessmen who cared little about politics
remained extremely sensitive to the economic effects of political
pressures. Thus, Atchison's rhetoric failed to dampen their enthusiasm about St. Louis outlets, but reports that the senator's supporters had disrupted commerce sparked immediate concern. Moreover,
predictions that slavery would retard the economic development of
cities alarmed New York investors, and these interpretations became
extremely common during this period, as observers analyzed the St.
Louis marketplace in terms of the larger political currents of the
day.[240] For example, the Wisconsin politician and newspaper editor
Carl Schurz, who later moved to Missouri and represented the state
in the U.S. Senate, concluded that "the existence of slavery cast its
shadow over the industrial and commercial development of the
city."[241] Similarly, William Rey, a French traveler, attributed St.
Louis's sluggish economic development to the "moral atmosphere"

surrounding slavery.[242] The *New York Daily Tribune* suggested that investments in St. Louis would come to resemble investments in Alabama, and the *New York Independent* explained that Missouri businesses were doomed and warned Yankees to "stand from under."[243]

St. Louis's problems also seemed to confirm the wisdom of Free Soil predictions. Northern writers reveled in comparing the slow population growth, degraded workers, undeveloped economy, weak manufacturing sector, and unimproved lands of Missouri with those of the vigorous, dynamic, prosperous free states surrounding it.[244] Moreover, when rural Missourians embraced Southern politics, Northern editors and financial writers ceased comparing St. Louis to New York and Boston. Instead, they compared the river city to Norfolk and Charleston.[245] Like other "slave breeding depots," St. Louis appeared destined to be "wasted to a dwarf by devotion to slavery."[246] Thus, the commercial decline of the Missouri city supported Free Soil forecasts, heightening Yankee concerns about local ventures.

Pragmatic Northern entrepreneurs began to avoid investing in a city that seemed shackled to a "blighted" economic system. One local editor explained that "capitalists began to be chary of [St. Louis] investments and to withdraw capital that was deemed no longer safe."[247] Furthermore, Free Soil prophesies became self-fulfilling in St. Louis during this period. As Yankee merchants bypassed the city's market, the local economy deteriorated, exacerbating concerns about remaining investments, confirming antislavery predictions, and reinforcing the shift of resources away from St. Louis. Although Yankee dollars had "created" St. Louis during the preceding decade, the much-lauded marriage between St. Louis and Boston and New York appeared to be in grave danger during the mid-1850s.[248]

When Northern attitudes toward investing in a turbulent slave state shifted, Yankee involvement in the local marketplace declined. More than ever before, unsuccessful New York entrepreneurs returned to the Northeast. At the same time, well-backed Yankee merchants stopped migrating to St. Louis. During the late 1840s New Yorkers and Bostonians had started over half of the businesses in the city. By comparison, they established fewer than one-third of the firms that opened in St. Louis during the mid-1850s and fewer than one-sixth of the businesses that began during the height of the Kansas turmoil. Yankees established fewer firms between 1854 and 1856 than during any three-year period since the start of the local economic recovery in 1844. As a result, their control of the local economy waned, and the portion of the marketplace dominated by these migrants withered.[249]

Table 6.1 *Merchant's origin by date of opening of business*

Place of origin	1842–50 (percent)	1851–53 (percent)	1854–56 (percent)	1857–60 (percent)
New England	20	15	9	8
New York	36	31	24	16
Midwest and Southwest	19	26	38	47
West	–	8	10	16
Other	24	26	19	13

Source: Missouri Vols. 36–38, R. G. Dun and Company Collection, Baker Library, Harvard University Graduate School of Business Administration.

These changes dramatically reshaped the economy of St. Louis. Yankee disdain for "Southern" investments weakened the largest and most dynamic sector of the St. Louis economy. Since New York and Boston managers operated most of the large-scale ventures in the city, the upper stratum of the local marketplace declined sharply during this period. Very few sizable enterprises opened in St. Louis after the cessation of Yankee migration. The proportion of large businesses in the marketplace, for example, fell by 44 percent during this period, and the proportion of the largest businesses in the market (firms considered "enormous" by local credit reporters) declined still more dramatically, dropping by 88 percent during the Kansas years. Before the border war, credit investigators found that such mammoth businesses comprised 3 percent of the commercial ranks. After the sack of Lawrence, however, fewer than one new firm in three hundred was termed "enormous." Because success was directly related to scale in antebellum St. Louis, the proportion of successful commercial ventures in the city plunged when Yankee involvement in the local marketplace fell.[250]

In short, the Kansas turmoil frayed the economic cords that linked the St. Louis marketplace to the national economy. Yankee entrepreneurs, operating large-scale ventures, had forged these ties. When they left the city, the mechanisms that had connected St. Louis to distant commercial centers nearly vanished as well. Western outlets, the principal conduits for the flow of eastern goods to St. Louis, gradually disappeared from the local marketplace. Prior to 1854 branch concerns had compromised over one-third of the city's businesses, but after the passage of the Kansas-Nebraska bill fewer than one new firm in eleven operated as an outlet for an eastern house.

With this sharp decline, St. Louis's direct ties to New York, Boston, and European markets deteriorated, and long-distance commerce languished.[251] Commission houses, another arrangement designed to facilitate long-distance trade, also declined during this period. The proportion of transshipping businesses fell by nearly 50 percent. Thus, the changing winds of Northern opinion reduced Yankee involvement in the St. Louis marketplace, robbing the city of its largest and most profitable businesses. "The burden of the fireside talk in eastern homes," the *Missouri Democrat* lamented in 1856, "has severed our business relations . . . on Wall Street."[252] In 1856, despite a decade of prosperity, the economy of St. Louis was in disarray.

The departure of Yankee merchants weakened the local economy in other ways as well. The slavery agitation, for example, exacerbated the capital shortages that had stunted the St. Louis economy before the arrival of New York and Boston entrepreneurs. Yankee involvement in the local economy had enabled the city to grow without banks or indigenous capital sources. Instead, New York merchants, by sending Wall Street dollars to their sons, had fueled the expansion of the local economy. When Yankee outlets in the city closed, eastern capital returned to Wall Street and State Street vaults, leaving local traders without access to financial resources and exaggerating the effects of this changing migration pattern.[253] Because they could no longer rely on Yankee capital or commercial networks, St. Louis merchants experienced increasing difficulty procuring goods from eastern markets.[254] Shopkeepers encountered even greater problems, however, finding customers.[255]

Badly strained under the weight of the sectional controversy, the economy of St. Louis collapsed in 1856. Both retail and wholesale trades contracted, and country traders directed agricultural produce to other commercial centers.[256] Even the city's real estate market, long a source of pride for local boosters, lurched during this period, as the economy spiraled downward.[257] The *New York Times* termed the slump "commercial retribution."[258]

The truncated St. Louis economy grew weaker and assumed an increasingly regional orientation. For example, merchants from Missouri or the Mississippi valley established almost 40 percent of the firms that opened during the Kansas years. The combination of the flight of Yankee merchants and the relative increase in the proportion of locally and regionally oriented firms created a commercial environment in which the most fragile and vulnerable businesses became dominant.[259] Before the border war, nearly a quarter of the city's businesses had survived for more than ten years. By comparison, among firms that opened after the turmoil, fewer than one business in twelve operated for a decade. Those who remained active in the St. Louis commercial district, most often men with scant capital, impaired credit, and few connections to outside suppliers, struggled against declining markets in a depressed region.[260] The proportion of merchants who relied on very limited local or regional capital sources skyrocketed, increasing by nearly 80 percent during the Kansas years. As a result, the bankruptcy rate in St. Louis rose, and the average life span for commercial ventures dropped by nearly 40 percent. Thus, the decaying image of the St. Louis marketplace became both self-perpetuating and increasingly accurate.

The decline in the economy and the disruption in the flow of settlers to the city nearly arrested population growth during this period. Between 1845 and 1852 the annual population increase in the city had averaged 14 percent. Even during the cholera epidemic newcomers had poured into St. Louis. The adverse publicity surrounding the Kansas war, however, interrupted population growth. In 1855, for example, the number of local inhabitants increased by less than 3 percent. The sack of Lawrence and the Dred Scott controversy chilled urban growth still more dramatically. The population of St. Louis increased by less than 1 percent during 1856. Outmigration from the city exceeded the flow of newcomers to St. Louis; only natural increase prevented the local population from falling. The number of German settlers traveling from the port of New Orleans fell by 35 percent in 1855 and by another 45 percent during 1856.[261] Local doctors, whose quarantine facilities recorded "emigrant arrivals" in order to track the spread of cholera, reported that the tide of travelers to the city fell by 60 percent.[262] Native migration to St. Louis nearly ceased, and the local population of transplanted Yankees fell during the Kansas years.

Changing New York and Boston perceptions of St. Louis crippled the city in its war with Chicago. During the mid-1850s each city fought to enlarge its economic sphere by extending railroad lines toward eastern markets and deep into the surrounding countryside. Railroad construction, however, required enormous pools of capital, and at the height of the battle, St. Louis lost its principal backers. Without Yankee dollars, Missouri roads could not be built.[263]

Not surprisingly, Missouri railroad bonds attracted scant interest during the Kansas years. Rather, with each border "outrage," the value of the state bonds that financed railroad construction sank lower, slowing the pace of construction and impairing St. Louis in its battle for regional supremacy.[264] Prior to the settlement of the new territories, Missouri railroad bonds had sold for $107 in New York markets. By 1856, however, the bonds had fallen to $86, and during the following year Missouri railroad bonds plunged to $60.[265] In total, the market value of the bonds dropped by 44 percent in three years, and Missouri railroad construction nearly stopped. Eli Thayer and

William Cullen Bryant reported the decline with undisguised glee. "The late robbery committed on the Missouri will doubtless have the tendency of still further depressing the railway stocks of that state," the *New York Evening Post* announced in 1856.[266] "Let there be another inroad into Kansas," William Cullen Bryant warned, "and the credit of Missouri would sink yet lower."[267] Thayer explained that he had struck a "heavy blow for freedom at the brokering board . . . the Border Ruffians who have taken steps towards destroying the crediting of Missouri and thus making progress in internal improvements impossible."[268]

Although Thayer claimed credit for the depreciation, other observers concluded that the plummeting value of Missouri railroad bonds reflected the declining reputation of St. Louis and the "maligning" influence of the peculiar institution.[269] "Because we live in a slave State," the *Missouri Republican* concluded, "eastern capital cannot be relied upon to build our railroads."[270] "Kansas has been the stumbling block," a local merchant added.[271] New York entrepreneurs expressed little desire to finance the construction of a railroad system to serve a slumping city that was tied to an unstable and perhaps dying economic system.[272]

The capital withdrawn from the St. Louis marketplace, however, did not lie idle. Instead, Boston and New York merchants searched for alternate investments during this period. "Capitalists, who are always exceedingly cautious, nay timid, were shaken in their faith regarding our city," the *Missouri Democrat* explained. "And so they turned their faces in other directions."[273] Some of the men who had been involved in St. Louis ventures earlier in the decade turned to Chicago investments after the border war.[274] In addition, new investors in western businesses chose Chicago enterprises.[275] Just as New York merchants withdrew the capital from ventures in the Missouri city, Yankee capital poured into the Illinois city.

This capital, some of which had "belonged" to St. Louis, accelerated the construction of Chicago's railroad network. Again and again, eastern commercial writers warned that "capital is timid." Until the Kansas turmoil, St. Louis had held a clear advantage in the battle for regional economic supremacy. In 1851, for example, St. Louis shippers handled four times more wheat and flour, six times more beef, and fifteen times more molasses than their Chicago counterparts.[276] The Missouri city was well established at a time when Chicago was best known for its perpetually mud-covered streets. Although some eastern merchants chose to speculate on the growth of Chicago, more often cautious capitalists opted for safer St. Louis investments.[277] Chicago railroads, like Chicago commercial ventures, remained relatively starved for eastern support until timid Yankee entrepreneurs became concerned about the future of their St. Louis investments. During the mid-1850s, however, investment patterns abruptly changed. Suddenly, St. Louis ventures had become risky. Because of the slavery agitation, the *Missouri Republican* complained, "Chicago is now a favorite among Eastern capitalists."[278] Eli Thayer had anticipated this shift, boasting to Edward Everett Hale that as a result of his crusade "Chicago will laugh and St. Louis will rage."[279]

Thus, the problems of St. Louis redounded to the benefit of Chicago, and the latter city triumphed in part because the former lost its appeal in New York financial circles.[280] The small stream of Yankees who migrated to Chicago during the early 1850s increased the eastern pool of knowledge about the city, and when Yankees turned away from St. Louis investments, an alternate site was both widely known and readily available. Yankee branch managers, drawn from the same mold as the eastern merchants who had flooded St. Louis a decade earlier, migrated to Chicago during the mid-1850s. In many cases, the same families were involved. For example, in 1842 Luther Laflin sent his son Sylvester to St. Louis in order to establish an outlet of his New York milling factory. Fifteen years later Laflin sent his son Solomon to Chicago in order to open a branch.[281] New York importers and Boston shoe manufacturers began to establish western outlets in the Illinois boomtown.[282] According to *Chicago Magazine*, the flow of Yankee businessmen entailed a "colonization."[283]

Backed by vast pools of eastern dollars, the economy of Chicago blossomed during the Kansas years. Yankee merchants financed the construction of three railroad lines to eastern markets, and Chicago established direct rail communications with New York and Boston, enhancing the commercial relationship between the cities and diverting trade from St. Louis.[284] "With the aid of eastern capital," the *Missouri Republican* conceded in 1855, "Chicago is evidently beginning to take the lead, and will doubtless soon distance the Mound City."[285] In short, the Kansas war channeled Yankee commercial interest and capital to Chicago. The fall of St. Louis accelerated the rise of Chicago, and the increasing development of the free-soil trading center hastened the decline of its slaveholding counterpart. The Missouri city remained a large urban center, though its rival captured New York capital and became the principal western cog in the national economy.

St. Louis reached its peak in the years immediately before the passage of the Kansas-Nebraska Act. At the height of the midcentury boom St. Louis commanded the West. New York capital poured into the local marketplace; well-bred Yankee merchants dominated the commercial district; and St. Louis was known as one of the fastest-growing and most "vigorous" cities in the nation. Steamboat arrivals, lead production, and local commercial receipts achieved unprecedented levels during this period – and plunged thereafter.[286] The sectional crisis undermined the economic foundation of St. Louis and remade the urban West.

The political and ideological war that began on the western border of Missouri transformed the relationship between New York and its outpost on the Mississippi River. Because St. Louis remained so dependent on the Northeast, the shift in migration and investment profoundly affected the local marketplace. When Yankee commercial involvement waned, St. Louis lost the lion's share of its capital, its most profitable markets, and its strategic role in the national economy. By 1856 New Yorkers and Bostonians believed that St. Louis was a dying city, and for the remainder of the antebellum period the reputation of the Missouri city plummeted and the local economy deteriorated. Shortly after peace returned to Kansas, a leading New York commercial journal reported that one western city "is destined to be the largest commercial and banking city west of New York. She offers inducements to the capitalist and banker, which, perhaps, no other city in the Union can afford." That city, *Hunt's Merchants' Magazine* concluded, was Chicago.[287]

Yankee merchants built the urban West, though they assumed a more permanent role in the development of St. Louis's principal rivals. Just as New Yorkers fueled the ascent of St. Louis, businessmen from the Atlantic coast directed the commercial development of other western cities during this period. New York and Boston capitalists financed the construction of Chicago's railroad system, and Massachusetts merchants were among the first traders to arrive in San Francisco.[288] These entrepreneurs, however, remained active in both cities for decades, gradually forming local attachments and establishing indigenous institutions. Branch managers became resident partners and matured with their adoptive cities; a homegrown generation of business leaders emerged. While preserving important economic ties to eastern commercial centers, these men developed deepening attachments to the local marketplace and abiding loyalties to local society.[289] Although violence and turmoil punctuated the development of most cities, neither Chicago nor San Francisco lost its eastern backing or collapsed as a result of local or regional problems.

Why were Yankee entrepreneurs so willing to abandon St. Louis during the mid-1850s? Most important, the force of sectional feelings far exceeded the problems experienced by rival cities; economic, political, and ideological concerns reinforced one another during the antebellum period, producing an explosive new mixture. Free Soil explanations of life under the peculiar institution, for example, both discouraged eastern capitalists from pursuing St. Louis investments and exaggerated the city's new-found reputation for violence, particularly violence against Yankees.[290]

If Wall Street's waning interest in St. Louis is understandable, the departure of branch managers is less easily explained. Most of these merchants had accumulated impressive profits during their years in St. Louis. Although many anxious Yankee investors – and fathers – "recalled" their outlet operators, few of these transplanted easterners balked at the suggestion. Men who had expended considerable energy developing the St. Louis marketplace readily fled from the city during the Kansas years.

Within a decade the economy of St. Louis blossomed and wilted. Unlike rival western cities, St. Louis's commercial reign proved to be short-lived; so short-lived, in fact, that the merchants who triggered and sustained the midcentury boom never became rooted in the city. Most Yankee entrepreneurs spent only a few years in St. Louis. The Kansas turmoil followed so closely on the heels of prosperity – and the Yankee influx – that well-bred eastern newcomers returned to the Atlantic coast before they had become established residents of St. Louis. Few felt sufficiently "settled" in the city to defend the Missouri city or to endure local problems.[291] Nor did their years in the West exert a sustained influence on the young businessmen. For example, William Claflin spent three years in St. Louis managing a branch of his father's shoe business. Upon returning to Massachusetts in 1850, Claflin assumed independence and fit smoothly into middle-class circles. Five years later the young shoe manufacturer, along with other publicly minded Yankees, subscribed to stock in a local reform organization; Claflin pledged to purchase five shares of stock in the New England Emigrant Aid Company.[292]

A peculiar combination of state policies and national events made St. Louis less resilient than other western urban centers. Xenophobic Missouri legislation exaggerated the city's dependence on Yankee economic intervention at a time when national politics jeopardized the future of a commercial city in a border state. For nearly a century observers had agreed that nature had blessed St. Louis. Just as the city mushroomed, however, sectionalism radically altered the relationship between geography and urban growth. Thus, the slavery controversy crippled St. Louis before the city outgrew its colonial status. A decade of close commercial ties between a Yankee city in the Far West and its trading partners on the Atlantic coast was rapidly forgotten during the years immediately preceding the Civil War, and Northern merchants cast St. Louis in new and foreboding terms. When rural Missourians tilted to the South, St. Louis became, in the minds of New York merchants, a Southern city. As a result, Yankee entrepreneurs severed their economic ties with St. Louis, just as they did with Mobile and with other Yankee colonies in the South.[293]

7 Rebirth

The battle between St. Louis and Chicago was not necessarily a zero-sum game. The Illinois city would have grown even if the Missouri entrepôt had continued to flourish. Well before David Atchison led his ruffians into Kansas, Chicago merchants began invading St. Louis's commercial hinterland.[1] Moreover, some northeastern capitalists, such as John Murray Forbes, had become interested in Illinois railroads prior to the settlement of the new western territories.[2] Although neither city had to collapse for the other to thrive, they competed for markets, migrants, and capital, and only one urban center could dominate the western economy.

The Kansas turmoil, however, transformed the development of both cities. Historians cannot know if Chicago would have supplanted St. Louis without the disruption spawned by Thayer, Atchison, and their followers; neither city's fate was inevitable. Nonetheless, the sectional controversy tipped an important balance in the Illinois city's favor. Between 1854 and 1856 political tensions sapped the commercial strength of St. Louis and dramatically accelerated the ascent of Chicago. Gradual shifts in investment, marketing, and migration patterns became abrupt changes, and the contest for economic control of the West became increasingly one-sided. New York and Boston capital poured into Illinois businesses; Chicago merchants gained control of important hinterland markets; and settlers made the lake city the new gateway to the West. Although St. Louis need not have declined for Chicago to grow, the cities fought for many of the same upper midwestern markets and for similar – and limited – pools of Wall Street capital and northeastern migrants.[3] Moreover, following the border war the Missouri city was unable to compete, and by 1856 Chicago captured the lion's share of crucial resources. The fates of the urban centers, therefore, were linked, though they were not inseparable.

Equally important, this process was self-perpetuating. Short-term disruptions in the St. Louis marketplace exaggerated concerns about the city's future, reinforced the flow of goods, migrants, and money to Chicago, and thus evolved into long-term disruptions. When New York entrepreneurs withdrew their capital from St. Louis businesses, they retarded the development of the Missouri city. But because many of these entrepreneurs transferred their capital from St. Louis enterprises to Chicago ventures, their activities also stimulated the development of the Illinois trading center.[4] As a consequence, St. Louis's problems and Chicago's prosperity became overlapping and cumulative.

Changes in the relationship between New York and St. Louis profoundly affected social, cultural, and political life in the Missouri city. Residents of the river entrepôt responded to Yankee judgments and Wall Street strategies in ways that transformed the character of the city. Reactions to the border war influenced the tone of booster-ism, the activities of municipal government, assumptions about local culture, and even perspectives on the future of the city. Outside forces altered both New York's view of St. Louis and St. Louis's view of itself. At midcentury, for example, St. Louis residents had proudly asserted that they lived in a Yankee city. A decade later an increasing number of residents insisted that St. Louis was a Southern city. Sectionalism remade antebellum St. Louis.

The political turmoil of the mid-1850s cast a foreboding shadow over Yankee St. Louis. Transplanted Northerners watched in horror as New York and Boston suppliers diverted manufactured goods to Chicago markets, and the economy of St. Louis stagnated. At the same time, the cessation of Yankee migration to the city exaggerated St. Louis's problems. Without an influx of Northern newcomers, conservative politics and proslavery institutions, they feared, would soon overwhelm the city's Yankee population.

Most Northern-born residents believed that St. Louis could not prosper in a proslavery environment. Capital, they noted, followed Yankee migration, and New Yorkers "will see no inducements to carry . . . their enterprise to a place where regression is the order of the day."[5] According to the *Missouri Democrat*, migrants would "not venture into a land over which the cloud of degraded servitude and a repressing [sic] labor system had spread."[6] Instead, Yankees and their capital were "flowing round us everywhere and everywhere avoiding us."[7] As long as slaveholders ruled Missouri, St. Louis would languish.[8]

Although the sectional controversy had undermined the local econ-omy and dimmed the chances for recovery, transplanted Yankees believed that the slavery issue offered a solution to the city's problems as well. "Redemption," they argued, would reverse the decline and restore St. Louis to its "position as the future metropolis of the West." Antislavery leaders and local businessmen agreed that encouraging Yankee migration could redeem Missouri from the slave power and revive St. Louis's sagging economy.[9] For example, an influx of Northerners promised to "fill the coffers of the treasury, reduce taxation to a minimum, and secure an ample fund to protect and promote internal improvements, agricultural encouragements and common school interests."[10] Transplanted Yankees argued that such newcomers would rekindle the passenger trade and even stimulate the construction of a railroad system, enabling St. Louis to compete with Chicago once again.[11]

Yankee migrants would also supply the capital needed to fuel St. Louis's economic recovery. As in the mid-1840s, they would relieve the capital shortages that paralyzed the economy and trigger a boom. "The incoming of capital," the *Missouri Democrat* suggested, would "surpass the wildest hopes of the most sanguine."[12] Such an influx of resources also promised to spur manufacturing and to reestablish commercial ties with New York and Boston. Northern migrants, B. Gratz Brown concluded, will "render her the great inland city of the United States."[13]

Equally important, many St. Louis residents believed that this migration would overwhelm proslavery political forces and undermine slavery in the state. In 1858, for example, a proslavery Missourian concluded that Yankees could only control the state "by introducing emigrants from the North."[14] Another writer predicted that the arrival of Yankee newcomers would transform local institutions, and "Missouri will slough off the niggers in a few years."[15] Once St. Louis was freed from the blighting influence of the peculiar institution, the city would enjoy "unprecedented" prosperity.[16] In short, migration would redeem St. Louis and crush the slave power in the Far West. "Surely this terrible Upas tree which all avoid, and which is blighting the whole of Missouri and everyone within its borders," the *Missouri Democrat* announced in 1857, "may be girded about so as to eventually destroy it."[17]

Thus, St. Louis merchants and editors struggled to rekindle Yankee interest in the city. But with each passing day the local economy deteriorated, Southern interests in the area gained power, and the task of attracting Northerners to Missouri became more difficult. Some St. Louis writers hoped that advertising the city's advantages would stimulate Yankee attention. Boosters labored to "remind our Northern neighbors that . . . they will find Missouri much more congenial to them than Kansas."[18] B. Gratz Brown, for example, implored "Eastern journals . . . to direct the attention of immigrants hitherward," and merchants and editors urged municipal leaders to court the "public esteem" of New Yorkers and Bostonians.[19] Similarly, the *Missouri Democrat* recommended that city officials issue "a series of publications to acquaint the industrial population of the east with the unrivaled inducements to immigration which exist in Missouri."[20] Such tracts could be distributed throughout the cities of the Northeast.[21] Once apprised of the extraordinary advantages of St. Louis, "a rush of movers," particularly Yankee capitalists and farmers, would pour into the region, according to local writers, and restore St. Louis's failing health.[22]

Few Northern newspapers, however, championed the attractions of Missouri, and few Yankees moved to the state or its leading city. The fears that had diverted migration during the border war loomed still larger during the politically charged years following the Kansas turmoil. Moreover, Northerners continued to associate St. Louis with Missouri and with the slave economy. One Massachusetts resident, for example, warned St. Louis officials that New Englanders "will never come to place themselves and their families in contact with slavery."[23] An Ohio resident agreed, noting that "Missouri is the best State in the Union – only for slavery."[24] Transplanted Northerners quickly recognized that Yankees would not migrate until St. Louis was "disenthralled" from Southern "chains," and Southern interests could be defeated only if Yankees migrated to the city.[25]

Many St. Louis residents believed that Republican politics offered a solution to the city's problems. Local concerns, however, shaped the character of Missouri Free Soilism. In the North, free labor prescriptions represented a theoretical formulation, a vision of an open, expanding, middle-class republic. Inexpensive, fertile western land provided a kind of safety valve for the North, offering opportunity and symbolizing economic independence. Republican ideology set forth a model of a harmonious society – rather than a description of antebellum America. Although tenant farmers and the industrious poor had no clear place in this formulation, Free Soil writers focused their attention on the glorious potential of an open society of producers.[26]

In St. Louis during the late 1850s, free-labor ideology represented a pragmatic response to local problems. Missouri Republicans seldom discussed the inherent value of work. Nor did they celebrate the virtues of a fluid, expanding society. Instead, Missouri Republicans used free-labor rhetoric as a tool to stimulate Yankee migration to St. Louis. Local Republicans urged St. Louis residents to support the Free Soil ticket because a Republican victory would constitute "an emphatic voice" that "we are under no thraldom [sic] of slave propagandism."[27] Electoral triumphs, according to St. Louis Free Soilers, "shall ring throughout every state of the union" and trigger "an irrepressible exodus of slaves from the borders of Missouri."[28] According to the Missouri Democrat, a Republican majority will be "unfurled to the breeze"; the banner of free labor will provide a "signal for an influx of population."[29]

In short, Republican politics represented an effort to assure Yankee observers that slavery was disappearing from the state, and the principal goal of local Republicans was to attract Northerners to the city, both to revive the local economy and ultimately to overwhelm the slave power. For example, the city's Free Soil newspaper reported that Republican victories demonstrated "that our city is permanently redeemed from slavery, and that the State is in the process of a similar redemption," and this news would attract Northern capital and Northern capitalists.[30] Similarly, B. Gratz Brown promised St. Louis residents that a victory for John Wimer, the Free Soil candidate in the 1857 race for mayor, "will be a perpetual pronouncement for the future, inviting capital and labor and arts and manufactures here to build up the Central City of the Valley of the Mississippi."[31] If Wimer triumphed, according to local Republicans, Yankee migration would begin anew. Specific prescriptions fueled Republican politics in antebellum St. Louis.

Indeed, Free Soil victories in St. Louis attracted widespread Northern attention. For example, when John Wimer captured the top office in the city, the New York Daily Tribune reprinted part of the Missouri Democrat's analysis of the event. The editor termed the victory "a triumph that in Rome would have crowned the victor with a wreath of glory as he went up the Appian way – in Greece would have led to Olympian games in his honor. . . ."[32] St. Louis's Republican newspaper claimed to receive dozens of letters from Yankee observers who wanted to congratulate local merchants and community leaders.[33] According to the Missouri Democrat, "one of the largest capitalists in New York" praised St. Louis Free Soilers for their "glorious triumph."[34] Ironically, this "capitalist" was a former resident who had recently fled from St. Louis. Nonetheless, businessmen and boosters anticipated that the election of 1857 would revive the city's flagging fortunes.

Many Northern editors joined in the chorus of praise for local Republicans, though their reports cast St. Louis in damning terms. So Southern was St. Louis, in the minds of Yankee editors, that they argued that Wimer's victory signaled the decline of the South – rather than the rebirth of a border city; the election underscored St. Louis's

"Southern-ness."[35] The *New York Daily Tribune*, for example, explained that Wimer's triumph suggested that "St. Louis is almost the first Southern town which has outgrown, or which has felt itself to have outgrown this condition of shop-keeping vassalage" to planters.[36] The election indicated that St. Louis voters were challenging the "country planters, who have hitherto ruled in St. Louis with the same authority almost as on their own plantations."[37] Similarly, the *Rock Island Advertiser* concluded that "St. Louis nobly and independently stands in the van of all southern cities."[38] Thus, antislavery victories reinforced the belief that Southern politics and Southern interests dominated the city as well as the state.

Instead of celebrating the final victory for the city, Northern editors emphasized the modest progress of the section. According to most accounts, St. Louis Free Soilers were brave souls fighting an uphill battle against overwhelming odds; Republican victories represented faint, flickering beacons in a dark land. The *New York Daily Tribune*, for example, termed Wimer's election the "first bold push."[39] Moreover, Northern journalists predicted that prosperity would return to St. Louis only "upon the fact of slavery's extinction."[40] Another Free Soil victory prompted a Philadelphia newspaper to conclude that "upon some future day on which the absolute cessation of slavery should occur, its [St. Louis's] real estate would double in two years."[41] Similarly, a Chicago editor looked forward to the "final triumph" of the "free State movement of Missouri."[42] Northerners remained guarded; the battle had barely begun. The editor of the *Boston Journal* explained that "we do not wish to over-estimate the importance of the recent victory [of Wimer] in Missouri."[43]

While Free Soilers struggled for Pyrrhic victories in St. Louis, proslavery interests enjoyed increasing success in local elections. The Democratic Party, for example, carried the city in 1858. "The day has come," a St. Louis politician conceded, "that no man can get an office who does not charge around, holler nigger and commence pulling negro wool over everybody's eyes."[44] The relative decline of the population of transplanted Yankees and the growing population of midwestern, Southern, and Irish voters enhanced "conservative" political strength in the city.[45] Although the two camps traded victories, each Democratic victory brought sighs of resignation from Yankee observers. The heroic battle, antislavery editors announced, was lost.

Just when an influx of Northern traders and Free Soil voters became most crucial, the prospects for such a migration became most unlikely. With Yankee politics on the defensive and Yankee commercial interests in the city waning, few New Yorkers or New Englanders settled in St. Louis. In 1858 W. A. Scay, writing for *De Bow's Review*, assessed the antislavery position in the area. "Their only chance," he noted, "is in immigration – in overwhelming the present conservative power of the State. . . . Who is so insane as to believe they will ever accomplish their purpose," Scay concluded. "No effects of ours," a local editor agreed, "can turn into Missouri the volume of those waters . . . of Northern emigration."[46]

Moreover, increasing numbers of Yankees left St. Louis during the late 1850s. Many northerners, like the successful attorney and aspiring politician John Kasson, tired of daily life in "strife-torn" St. Louis. In 1857 Kasson "plotted a course" out of the city and migrated to Des Moines.[47] Yankee merchants left the city as well. Some New York and Boston businessmen closed their offices and returned to the Northeast.

A surprising number of these entrepreneurs transferred their western branches from St. Louis to Chicago during this period. For a few, this involved a two-step process. Initially, they established Chicago offices, and gradually these men shifted their resources to the Illinois branches and closed the Missouri outlets. Other St. Louis merchants, such as William Funkhouser, began investing surplus capital in Chicago businesses.[48] More often, however, branch managers, probably following the instructions of their fathers in New York, simultaneously closed St. Louis businesses and opened Chicago offices. Thus, New York outlet managers with experience in St. Louis became numerous in the burgeoning Chicago business district.[49] Independent entrepreneurs flocked to the Illinois trading center as well. James Sanger, for example, moved from the Pittsburgh area to St. Louis in 1854 to establish a business that built carriages for railroads. In February of 1858, Sanger opened a Chicago office, and eight months later he closed the St. Louis house.[50] This process shifted scarce capital and experienced businessmen from St. Louis to Chicago, reinforcing the larger changes in both cities and dovetailing with the increasing flow of Yankee capital to the Illinois trading center.

The Yankee exodus included many prominent residents. Some of these transplanted northeasterners migrated to Chicago. For example, Eliphalet W. Blatchford, the first president of the St. Louis Young Men's Christian Association, moved to Chicago in late 1855.[51] Like many St. Louis merchants, Blatchford relocated in order to establish and manage the Chicago branch of a Missouri business. In 1859, however, the Connecticut native severed his ties with the Missouri office and with St. Louis.[52] Other influential residents, such as Robert M. Henning, returned to the Northeast. The president of the St. Louis Chamber of Commerce and one of the most successful merchants in the city, Henning resettled in New York in 1856. According to the *Missouri Republican*, "he leaves this community to unite himself more closely with . . . his house in New York."[53]

The exodus of businessmen weakened the community of Yankees in St. Louis. Prominent clergymen, northerners who migrated to the city to tame the Far West and to serve the spiritual needs of well-bred Yankees, soon followed their parishioners to Chicago. In 1856, for example, the Congregational minister Truman Post left St. Louis to "connect himself" with the Chicago Theological Seminary. The new president of the seminary's board of trustees, Eliphalet W. Blatchford, persuaded Post to migrate.[54] Similarly, the Presbyterian clergyman Nathan L. Rice accepted "a call to Chicago" in 1857. "We are convinced," Rice explained, "that we can accomplish more for the cause of Christ, and for the cause of Presbyterianism, by settling in Chicago, than by remaining in St. Louis."[55] During the late 1850s St. Louis held little for prominent Yankees, and the proportion of northerners in the city's population fell by over 40 percent during the decade; by 1860 fewer than 6 percent of St. Louis residents hailed from the Northeast.

The Panic of 1857 accelerated the exodus of Yankee merchants from St. Louis. The end of the Crimean War disrupted European demand for American goods, and the value of stocks and securities plummeted. Exporters experienced increasing difficulty meeting their obligations; railroad investors grew "chary"; and by October the panic had gripped New York. Although the depression had little immediate effect on most St. Louis merchants, it crippled businessmen with commercial ties to New York and Boston.[56]

Many of the strongest houses in St. Louis, firms that had survived the Kansas turmoil, collapsed in 1857. Some businesses failed when their New York offices suspended operations or declared bankruptcy. E. W. Clarke, one of the wealthiest Yankees in St. Louis, closed his firm "because of the suspension of the house in New York," though the collapse of the Boston branch – J. W. Clarke and Company – precipitated the decline of the New York office.[57] The economic ties that sustained branches during local crises became deadly shackles in 1857. For example, branch outlets failed twice as often as independent firms as a result of the panic, and those eastern houses that survived the financial pressure most often escaped badly impaired. Moreover, for many New York merchants, closing western branches – or withdrawing support from relatively unprofitable far-flung ventures – represented an austerity measure. Other Yankee houses consolidated their western outlets and transferred stock and personnel to hardier Chicago offices.[58]

Nearly all firms with northeastern ties suffered during the Panic of 1857. Ninety-four percent of the businesses operated by transplanted Bostonians either failed in 1857 or faced extreme financial problems during the tortured months following the financial downturn. Like many Yankee entrepreneurs, John McNeil "never recovered from the embarrassments of 1857." McNeil, a wealthy New Yorker, arrived in St. Louis in 1845. Relying on friends in New York, he forged a small empire in the Far West. McNeil operated a number of local hat businesses, owned nearly $60,000 worth of real estate, and sat as the director of a local bank. The depression in New York, however, consumed McNeil's riches. The credit rating of his businesses tumbled; assistance from friends was inadequate; and in 1860 McNeil declared bankruptcy.[59] For Augustus Pomeroy, the panic was still more devastating. A Massachusetts native, Pomeroy, like McNeil and hundreds of Yankee merchants, migrated to St. Louis in 1845. During the next dozen years, Pomeroy's wealth grew and multiplied. By the mid-1850s local credit investigators considered him a very wealthy man. Pomeroy's Atlantic coast connections, his springboard to commercial success, rapidly disintegrated when the depression paralyzed New York and Boston. Anticipating the demise of his financial empire, the entrepreneur, according to credit reporters, became insane. In January of 1858 Pomeroy collapsed and died, the result of "anxiety occasioned by the panic."[60]

Because the depression centered in New York, wealthy St. Louis merchants suffered financial reverses. Entrepreneurs who engaged in high-volume trade with northeastern houses fared particularly badly in 1857. The financial crisis crippled the largest firms in St. Louis and "embarrassed" the wealthiest Yankees in the city. According to the clergyman Montgomery Schuyler, "men stood aghast and watched in hopeless despair [as] the fair fabric of their well built fortunes crumbled into ruins."[61] The paradoxical effects of the New York depression, Edward Miller observed, rendered October 6, 1857 "the darkest day financially that St. Louis ever knew."[62] The panic also intensified the flow of Yankees out of St. Louis.

Many residents of the city blamed transplanted northeasterners for the city's economic problems. Because the depression exaggerated the commercial decline of the mid-1850s and continued long after the national financial crisis subsided, local observers searched for more general explanations for the city's economic problems, and they traced the "embarrassments" to New York jobbers, claiming that the "imprudent speculations" of St. Louis's Yankee traders had undermined the local economy.[63] The growing financial difficulties experienced by branch operators confirmed this view. Even antislavery spokesmen admitted that Yankee traders had exposed the local economy to the speculative mania that culminated in the Panic of 1857.[64] In addition, Missourians recalled that Northern moral proscriptions had accelerated the loss of the passenger and provisions trades, and St. Louis residents of all political leanings began to question the motives of those "wandering Jews" and "renegade Yankees" who abandoned St. Louis during the late 1850s.

The economic ascent of Chicago seemed to be connected to this migration, and the increasing flow of New York and Boston businessmen from St. Louis to Chicago pointed to a conspiracy. "The fact can no longer be concealed that New York and Boston have steadily come into competition with St. Louis," the river city's Free Soil newspaper admitted in 1859.[65] Rural Missourians and St. Louis residents joined forces during this period, calling attention to the "systematic attempts . . . in Eastern cities to divert capital from our borders."[66] The centerpiece of the Yankee plan to destroy St. Louis, according to Missourians, was a campaign of economic warfare.

Angry St. Louis residents found abundant evidence of the Yankee conspiracy. First, financial observers recognized that New York capital poured into Chicago during this period. Beginning in the mid-1850s, northeastern merchants shifted their investment strategies and used their economic influence to build the Illinois city. "Chicago [is] the pampered child of a rich and indulgent East," a St. Louis resident noted.[67]

Yankee involvement in Chicago railroads, however, confirmed their suspicions. Even before the Kansas crisis, the Hannibal and St. Joseph Railroad, an extension of the Chicago, Burlington, and Quincy line, had received generous support from John Murray Forbes and a group of Boston capitalists.[68] In fact, the line's board of directors held monthly meetings alternately in Boston and Hannibal.[69] Crossing the richest agricultural section in Missouri, this road used Yankee capital to divert much of the region's farm produce to Chicago markets.[70]

Moreover, St. Louis residents believed Yankees "governed and directed" these roads for the "sole purpose of injuring St. Louis."[71] "Eastern Railroad men were killing" St. Louis in order to "contribute to the commercial expansion of Chicago and Boston."[72] Suddenly, Eli Thayer's crusade, William Cullen Bryant's invectives, the sizable stream of prominent residents that abandoned St. Louis after the Panic of 1857, and the rapid growth of Chicago appeared to be parts of a vast plan. Yankee manipulators had stunted the growth of St. Louis and undermined the construction of Missouri railroads. In 1857 less than two hundred miles of railroad lines operated in the state; by comparison, Chicago's "system" included nearly four thousand miles of track.[73] Thus, St. Louis residents traced the rise of Chicago and the economic collapse of St. Louis to Yankee capitalists. "Eastern capital" a local writer announced, "pushed her [Chicago's] railroads out in all directions, largely taking away the trade" of St. Louis.[74]

Two ominous processes seemed to overlap. First, New York branch managers and capitalists fueled the ascent of Chicago. But Missourians also concluded that Yankee manipulators and their agents had invaded St. Louis's commercial domain, sharply narrowing the river city's hinterland. As a result, agricultural receipts from the region to the north fell during the mid- and late 1850s.[75] Corn receipts dropped by nearly 50 percent; flour receipts fell by 37 percent; and both wheat and barley receipts declined by almost 20 percent.[76] Yankee dollars, St. Louis residents noted, had linked the upper Mississippi, the Illinois River, and the Missouri River to Chicago railheads and to eastern transshippers, robbing St. Louis of its northern hinterland.[77] Even the *Missouri Democrat*, whose editor supported antislavery politics, predicted that "the capitalists of Wall Street will narrow the commercial territory of St. Louis to a very limited compass."[78] Armed with the financial muscle of Wall Street, Chicago appeared invincible, and more and more St. Louis residents admitted commercial defeat and braced for the worst.[79]

By 1858 Chicago had captured much of the upper Midwest, "claiming" most of Iowa, Minnesota, northern Illinois, and northern Missouri. According to William Kingsford, the Illinois city had become "the ruling market in western commercial operations."[80] Because railroads invaded the most commercially productive regions of the upper Mississippi valley, prosperous areas were gradually drawn into Chicago's commercial sphere. Northern Illinois, northern Missouri, and southern Iowa country merchants increasingly patronized Chicago's markets, and interior traders from Peoria, Jacksonville, Springfield, Dubuque, Galena, and Hannibal contributed to the flood of rural businessmen who abandoned the St. Louis provisions market during the late 1850s.[81] Conversely, depressed sections of the region often remained dependent on river transportation and the St. Louis marketplace. As a result, the St. Louis market stagnated while much of the Old Northwest and the upper valley blossomed and Chicago flourished.[82] The small economic shift that began during the Kansas turmoil became a ground swell in the years following the sack of Lawrence.[83]

The St. Louis marketplace thus underwent a dramatic transformation. Before the passage of the Kansas-Nebraska bill St. Louis had been a major cog in the national economy, with close commercial ties to New York and Boston. During the next three years political changes and the Panic of 1857 weakened those connections and nearly severed the commercial bonds that linked St. Louis to northeastern markets. The Missouri city became a regional entrepôt, possessing strong ties to a small hinterland and only weak ties outside of the region. Local newspaper editors and commercial writers admitted that the provisions and passenger trades were irretrievably lost. So too was the rich agricultural region to the north of the city. According to the *Missouri Democrat*, the completion of the Chicago, Burlington, and Quincy line in 1856 and the St. Joseph and Hannibal railroad in 1859 "dismembered" St. Louis.[84]

Only small, protected areas, pockets of settlement beyond the reach of Illinois railroads and Chicago drummers, remained within the domain of St. Louis. Scattered markets in southern Illinois, southern Missouri, Arkansas, Tennessee, and Kentucky sustained the St. Louis economy during this period. Local merchants discovered that country traders from the city's southern hinterland became their best and their steadiest customers. During the early 1850s, for example, merchants from southern Missouri comprised only 20 percent of the country traders who visited St. Louis each spring. By 1859, however, nearly half of the interior businessmen who patronized the city's spring market hailed from this area.[85]

Changing credit networks reflected this transformation and reinforced structural shifts in the local economy. Prior to the border "disturbances," most local merchants had relied on northeastern credit – and New York relatives – to purchase manufactured goods. Deeds of assignment, promissory notes, and bankruptcy declarations revealed the close relationship between St. Louis entrepreneurs and their suppliers on the Atlantic coast. During the mid-1850s, however, fewer New York manufacturers traded with St. Louis businessmen, and local merchants became less indebted to Yankee merchants. By the end of the decade scant traces remained of this once-vibrant trading network. Instead, St. Louis merchants increasingly relied on midwestern jobbers and regional suppliers. Local merchants or interior traders financed more than two-thirds of all the firms that opened their doors in St. Louis during the late 1850s. They had financed only 17 percent of new firms during the 1840s.

Although local capitalists assumed an increasing role in the city's marketplace, St. Louis, as a result of its colonial relationship with New York, lacked the kind of commercial elite that financed commercial ventures in older cities. The wealthiest residents of St. Louis invested in many businesses, but the group was small and most active in real estate and similar enterprises. Pierre Chouteau retained his influence in the business district, and local entrepreneurs such as

Table 7.1 *Source of capital by date of opening of firm*

Source of capital	1842–50 (percent)	1851–53 (percent)	1854–56 (percent)	1857–60 (percent)
New England	19	9	5	5
New York	39	24	18	8
Pennsylvania	10	14	9	4
Local and Midwest	17	38	55	68
Far West	2	7	7	10
Other	13	8	6	5

Source: Missouri Vols. 36–38, R. G. Dun and Company Collection, Baker Library, Harvard University Graduate School of Business Administration.

James Eddy, who was a silent partner in a large number of St. Louis dry goods firms, remained involved in local economic affairs, though neither these men nor their associates could fill the vacuum created by the Yankee exodus.[86] Instead, the new capitalists were often residents such as August Nedderhut, a "returned Californian." Like many men of small means, Nedderhut, a young German immigrant, contracted California fever and invaded the Pacific goldfields during the early 1850s. Unlike most fortune seekers, however, Nedderhut realized his dreams; he returned to St. Louis triumphant, bringing home "considerable [gold] dust." Nedderhut immediately became a "capitalist" and the silent partner in a number of small ventures. His wealth, however, was modest.[87] Most successful gold seekers accumulated only a few thousand dollars; their financial resources remained limited, and they continued to lack the experience and the "acquaintances" to enter lucrative industries. Such new wealth did not compensate for the loss of Yankee capital.

The meager capital reserves of St. Louis merchants and their hinterland trading partners sharply limited the scale of new businesses and restricted them to regional enterprises. While large firms comprised over one-third of the businesses in operation in St. Louis before the border war, after the "agitation" fewer than one new business in six was considered a large venture. Small firms with limited financial reserves controlled an increasing share of the local marketplace, and continuing capital shortages insured that most St. Louis ventures would remain modest enterprises. Far-flung business enterprises designed to compete with Chicago traders or to extend St. Louis's economic sphere deeper into the city's agricultural hinterland were impossible.

Moreover, the increasing dominance of small, poorly financed firms contributed to the failure rate among local businesses, which rose by 74 percent between the invasion of Kansas and the assault on

Fort Sumter in 1861. Not only did more firms fail, but they did so faster than ever before. The average life span for local businesses fell by 39 percent during the late 1850s, and three-fourths of all ventures failed within four years – compared to only 43 percent of firms that failed during the mid-1840s.

Local financial writers urged merchants to take advantage of the city's "protected" domain and to concentrate their investments on regional businesses. They argued that the hinterland trade offered a glimmer of hope for stabilizing the failing economy. Editors and commercial writers implored local merchants to "secure" the "dominion which nature has bequeathed" to St. Louis and to develop this safe and steady trade.[88] Kentucky, Missouri, Tennessee, and Arkansas markets, the *Missouri Republican* noted in 1857, "naturally belong to St. Louis."[89] "Our city is nearer to them [than Chicago] and more accessible."[90] Although such recommendations provided a source of optimism for local manufacturers, commercial writers increasingly conceded that Chicago commanded the West.

The declining and regionally oriented local economy provided little opportunity for newcomers during the late 1850s, and the population of the city, as in the mid-1850s, barely increased. The municipal census of 1857, for example, revealed only one thousand new residents in the city, the vast majority of whom were St. Louis-born infants.[91] Although the population grew by over 25 percent during the second half of the decade, the annexation of outlying areas and natural increase accounted for most of this growth. Thousands of boom-period immigrants, for example, began families during this period. While the proportion of newcomers in the population fell by 43 percent, the proportion of residents under the age of ten increased by 41 percent during the decade. In 1850 St. Louis was a city of young, unattached newcomers and fortune seekers. A decade later, sex ratios had evened, family size had increased by 53 percent, the proportion of residents owning real estate had doubled, boarding-house life had virtually disappeared, and most adult residents were married and parents. The vast majority of the people who lived in the city in 1860 had arrived before the Kansas ordeal. St. Louis was no longer a lodestone.

Growing ties with the hinterland transformed migration patterns. Only a small stream of migrants moved to the city during the late 1850s, though these newcomers accelerated important changes in the economy of St. Louis. Nearly three-fourths of the migrants who settled in the city during this period had traveled there from the lower Mississippi valley or the lower Ohio valley. Rural Kentuckians and

Missourians, rather than the Bostonians and the New Yorkers of the boom era, peopled St. Louis after the Panic of 1857.

Some of these newcomers were merchants who responded to the growing economic relationship between St. Louis and the city's southern hinterland. Midwestern newcomers established almost two-thirds of the businesses that opened in the city during the late 1850s. Many successful country traders, merchants whose ventures flourished with the growth of the hinterland trade, migrated to St. Louis in order to expand their businesses. Lee Shrylock, for example, enjoyed considerable success in his western Kentucky country dry goods business. He operated a small store in Hopkinsville, Kentucky, between 1824 and 1846. The following year Shrylock added a partner and expanded his business. During the late 1850s he "began to cast his eyes about for a more extended field of operation" and established a business in St. Louis.[92] Similarly, James Butler settled in St. Louis in 1859 to enlarge his Lexington, Missouri, boot and shoe firm. Long a successful merchant in western Missouri, Butler was already well known in St. Louis when he migrated to the city.[93] Many migrants established shipping firms or commission houses, both tapping and strengthening the commercial relationship between interior traders and the St. Louis market. John Roe, for example, transshipped pork from his native Clark County, Missouri, to St. Louis merchants.[94]

River towns, such as Memphis, assumed a new importance in St. Louis's hinterland trade, and more and more Tennessee and Kentucky merchants migrated to St. Louis. Charles Mety, for example, moved to St. Louis in 1859 in order to expanded his Memphis wholesale shoe business.[95] Cincinnati and Louisville, trading centers largely bypassed by northern rail lines, also forged growing ties with St. Louis merchants during the late 1850s. As a result, many small manufacturers in Cincinnati marketed their goods in St. Louis, and a small stream of agents and salesmen traveled between the cities. In 1858 James Calm migrated from Cincinnati to St. Louis in order to sell the "fancy goods" produced by his brother in Ohio.[96] Over 40 percent of the midwestern merchants who settled in St. Louis during the late 1850s migrated from Cincinnati. Since well-backed and prosperous merchants continued to prefer Chicago ventures and New York trading partners, only poorer merchants and weaker, regionally oriented firms operated in the modest southern river trade.

Regional commerce proved to be particularly appealing to clerks and aspiring entrepreneurs from St. Louis's rural hinterland. Hundreds of midwestern and southern salesmen and clerks migrated to St. Louis and started small businesses during the late 1850s. Most of these men traveled from small towns.[97] The contrast with the boom-era migrants was dramatic. At midcentury St. Louis attracted wealthy merchants from a handful of eastern commercial centers. By the late 1850s, however, most middle-class migrants were men of modest means from small towns located near waterways. The logistical and economic factors that had discouraged poor merchants from engaging in long-distance commerce had little effect on hinterland migration or regional trade. Thus, aspiring merchants traveled short distances, from Missouri, Arkansas, Tennessee, southern Illinois, and Ohio to St. Louis, in order to test the commercial waters in the region's trading capital.

Virtually all of these entrepreneurs, however, lacked capital, and most merchants, according to local credit reporters, possessed scant experience in the trade. William Shepperd, for example, left a clerking position in Napoleon, Arkansas, to start a commission business in St. Louis. Shepperd's one hundred fifty dollars of capital proved to be inadequate, and within months his firm had failed.[98] The distribution of an estate or a similar sudden windfall often prompted midwestern town dwellers to migrate to the nearest commercial entrepôt and establish a small business. For example, in 1857 C. S. Sanderson, a Cincinnati stage agent, inherited two thousand dollars from his father's estate. Sanderson immediately left Ohio, migrated to St. Louis, and purchased a small grocery business. The concern quickly consumed Sanderson's legacy, and after only three months he closed the business.[99] Other midwesterners migrated from one city within the region to the next. Thus, many Louisville, Natchez, and Lexington men, usually with little wealth, moved to St. Louis and established businesses. Few hinterland traders, however, could overcome capital shortages, their own inexperience, or the depressed condition of regional markets. Almost 80 percent of these firms failed within three years.

Merchants such as Sanderson and Shepperd reinforced shifts in the marketplace. The difficulties experienced by country traders inflated the local failure rate, further blackening the city's commercial reputation and doubling the resolve of Yankee traders to avoid St. Louis ventures. Without New York capital or commercial networks, the scale and breadth of the local economy continued to decline. During the late 1850s the top-heavy character of the boom-era economy disappeared. According to local credit reporters, the proportion of new businesses established by wealthy entrepreneurs fell by 55 percent during the course of the decade. In place of enormous Yankee houses, country traders and rural clerks established small, regional concerns, and small-scale and poorly backed firms dominated the St.

Louis marketplace. Even successful newcomers, such as Lee Shrylock, operated within the city's immediate hinterland. Credit networks seldom extended further west than the Kansas border or
further east than Cincinnati, and few St. Louis merchants operated
outside the region during this period. By the start of the Civil War St.
Louis was a declining regional entrepôt, bound to a narrow – and
shrinking – hinterland.

The growing interdependence between the city and its region
influenced perceptions of St. Louis as well. If Yankees viewed the city
as a declining, second-rate trading center linked to a stagnant and
politically backward area, the inhabitants of the lower Ohio and
Mississippi valleys saw St. Louis in very different terms. The increasingly regional orientation of the local economy made the city attractive and even alluring to hinterland migrants. More than ever before,
rural midwesterners became familiar with the advantages of St.
Louis. For decades interior farmers had believed that northern "vampires," speculating agents for "New York sharpers," controlled the
St. Louis marketplace.[100] The Kansas turmoil and the close ties between western outlet managers and their backers in the North reinforced stark images of Wall Street capitalists manipulating the
Missouri economy. Moreover, the exodus of Yankee merchants from
the city had little effect on these perceptions; midwesterners continued to view St. Louis in foreboding terms. The new interdependence between St. Louis and its hinterland, however, changed these
images. During the late 1850s rural Missourians had increasing contact with St. Louis, and many country dwellers knew merchants who
had migrated to St. Louis. Such informal networks proved to be
important conduits of information, gradually transforming the image
of the city.

St. Louis became a midwestern – rather than a Yankee – city during
this period, and rural Missourians and Kentuckians increasingly
considered the city a regional capital. Country editors chronicled the
triumphs of local migrants in the big city, and articles celebrated the
attractions of life in St. Louis.[101] Interior newspapers told of the high
wages, the extraordinary opportunities, and the boundless excitement of St. Louis. Moreover, men who had visited the city regaled
rural friends with descriptions of opulent houses, busy shops,
mobbed thoroughfares, and savory temptations. The rural pool of
knowledge about St. Louis expanded enough to replace frightening
stereotypes with images of enchantment. According to Hannibal-
native Mark Twain, his father "was always talking about St. Looy like
an old citizen." Twain also recalled that "two or three of the boys had
long been persons of consideration among us because they had been

to St. Louis once and had a general knowledge of its wonders."[102] Ironically, just as St. Louis became a declining, regional entrepôt, hinterland observers associated the city with progress, refinement, and opportunity.

The advantages of St. Louis seemed doubly attractive in view of the economic problems that beset farmers living in much of the city's hinterland. Eastern migrants settled the southern tier of the Midwest early in the century. Cincinnati commanded the Far West during the Jacksonian period, and Lexington and Louisville offered familiar western vigor and promise. By midcentury, however, the region was demographically mature, and population pressures made the Ohio valley states "net exporters of human resources."[103] Increasingly, Ohio, Indiana, Illinois, and Kentucky farmers left their homes in search of fertile land and greater employment opportunities. At the same time, northern railroads disrupted the commercial networks that linked these farmers to eastern and European markets; produce from the rapidly growing northern areas tied to Chicago railroads flooded eastern markets and hastened the economic decline of the lower Ohio valley and the lower Mississippi valley.[104] With farm prices falling, currency in short supply, and unemployment legion, more and more midwesterners considered migration.

Logistical factors increased the appeal of migration during this period. Steamboat fare, once quite expensive for agricultural workers, fell sharply on Ohio valley routes. In response to increasing competition and declining river traffic, boat owners engaged in price wars during the second half of the 1850s. Passage from Cincinnati to St. Louis, including a stateroom, meals, and "full hotel accommodations," fell to one dollar, making migration affordable for all midwesterners.[105]

Although hinterland farmers hardly thronged St. Louis during the late 1850s, each year a few thousand country men traveled "to this city from one of the back counties of an adjoining State" in search of employment.[106] Migration often represented a desperate response to hard times. Barney Igo, for example, chose to settle in St. Louis after all his cattle died and he found himself unable to feed his seven children. A resident of Winona, Minnesota, one of the small northern pockets that remained tied to Mississippi River commerce and thus St. Louis markets, Igo hoped "to migrate hither and remain until he could restock his farm." Like many migrants, Igo chose St. Louis because of favorable descriptions he had read. A Minnesota newspaper, he reported, gave "seductive accounts of high wages and abundant work in St. Louis."[107] The sagging economy of the city, however, offered few opportunities during this period, and, like many newcomers, Igo found no work in the city. He eventually turned to a municipal asylum for assistance.[108]

Deepening rural poverty increased the stream of country migrants to St. Louis during the late 1850s and exacerbated the unemployment problem in the city that began during the Panic of 1857. The *Missouri Republican*, for example, predicted "a vast migration from Kentucky, Virginia, Pennsylvania and Tennessee, where they have no money."[109] Hinterland paupers poured into the city in search of work or relief.[110] Just when the local economy was least able to absorb poor newcomers, orphans, widows, and destitute farmers migrated to the city. The number of unemployed men in St. Louis soared after 1857, and local asylums overflowed. The decline of the city's economy bound St. Louis to its hinterland, stimulating a stream of destitute country migrants that increased as the regional economy sagged. The Panic of 1857 exaggerated the problems generated by the Kansas turmoil, and the hinterland migration magnified the economic and unemployment crisis triggered by the panic.

Too poor to travel to Chicago, destitute midwesterners migrated to St. Louis during the late 1850s. Nearly three-fourths of the newcomers to the city were manual workers, and most were clustered in semiskilled or unskilled callings.[111] By the late 1850s, St. Louis conformed to the eastern model of internal migration. Like older eastern cities, the majority of St. Louis's newcomers were manual workers who migrated from the city's immediate hinterland. While rapidly growing, younger western cities continued to attract wealthy migrants from Boston and New York, St. Louis increasingly represented a maturing regional entrepôt, lacking the excitement or vitality of its youthful days.[112] Thus, this hinterland migration reflected the dawn of a new age in the city's history.

The growing hinterland migration also affected the character of the city. Transplanted rural and small-town midwesterners comprised a rapidly increasing proportion of the city's population. Democratic views, therefore, gained greater popularity within the city, and the well-established battle between city merchants and rural Missourians faded. The exodus of Yankees and the arrival of rural Kentuckians and interior Missourians gave new political force to proslavery, hard money, and anti-eastern sentiment in St. Louis, and for the first time Democratic landslides became common in municipal elections.[113] After 1857, even the city's Republican newspaper endorsed conservative economic thinking, moderation on the slavery agitation, and regional agendas. For example, the editor termed Massachusetts railroad builders "wandering Jews," and he warned municipal officials to beware of Yankee machinations designed to make St. Louis a "fief" of Boston.[114] While the economy assumed a decidedly regional orientation, the character of St. Louis gradually followed suit.

Two smaller streams of migration reinforced the regional character of the city. First, German immigrants comprised nearly 40 percent of the newcomers who settled in St. Louis during the late 1850s. Many of these migrants traveled from the Midwest, and they differed little from other midwestern newcomers. Most were poor and unskilled, and some migrated out of desperation. Other Germans, however, traveled longer distances to settle in St. Louis. Despite local conditions, St. Louis maintained its reputation as a German city. Stories of "Latin farmers," for example, persisted, and many Germans knew of the city's renowned German schools, its Lutheran churches, and its Free Thinker newspaper. St. Louis's vast array of problems, however, cut deeply into the flow of German migration to the city; fewer immigrants traveled to the city, and wealthier Germans, like their native-born counterparts, increasingly chose to settle in Chicago.[115] Nonetheless, a small current of Germans, most often working-class immigrants, migrated to the city during the late 1850s.

Germans comprised nearly a quarter of the newcomers who arrived in the city from the Old Northwest and the upper Mississippi valley states. While most native-born migrants from this region hailed from isolated agricultural areas bypassed by railroad lines, German immigrants often traveled from prosperous and growing trading centers. Nicholas Willei, for example, left Davenport, Iowa, in 1860 to resettle in languishing St. Louis.[116] Similarly, Thomas Sauter, a thirty-year-old laborer from Baden, lived in Philadelphia and Iowa City before migrating to St. Louis in 1859.[117] Cultural attractions persisted long after economic enticements faded.

German immigrants from as far away as the Atlantic coast also resettled in St. Louis during the late 1850s. In fact, immigrants comprised the majority of the migrants who traveled to the city from the Northeast during this period.[118] Most of these newcomers were manual workers, and this new migration from the Atlantic coast assumed a working-class and an immigrant character. Gottlieb Bentz, for example, settled in St. Louis in 1860. A Wurttemberg-born butcher, Bentz lived in Philadelphia for nearly a decade before traveling to St. Louis with his wife and two young children. Like many skilled workers, Bentz was unable to find employment in his calling in St. Louis. Instead, he endured low wages and seasonal unemployment, working as a day laborer in the city.[119] While some small-town midwestern newspaper editors announced the advantages of the regional capital during this period, few Philadelphia journals cele-

brated the virtues of St. Louis during the late 1850s. Men such as
Bentz migrated for cultural reasons.

Ironically, the growing German population of St. Louis exaggerated the regional character of the city. In 1860 German immigrants
and their children comprised 44 percent of the city's population. Until
the mid-1850s, when the alliance between Benton Democrats, Whigs,
and Know-Nothings collapsed, religious and cultural fissures had
fragmented St. Louis's German community.[120] The Free Soil cause,
however, unified the city's diverse German population, and the
immigrants rallied behind the Republican banner, becoming a powerful force in local politics. In fact, with the exodus of Yankees from the
city, Germans provided the backbone of the antislavery movement in
St. Louis.[121] As these immigrants became more radical, native-born
residents became more conservative, and new divisions arose in
municipal politics. According to many city dwellers, Germans fanned
the slavery agitation, diverting northern trade and alienating southern commerce with their "abolitionist fanaticism." One observer
noted that residents termed Germans the "Damned Dutch – uttering
the words with that ferocious emphasis which they usually reserve
for the Damned Yankee."[122]

In 1860 William Seward visited St. Louis and delivered a vitriolic
and peculiarly threatening message. Noting the blighting influence of
slavery, Seward expressed his amazement that "in Missouri, with
such a vast territory and such great resources, there is after so long a
settlement, so little of population, improvement and strength to be
found." On the abolition question, Seward suggested that "you [St.
Louis residents] are in a way being Germanized into it."[123] Few
Missourians or transplanted Kentuckians relished the thought of
being "Germanized" into antislavery "fanaticism," and increasingly,
residents charged that the immigrants challenged local political culture and threatened local values. Thus, native-born residents supported conservative, regional causes and the Democratic Party in
order to protect their city from the "damned Dutch" and their Union-
ist fanaticism.

A second small stream of long-distance migrants inspired a still
more defensive reaction from native-born residents. For these travelers, St. Louis possessed a kind of negative appeal. In 1850 well-bred
merchants had poured into the city from New York and Boston. A
decade later, few native-born migrants traveled from the Northeast to
St. Louis, and only one northeastern newcomer in six worked in a
commercial calling. This tiny group of merchants, in sharp contrast
to their earlier counterparts, consisted of poor and unsuccessful

businessmen. Many of these men probably chose St. Louis because its markets were quiet and its commercial district contained few Yankees. Hugh Thompson, for example, migrated to the city from Greenfield, Massachusetts, in 1857, after "he was unfortunate in business there."[124] Thompson may have hoped to start anew – in a setting where his previous failures would remain unknown. Other Yankee merchants preferred to dodge old creditors by hiding in a city with relatively few familiar faces, and St. Louis proved to be an ideal choice. A small current of unsuccessful entrepreneurs from outside of the city's hinterland, including many forgers, swindlers, and "pigeon droppers," escaped to St. Louis during this period. Prosperous merchants continued to migrate to Chicago, while unsuccessful traders from the Northeast and the northern tier of the Midwest moved to St. Louis.

St. Louis residents became increasingly suspicious of all Yankee merchants. Most "unknown" New Yorkers were branded "transients," a label that implied "rascality," and local boosters and credit investigators repeatedly warned St. Louis merchants about New York "sharpers" and Boston "scoundrels."[125] St. Louis merchants and municipal leaders began to shun all contact with eastern commerce; ties to New York or Boston became sources of fear and causes for concern. "Don't trust even the liberality of the Yankee," the *Missouri Republican* counseled in 1859.[126] The behavior of eastern sharpers also revived painfully fresh memories of other Yankee betrayals – the New York railroad betrayal, the Chicago exodus, and the "over-trading" hysteria preceding the panic. At all levels, contact with Yankee merchants and their commercial centers seemed pernicious. While municipal leaders struggled to steady the rocky economy and to restore stability to local society, Yankee merchants, even honest eastern traders, seemed to introduce instability. Speculation, "over-trading," and "long-credit," the tools of aggressive Yankee entrepreneurs, symbolized the vulnerability of the local economy and the downfall of the city.[127]

Reacting to these fears, St. Louis city officials and leading merchants self-consciously rejected the "go-ahead" eastern model of "commercial progress" during the late 1850s. No longer did they affirm their ties to Wall Street or celebrate their "marriage" to New York and Boston. More important, community leaders repudiated the dynamic, vigorous vision of urban development that they had associated with the great commercial centers of the Northeast and that they had attempted to emulate earlier in the decade. Instead, they charted the future of St. Louis in direct contradistinction to the aggressive course pursued by New York and its "fiefs."

St. Louis writers denounced Yankee notions of success and prosperity during this period. The growth of Wall Street's colonies, local writers charged, too often proved to be artificial and "bloated."[128] According to St. Louis editors, Chicago possessed the characteristic flaws of a Yankee-built town. Local newspapers warned that "Chicago is mortgaged to eastern capitalists."[129] Its growth, a St. Louis editor added in 1858, "has not been . . . healthy."[130] "The capital of Eastern cities has been poured into them [Chicago and other western urban centers] on speculation."[131] As a result, the city is "greatly dependent on foreign control" and "foreign lords." "Chicago seems to be gassy, inflated – puffed up," the *Missouri Democrat* warned.[132]

Rather than imitating Chicago's "bloated" growth or the unhealthy development of other Yankee "fiefs," St. Louis officials vowed to make their city "solid and stable." They promised to chart an independent course, free from the machinations of Wall Street speculators. In order to avoid corrupting outside bonds, local merchants began to shun "foreign" capital sources, remaining "self-reliant, prudent and sagacious."[133] Instead of "submitting" to foreign control, "the people of St. Louis," according to the *Missouri Republican*, "have determined to rely upon themselves."[134]

The results, according to local writers, were dramatic. The compiler of a city directory, for example, boasted that "Saint [sic] Louis presents to the eye of the stranger who first visits it, the idea of great solidity."[135] Similarly, a local newspaper editor bragged that "St. Louis is evidently solid-built and being built on a sure foundation."[136] "All business here," a traveler reported in 1859, "seems to be founded on a sure basis, but few banks; all trade being dependent on its own resources."[137] Unlike Chicago, "St. Louis was on a solid foundation," another writer explained.[138] It was "more conservative than other Western cities . . . satisfied to grow steadily, but surely," a local editor boasted.[139]

St. Louis's self-image became tied to conservative ideals. Every discussion of the city's future included a condemnation of Yankee practices and an affirmation of local spirit and rectitude.[140] If speculation symbolized Wall Street evils, cash transactions became a badge of honor and independence in the losing war against New York speculators. Conservative St. Louis merchants preferred a "safe and prudent" trading system – a cash economy.[141] According to local financial observers, St. Louis businessmen, unlike their credit-encumbered Yankee counterparts, never swindled their customers and avoided risky ventures, long credit, and overtrading. St. Louis merchants condemned the "little tricks which to [a] considerable extent, mark some business men, or rather men in business in some other places."[142] Similarly, while Chicago traders hired Yankee agents, St. Louis businessmen, always "conservative and steady," relied on local men, thus "sustaining to the fullest extent the present elevated character of the St. Louis merchants."[143] Not surprisingly, the Missouri city "has a better class of men for merchants than Chicago," a local editor explained in 1859.[144]

When more vigorous ideals became unattainable, St. Louis boosters made a virtue out of necessity and celebrated the prudence of their business class. Much of this new emphasis on solidity and independence was born of resignation.[145] Castigating Yankee practices served both to rebuke Northern influence and to generate community pride in the city. Local merchants, for example, denounced the evils of foreign backing just as Yankee merchants eschewed St. Louis investments. But if market forces had denied local entrepreneurs access to external capital, this rhetoric enabled St. Louis men to argue that the decision had been their own; they controlled the fate of the city, and they had chosen rectitude over speculation. "Standards of commercial honor" – not Wall Street – had "inclined [local merchants] to an excess of caution than to an excess of enterprise," and St. Louis boosters applauded the course that residents had "chosen."[146]

Even though local editors acknowledged that "Chicago, for her age, has outstripped St. Louis," community leaders championed their city's "solidity."[147] Similarly, in May, 1857 – months before the depression – a local editor proclaimed that "St. Louis is known as the most solvent city in the Union," and the following year the city controller announced that "we can point with pride to the fact that the city of St. Louis has never been protested on her bonds or interest."[148] Earlier in the decade municipal leaders had coveted loftier goals.

Such efforts to generate local pride increasingly entailed an explicit rejection of all things associated with the Northeast. Writers began to wonder why "every charity measure of New York ladies is copied among us," and newspaper editors contrasted the "sycophancy" of Yankee politics with the strong-willed, independent course of Missouri politics.[149] Community leaders also urged residents to reject the "monopolizing system" of eastern letters and to "cultivate home talent."[150] In November, 1859 the *Missouri Republican* even asked local lawmakers to consider "a different day on which to manifest our thankfulness to God for his many blessings during the year." The newspaper's editor urged Missourians to be "independent" from Yankee Thanksgiving celebrations.[151]

Community leaders transformed the tone of boosterism during the late 1850s. Earlier in the decade, writers had directed their rhetoric toward the East, emphasizing the vitality of St. Louis and hoping to attract Yankee capital and capitalists. After the collapse of the local economy, however, boosterism served a new and internal purpose. Editors and community leaders introduced ideals that demonstrated the moral and ethical chasm separating conservative St. Louis from speculating, mercenary Yankee trading centers. No longer a mechanism to attract outsiders, boosterism became a tool designed to generate internal cohesion and to serve local needs.

The new character of the city affected the scope of city government as well. During the boom municipal officials had worked to spur local growth and prosperity. Their task had been to provide institutional inducements for outside investors and migrants and to enact statutory safeguards to protect the economic well-being of the city. After the crisis of the mid-1850s, however, residents demanded that municipal officials insulate St. Louis from foreign shocks. Community leaders argued that local control might provide a buffer against the turbulent world of Yankee speculators, New York commerce, and other disruptive outside forces.[152] Local pride, resignation, regional character, and a welling animosity toward New York and Chicago combined in a powerful mixture that transformed ideas about growth, progress, and local culture.

Pervasive fears of outsiders reshaped local institutions in ironic ways. St. Louis residents demanded legislative solutions to the city's problems, and local lawmakers sought institutional mechanisms to restore stability to the flagging economy.[153] A legislative revolution, reflecting the changing vision of community leaders, spearheaded this campaign, and municipal lawmakers enacted new statutes and bolstered old laws in order to repel "dangerous" outside elements. City ordinances, particularly vagrancy and anti-pauper statutes, became the chief municipal weapons in this war against outside "vampires."[154] This device was a familiar tool for local policy makers, but the focus and purpose of such statutes changed dramatically during the crisis of the late 1850s.

Vagrancy acts had long enabled law enforcers to control dangerous elements in the community, though the cultural pressures of the period redefined the nature of dangerous behavior. During the boom period, for example, legislators, policymakers, and police officers had used vagrancy statutes to protect the local economy. Beginning in the mid-1840s, just as the marketplace burgeoned, they revised these ordinances in order to safeguard the city from individuals who might disrupt commerce.[155] Thus, municipal officials tolerated drunkards, prostitutes, and laggards but bolstered vagrancy laws to control pickpockets and safe crackers.[156] Legislators drew a sharper distinction between criminals and mere idlers during this period, and the vagrant statute, which had been used to repel deviants and paupers, became a mechanism for convicting thieves, confidence men, and burglars when other, more traditional laws proved to be ineffective.[157] In fact, city officials broadened the definition of vagrancy to include persons having the "reputation of being thieves, burglars, or pickpockets."[158] Vagrancy became an economic crime during this period, and the overwhelming majority of those charged with the offense had either committed crimes against the marketplace or possessed reputations for engaging in such activities.[159] For example, law enforcers permitted brothels to operate in the city and ignored beggars. But if the "nymphs du pave" robbed their patrons and if beggars bothered shoppers in the business district, the police "vindictively" enforced the local vagrant act.[160]

During the late 1850s the city's problems ballooned, and local lawmakers expanded vagrancy statutes to deal with a growing range of ills. Residents increasingly feared all outsiders during this period – not just thieves and burglars. Groping for a legislative panacea, lawmakers added "procurers or agents for bawds, women who live in houses of bad repute, women who frequent beer houses, notorious loafers, bawds, courtesans, and men who live in bawdy houses" to the list of "characters" within the scope of the vagrant act.[161] Law enforcers also arrested "whiskey-suckers," idlers, and paupers, believing that transients "are a contaminating leprosy."[162] Similarly, they "vagged" loafers and deviants for presenting "a deadly poison in the way of our youth."[163] During the late 1850s men like William Bushel and John Burns became the principal targets of the vagrant act. In 1858 the police found Bushel and Burns "sleeping together in a deserted house" and arrested them on vagrancy charges.[164] These statutes were increasingly used to arrest anyone who threatened social mores or public order. Deviants and drunkards replaced forgers and confidence men as the principal threats to St. Louis. Shifts in the economy and in local culture exerted a powerful and abrupt influence on law enforcement.

City officials no longer welcomed newcomers to St. Louis. Instead, community leaders sought mechanisms to repel strangers and the evils that migrated with them. The legislative assault on "foreign" influences extended beyond bolstered vagrancy ordinances. For example, in 1861 the city council strengthened anti-paupers statutes.[165] Moreover, local politicians charged that other cities, particularly – and not surprisingly – New York and Chicago, were shipping their undesirables to St. Louis. Law enforcers became concerned about the

influx of pregnant women without husbands, the old, and the in-
firmed.[166] All strangers seemed to challenge the stability of St. Louis;
Yankee merchants introduced economic and social instability, paupers upset local institutions, and strangers brought a bevy of evils. The
economic concerns that followed the Panic of 1857 transformed perceptions of the outside world, and conservative ideas became xenophobic proscriptions in the late 1850s.

These perceptions reinforced the growing cultural bond between
St. Louis and the lower Mississippi valley. City dwellers did not share
the world view of the residents of Mississippi or Alabama, though St.
Louis merchants and workers expressed a growing – if somewhat
superficial – sympathy for Southern culture and for Southern ideas
about urban development. The new emphasis on honor and solidity
and the surging anti-Yankee sentiments of St. Louis residents meshed
well with the values that Missourians associated with the South.
Economic and social forces, however, also forged a new connection
between St. Louis residents and the slave states during the late 1850s.

An increasing number of St. Louis merchants turned to Southern
markets during this period. As Chicago drummers captured the
Missouri city's northern and western hinterlands and as local entrepreneurs shunned high-risk business ventures, the "Southern trade"
became more attractive and more important. This market, according
to local financial writers, promised prosperity without instability. The
Missouri Republican argued that Southern merchants "are a safe community to deal with" and the South is "legitimately within the scope of
our enterprises."[167] Expanding this commerce would require neither
credit nor speculation nor "over-trading," and local merchants believed that St. Louis ventures "may defy competition" in the "States
to the south."[168] More important, St. Louis writers and businessmen
argued that entering Southern markets would help compensate for
the loss of Northern markets.[169]

Increasing commercial ties with the South, however, required
political changes – or at least greater subtlety in political affairs.
Merchants throughout the lower Mississippi valley reminded their
counterparts in St. Louis that commerce and politics were indeed
closely related. "If your city desires the trade of the South," the
Memphis Bulletin warned, "let it respect the rights of the Southern
people and be what nature intended it to be – a city of the South."[170]
Other editors in the region echoed this message, assuring St. Louis
merchants that political support or even political sympathy with the
slave states would yield enormous economic dividends and that
Southern businessmen would prefer to trade with men in another
slave state.[171] Community leaders urged St. Louis entrepreneurs to

"mak[e] a favorable impression on the southern mind."[172] For practical reasons, St. Louis merchants and even antislavery political leaders softened their public positions on slavery and established greater connections with the South.

Commerce with the lower Mississippi valley and with the products of the slave economy assumed growing importance in St. Louis. Local financial writers reported that "the old States – Kentucky, Tennessee, Georgia, South Carolina, and others – are interchanging commodities with us on a constantly increasing scale."[173] At a time when receipts of foodstuffs from the northern and western hinterlands fell, tobacco and hemp receipts soared.[174] The city became a major distribution center for Tennessee cotton, and Georgia buyers buoyed the St. Louis corn market.[175] According to the local merchants' exchange in 1860, "trade with the plantations, towns and cities of the South is becoming every season of greater importance to the commerce of St. Louis."[176] Even Yankee financial writers recognized the change. For example, *Hunt's Merchants' Magazine* suggested that the "peculiar" character of St. Louis's "facilities" accounted for its "steadily increasing" Southern trade.[177]

These economic changes reinforced cultural shifts and migration patterns. A small stream of Southerners moved to St. Louis during the years before the Civil War, contributing to Democratic and proslavery voting strength in the city. Newspaper advertisements, often emphasizing "Southern acquaintances," bore evidence of the process. For example, in 1860 "a young man from the South" placed an employment notice in the *Missouri Republican*. Possessing eight years of experience, he was "desirous of building up a business with Tennessee, Georgia and South Carolina, as [I] have a considerable acquaintance in each of those States."[178] The number of merchants who migrated from the lower Mississippi valley nearly doubled during the 1850s as well, exaggerating the regional – and the sectional – orientation of the economy.

By the early 1860s surprisingly few traces remained of the Yankee city of the early 1850s, and St. Louis residents often actively rebuffed connections to Yankee politics and culture. For example, when Frank Blair, a local congressman, returned to the city from the Republican convention in 1860 and announced his support for Abraham Lincoln, a riot erupted. Mobs pelted local Republicans with stones, bellowed "blasphemous yells," and screeched "hellish imprecations" at antislavery spokesmen.[179] The same year, the local Mercantile Library Association invited Henry Ward Beecher to deliver "a course of lectures." But the organizers of the visit demanded that the clergyman "eschew all matters pertaining to politics and religion."[180] A year later Horace Greeley canceled a speaking engagement in St. Louis at the insistence of local Republicans. "I was advised," Greeley reported, "that I would probably be mobbed if I were to attempt to lecture."[181] Although most St. Louis residents acknowledged that "the interests of Missouri are not identical to those of South Carolina," native-born voters increasingly supported the Southern cause and embraced Southern culture; only the hated "damned Dutch" and a small group of stubborn Yankees, still led by William Greenleaf Eliot, sustained Yankee culture.[182] In 1860 the *St. Louis Bulletin* reported that "Southern wealth and Southern enterprise" built St. Louis and Missouri. "She is one with the South."[183]

A new city was born during the late 1850s. Sectionalism destroyed Yankee St. Louis, and a regional capital emerged. While Chicago captured northern attention and Wall Street dollars, St. Louis became culturally, politically, and economically tied to its hinterland. The city offered few attractions to outsiders and, in fact, local lawmakers erected institutional barriers to repel suspicious newcomers. Instead, hinterland farmers patronized St. Louis markets, and interior migrants settled in the city during this period. Thus, the conservative, Democratic, and regional character of the city increased with time. St. Louis belonged to the lower Mississippi valley, though Southern culture and politics exerted an increasing influence on the character of the city as sectional passions flared.

On April 12, 1861, General Pierre Beauregard issued orders to open fire on Fort Sumter, and that volley sealed the fate of St. Louis. Although Missourians rejected secession, the Civil War completed the revolution that had begun in 1854.[184] Men of means fled from St. Louis at the first sign of war. "Our best people will leave as soon as they can arrange their business," a local merchant predicted in 1860.[185] More than ever before, only merchants with modest, regionally oriented businesses operated in St. Louis's marketplace. In 1861 soldiers blockaded the Mississippi River, reducing St. Louis's river trade, the lifeblood of the failing economy, "to about one third of its former amount." Local reporters termed the levee a "graveyard," and the city's merchants became totally dependent on their Southern customers.[186] When the war ended, St. Louis's rebirth was complete.

In 1867 a Boston journalist traveled to St. Louis to write an article about the Missouri city for the *Atlantic Monthly*. James Parton interviewed merchants and editors and wandered the streets of the city, hoping to capture the character of the city. His descriptions of St. Louis reflected a blend of Yankee stereotypes and local boosterism.[187] Ironically, the two images proved to be nearly identical. St. Louis residents saw themselves very much as Yankee observers saw them.

To Northern readers who were unfamiliar with St. Louis, Parton portrayed a "solid," "stable" city of Southern gentlemen. "The wealth, the social influence, the planting interest, and much of the cultivated brain of the city and the State," the writer explained, "were in the fullest sympathy with the Secessionists."[188] "It is so pleasant to a Northern traveller [sic]," he noted, "to reside for a while in the Southern States."[189]

The contrast between St. Louis and Yankee commercial centers fascinated Parton. "Chicago amuses, amazes, bewilders, and exhausts the traveller [sic]," Parton reported.[190] St. Louis "rests and restores him."[191] Nor were St. Louis merchants cut from the same cloth as aggressive Yankee entrepreneurs. Unlike their Chicago counterparts, they "do not know . . . and push and advertise and vaunt as much."[192] Instead, they "take life more easily."[193] St. Louis businessmen, Parton added, remained staunchly independent, "not borrow-[ing] from abroad."[194] This solidity and honor, the self-styled trademarks of local merchants, gave them a certain "charm," like that of the "country gentleman."[195] More than any other cause, Parton concluded, it was Southern culture that distinguished St. Louis residents from Yankee city dwellers. "As the chief city of a State that shared and deliberately chose to share, the curse of slavery, it has much of the languor and carelessness of being served by slaves."[196] The marketplace seemed "tranquil."[197] It "needs a few more Yankees," Parton noted.[198]

Within two decades St. Louis had burgeoned, collapsed, and reemerged. The economic crisis of the mid-1850s, however, permanently reshaped the character of the new city. During the 1840s New York dollars built St. Louis, and a decade later Yankee whims undermined the city's preeminence. This final transformation sparked powerful political and cultural changes during the late 1850s. Helpless to stem the decline, St. Louis boosters and municipal officials recast community ideals and embraced stark anti-Yankee images as the first great commercial center of the Midwest succumbed to the pressures of sectionalism. Between the invasion of Kansas and the assault on Fort Sumter, St. Louis became a midwestern city with a very strong Southern flavor.

Conclusion

Sectionalism remade the urban West. The debate over the future of slavery triggered the fall of St. Louis, the first major commercial center of the trans-Mississippi West. It transformed the principal western cog in the national economy into a declining, inward-looking city served by a shrinking hinterland. Moreover, the sectional crisis spurred the development of Chicago. When Yankee merchants abandoned St. Louis and began to direct their attention to Chicago, the Illinois city mushroomed. Towns and cities within Chicago's hinterland enjoyed new prosperity as well. Thus, Chicago supplanted St. Louis during the late 1850s, becoming the major eastern outlet in the West and the greatest boomtown in the nation.

Yankee merchants forged the growth of western cities in antebellum America. Although geography and natural "zodiacs" influenced urban development, human factors elevated Chicago to greatness, trapped Cairo in its infancy, and triggered the dramatic rise and the relative fall of St. Louis. Young western cities lacked institutions, capital markets, and commercial networks. Migrants supplied these needs, and the city that captured eastern favor flourished and dominated its rivals. Yankee newcomers, bringing venture capital, economic power, and eastern cultural conventions, affected the urban West by choosing to migrate to one city over the next. The force of such decisions became self-perpetuating, and well-established migration patterns brought regional dominance to some cities while crushing the ambitions of other promising towns. The attractions of Cincinnati retarded the growth of Louisville; the preeminence of St. Louis crushed Alton and limited the early development of Chicago; and the subsequent rise of Chicago crippled its former nemesis. As long as St. Louis served as the principal Yankee outpost in the region, cities such as Quincy, St. Charles, and Chicago remained starved for economic sustenance and underdeveloped.

But the sectional crisis recast the relationship between the East and the urban West. Although prominent Northern merchants, such as

175

Lewis Tappan and Amos Lawrence, assumed central roles in the crusade against slavery, most of the businessmen who invested in western cities cared little about politics. Rather, economic considerations governed their investment strategies. These men, however, made financial decisions at a time in which political pressures informed every aspect of life, and sectionalism molded the perceptions that determined economic strategies. In large part, St. Louis businesses languished not because trade, profits, or bond values declined but because New York merchants believed that the commercial foundations of the marketplace would soon crumble. Their subsequent decisions made such forecasts self-fulfilling. Political forces, therefore, reshaped perceptions in a way that altered economic activities, accelerating the decline of St. Louis and the rise of Chicago. Railroad construction, investment and migration patterns, and boosterism were effects, not causes, of this process.

The debate over the future of slavery also imposed a sectional perspective on urban development. Capitalists in New York and merchants in Memphis attempted to control the character of St. Louis by demanding that the city choose a Northern or a Southern orientation. They measured the commercial potential of trading partners in terms of profits, stability, and an environment amenable to sectional development. St. Louis succumbed because the border turmoil made Missouri investments appear risky and because Yankee entrepreneurs feared that the city had chosen a political path that was antithetical to Northern commercial interests. As St. Louis seemed to become Southern, Northern capital flowed out of the city – and often into Chicago, reinforcing shifts in regional growth. Moreover, when regional pressures and Wall Street investment strategies compelled St. Louis to stake its future with the lower Mississippi valley, local boosters forged a new vision of urban development, rejecting the Northern model in favor of a perspective consonant with the region and sympathetic to the South.

In sum, sectionalism profoundly transformed the development of the urban West. The fall of St. Louis and rise of Chicago represented the most dramatic effects of a process that altered the nature of western urbanization. Political forces rechanneled the flow of migrants to the region, remolding the cultural and institutional ties between the Northeast and the West. Similarly, the debate over the extension of slavery upset investment patterns and capital flows. This not only shaped the growth of the leading cities of the West but also influenced the economic character of the nation. Northeastern interest in financing a rail network around the new Yankee colony was one effect of this shift. The rapid decline of the steamboat probably reflected this change as well. The surge in the pace of railroad construction coincided with the rise of Chicago. Capital that otherwise would have been invested in enterprises that served St. Louis, including railroads but also steamboats, flowed into Chicago ventures. As a consequence, rail construction received more of the available funds, railroad ties cemented Chicago's relationship with New York and Boston, towns in the upper Mississippi valley boomed, and the locus of economic activity in the Midwest shifted to the North. Although the slavery controversy initiated a process that centered in St. Louis, the effects of this process extended far beyond the Missouri city. In short, the sectional crisis redefined the relationship between Yankee merchants and their St. Louis colony. As a result, it remade the urban West.

Notes

Chapter 1: Introduction

1 See *De Bow's Review* 24 (March 1858): 255. For an interesting analysis of the role of regional nodes in an urban system, see David Ralph Meyer, "A Dynamic Model of the Integration of Frontier Urban Places into the United States System of Cities," *Economic Geography* 56 (April 1980): 132–36. For a study of urban growth and farming, see Michael Conzen, *Frontier Farming in an Urban Shadow* (Madison, Wis., 1971).

2 The historical literature on urban failure is scant; historians have demonstrated more interest in nineteenth-century urban growth than in urban decline. For a few very good examples, see Don Harrison Doyle, *The Social Order of a Frontier Community* (Urbana, Ill., 1978); id., *New Men, New Cities, New South* (Chapel Hill, N.C., 1990); Herman R. Lantz, *A Community in Search of Itself* (Carbondale, Ill., 1972); Merl E. Reed, *New Orleans and the Railroads* (Baton Rouge, La., 1966). Similarly, scholars have devoted little attention to changes in "structural patterns of interdependencies." See Allan Pred, *City-Systems in Advanced Economies* (New York, 1977), 12–13.

3 Because the book explores the processes that shaped the development of St. Louis, many events and dynamics that influenced local culture receive little attention. For example, St. Louis had a large and vibrant German community during the antebellum period. Although this group influenced the history of the city in many ways, its impact on the rise and fall of St. Louis was indirect more often than it was direct. For analyses of St. Louis's German community, see George Helmuth Kellner, "The German Element on the Urban Frontier: St. Louis, 1830–1860" (Ph.D. dissertation, University of Missouri–Columbia, 1973); Audrey Louise Olson, "St. Louis Germans, 1850–1920: The Nature of an Immigrant Community and Its Relation to the Assimilation Process" (Ph.D. dissertation, University of Kansas, 1970). For an excellent discussion of German immigrants in the urban West, see Kathleen Neils Conzen, *Immigrant Milwaukee*, 1836–1860 (Cambridge, Mass., 1976). Nor does this study deal explicitly with gender or with women in the city. In part, this reflects the imbalance in sex ratios. But more important, it reflects the nature of the issues that form the foundation of the book. Women affected the development of the city in numerous ways. Nonetheless, they did not assume a central role in the flow of capital to the urban West or in the economic connection between St. Louis and New York.

4 See Charles A. Dana, *The Great West* (Boston, 1857), 172; Adolphus M. Hart, *History of the Valley of the Mississippi* (Cincinnati, 1853), 132; W. Williams, *Appleton's Southern and Western Traveller's Guide* (New York, 1849), 44; Patrick Shirreff, *A Tour Through North America* (Edinburgh, 1835), 263 . Also see Glen E. Holt, "The Shaping of St. Louis, 1763–1860"

(Ph.D. dissertation, University of Chicago, 1975), 156; Charles N. Glaab and A. Theodore Brown, *A History of Urban America* (London, 1967), 74.

5 For example, see Truman Marcellus Post, 1833, quoted in T. A. Post, *Truman Marcellus Post, D. D.* (Boston, 1891), 45; Narcissa Whitman to Mother, March 29, 1836, in "Letters Written by Mrs. Whitman From Oregon to Her Relatives in New York," in *Transactions of the Nineteenth Annual Reunion of the Oregon Pioneers Association for 1891* (Portland, Oreg., 1891), 81. For an interesting treatment of gateway cities, see A. F. Burghardt, "A Hypothesis About Gateway Cities," *Annals of the Association of American Geographers* 61 (June 1971): 269. Also, see Meyer, "A Dynamic Model of the Integration of Frontier Urban Places into the United States System of Cities," 132.

6 *Missouri Republican*, July 9, 1845. Also see ibid., September 5, 1848; ibid., September 16, 1843.

7 Ibid., June 22, 1849.

8 *Missouri Democrat*, May 10, 1853; ibid., February 8, 1854; *Missouri Republican*, September 6, 1844.

9 Captain Frederick Marryat, *Diary in America*, ed. Jules Zanger (1839; reprint, Bloomington, Ind., 1960), 254.

10 Charles Dickens, *American Notes for General Circulation* (New York, 1842), 90.

11 *Annual Review: The History of St. Louis, Commercial Statistics, Improvements of the Year and Account of Leading Manufactures, etc., From the Missouri Republican, January 10, 1854* (St. Louis, 1854), 11.

12 Olson, "St. Louis Germans, 1850–1920," 13. For a detailed treatment of this problem, see Timothy R. Mahoney, *River Towns in the Great West* (New York, 1990), 73–76.

13 James Neal Primm, *Lion of the Valley* (Boulder, Colo., 1981), 174.

14 *Missouri Republican*, May 26, 1849.

15 James Neal Primm, *Economic Policy in the Development of a Western State* (Cambridge, Mass., 1954), chaps. 2–3. Also see Simon F. Kropp, "The Struggle for Limited Liability and General Incorporation Laws in Missouri to 1849" (M.A. thesis, University of Missouri–Columbia, 1939).

16 Ibid. Also see *Missouri Republican*, June 28, 1836; ibid., April 12, 1841; Allan Pred, *Urban Growth and City-Systems in the United States, 1840–1860* (Cambridge, Mass., 1980), 220. For other regions and cities, see Harry N. Scheiber, "Urban Rivalry and Internal Improvements in the Old Northwest, 1820–1860," in Alexander B. Callow, Jr., ed., *American Urban History: An Interpretive Reader with Commentaries*, 2d ed. (New York, 1973): 135–46; id., *Ohio Canal Era* (Athens, Ohio, 1969); Carl Abbott, *Boosters and Businessmen* (Westport, 1981); David M. Gold, "Public Aid to Private Enterprise Under the Ohio Constitution," *University of Toledo Law Review* 16 (Winter 1985): 405–505; Hendrik Hartog, *Public Property and Private Power* (Ithaca, N.Y., 1983); Kermit L. Hall, *The Magic Mirror* (New York, 1989), chaps. 5–6; Morton J. Horwitz, *The Transformation of American Law, 1780–1860* (Cambridge, Mass., 1977); Ronald E. Seavoy, *The Origins of the American Business Corporation, 1784–1855* (Westport, Conn., 1982), 258; Thomas C. Cochran, *Frontiers of Change* (New York, 1981).

17 See John W. Million, *State Aid to Railways in Missouri* (Chicago, 1896); Paul W. Gates, "The Railroads of Missouri, 1850–1870," *Missouri Historical Review* 26 (January 1932): 126–41. Primm, *Economic Policy*, chap. 5; J. Christopher Schnell, "Chicago Versus St. Louis," *Missouri Historical Review* 71 (April 1977): 252–58.

18 Primm, *Lion of the Valley*, 219–20.

19 Primm, *Economic Policy*, chaps. 1, 3.

20 John A. Kasson, quoted in Edward Younger, *John A. Kasson* (Iowa City, Iowa, 1955), 59.

21 Allan R. Pred, "American Metropolitan Growth: 1860–1914, Industrialization, Initial Advantage," in *The Spatial Dynamics of U.S. Urban-Industrial Growth, 1800–1914* (Cambridge, Mass., 1967), 12–85; id., "The American Mercantile City: 1800–1840: Manufacturing, Growth, and Structure," in *The Spatial Dynamics of U.S. Urban-Industrial Growth, 1800–1914*, 143–215; id., *City-Systems in Advanced Economies*, 12; Diane Lindstrom and John Sharpless, "Urban Growth and Economic Structure in Antebellum America," in Paul Uselding, ed., *Research in Economic History* 3 (1978): 211; Meyer, "A Dynamic Model of the Integration of Frontier Urban Places into the United States System of Cities," 136.

22 During the 1850s the economy of St. Louis declined, and the city never regained its regional or national prominence. Nonetheless, it remained a major urban center. St. Louis's collapse was relative rather than absolute.

23 For interesting treatments of initial advantage and regional dominance, see Meyer, "A Dynamic Model of the Integration of Frontier Urban Places into the United States System of Cities," 132–36; Pred, *City-Systems in Advanced Economies*, 12.

24 For a few notable exceptions, see Timothy R. Mahoney, *River Towns in the Great West*; id., "Urban History in a Regional Context: River Towns on the Upper Mississippi, 1840–1860," *Journal of American History* 72 (September 1985): 318–39; id., "River Towns in the Great West, 1835–1860" (Ph.D. dissertation, University of Chicago, 1982); Roberta Balstad Miller, *City and Hinterland* (Westport, Conn., 1979); Thomas M. Doerflinger, *A Vigorous Spirit of Enterprise* (Chapel Hill, N.C., l986).

25 For example, William Gilpin, "The Cities of Missouri," *The Western Journal and Civilian* 11 (October 1853): 39–40; Charles N. Glaab, "Visions of Metropolis: William Gilpin and Theories of City Growth in the American West," *Wisconsin Magazine of History* 45 (Autumn 1961): 21–31; Thomas L. Karnes, *William Gilpin, Western Nationalist* (Austin, 1970).

26 See Wyatt Winton Belcher, *The Economic Rivalry Between St. Louis and Chicago, 1850–1880* (New York, 1947); Abbott, *Boosters and Businessmen*, 111.

27 Robert Sears, *A Pictorial Description of the United States* (New York, 1852), 572.

28 See William Gilpin, *The Central Gold Region* (Philadelphia, 1860); id., "The Cities of Missouri," *The Western Journal and Civilian* 11 (October 1853): 39–40; Karnes, *William Gilpin*; Lawrence H. Larson, *The Urban West at the End of the Frontier* (Lawrence, Kans., 1978), 3; Glaab and Brown, *A History*

of Urban America (London, 1967), 78; Charles N. Glaab, *Kansas City and the Railroads* (Madison, Wis., 1962), 24–27.

29 Larson, *The Urban West at the End of the Frontier*, 3, 6; Karnes, *William Gilpin*, 214; Glaab, "Visions of Metropolis."

30 Charles N. Glaab, "Jessup W. Scott and a West of Cities," *Ohio History* 73 (Winter 1964): 5; Larson, *The Urban West at the End of the Frontier*, 6–7; Abbott, *Boosters and Businessmen*, 111.

31 For example, see *De Bow's Review* 17 (October 1854): 395; Humphrey Phelps, *Phelps' Hundred Cities and Large Towns of America* (New York, 1853), 74; Amos Andrew Parker, *A Trip to the West and Texas* (Concord, N.H., 1835), 75.

32 For example, see *New York Journal of Commerce*, September 2, 1856; Mrs. Isabella Bishop, *The Englishwoman in America* (London, 1856), 156, 158; *The Rail-Roads, History and Commerce of Chicago* (Chicago, 1854), 69.

33 For a thoughtful discussion of some of these issues, see Schnell, "Chicago Versus St. Louis," 260. Locational forces and changing currents contributed to this process, though they did not operate in isolation. Also see Bessie Louise Pierce, "Changing Urban Patterns in the Mississippi Valley," *Journal of the Illinois Historical Society* 43 (Spring 1950): 49; id., *A History of Chicago* (New York, 1940), 2:35–76. For an interesting analysis of some of the forces behind changing currents of trade and transportation, see Mahoney, *River Towns in the Great West*, 209–42.

34 Louise Carroll Wade, *Chicago's Pride* (Urbana, Ill., 1987), 13.

35 Pierce, "Changing Urban Patterns in the Mississippi Valley," 49.

36 Frederic Cople Jaher, review of *Chicago 's Pride*, by Louise Carroll Wade, *American Historical Review* 93 (June 1988): 778.

37 Primm, *Lion of the Valley*, 235.

38 William Gilpin, "The Cities of Missouri," *Western Journal and Civilian* 11 (October 1853):. 31–40.

39 Glaab, *Kansas City and the Railroads*, 25–28.

40 For Cairo, see Herman R. Lantz, *A Community in Search of Itself*, 5. Also see Schnell, "Chicago Versus St. Louis."

41 *Annual Review of the Trade and Commerce of St. Louis, for the Year 1848* (St. Louis, 1849), 3; William Gilpin, "The Cities of Missouri," *Western Journal and Civilian* 11 (October 1853): 40; Glaab, *Kansas City and the Railroads*, 25.

42 Lindstrom and Sharpless, "Urban Growth and Economic Structure in Antebellum America," 211.

43 For example, see *Missouri Democrat*, August 1, 1860.

44 For example, see Abbott, *Boosters and Businessmen*, 97; John Lauritz Larson, *Bonds of Enterprise* (Cambridge, Mass., 1984), 114–15; H. Craig Miner, *The St. Louis-San Francisco Transcontinental Railroad* (Lawrence, Kans., 1972), 18; Belcher, *The Economic Rivalry Between St. Louis and Chicago*, 182–94; Lawrence H. Larson, "Chicago's Midwest Rivals," *Chicago History* 5 (Fall 1976): 141.

45 Belcher, *The Economic Rivalry Between St. Louis and Chicago*, 15.

46 Ibid., 193. To be sure, boosters in the respective cities need not have shared an identical vision of the future, though Belcher's analysis caricatures the

process. For well-conceived discussions of local conditions and different booster strategies, see Abbott, *Boosters and Businessmen*, 41, 200; Mahoney, *River Towns in the Great West*, 106.

47 For example, a number of excellent urban history textbooks cite Belcher's interpretation. See Glaab and Brown, *A History of Urban America*, 110; David Ward, *Cities and Immigrants* (New York, 1971), 35; Howard P. Chudacoff and Judith E. Smith, *The Evolution of American Society*, 3d ed. (Englewood Cliffs, N.J., 1988), 45; David R. Goldfield and Blaine A. Brownell, *Urban America*, 2d ed. (Boston, 1990), 100.

48 *Annual Review of the Trade and Commerce of St. Louis, for the Year 1848*, 2.

49 Constance M. Green, *American Cities in the Growth of the Nation* (New York, 1957), 59. Also see Schnell, "Chicago Versus St. Louis," 247.

50 John Hogan, *Thoughts About the City of St. Louis, Her Commerce, Manufactures, Railroads, etc.* (St. Louis, 1854), 7. Also see *A Review of the Commerce of St. Louis, for the Year 1849*, 2; *Missouri Democrat*, November 30, 1854; *Missouri Republican*, December 13, 1854; Primm, *Lion of the Valley*, 234–38.

51 *Missouri Democrat*, October 28, 1854; ibid., November 23, 1854; Primm, *Economic Policy*, 96.

52 Doyle, *The Social Order of a Frontier Community*, 255–59.

53 Ibid. For other studies that consider the impact that local conditions exerted on boosterism, see Doyle, *New Men, New Cities, New South*, 20–21; Doerflinger, *A Vigorous Spirit of Enterprise*, chap. 8; Burton W. Folsom, Jr., *Urban Capitalists* (Baltimore, 1981).

54 Doyle, The Social Order of a Frontier Community, 255–59.

55 For example, see *Missouri Democrat*, May 28, 1857; ibid., October 20, 1856; ibid., December 15, 1858; ibid., April 7, 1850.

56 For example, see Hogan, *Thoughts About the City of St. Louis*. For another critique of the booster interpretation, see Eric H. Monkkonen, *America Becomes Urban* (Berkeley, 1988), 269 n. 15.

57 For works that emphasize the influence of outside forces, see Miller, *City and Hinterland*, 155; Glen E. Holt, "The Birth of Chicago," *Journal of the Illinois Historical Society* 76 (Summer 1983): 94. For an analysis of regional forces, see Mahoney, *River Towns in the Great West*, 209–72.

58 John D. Haeger, "Capital Mobilization and the Urban Center," *Mid-America* 60 (April–July 1978): 92–93; id., "Eastern Money and the Urban Frontier," *Journal of the Illinois Historical Society* 64 (Autumn 1971): 284. Also see id., "The Abandoned Townsite on the Midwestern Frontier," *Journal of the Early Republic* 3 (Summer 1983): 165–83 ; id., *The Investment Frontier* (Albany, N.Y., 1981); Stuart M. Blumin, "When Villages Become Towns," in *The Pursuit of Urban History*, eds. Derek Fraser and Anthony Sutcliffe (London, 1983), 64. For a very different kind of an analysis that makes a similar argument about the relationship between urbanization and external, particularly long-distance, forces, see Paul M. Hohenberg and Lynn Hollen Lees, *The Making of Urban Europe* (Cambridge Mass., 1985). Another interesting analysis can be found in Meyer, "A Dynamic Model of the Integration of Frontier Urban Places into the United States System of Cities," 136.

59 For example, see Pred, *Urban Growth and City-Systems*, 30.

60 Primm, *Economic Policy*, 29; Cable, *The Bank of the State of Missouri*, 146–48.

61 For Philadelphia, see Diane Lindstrom, *Economic Development in the Philadelphia Region, 1810–1850* (New York, 1978).

62 Haeger, "Capital Mobilization and the Urban Center," 88–93; id., "Eastern Money and the Urban Frontier," 267–84. Also see Peter R. Decker *Fortunes and Failure* (Cambridge, Mass. 1978).

63 For example, see Haeger, "Capital Mobilization and the Urban Center," 88; id., "Eastern Money and the Urban Frontier," 267–84; id., "The Abandoned Townsite on the Midwestern Frontier," 165–83; Pred, *Urban Growth and City-Systems*, 220.

64 See Henry Nash Smith, *Virgin Land* (Cambridge, Mass., 1950); Lewis O. Saum, *The Popular Mood of Pre-Civil War America* (Westport, Conn., 1980), chap. 8; Ray Allen Billington, *Land of Savagery, Land of Promise* (New York, 1981). For a more general discussion of the middle class and its influence on urban society, see Stuart M. Blumin, *The Emergence of the Middle Class* (New York, 1989).

65 For example, see John Mason Peck, *A New Guide for Emigrants to the West* (Boston, 1837), 324; *Home Missionary* 5 (July 1832): 80; ibid. 15 (September 1842): 104–5; ibid. 19 (January 1847): 218; Lyman Beecher, *A Plea for the West* (Cincinnati, 1835).

66 For example, see Richard Slotkin, *Regeneration Through Violence* (Middletown, Conn., 1973).

67 Rush Welter, "The Frontier West as Image of American Society," *Mississippi Valley Historical Review* 46 (March 1960): 593–614.

68 Welter, "The Frontier West as Image of American Society," 612.

69 For example, see William Greenleaf Eliot, "Sermon to the Boston Church," William Greenleaf Eliot Papers, Missouri Historical Society, St. Louis, Missouri.

70 Welter, "The Frontier West as Image of American Society," 613.

71 Ministers were the most vocal and self-conscious proponents of this view. For example, see Truman Marcellus Post, "The New Settlements of the West," May, 1854, quoted in T. A. Post, *Truman Marcellus Post, D. D.* (Boston, 1891), 216. Many scholars have noted that migrants suspend their value systems in new destinations. See Michael J. Piore, *Birds of Passage* (New York, 1979), 81. There is some evidence of such behavior in antebellum St. Louis. For example, see J. Davis to Lewis Bristol, July 22, 1838, St. Louis History Collection, Missouri Historical Society, St. Louis, Missouri. Most eastern migrants, however, remained intent on returning to the East. See the correspondence of Elizabeth Sargent, St. Louis History Collection, Missouri Historical Society, St. Louis, Missouri.

72 St. Louis observers used the term "Yankee" to describe individuals from both New York and New England. Thus, I have relied on this definition throughout the text.

73 See Belcher, *The Economic Rivalry Between St. Louis and Chicago*, chap. 8; Primm, *Lion of the Valley*, chap. 7. For a sample of studies that examine sectionalism and cities, see William H. Pease and Jane H. Pease, *The Web*

of *Progress* (New York, 1985); James Michael Russell, *Atlanta, 1847–1890* (Baton Rouge, 1988); Gary Lawson Browne, *Baltimore in the Nation, 1789–1861* (Chapel Hill, N.C., 1980); D. Clayton James, *Antebellum Natchez* (Baton Rouge, La, 1968); David R. Goldfield, *Cotton Fields and Skyscrapers* (Baton Rouge, La., 1982); id., *Urban Growth in the Age of Sectionalism* (Baton Rouge, La., 1977); Reed, *New Orleans and the Railroads;* Doyle, *New Men, New Cities, New South.*

74 For example, see *Home Missionary* 15 (June 1842): 35; Reverend George Lewis, *Impressions of America and American Churches* (Edinburgh, 1848), 253.

75 For example, see *Memphis Bulletin,* quoted in *Missouri Republican,* June 1, 1859; R. A. Chapman to the New England Emigrant Aid Company, October 20, 1855, New England Emigrant Aid Company Correspondence, 1854–1858, New England Emigrant Aid Company Papers, microfilm, reel l; Amos A. Lawrence to Samuel C. Davis, July 17, 1854, Letter Book of Amos A. Lawrence, p. 11, New England Emigrant Aid Company Papers, microfilm, reel 4; Eli Thayer, *A History of the Kansas Crusade* (1889; reprint, Freeport, N.Y., 1971), 208.

76 With regard to St. Louis and to Missouri, see Thayer, *A History of the Kansas Crusade; New York Daily Tribune,* August 11, 1856; *Missouri Democrat,* April 7, 1857; *Anzeiger des Westens,* February 4, 1861, quoted in Steven Rowan ed. and trans. and James Neal Primm, ed., *Germans for a Free Missouri* (Columbia, Mo., 1983), 164; *Chicago Press and Tribune,* April 6, 1859.

77 See Eric Foner, *Free Soil, Free Labor, Free Men* (New York, 1970). I should note that I have capitalized words such as Northern and Southern when they refer to regional culture, politics, and economics in the context of the sectional crisis.

78 See *New York Evening Post,* February 14, 1856.

79 For example, see *Memphis Bulletin,* quoted in *Missouri Republican,* June 1, 1859.

Chapter 2: *"These Yankee notions will not suit Missouri'*

1 See John D. Haeger, "Capital Mobilization and the Urban Center," *Mid-America* 60 (April–July 1978): 88; Glen E. Holt, "The Birth of Chicago," *Journal of the Illinois Historical Society* 76 (Summer 1983): 94. For a discussion of regional forces and urban growth, see Timothy R. Mahoney, *River Towns in the Great West* (New York, 1990), 209–42.

2 See Missouri Vols. 36–38, R. G. Dun and Company Collection, Baker Library, Harvard University Graduate School of Business Administration, Boston, Massachusetts; *Missouri Democrat,* October 20, 1858; *Missouri Republican,* August 16, 1857.

3 For example, see *Annual Review of the Trade and Commerce of St. Louis for the Year 1848* (St. Louis, 1849), 10; Reverend T. M. Cunningham, *Address Before the St. Louis Young Men's Christian Association* (St. Louis, 1853), 5;

Truman Marcellus Post, "The New Settlement of the West," May, 1854, quoted in T. A. Post, *Truman Marcellus Post, D.D.* (Boston, 1891), 216; *Missouri Democrat*, August 15, 1859.

4 Perry McCandless, *A History of Missouri, 1820–1860* (Columbia, Mo., 1972), 135; Russel L. Gerlach, *Settlement Patterns in Missouri* (Columbia, Mo., 1980), 19; John Vollmer Mering, *The Whig Party in Missouri* (Columbia, Mo., 1967); *Sixth Census or Enumeration of the Inhabitants of the United States, As Corrected At the Department of State, in 1840* (Washington, D. C., 1841), 417.

5 Gerlach, *Settlement Patterns in Missouri*, 22; William O. Lynch, "The Influence of Population Movements in Missouri Before 1861," *Missouri Historical Review* 16 (July 1922): 512–15. Also see Michael J. O'Brien, ed., *Grassland, Forest, and Historical Settlement* (Lincoln, Nebr., 1984).

6 Richard C. Wade, *The Urban Frontier* (Cambridge, Mass., 1959), 1.

7 James Neal Primm, *Lion of the Valley, St. Louis, Missouri* (Boulder, Colo., 1981), 9.

8 Ibid.

9 Wade, *The Urban Frontier*, 3.

10 Henry Marie Brackenridge, *Views of Louisiana* (Pittsburgh, 1814), 120–23. Also see Glen E. Holt, "The Shaping of St. Louis, 1763–1860" (Ph.D. dissertation, University of Chicago, 1975), 100.

11 Hiram Martin Chittenden, *The American Fur Trade of the Far West* (New York, 1935), 1:106.

12 Ibid., 131–32; Richard E. Oglesby, *Manual Lisa and the Opening of the Missouri Fur Trade* (Norman, Okla., 1963), 153.

13 Chittenden, *The American Fur Trade of the Far West*, 1:106.

14 J. Thomas Scharf, *The History of St. Louis City and County* (Philadelphia, 1883), 1:287.

15 Chittenden, *The American Fur Trade of the Far West*, 1:58.

16 Holt, "The Shaping of St. Louis," 133.

17 Brackenridge, *Views of Louisiana*, 122. Also see Holt, "The Shaping of St. Louis," 69.

18 Brackenridge, *Views of Louisiana*, 121–23.

19 Robert V. Hine, *The American West* (Boston, 1973), 44.

20 Primm, *Lion of the Valley*, 129; Holt, "The Shaping of St. Louis," 107.

21 Wade, *The Urban Frontier*, 61.

22 Primm, *Lion of the Valley*, 133; Glen E. Holt, "St. Louis's Transition Decade, 1819–1830," *Missouri Historical Review* 76 (July 1982): 370.

23 Chittenden, *The American Fur Trade of the Far West*, 1:57–58.

24 Kenneth Porter, *John Jacob Astor* (Cambridge, Mass., 1931), 2:693.

25 Chittenden, *The American Fur Trade of the Far West*, 1:109.

26 Ibid.

27 Holt, "The Shaping of St. Louis," 66; Primm, *Lion of the Valley*, 108.

28 Ronald L. F. Davis, "Community and Conflict in Power," *Western Historical Quarterly* 10 (July 1979): 340.

29 Holt, "The Shaping of St. Louis," 75; Wade, *The Urban Frontier*, 63.

30 Holt, "St. Louis's Transition Decade," 366; id., "The Shaping of St.

Louis," 75; Primm, *Lion of the Valley*, 107; Timothy Flint, *A Condensed Geography and History of the Western States or the Mississippi* (Cincinnati, 1828), 2:110.

31 Gerlach, *Settlement Patterns in Missouri*, 18.

32 Ibid., 13; William Greenleaf Eliot, "Gazetteer of the State of Missouri," *North American Review* 48 (April 1839): 520; James N. Primm, *Economic Policy in the Development of a Western State* (Cambridge, Mass., 1954), 132; Holt, "The Shaping of St. Louis," 61; Hattie M. Anderson, "Missouri, 1804–1828," *Missouri Historical Review* 31 (January 1937): 166.

33 Diarist, quoted in Scharf, *St. Louis*, 1:298. Also see Eliot, "Gazetteer of the State of Missouri," 520.

34 Holt, "The Shaping of St. Louis," 77. Also see Flint, *A Condensed Geography*, 2:110.

35 John Mason Peck, *Forty Years of Pioneer Life*, ed. Rufus Babcock (1864; reprint, Carbondale, Ill., 1965), 146.

36 Lewis C. Beck, "A Gazetteer of the States of Illinois and Missouri, " 1823, reprinted in *The Early Histories of St. Louis*, ed. John F. McDermott (St. Louis, 1952), 80; Holt, "St. Louis's Transition Decade," 368; Davis, "Community and Conflict in Power," 339.

37 Joseph P. Nicollet, "Sketch of Early St. Louis," 1832, reprinted in *The Early Histories of St. Louis*, 160; Beck, "A Gazetteer of the States of Illinois and Missouri," 80. Also see Peck, *Forty Years of Pioneer Life*, 87.

38 William Nisbet Chambers, *Old Bullion Benton* (Boston, 1956), 61; Scharf, *St. Louis*, 1:567.

39 Holt, "The Shaping of St. Louis," 96; Scharf, *St. Louis*, 2:1096–97; Davis, "Community and Conflict in Power," 339.

40 Peck, *Forty Years of Pioneer Life*, 78; Holt, "The Shaping of St. Louis," 78; John Ray Cable, *The Bank of the State of Missouri* (New York, 1923), 18–19.

41 Holt, "The Shaping of St. Louis," 96. Also see Maximilian Ivan Reichard, "The Origins of Urban Police" (Ph.D. dissertation, Washington University, 1975), chap. 7.

42 Brackenridge, *Views of Louisiana*, 120.

43 Davis, "Community and Conflict in Power," 341.

44 Ibid.; Holt, "St. Louis's Transition Decade," 380.

45 See Davis, "Community and Conflict in Power"; Lewis E. Atherton, *The Pioneer Merchant in Mid-America* (New York, 1939), 89; Mahoney, *River Towns in the Great West*, 162–63.

46 See Davis, "Community and Conflict in Power," 345–55; Wade, *The Urban Frontier*, 108.

47 Wade, *The Urban Frontier*, 108; Cable, *The Bank of the State of Missouri*, 50–51; Scharf, *St. Louis*, 2:1390.

48 See William G. Shade, *Banks or No Banks* (Detroit, 1972); Wade, *The Urban Frontier*, chap. 2; George R. Taylor, *The Transportation Revolution* (New York, 1951), chap. 15; Peter Temin, *The Jacksonian Economy* (New York, 1969).

49 Cable, *The Bank of the State of Missouri*, 23; Primm, *Lion of the Valley*, 109.

50 Primm, *Lion of the Valley*, 108–9; Cable, *Bank of the State of Missouri*, 53.

51 Cable, *The Bank of the State of Missouri*, 50–51; Primm, *Lion of the Valley*, 109.
52 Flint, *A Condensed Geography*, 2:110; Holt, "The Shaping of St. Louis," 105.
53 Primm, *Economic Policy*, 2; id., *Lion of the Valley*, 110; Holt, "St. Louis's Transition Decade," 368; Cable, *Bank of the State of Missouri*, 56. For a discussion of the mismanagement issue, see Cable, *Bank of the State of Missouri*, 68–69.
54 Flint, *A Condensed Geography*, 2:110.
55 Holt, "The Shaping of St. Louis," 104; John O'Fallon, quoted in Wade, *The Urban Frontier*, 173; Flint, *A Condensed Geography*, 2:112; Eliot, "Gazetteer of the State of Missouri," 521.
56 Justus Post, quoted in William E. Foley, "Justus Post: Portrait of a Frontier Land Speculator," *Bulletin of the Missouri Historical Society* 36 (October 1979): 25.
57 Flint, *A Condensed Geography*, 2:111–12; Holt, "The Shaping of St. Louis," 104, 129.
58 Justus Post, 1820, quoted in Foley, "Justus Post," 25.
59 Ibid.
60 *Niles Weekly Register* 43 (September 15, 1832): 38.
61 For example, see *Missouri Intelligencer*, July 31, 1821; R. W. Wells, "A Review of the New Constitution of Missouri," in *Journal of the Convention of the State of Missouri* (Jefferson City, Mo., 1845), 7. For a more general discussion of this issue, see J. Mills Thornton III, *Politics and Power in a Slave Society* (Baton Rouge, La., 1978); Larry Schweikart, *Banking in the American South from the Age of Jackson to Reconstruction* (Baton Rouge, La., 1987).
62 See Holt, "St. Louis's Transition Decade."
63 For example, see *Missouri Intelligencer*, July 31, 1821; *Missouri Gazette*, December 6, 1820; Primm, *Economic Policy*, 7–8.
64 Cable, *The Bank of the State of Missouri*, 72, 148. Also see Thornton, *Politics and Power in a Slave Society*, 57.
65 *Niles Weekly Register*, quoted in Cable, *The Bank of the State of Missouri*, 68.
66 *Missouri Gazette*, December 6, 1820.
67 Mering, *The Whig Party in Missouri*, 72
68 Primm, *Economic Policy*, 18.
69 For other areas, see Harry N. Scheiber, "Urban Rivalry and Internal Improvements in the Old Northwest, 1820–1860," in Alexander B. Callow, Jr., ed., *American Urban History: An Interpretive Reader with Commentaries*, 2d ed. (New York, 1973): 135–146; id., *Ohio Canal Era* (Athens, Ohio, 1969); Kermit L. Hall, *The Magic Mirror* (New York, 1989), chaps. 5–6; Morton J. Horwitz, *The Transformation of American Law, 1780–1860* (Cambridge, Mass., 1977); Ronald E. Seavoy, *The Origins of the American Business Corporation, 1784–1855* (Westport, Conn., 1982), 258; Thomas C. Cochran, *Frontiers of Change* (New York, 1981); David M. Gold, "Public Aid to Private Enterprise under the Ohio Constitution," *University of Toledo Law Review* 16 (Winter 1985): 405–505; Hendrik Hartog, *Public*

Property and Private Power (Ithaca, N.Y., 1983); Atherton, *The Pioneer Merchant*, 84.

70   Primm, *Economic Policy*, 34.
71   Richard P. McCormick, *The Second American Party System* (Chapel Hill, N. C., 1966), 304; McCandless, *A History of Missouri*, 9.
72   Harry S. Gleick, "Banking in Early Missouri, " *Missouri Historical Review* 61 (July 1967): 439.
73   Cable, *The Bank of the State of Missouri*, 37.
74   *Missouri Intelligencer*, July 31, 1821.
75   Ibid.
76   Primm, *Lion of the Valley*, 122.
77   Ibid.; Flint, *A Condensed Geography*, 2:111.
78   Primm, *Economic Policy*, 13.
79   Ibid. Also see Simon F. Kropp, "The Struggle for Limited Liability and General Incorporation Laws in Missouri to 1849" (M.A. thesis, University of Missouri–Columbia, 1939).
80   *Missouri Republican*, May 7, 1836. Also see Kropp, "The Struggle for Limited Liability";Dorothy B. Dorsey, "The Panic and Depression of 1837–1843 in Missouri," *Missouri Historical Review* 30 (October 1935): 132–61; Cable, *The Bank of the State of Missouri*; Gleick, "Banking in Early Missouri."
81   Holt, "The Shaping of St. Louis," 107; Primm, *Lion of the Valley*, 128.
82   Brackenridge, *Views of Louisiana*, 94; Chittenden, *The American Fur Trade of the Far West*, 1: chaps. 13–16; Primm, *Lion of the Valley*, 132.
83   Porter, *John Jacob Astor*, 2:693.
84   Ibid.
85   Reichard, "The Origins of Urban Police," 9; Cable, *The Bank of the State of Missouri*, 21; Primm, *Lion of the Valley*, 132.
86   John A. Paxton, "St. Louis Directory and Register, 1821," reprinted in *The Early Histories of St. Louis*, 72; Primm, *Lion of the Valley*, 130–33.
87   Foley, "Justus Post," 25.
88   Holt, "St. Louis's Transition Decade," 372.
89   Holt, "The Shaping of St. Louis," 129.
90   Ibid., 127.
91   Michael Chevalier, *Society, Manners and Politics in the United States* (1835; reprint, Ithaca, N. Y., 1961), 208; Eric F. Haites, James Mak, and Gary Walton, *Western River Transportation* (Baltimore, 1975), chap. 1; Louis C. Hunter, *Steamboats on the Western Rivers* (Cambridge, Mass., 1949), passim.
92   See Wyatt Winton Belcher, *The Economic Rivalry Between St. Louis and Chicago 1850–1880* (New York, 1947), 29–31; Haites, et al., *Western River Transportation*, chap. l; Hunter, *Steamboats on the Western Rivers*, passim; James Hall, *The West* (Cincinnati, 1848), 247.
93   McCandless, *A History of Missouri*, 136.
94   Primm, *Lion of the Valley*, 138.
95   *Missouri Republican*, January 1, 1834; ibid., January 10, 1854; Holt, "The Shaping of St. Louis," 121, 148; Reichard, "The Origins of Urban Police," 11; McCandless, *A History of Missouri*, 137.

96 Primm, *Lion of the Valley*, 138; Holt, "The Shaping of St. Louis," 121.

97 Holt, "The Shaping of St. Louis," 121.

98 Haites, et al., *Western River Transportation*, 4. Also see Hunter, *Steamboats on the Western Rivers*.

99 Hunter, *Steamboats on the Western Rivers*, 420; Thomas E. Parks, "The History of St. Louis, 1827–36" (M.A. thesis, Washington University, 1948), 38.

100 Ibid.

101 Mrs. Marcus, "Letters," in *The First White Women Over the Rockies*, ed. Clifford M. Drury (Glendale, Calif., 1963), 42.

102 Holt, "The Shaping of St. Louis," 118; id., "St. Louis's Transition Decade," 375; Flint, *A Condensed Geography*, 2:113.

103 *Missouri Republican*, April 17, 1835.

104 Ibid., November 7, 1835. Also see ibid., October 4, 1836.

105 *St. Louis Bulletin*, April 11, 1836, quoted in *Niles Weekly Register* 14 (April 30, 1836): 145.

106 Frances Fackler to Mrs. Ann Burruss, February 13, 1834, Missouri History Collection, Missouri Historical Society, St. Louis, Missouri. Also see Adolph Greer, "Letter," December 16, 1833, in "The Followers of Duden," ed. and trans. William G. Bek, *Missouri Historical Review* 14 (January 1920): 218.

107 Cable, *The Bank of the State of Missouri*, 82; Atherton, *The Pioneer Merchant*, 60–61. Also see Timothy R. Mahoney's fine doctoral dissertation. Timothy R. Mahoney, "River Towns in the Great West, 1835–1860" (Ph.D. dissertation, University of Chicago, 1982), 256.

108 *Missouri Intelligencer*, November 6, 1830, quoted in Cable, *The Bank of the State of Missouri*, 106.

109 Local merchants often paid their eastern debts by filling packages with notes and entrusting them to forwarding houses. John Darby recalled that in 1829 a St. Louis dry goods merchant committed suicide after learning that the contents of his package of notes had disappeared in transit. See John F. Darby, *Personal Recollections* (St. Louis, 1880), 175.

110 Dorsey, "The Panic and Depression of 1837–1843 in Missouri," 134; Cable, *The Bank of the State of Missouri*, 87. Cable quotes 1832 figures for the flow of notes to branch banks. Over one-half of the value of all bills of exchange remitted by St. Louis merchants in 1832 were payable in either Pittsburgh, Louisville, or Cincinnati. The combined value of Atlantic coast bills accounted for only 30 percent of the indebtedness of the merchants of St. Louis.

111 Gottfried Duden, *Report on a Journey to the Western States of North America*, ed. James Goodrich, trans. George Kellner, Elsa Nagel, Adolf E. Schroeder, and W. M. Senner (1829; reprint, Columbia, Mo., 1980), 182.

112 See Dorsey, "The Panic and Depression of 1837–1843 in Missouri," 134; Cable, *The Bank of the State of Missouri*, 87.

113 Holt, "The Shaping of St. Louis," 119–20; id., "St. Louis's Transition Decade," 376.

114 See Holt, "St. Louis's Transition Decade," 372; Cable, *The Bank of the State of Missouri*, 19; Wade, *The Urban Frontier*, 201; Mahoney, "River Towns in the Great West, 1835–1860," 152.

115 Holt, "St. Louis's Transition Decade," 366, 379.

116 *Niles Weekly Register* 39 (October 30, 1830): 157; *De Bow's Review* 1 (January 1846): 149.

117 Maximilian Ivan Reichard, "Urban Politics in Jacksonian St. Louis," *Missouri Historical Review* 70 (April 1976): 270–71; Davis, "Community and Conflict in Power," 342.

118 Davis, "Community and Conflict in Power," 350–52.

119 For example, see Holt, "The Shaping of St. Louis," 140–44; Logan U. Reavis, *St. Louis* (St. Louis, 1875), 44–46. In addition to municipal institutions, the St. Louis Theatre, the Central Fire Company, the *Missouri Republican*, the St. Louis Hotel, the St. Louis Gas Light Company, and the Missouri Insurance Company were founded during the 1830s. Moreover, during this decade the city began to restrict the presence of livestock within the corporate limits. See St. Louis City Council: Board of Delegates, July 29, 1839, manuscript, 102, Missouri Historical Society, St. Louis, Missouri.

120 See Charles H. Cornwell, *St. Louis Mayors* (St. Louis, 1965), 1–2.

121 Ibid.; Wade, *The Urban Frontier*, 320; Scharf, *St. Louis*, 1:654.

122 See Scharf, *St. Louis*, 1:654 ; Primm, *Lion of the Valley*, 124–25; Wade, *The Urban Frontier*, 270, 279, 320.

123 Ibid.; Minutes, June 12, 1829, St. Louis Board of Alderman Minutes, 1827–1830, 372, typescript, State Historical Society of Missouri, Columbia, Missouri.

124 Primm, *Lion of the Valley*, 125. For a brief discussion of Philadelphia's role in the early economic development of the region, see David Ralph Meyer, "A Dynamic Model of the Integration of Frontier Urban Places into the United States System of Cities," *Economic Geography* 56 (April 1980): 133.

125 Reichard, "The Origins of Urban Police," 165.

126 St. Louis City Council Minutes, June 26, 1828, quoted in Wade, *The Urban Frontier*, 316. Also see Reichard, "The Origins of Urban Police," 165.

127 Minutes, June 12, 1829, St. Louis Board of Alderman Minutes, 1827–1830, 372, typescript, State Historical Society of Missouri, Columbia, Missouri.

128 Cornwell, *St. Louis Mayors*, 2.

129 Primm, *Lion of the Valley*, 123.

130 *Niles National Register* 7 (November 23, 1839): 207; Primm, *Economic Policy*, 33; id., *Lion of the Valley*, 114.

131 Holt, "The Shaping of St. Louis," 170; Reavis, *St. Louis*, 44–46.

132 Joseph Charles Latrobe, *The Rambler in North America* (London, 1835), 235.

133 G[eorge]. W[illiam]. Featherstonhaugh, *Excursion Through the Slave States* (New York, 1844), 63–64. Also see Edmund Berkeley and Dorothy

Smith Berkeley, *George William Featherstonhaugh* (Tuscaloosa, Ala., 1988).
134 Mering, *The Whig Party in Missouri*, 45.
135 Archy Kasson to Sarah and John Townsend, February 17, 1831, Archy Kasson Papers, Joint Collection, University of Missouri Western Historical Manuscript Collection–Columbia and State Historical Society of Missouri Manuscripts, Columbia, Missouri; Anderson, "Missouri, 1804–1828," 174; McCandless, *A History of Missouri*, 37; Gerlach *Settlement Patterns in Missouri*, 20–22; Robert William Duffner, "Slavery in Missouri River Counties, 1820–1865" (Ph.D. dissertation, University of Missouri–Columbia, 1974), 5; Reminiscences of Mrs. Adele B. Gratiot, typescript, 4, Gratiot Papers, Missouri Historical Society, St. Louis, Missouri; John Mason Peck, *A New Guide for Emigrants to the West* (Boston, 1837), 324.
136 Gerlach, *Settlement Patterns in Missouri*, 22.
137 Ibid., 19, 22.
138 Ibid., 19–20.
139 James Shortridge, "The Expansion of the Settlement Frontier in Missouri," *Missouri Historical Review* 75 (October 1980): 70.
140 *Niles Weekly Register* 43 (September 15, 1832): 38.
141 *Sixth Census*, 417; Harrison A. Trexler, *Slavery in Missouri, 1804–1865* (Baltimore, 1914), 225–26.
142 McCandless, *A History of Missouri*, 135.
143 *Sixth Census*, 417; Mering, *The Whig Party in Missouri*, 63.
144 *Sixth Census*, 310–12, 417. Also see Allan Pred, *Urban Growth and the Circulation of Information* (Cambridge, Mass., 1973), 99.
145 *Sixth Census*, 310–21, 412–13, 418.
146 McCandless, *A History of Missouri*, 90–91.
147 Ibid.
148 McCormick, *The Second American Party System*, 309.
149 Ibid., 308; *Missouri Argus*, December 2, 1837; Mering, *The Whig Party in Missouri*, 1, 44–45.
150 Mering, *The Whig Party in Missouri*, 60.
151 Ibid., 54; James Roger Sharp, *The Jacksonians Versus the Banks* (New York, 1970), 325.
152 McCormick, *The Second American Party System*, 309.
153 Kenneth M. Stampp, *The Peculiar Institution* (New York, 1956), 30.
154 *Sixth Census*, 416–17; *Niles Weekly Register* 43 (September 15, 1832): 38; Trexler, *Slavery in Missouri*, 225–26.
155 See McCandless, *A History of Missouri*, 37; Gerlach, *Settlement Patterns in Missouri*, chap. 3. Also see Thornton, *Politics and Power in a Slave Society*; Schweikart, *Banking in the American South*.
156 Gerlach, *Settlement Patterns in Missouri*, 19–22.
157 Primm, *Economic Policy*, 32. Also see Kropp, "The Struggle for Limited Liability"; Thornton, *Politics and Power in a Slave Society*, 52, 54; Shade, *Banks or No Banks*, 144, 173.
158 For example, see *Missouri Argus*, May 20, 1836.

159 *Missouri Republican,* December 10, 1833; Primm, *Economic Policy,* 20.

160 *Missouri Republican,* December 10, 1833.

161 *Missouri Argus,* June 17, 1836; ibid., August 26, 1836.

162 Ibid., August 26, 1836; ibid., May 6, 1836.

163 Primm, *Economic Policy,* 25; Cable, *The Bank of the State of Missouri,* 125; *Missouri Argus,* June 17, 1836; ibid., August 26, 1836; Governor Lilburn W. Boggs, "First Biennial Message," November 22, 1836, in *The Messages and Proclamations of the Governors of the State of Missouri,* eds. Buel Leopard and Floyd C. Shoemaker (Columbia, Mo., 1922), 1:313.

164 Primm, *Economic Policy,* 25.

165 Chambers, *Old Bullion Benton,* 61; Primm, *Lion of the Valley,* 109, 111.

166 Cable, *The Bank of the State of Missouri,* 55, 72–73.

167 Chambers, *Old Bullion Benton,* chap. 12; Cable, *The Bank of the State of Missouri,* 72; John B. C. Lucas, *The Letters of Hon. J. B. C. Lucas From 1815 to 1832* (St. Louis, 1905), passim; Primm, *Lion of the Valley,* 111.

168 Ibid.

169 *Missouri Argus,* June 17, 1836; Primm, *Economic Policy,* 138.

170 *Missouri Argus,* May 20, 1836; Primm, *Economic Policy,* 143. Also see Sharp, *The Jacksonians Versus the Banks,* 322; Schweikart, *Banking in the American South.*

171 Cable, *The Bank of the State of Missouri,* 145–68. Also see Thornton, *Politics and Power in a Slave Society,* 48; Schweikart, *Banking in the American South;* Sharp, *The Jacksonians Versus the Banks,* 277, 284.

172 *Missouri Argus,* May 20, 1836.

173 Governor Lilburn W. Boggs, "First Biennial Message," November 22, 1836, in *Messages and Proclamations,* 1:313. Alexander McNutt, quoted in Schweikart, *Banking in the American South,* 25.

174 Select Committee, 1833, quoted in Cable, *The Bank of the State of Missouri,* 109.

175 Primm, *Economic Policy,* 28–30; Cable, *The Bank of the State of Missouri,* 153, 159; John Denis Haeger, *The Investment Frontier* (Albany, N.Y., 1981), chap. 7; Shade, *Banks or No Banks,* chaps. 1, 6.

176 Primm, *Economic Policy,* 29; Cable, *The Bank of the State of Missouri,* 145–48, 157; Haeger, *The Investment Frontier,* chap. 7.

177 Primm, *Economic Policy,* 28; Cable, *The Bank of the State of Missouri,* 134–68.

178 Primm, *Economic Policy,* 27, 30; Cable, *The Bank of the State of Missouri,* 134–68.

179 Cable, *The Bank of the State of Missouri,* 95–99.

180 Ibid., 95.

181 *Missouri Republican,* April 7, 1841. Also see Charter Bill, 1837, quoted in Cable, *The Bank of the State of Missouri,* 142–43.

182 Dorsey, "The Panic and Depression of 1837–1843 in Missouri," 137; Cable, *The Bank of the State of Missouri,* 149; Holt, "The Shaping of St. Louis," 270.

183 Thomas Hart Benton, 1837, quoted in Chambers, *Old Bullion Benton,* 223.

184 Dorsey, "The Panic and Depression of 1837–1843 in Missouri," 137; Sharp, *The Jacksonians Versus the Banks*, 197.

185 Governor Thomas Reynolds, "Inaugural Address," November 18, 1840, in *Messages and Proclamations*, 1:457; Dorsey, "The Panic and Depression of 1837–1843 in Missouri," 137; Cable, *The Bank of the State of Missouri*, 149; Chambers, *Old Bullion Benton*, 223.

186 *Missouri Argus*, December 23, 1837.

187 Whittelsey, "Missouri and Its Resources," *Hunt's Merchants' Magazine and Commercial Review* 8 (June 1843): 542. Also see Governor Thomas Reynolds, "Inaugural Address," November 18, 1840, in *Messages and Proclamations*, 1:457; Governor Daniel Dunklin, "First Biennial Address," November 18, 1834, in *Messages and Proclamations*, 1:245. Also see Thornton, *Politics and Power in a Slave Society*, 52.

188 Paul W. Gates, "The Railroads of Missouri, 1850–1870," *Missouri Historical Review* 26 (January 1932): 128; Primm, *Economic Policy*, 91.

189 Alphonso Wetmore, *Gazetteer of the State of Missouri* (St. Louis, 1837), 23.

190 Cable, *The Bank of the State of Missouri*, 149; *Missouri Argus*, November 27, 1840; Dorsey, "The Panic and Depression of 1837–1843 in Missouri," 139, 148. "On October 1, 1840, the State debt [of Missouri] amounted to $404,631.27 – a sum considerably less than the annual interest payment on the State debt of Illinois, which in 1841, was $17,000,000." See Primm, *Economic Policy*, 87. Also see J. Christopher Schnell, "Chicago Versus St. Louis," *Missouri Historical Review* 71 (April 1977): 252.

191 *Missouri Argus*, March 3, 1835.

192 *Missouri Republican*, April 12, 1841.

193 Cable, *The Bank of the State of Missouri*, 179.

194 Ibid.

195 *Missouri Argus*, November 22, 1839; Primm, *Lion of the Valley*, 142; Cable, *The Bank of the State of Missouri*, 179.

196 Primm, *Economic Policy*, 41; Cable, *The Bank of the State of Missouri*, 179; Dorsey, "The Panic and Depression of 1837–1843 in Missouri," 144.

197 For example, see *Missouri Republican*, December 10, 1841; ibid., July 1, 1842.

198 *Missouri Republican*, May 18, 1841; Cable, *The Bank of the State of Missouri*, 186.

199 *Hunt's Merchants' Magazine* 8 (February 1843): 177; *Missouri Republican*, July 1, 1842.

200 *Missouri Republican*, July 1, 1842.

201 *Home Missionary* 13 (August 1840): 77–78.

202 *Missouri Republican*, July 1, 1842.

203 Ibid., February 4, 1842.

204 Ibid., December 10, 1841.

205 Ibid., February 14, 1840.

206 Emil Mallinckrodt to Edward Mallinckrodt, December 28, 1842, Emil Mallinckrodt Papers, translated typescript, Missouri Historical Society, St. Louis, Missouri. Also quoted in Herbert Theodore Mayer, "The

History of St. Louis, 1837–47" (M.A. thesis, Washington University, 1949), 27.

207 *Annual Review of the Commerce of St. Louis for the Year 1853* (St. Louis, 1854), 13.
208 *Missouri Argus*, May 19, 1837.
209 *Missouri Republican*, May 18, 1841.
210 *Niles National Register* 6 (June 1, 1839): 211; *Missouri Republican*, February 6, 1840; Cable, *The Bank of the State of Missouri*, 122.
211 Dorsey, "The Panic and Depression of 1837–1843 in Missouri," 151.
212 Primm, *Lion of the Valley*, 142–43; Cable, *The Bank of the State of Missouri*, 185; Mering, *The Whig Party in Missouri*, 104.
213 *Missouri Republican*, November 2, 1841.
214 Ibid., January 28, 1840.
215 Ibid., May 18, 1841.
216 Cable, *The Bank of the State of Missouri*, 241.
217 *Missouri Republican*, November 2, 1841; ibid., November 9, 1841.
218 Ibid., February 8, 1842.
219 Dorsey, "The Panic and Depression of 1837–1843 in Missouri," 145, 156.
220 Cable, *The Bank of the State of Missouri*, 122; *Niles National Register* 6 (June 1, 1839): 211; *Missouri Republican*, February 6, 1840; *Jefferson Inquirer*, April 14, 1842; ibid., May 19, 1842.
221 *Home Missionary* 13 (August 1840): 77–78.
222 *Columbia Patriot*, August 12, 1842, quoted in Dorsey, "The Panic and Depression of 1837–1843 in Missouri," 156.
223 *Jefferson Inquirer*, September 15, 1842. Also see Dorsey, "The Panic and Depression of 1837–1843 in Missouri," 156.
224 For example, see *Jefferson Inquirer*, December 17, 1840; ibid., December 24, 1840; ibid., April 22, 1841; ibid., September 22, 1842; Governor Thomas Reynolds, "First Biennial Address," November 22, 1842, in *Messages and Proclamations*, 1:465.
225 See Governor Thomas Reynolds, "Inaugural Address, " November 18, 1840, in *Messages and Proclamations*, 1:454; Governor Thomas Reynolds, "First Biennial Address," November 22, 1842, in *Messages and Proclamations*, 1:465; *Jefferson Inquirer*, December 24, 1840; ibid., April 22, 1841; ibid., November 25, 1841; ibid., September 22, 1842; ibid., October 13, 1842.
226 *Jefferson Inquirer*, November 25, 1841. Also see Chambers, *Old Bullion Benton*, 233.
227 Dorsey, "The Panic and Depression of 1837–1843 in Missouri," 153.
228 *Jefferson Inquirer*, July 14, 1842.
229 Ibid., December 3, 1840. Also see Governor Thomas Reynolds, "Inaugural Address," November 18, 1840, in *Messages and Proclamations*, 1:454; C. F. Jackson, "Report of the Committee on Banks and Corporations," Appendix, *Journal of the Convention of the State of Missouri* (Jefferson City, Mo., 1845), 9.
230 *Jefferson Inquirer*, October 13, 1842. Historians of Missouri have been generally uncritical of this view; many have, in fact, concurred. For

example, see Dorsey, "The Panic and Depression of 1837–1843 in Missouri," 153, and Primm, *Economic Policy*, 41. Few modern writers on the subject, however, have examined the tenuous relationship between eastern capitalists and western merchants.

231 R. W. Wells, *A Review of the New Constitution of the State of Missouri* (Jefferson City, Mo., 1846), 6–7. Also see *Jefferson Inquirer*, December 17, 1840; ibid., April 22, 1841; Chambers, *Old Bullion Benton*, 267; Dorsey, "The Panic and Depression of 1837–1843 in Missouri"; Primm, *Economic Policy*, 48.

232 *Jefferson Inquirer*, December 17, 1840. Also see ibid., March 23, 1843; Mering, *The Whig Party in Missouri*, 111–12.

233 Primm, *Economic Policy*, 52.

234 McCandless, *A History of Missouri*, 231. Also see R. W. Wells, *A Review of the New Constitution of the State of Missouri* (Jefferson City, Mo., 1846).

235 Primm, *Economic Policy*, 44–47; *Missouri Republican*, April 12, 1841; ibid., June 20, 1843. Also see Shade, *Banks or No Banks*, 100–1.

236 Primm, *Economic Policy*, 45–49; Kropp, "The Struggle for Limited Liability," 40; McCandless, *A History of Missouri*, 229. Also see George D. Green, *Finance and Economic Development in the Old South* (Stanford, Calif., 1972), 103, 118, 126.

237 Primm, *Economic Policy*, 47; McCandless, *A History of Missouri*, 229.

238 Governor John C. Edwards, "Inaugural Address," November 24, 1844, in *Messages and Proclamations*, 2:49; Jackson, "Report of the Committee on Banks and Corporations," Appendix, *Journal of the Convention of the State of Missouri*, 9; Primm, *Economic Policy*, 40, 48.

239 Primm, *Economic Policy*, 47.

240 *Missouri Republican*, April 12, 1841.

241 *Jefferson Enquirer*, December 17, 1840. The newspaper changed the spelling of its name.

242 McCandless, *A History of Missouri*, 255; Mering, *The Whig Party in Missouri*, 139; Primm, *Economic Policy*, 50–51.

243 *Jefferson Enquirer*, December 17, 1840; Kropp, "The Struggle for Limited Liability," 56. For a different interpretation, see Primm, *Economic Policy*, 138, n. 68. Also see Wells, *A Review of the New Constitution of the State of Missouri*, 9; McCandless, *A History of Missouri*, 255; Mering, *The Whig Party in Missouri*, 140.

244 See Whittelsey, "Missouri and Its Resources," 537; *Missouri Argus*, May 20, 1836; *Missouri Republican*, April 7, 1841. For an interesting discussion of similar issues, see Thomas M. Doerflinger, *A Vigorous Spirit of Enterprise* (Chapel Hill, N.C., 1986).

245 Primm, *Lion of the Valley*, 142–43.

246 *Missouri Republican*, September 30, 1842.

247 Ibid., August 29, 1843.

248 Ibid., February 8, 1842. Also see ibid., September 30, 1842.

249 J. H. James, *Rambles in the United States and Canada During the Year 1845* (London, 1847), 144.

250 See *Hunt's Merchants' Magazine* 6 (June 1842): 566; *Missouri Republican*,

November 6, 1843; Dorsey, "The Panic and Depression of 1837–1843 in Missouri," 159; Hunter, *Steamboats on the Western Rivers*, 49.

251 *Niles National Register* 9 (November 28, 1840): 197.

252 Primm, *Lion of the Valley*, 144; Holt, "The Shaping of St. Louis," 271; Dorsey, "The Panic and Depression of 1837–1843 in Missouri," 146–47.

253 Gustavus Wulfing to Mother, February 14, 1843, *The Letters of Gustavus Wulfing*, ed. Eugene Tavenner and trans. Carl Hirsch (Fitch, Mo., 1941), 196.

254 Gottfried Duden, March, 1827, "Duden's Report," trans. William G. Bek, *Missouri Historical Review* 13 (January 1919): 178; Gottfried Duden, *Report on a Journey to the Western States of North America*, ed. James W. Goodrich, trans. George H. Kellner, Elsa Nagel, Adolf E. Schroader (1829; reprint, Columbia, Mo., 1980), 182.

255 Frederick Graff to Charles Graff, June 29, 1838, St. Louis History Collection, Missouri Historical Society, St. Louis, Missouri; Duden, *Report on a Journey to the Western States of North America*, 255.

256 Stephen A. Douglas, 1838, *The Letters of Stephen A. Douglas*, ed. Robert W. Johannsen (Urbana, Ill., 1961), 60.

257 *Missouri Republican*, February 8 , 1842; ibid., May 18, 1841.

258 *Missouri Republican*, April 12, 1841; Primm, *Economic Policy*, 46.

259 *Missouri Republican*, November 9, 1841.

260 Atherton, *The Pioneer Merchant in Mid-America*, 48, 71; Cable, *The Bank of the State of Missouri*, 170.

261 *Missouri Republican*, April 17, 1835.

262 For an interesting discussion, see Harriet E. Amos, *Cotton City* (University, Ala., 1985); Merl E. Reed, *New Orleans and the Railroads* (Baton Rouge, La., 1966); Schweikart, *Banking in the American South*; Green, *Finance and Economic Development in the Old South*.

263 *Greensborough Patriot*, August, 13, 1839 in "North Carolinians Comment on Missouri,"*Missouri Historical Society: Glimpses of the Past* 1 (August 1934): 72; J[ames]. S[ilk]. Buckingham, *The Eastern and Western States of America* (London, 1842), 3:147; Amos Andrew Parker, *Trip to the West and Texas* (Concord, N.H., 1835), 79.

264 Marbel Camden to Wife, 1834, quoted in John F. McDermott, "Dr. Brown's St. Louis," *Missouri Historical Review* 54 (April 1960): 247.

265 Hall, *The West*, 250, 256.

266 Whittelsey, "Missouri and its Resources," 544.

267 Ibid.

Chapter 3: Savagedom, destiny, and the isothermal zodiac

1 Although the fight for resources was not a zero-sum game, eastern capital was limited, and the town that captured the attention of investors usually dominated its rivals. See John D. Haeger, "The Abandoned Townside on the Midwestern Frontier," *Journal of the Early Republic* 3 (Summer 1983): 165–83; id., "Capital Mobilization and the Urban Center," *Mid-America* 60

(April-July 1978): 75–93; id., "Eastern Money and the Urban Frontier," *Journal of the Illinois Historical Society* 64 (Autumn 1971): 267–84.

2 For example, see Reverend George Lewis, *Impressions of America and the American Churches* (Edinburgh, 1848), 248.

3 J[ames]. S[ilk]. Buckingham, *The Eastern and Western States of America* (London, 1842), 3:208.

4 Harriet Martineau, *Retrospect of Western Travel* (New York, 1838), 2:21.

5 Patrick Shirreff, *A Tour Through North America* (Edinburgh, 1835), 226.

6 *De Bow's Review* 24 (March 1858): 255.

7 "The Diary of Reverend Edward Evans Parrish," in "Crossing the Plains in 1844, " *Transactions of the Sixteenth Annual Reunion of the Oregon Pioneers Association* (Portland, Oreg., 1888), 83.

8 Narcissa Whitman to Mother, March 29, 1836, in "Letters Written by Mrs. Whitman From Oregon to Her Relatives in New York," *Transactions of the Nineteenth Annual Reunion of the Oregon Pioneers Association for 1891* (Portland, Oreg., 1891), 81.

9 G[eorge]. W[illiam]. Featherstonhaugh, *Excursion Through the Slave States* (New York, 1844), 64.

10 Truman Marcellus Post, 1833, quoted in T. A. Post, *Truman Marcellus Post* (Boston, 1891), 45.

11 Ibid., 46.

12 See, for example, C[arter]. A. Goodrich, *The Family Tourist* (Hartford, 1848), 463; John Lewis Peyton, *Over The Alleghenies* (London, 1870), 251.

13 Francis Parkman, *The Oregon Trail* (Boston, 1880), 1.

14 T. A. Richards, ed., *Appleton's Illustrated Hand-book of American Travel, 1857*, quoted in Glen E. Holt, "The Shaping of St. Louis, 1763–1860" (Ph.D. dissertation, University of Chicago, 1975), 343.

15 See *A Young Traveller's Journal of a Tour in North and South America During the Year 1850* (London, 1852), 114; Amos Andrew Parker, *The Trip to the West and Texas* (Concord, N. H., 1835), 79; Louis C. Hunter, *Steamboats on the Western Rivers* (Cambridge, Mass., 1949), 274.

16 See Dr. Albert C. Koch, *Journey Through a Part of the United States of North America in the Years 1844–1846*, trans. Ernst A. Stadler (1846; reprint, Carbondale, Ill., 1972), 111; Charles Olliffe, *American Scenes*, trans. Ernest Falbo and Lawrence A. Wilson (1852; reprint, Painesville, Ohio., 1964), 14; Hunter, *Steamboats on the Western Rivers*, 274.

17 John J. Audubon, *Audubon and His Journals*, ed. Maria R. Audubon (New York, 1897), 1:450.

18 J. H. James reported that the "people are dying fast . . . from the murky atmosphere filled with the overladed miasma of a thousand swamps." See J. H. James, *Rambles in the United States and Canada During the Year 1845* (London, 1847), 149. Dickens also warned that St. Louis was "unhealthy." See Charles Dickens, *American Notes for General Circulation* (1842; reprint, Boston, 1867), 66.

19 Captain Frederick Marryat, *A Diary in America*, ed. Jules Zanger (1839; reprint, Bloomington, Ind., 1960), 233.

20 Charles Fenno Hoffman, *A Winter in the West* (New York, 1835), 2:72.

Also, see C. A. Goodrich, *The Family Tourist*, 463; Peyton, *Over the Alleghenies*, 251.

21 "Diary of Reverend H. H. Spalding," *Transactions of the Twenty-Fifth Annual Reunion of the Oregon Pioneers Association for 1897* (Portland, Oreg., 1897), 108.

22 Frederika Bremer, *The Homes of the New World*, trans. Mary Howitt (New York, 1853), 2:95.

23 For example, see John Darby, *Personal Recollections* (St. Louis, 1880), 180; William Clark Kennerly and Elizabeth Russell, *Persimmon Hill* (Norman, Okla., 1948), 32.

24 *Home Missionary* 17 (August 1844): 82.

25 *Niles National Register* 8 (June 13, 1840): 231.

26 Hoffman, *A Winter in the West*, 2:76. Washington Irving found St. Louis filled with "Indians and half-breeds" during his visit to the city. See J. Thomas Scharf, *The History of St. Louis City and County*, (Philadelphia, 1883), 2:1250. Also see Eduard Zimmerman, "Travel into Missouri In October, 1838," *Missouri Historical Society* 9 (January 1914): 34.

27 *Niles National Register* 8 (June 13, 1840): 231.

28 "The Journal of Henry B. Miller," ed. Thomas Maitland Marshall, *Missouri Historical Society Collections* 6 (June 1931): 215.

29 Theodor Engelmann, quoted in George Helmuth Kellner, "The German Element on the Urban Frontier: St. Louis, 1830–1860" (Ph.D. dissertation, University of Missouri–Columbia, 1973), 67.

30 See, for example, George H. Devol, *Forty Years a Gambler on the Mississippi* (New York, 1926); Hunter, *Steamboats on the Western Rivers*, chap. 9; John Morris [John O'Connor], *Wanderings of a Vagabond* (New York, 1873); Ray Allen Billington, "Anti-Catholic Propaganda and the Home Missionary Movement, 1800–1860," *Mississippi Valley Historical Review* 22 (December 1935): 361; Hoffman, *A Winter in the West*, 2:72; Parkman, *The Oregon Trail*, l; C. A. Goodrich, *The Family Tourist*, 463; Peyton, *Over the Alleghenies*, 251–52; Philip Hone, *The Diary of Philip Hone*, ed. Bayard Tuckerman (New York, 1889), 2:316. For a more general treatment of the subject, see Ray Allen Billington, *Land of Savagery, Land of Promise* (New York, 1981), chap. 12; Slotkin, *Regeneration Through Violence*, chap. 12; John D. Unruh, Jr., *The Plains Across* (Urbana, Ill., 1979), chap. 5.

31 For example, see William Claghorn to Emma Claghorn, June 23, 1847, St. Louis History Collection, Missouri Historical Society, St. Louis, Missouri; W. Goodell Bancroft to Edward W. Bancroft, undated, St. Louis History Collection, Missouri Historical Society, St. Louis, Missouri. Both men spent their first days in St. Louis unsuccessfully searching for the "western" excitement that travel writers had described. Also see J. Davis to Lewis Bristol, July 22, 1838, St. Louis History Collection, Missouri Historical Society, St. Louis, Missouri. Historians, including Turner, have viewed the West as "the land of unrestraint" as well. See Frederick Jackson Turner, quoted in Lewis O. Saum, *The Popular Mood of Pre–Civil War America* (Westport, Conn., 1980), 218; Richard Slotkin, *Regeneration Through Violence* (Middletown, Conn., 1973), chap. 2; Henry Nash Smith,

Virgin Land (Cambridge, Mass., 1950), chap. 6; Loren Baritz, "The Idea of the West," *American Historical Review* 66 (April 1961): 639.

32 Featherstonhaugh, *Excursion Through the Slave States*, 64.

33 For an important treatment of this issue, see Rush Welter, "The Frontier West as Image of American Society," *Mississippi Valley Historical Review* 46 (March 1960): 593–614.

34 Ibid.

35 John Mason Peck, *A New Guide for Emigrants to the West* (Boston, 1837), 325.

36 Ibid., viii.

38 For example, see Truman Marcellus Post, quoted in T. A. Post, *Truman Marcellus Post*, 216; Gottfried Duden, "Duden's Reports, 1824–1827," ed. and trans. William G. Bek, *Missouri Historical Review* 13 (January 1919): 174; "The Evangelization of the West," *New Englander* 4 (1846): 30.

39 Kellner, "The German Element on the Urban Frontier," 20.

40 See Gottfried Duden, "Duden's Reports, 1824–1827," ed. and trans. William G. Bek, *Missouri Historical Review* 13 (April 1919): 262; ibid., *Missouri Historical Review* 12 (October 1917): 22–31; James W. Goodrich, "Gottfried Duden: A Nineteenth-Century Missouri Promoter," *Missouri Historical Review* 75 (January 1981): 134; Kellner, "The German Element on the Urban Frontier," 20; Marcus Lee Hansen, *The Atlantic Migration, 1607–1860* (1940; reprint, New York, 1961), 149; Billington, *Land of Savagery, Land of Promise*, 291–92; Walter O. Forster, *Zion on the Mississippi* (St. Louis, 1951), 88.

41 Gottfried Duden, "Duden' s Reports, 1824–1827," ed. and trans. William G. Bek, *Missouri Historical Review* 13 (January 1919): 174; Kellner, "The German Element on the Urban Frontier," 14, 29; Hansen, *The Atlantic Migration*, 149; James W. Goodrich, "Gottfried Duden," 134; Kathleen Neils Conzen, "Germans," in *Harvard Encyclopedia of American Ethnic Groups*, ed. Stephan Thernstrom (Cambridge, Mass., 1980), 410–11. For a very different assessment of Duden's influence, see Walter D. Kamphoefner, *The Westfalians* (Princeton, 1987), 7, 94.

42 Gottried Duden, *Report on a Journey to the Western States of North America*, ed. James Goodrich, trans. George Kellner, Elsa Nagel, Adolf E. Schroeder, and W. M. Senner (1829; reprint, Columbia, Mo., 1980), 179. Also see Gottfried Duden, March, 1827, "Duden's Reports, 1824–1827," ed. and trans. William G. Bek, *Missouri Historical Review* 13 (January 1919): 174.

43 For example, see Gustavus Wulfing, *The Letters of Gustavus Wulfing*, ed. Eugene Tavenner and trans. Carl Hirsch (Fitch, Mo., 1941), 27; Kellner, "The German Element on the Urban Frontier," 86; Forster, *Zion on the Mississippi*, 88.

44 Zimmerman, "Travel Into Missouri," 35.

45 Kellner, "The German Element on the Urban Frontier," 88; Russel L. Gerlach, *Settlement Patterns in Missouri* (Columbia, Mo., 1986), 25.

46 Forster, *Zion on the Mississippi*, 250; Gerlach, *Settlement Patterns in Missouri*, 26.

47 "Saxon Emigration Code," quoted in Forster, *Zion on the Mississippi*, 567.

48 Duden, *Report on a Journey to the Western States of North America*, 52. Also see Kellner, "The German Element on the Urban Frontier," 14–15; Forster, *Zion on the Mississippi*, 88.

49 Duden, *Report on a Journey to the Western States of North America*, xiv; Gottfried Duden, quoted in Kellner, "The German Element on the Urban Frontier," 15.

50 Kellner, "The German Element on the Urban Frontier," 15.

51 Duden, *Report on a Journey to the Western States of North America*, 56, 172. Also see Kellner, "The German Element on the Urban Frontier," 17–18.

52 "Nicholas Hesse, German Visitor to Missouri, 1835–1837," ed. and trans. William G. Bek, *Missouri Historical Review* 41 (October 1946): 24; "The German Society of St. Louis," *Western Journal and Civilian* 5 (1851): 312; Gottfried Duden, quoted in Kellner, "The German Element on the Urban Frontier," 13.

53 Frederick Julius Gustorf, *The Uncorrupted Heart*, ed. Fred Gustorf (Columbia, Mo., 1969), 107.

54 Moritz Busch, *Travels Between the Hudson and the Mississippi, 1851–1852*, trans. Norman H. Binger (1854; reprint, Lexington, Ky., 1971), 231.

55 Kellner, "The German Element on the Urban Frontier," 171.

56 For example, see Carl Schurz, 1854, *The Autobiography of Carl Schurz* (New York, 1951), 122; Kellner, "The German Element on the Urban Frontier," 175; Forster, *Zion on the Mississippi*, 247.

57 Wulfing, *The Letters of Gustavus Wulfing*, 178.

58 For example, see Wulfing, *The Letters of Gustavus Wulfing*, 178; Kellner, "The German Element on the Urban Frontier," chap. 3; Forster, *Zion on the Mississippi*, chap. 5; Herman Steines to Parents, November 8, 1833, in "The Followers of Duden," ed. and trans. William G. Bek, *Missouri Historical Review* 14 (October 1919): 63.

59 Reverend Albert Barnes, 1849, quoted in Ray Allen Billington, *The Protestant Crusade, 1800–1860* (Chicago, 1938), 277.

60 *Home Missionary* 12 (August 1839): 73.

61 Ibid.; Lyman Beecher, *A Plea for the West* (Cincinnati, 1835), 108; Lyman Beecher, *The Autobiography of Lyman Beecher*, ed. Barbara M. Cross, (Cambridge, Mass., 1961), 2:167; Billington, *The Protestant Crusade*, 125.

62 For example, see Peck, *A New Guide for Emigrants*, viii; *Home Missionary* 15 (September 1842): 104–5; Smith, *Virgin Land*, 217.

63 See William Greenleaf Eliot, "Address Before the Franklin Society of St. Louis," *North American Review* 43 (July 1836): 288; id., "An Appeal for Aid to Build a Church in St. Louis," (Sermon delivered in Boston, May 10, 1835), William Greenleaf Eliot Papers, Missouri Historical Society, St. Louis, Missouri; Peck, *A New Guide for Emigrants*, viii; John Mason Peck, *Forty Years of Pioneer Life*, ed. Rufus Babcock, (1864; reprint, Carbondale, Ill., 1965), 304; *Home Missionary* 15 (September 1842): 104–5; Post, *Truman Marcellus Post*, 46; Reverend John A. Clark, *Gleanings By The Way* (Philadelphia, 1842), 89; "Missouri," *New England Magazine* 1 (October 1831):

350; Reverend James Finley, *Sketches of Western Methodism* (Cincinnati, 1855), 511; Billington, *The Protestant Crusade*, 255; Charles I. Foster, *An Errand of Mercy* (Chapel Hill, N.C., 1960), 197, 205–6.

64 Peck, *Forty Years of Pioneer Life*, x.

65 Peck, *A New Guide for Emigrants*, viii; *Home Missionary* 20 (June 1847): 39.

66 Clark, *Gleanings By The Way*, 89.

67 *Home Missionary* 17 (August 1844): 82–83.

68 I. H. Headlee to Samuel Headlee, June 13, 1849, St. Louis History Collection, Missouri Historical Society, St. Louis, Missouri.

69 Lewis, *Impressions of America* (Edinburgh, 1848), 268–69. Also see *North American Review* 43 (July 1836): 27–28.

70 Reverend T. R. Durfee, "A Plea For Missouri," *Home Missionary* 1 (November 1828): 115.

71 Ibid.

72 *Home Missionary* 5 (March 1833): 178–79.

73 Eliot, *Lectures to Young Men*, 12.

74 William Greenleaf Eliot, "The Religious and Moral Wants of the West," *American Unitarian Association Tracts*, series 1, number 117, vol. 10 (April 1837): 20; Billington, "Anti-Catholic Propaganda," 370–80; Foster, *An Errand of Mercy*, 206. Literary sources are filled with references to the Catholic presence in the region. For example, see "The Journal of Henry B. Miller," 258; Marbel Camden to Wife, 1834, quoted in John F. McDermott, "Dr. Brown's St. Louis," *Missouri Historical Review* 54 (April 1960): 247.

75 See Beecher, *A Plea for the West*, 31; *Home Missionary* 2 (April 1830): 192; Billington, *The Protestant Crusade*, chap. 5; Lewis, *Impressions of America*, 248.

76 Beecher, *A Plea for the West*, 69.

77 Ibid., 108.

78 Ibid., 11; Beecher, *Autobiography*, 2:167.

79 *Home Missionary* 6 (September 1833): 80.

80 Lewis, *Impressions of America*, 248. The *Home Missionary* frequently issued the same warning. For example, see ibid. 5 (July 1839): 35; ibid. 6 (September 1833): 80.

81 *Spirit of '76*, September 26, 1835, quoted in Billington, *The Protestant Crusade*, 128.

82 Many writers warned that French and Catholic customs retarded the moral and religious development of St. Louis. For example, see Lewis, *Impressions of America*, 252; Montgomery Schuyler, quoted in William Schuyler, *An Ambassador of Christ* (New York, 1901), 110.

83 Beecher, *A Plea for the West*, 57.

84 Lewis, *Impressions of America*, 253.

85 "Catholics in America," *Home Missionary* 5 (July 1832): 35.

86 "Agencies in the West," *Home Missionary* 15 (June 1842): 35.

87 See Foster, *An Errand of Mercy*, 207; Billington, "Anti-Catholic Propaganda," 361–62.

88   Billington, *The Protestant Crusade*, 129.
89   *Constitution of the American Home Missionary Society*, 1826, quoted in Foster, *An Errand of Mercy*, 184.
90   The American Sunday-School Union, for example, charged that "Catholic Europe is disgorging her priests and nuns . . . and systematic efforts are now making to control education." Quoted in Foster, *An Errand of Mercy*, 197, 206. The American Tract Society also expressed alarm at the Catholic presence in the Mississippi valley. The group's far western effort was centered in St. Louis. See Foster, *An Errand of Mercy*, 188; Lewis, *Impressions of America*, 253.
91   *Home Missionary* 15 (September 1842): 104–5; Lewis, *Impressions of America*, 253. Also see Schuyler, *An Ambassador of Christ*, 97.
92   Reverend W. W. Whipple, "Notices of Missouri as a Missionary Field," *Home Missionary* 19 (January 1847): 218.
93   *Home Missionary* 15 (September 1842): 104–5.
94   Whipple, "Notices of Missouri," 218.
95   *Home Missionary* 15 (September 1842): 104–5.
96   Ibid. 18 (January 1846): 203.
97   Ibid. 12 (August 1839): 73; Beecher, *A Plea for the West*, 31, 115.
98   William Claghorn, for example, held up his "hands in astonishment and wonder of [his] ignorance of the vast regions [of the west]." Claghorn lamented that he could find "not a single case of intoxication" and "no gambling" in St. Louis. The most exciting incident that he could report to his wife in Philadelphia was the singing of the "Dutch." See William Claghorn to Emma Claghorn, June 23, 1847, St. Louis History Collection, Missouri Historical Society, St. Louis, Missouri.
99   W. Goodell Bancroft to Edward W. Bancroft, undated, St. Louis History Collection, Missouri Historical Society, St. Louis, Missouri.
100 According to Charles Foster, nativism was a "logical embellishment" in the crusade to bring religion to the West. Fear, he notes, was an effective rhetorical tool. See Foster, *An Errand of Mercy*, 205. This image, however, was surprisingly rigid. Eastern editors demonstrated little interest in presenting other features of the region. For example, in 1836 William Greenleaf Eliot wrote a short article about the history of Missouri for the *North American Review*. Eliot noted that Missouri was a slave state and that the "people should have clothed themselves in sackcloth and ashes in view of the social and moral evil thus entailed upon them." To Eliot's horror, the magazine's editors omitted all references to slavery. See William Greenleaf Eliot, quoted in Walter Samuel Swisher, *A History of the Church of the Messiah* (St. Louis, 1934), 37.
101 Billington, *The Protestant Crusade*, 130.
102 Eliot, "Religious and Moral Wants of the West," 20.
103 Ibid.
104 Timothy Flint, *A Condensed Geography* (Cincinnati, 1828), 2:99.
105 C. A. Goodrich, *The Family Tourist*, 463.
106 Charles A. Dana, *The Great West* (Boston, 1857), 173. For another

example of this "borrowing," see Parker, *The Trip to the West and Texas*,
76; Buckingham, *The Eastern and Western States of America*, 3:147.

107 Daniel Webster, "Mr. Webster's Speech at St. Louis," *Niles Weekly
Register* 2, fifth series (July 15, 1837): 311.

108 Ibid.

109 Lieutenant-Colonel Arthur Cunyghame, *A Glimpse at the Great Western
Republic* (London, 1851), 154.

110 *De Bow's Review* 2 (December 1846): 411.

111 Dana, *The Great West*, 176.

112 Lady Emmeline Stuart-Wortley, *Travels in the United Stated During 1849
and 1850* (New York, 1851), 111.

113 Ibid.

114 Clark, *Gleanings By The Way*, 88.

115 William Greenleaf Eliot, "Gazetteer of the State of Missouri," *North
American Review* 48 (April 1839): 515.

116 Hiram Fuller, *Belle Briton On A Tour At Newport and Here and There* (New
York, 1858), 73; Erasmus Manford, *Twenty-Five Years in the West* (Chicago, 1867), 238; *Western Journal and Civilian* 3 (January 1849): 215,
quoted in Dale K. Doepke, "St. Louis Magazines Before the Civil War,
1832–1860" (Ph.D. dissertation, Washington University, 1963), 114;
William Gilpin, *The Central Gold Region* (Philadelphia, 1860), 193. Alex
Mackay even suggested that the "seat of general government" should
be transferred to St. Louis. See Alex Mackay, *The Western World* (Philadelphia, 1849), 2:130.

117 Buckingham, *The Eastern and Western States of America*, 3:147; "Statistics
of the Cities," *De Bow's Review* 3 (February 1847): 176. Similarly, Amos
Parker concluded that "it requires not the gift of prophecy to designate
this spot [St. Louis], as the site of the greatest city of the West." See
Parker, *Trip to the West*, 76.

118 Gilpin, *The Central Gold Region*, 112.

119 Ibid., 193. Also see Thomas L. Karnes, *William Gilpin, Western Nationalist* (Austin, Tex., 1970), 239–40.

120 Gilpin, *The Central Gold Region*, 133.

121 William Gilpin, "The Cities of Missouri," *Western Journal and Civilian* 11
(October 1853): 39–49. Also see Gilpin, *The Central Gold Region*, 97;
Charles N. Glaab and A. Theodore Brown, *A History of Urban America*
(London, 1967), 77.

122 Eliot, "Gazetteer of the State of Missouri," 515.

123 For example, see Robert Sears, *A Pictorial Description of the United States*
(New York, 1852), 572; Holt, "The Shaping of St. Louis," 274; Whitman,
"Letters Written by Mrs. Whitman," 81.

124 *De Bow's Review* 17 (October 1854): 395. Also see *Phelps' Hundred Cities
and Large Towns of America* (New York, 1853), 74.

125 John Mason to Emily Mason, June 1, 1841, quoted in Doris Ann Phelan,
"Boosterism in St. Louis, 1810–1860" (Ph.D. dissertation, St. Louis
University, 1970), 82.

126 Mrs. Elizabeth Ellet, *Summer Rambles in the West* (New York, 1853), 226.

127   Frank Blackwell Mayer, *With Pen and Pencil on the Frontier in 1851*, ed. Bertha Heilbron (St. Paul, Minn., 1932), 74; Mackay, *The Western World*, 2:129; Fuller, *Belle Briton on a Tour*, 3.

128   "Cities of the Valley of the Ohio and Mississippi Rivers," *De Bow's Review* 1 (February 1846): 147.

129   Alphonzo Wetmore, *Gazetteer of the State of Missouri* (St. Louis, 1837), 179.

130   Busch, *Travels Between the Hudson and the Mississippi*, 234.

131   *Home Missionary* 5 (March 1833): 178–79; Richard Smith Elliott, *Notes Taken in Sixty Years* (St. Louis, 1883), 165. Also, see Lewis, *Impressions of America*, 247; C. C. Whittelsey, "Missouri and its Resources," *Hunt's Merchants' Magazine and Commercial Review* 8 (June 1843): 544; James Hall, *The West* (Cincinnati, 1848), 250.

132   Post, *Truman Marcellus Post*, 149.

133   Charles Mackay, *Life and Liberty in America* (New York, 1859), 141.

134   Cunyghame, *A Glimpse at the Great Western Republic*, 160.

135   Luke Shortfield, *The Western Merchant* (Philadelphia, 1849), 212.

136   Frederick Graff to Charles Graff, June 29, 1838, St. Louis History Collection, Missouri Historical Society, St. Louis, Missouri.

137   Cunyghame, *A Glimpse at the Great Western Republic*, 160.

138   Gottfried Duden, March, 1827. "Duden's Reports, 1824–1827," ed. and trans. William G. Bek, *Missouri Historical Review* 13 (January 1919): 180. Duden responded to critics of his emigration plan by charging that many emigrants were unprepared for the journey. For a fuller discussion of this controversy, see Kellner, "The German Element on the Urban Frontier," 33.

139   Hermann Steines to Parents, November 8, 1833 in "The Followers of Duden," ed. and trans. William G. Bek, *Missouri Historical Review* 14 (October 1919): 64. Also see "Nicholas Hesse: German Visitor to Missouri, 1835–1837," ed. and trans. William G. Bek, *Missouri Historical Review* 41 (July 1947): 384.

140   For example, see Frederick Graff to Charles Graff, June 29, 1838, St. Louis History Collection, Missouri Historical Society, St. Louis, Missouri.

141   Ibid.

142   Truman Marcellus Post noted that St. Louis offered "marvelous attractions" for moral young men. See Post, *Truman Marcellus Post*, 149. Similarly, Gustavus Wulfing assured relatives in Germany that a young man with a "strong character" was bound to succeed in a vigorous place like St. Louis. See Wulfing, *The Letters of Gustavus Wulfing*, 332. William Greenleaf Eliot also insisted that such a dynamic city was ideal for young men. In St. Louis, Eliot declared, moral newcomers could shape the future. See Eliot, *Lectures to Young Men*, 17; Also see Kellner, "The German Element on the Urban Frontier," 270.

143   John Seaton to Father, January 30, 1844, St. Louis History Collection, Missouri Historical Society, St. Louis, Missouri.

144   John A. Kasson, 1851, quoted in Edward Younger, *John A. Kasson* (Iowa City, Iowa, 1955), 59.

145 Cunyghame, *A Glimpse at the Great Western Republic*, 160.
146 For example, see Post, *Truman Marcellus Post*, 149; Eliot, *Lectures to Young Men*, 17.

Chapter 4: Yankee newcomers and prosperity

1 For a perceptive analysis of the role that eastern capital played in the development of the urban West, see the work of John D. Haeger, particularly "Capital Mobilization and the Urban Center," *Mid-America* 60 (April–July 1978): 92–93; id., "Eastern Money and the Urban Frontier," *Journal of the Illinois Historical Society* 64 (Autumn 1971): 284; id., *The Investment Frontier* (Albany, N.Y., 1981).
2 John Lewis Peyton, *Over the Alleghenies* (London, 1870), 251–52.
3 *A Review of the Commerce of St. Louis for the Year 1849*, 3.
4 *Statistical View of the United States, Embracing Its Territory, Population – White, Free Colored, and Slave – Moral and Social Condition, Industry, Property, and Revenue; The Detailed Statistics of Cities, Towns, and Counties; Being A Compendium of the Seventh Census* (Washington, D. C., 1854), 399. Also see Audrey Louise Olson, "St. Louis Germans, 1850–1920: The Nature of an Immigrant Community and Its Relation to the Assimilation Process" (Ph.D. dissertation, University of Kansas, 1970), 13; *New York Daily Tribune*, March 12, 1856.
5 Unlike eastern urban centers, St. Louis did not draw migrants from its hinterland. In part this reflected the sparse population of the surrounding territory. See Richard Easterlin, "Population Change and Farm Settlement in the Northern United States," *Journal of Economic History* 36 (March 1976): 45–75. More important, St. Louis provided few attractions for manual workers during this period. The eastern pattern of internal migration reflects both the density of eastern population centers and the maturity – and decline – of eastern agriculture. For this eastern model of internal migration, see Stephan Thernstrom and Peter R. Knights, "Men in Motion," in *Anonymous Americans*, ed. Tamara K. Hareven (Englewood Cliffs, N.J., 1971), 17–47; Peter R. Knights, *The Plain People of Boston* (New York, 1971); John Modell, "The Peopling of a Working-Class Ward," *Journal of Social History* 5 (Fall 1971): 71–95; Michael B. Katz, Michael J. Doucet, and Mark J. Stern, *The Social Organization of Early Industrial Capitalism* (Cambridge, Mass., 1982), 102–30.
6 John D. Thompson to Amos A. Lawrence, July 22, 1857, Missouri History Collection, Missouri Historical Society, St. Louis, Missouri. St. Louis residents defined "Yankees" as migrants from New York or New England (and I have relied on this categorization).
7 For example, see Edward Younger, *John A. Kasson* (Iowa City, Iowa, 1955), 56; George M. Fredrickson, *The Inner Civil War* (New York, 1965), 33–35; Arthur M. Johnson and Barry E. Supple, *Boston Capitalists and Western Railroads* (Cambridge, Mass., 1967), 103.
8 John A. Kasson, 1851, quoted in Younger, *John A. Kasson*, 54.

9   Johnson and Supple, *Boston Capitalists and Western Railroads*, 9, 31, 58.

10 *The Teacher and Western Educational Magazine* I (February 1853): 36–37, quoted in Dale K. Doepke, "St. Louis Magazines Before the Civil War, 1832–1860" (Ph.D. dissertation, Washington University, 1963), 140.

11 John A. Kasson, quoted in Younger, *John A. Kasson*, 56.

12 For example, see *Home Missionary* 20 (June 1847): 38–40; Frederika Bremer, *The Homes of the New World* (New York, 1853), 2:95; C[arter]. A. Goodrich, *The Family Tourist* (Hartford, Conn., 1848), 463.

13 Fredrickson, *The Inner Civil War*, 33.

14 Ibid., 33–34.

15 For example, see Younger, *John A. Kasson*, 54–56; William Greenleaf Eliot, *Lectures to Young Men* (Boston, 1856), 52; Frederick Graff to Charles Graff, June 29, 1838, St. Louis History Collection, Missouri Historical Society, St. Louis, Missouri.

16 John A. Kasson, 1851, quoted in Younger, *John A. Kasson*, 56.

17 Logan U. Reavis, *St. Louis* (St. Louis, 1875), 654.

18 For example, see Lady Emmeline Stuart-Wortley, *Travels in the United States* (New York, 1851), 111; *Home Missionary* 17 (August 1849): 82.

19 Eliot, *Lectures to Young Men*, 17. Also, see "The Evangelization of the West," *New Englander* 4 (1846): 39.

20 Eliot, *Lectures to Young Men*, 52. For a discussion of opportunities in smaller cities, see John N. Ingham, "Rags to Riches Revisited," *Journal of American History* 63 (December 1976): 615–37.

21 For estimates of the cost of steamboat passage from the Atlantic coast to St. Louis, see *Missouri Republican*, January 17, 1843; ibid., July 22, 1850; J. S. Holliday, *The World Rushed In* (New York, 1981), 468.

22 For example, see Herman Steines to [unnamed] relative, November 8, 1833, in "The Followers of Duden: The Steines Family," trans. William G. Bek, *Missouri Historical Review* 14 (October 1919): 70; Stephen A. Douglas, 1838, *The Letters of Stephen A. Douglas*, ed. Robert W. Johannsen (Urbana, Ill., 1961), 60.

23 Gardner Folsome to Lewis Boynton, March 20, 1848, St. Louis History Collection, Missouri Historical Society, St. Louis, Missouri.

24 Frederick Graff to Charles Graff, June 29, 1838, St. Louis History Collection, Missouri Historical Society, St. Louis, Missouri.

25 Socio-economic status varied inversely with distance among migrants to St. Louis during the 1840s. For a general discussion of the relationship between socio-economic status and distance, see Everett S. Lee, "A Theory of Migration," in *Migration*, ed. J. A. Jackson (Cambridge, 1969), 294–96; E. G. Ravenstein, "The Laws of Migration," *Journal of the Royal Statistical Society* 48 (June 1885): 167–227. Also see Lawrence A. Brown, John Odland, and Reginald G. Golledge, "Migration, Functional Distance, and the Urban Hierarchy," *Economic Geography* 46 (July 1970): 77.

26 Allan Pred, *Urban Growth and the Circulation of Information* (Cambridge, Mass., 1973), 81.

27 For example, see *Hunt's Merchants' Magazine and Commercial Review* 15

(August 1846): 162–65; ibid. 24 (March 1851): 298; ibid. 26 (February 1852): 324–25; ibid. 28 (April 1853): 436–38; *De Bow's Review* 1 (January 1846): 79–80; ibid. 5 (April 1848): 370–73; ibid. 7 (August 1849): 178–81.

28 See Missouri Vols. 36–38, R. G. Dun and Company Collection, Baker Library, Harvard University Graduate School of Business Administration, Boston, Massachusetts (hereafter cited as RGD). Although the Dun ledger books do not provide a systematic treatment of migration, credit reporters investigated merchant's backgrounds carefully enough to provide strong evidence on migration patterns and "fields."

29 For example, see Eliot, *Lectures to Young Men*, 41; *Home Missionary* 5 (March 1833): 178; ibid. 20 (June 1847): 38

30 Henry Adams, quoted in Ernest Samuels, *The Young Henry Adams* (Cambridge, Mass., 1948), 57.

31 James S. Cowan to John W. Ellis, July 25, 1847, typescript, James S. Cowan Papers, Joint Collection, University of Missouri Western Historical Manuscript Collection–Columbia and State Historical Society of Missouri Manuscripts, Columbia, Missouri. Also see *The Teacher and Western Educational Magazine* 1 (February 1853): 36, quoted in Doepke, "St. Louis Magazines Before the Civil War," 140.

32 See Rush Welter, "The Frontier West as Image of American Society," *Mississippi Valley Historical Review* 46 (March 1960): 593–614.

33 John K. Lane to William Carr Lane, August 18, 1849, William Carr Lane Papers, Missouri Historical Society, St. Louis, Missouri.

34 [Jacob N.] Taylor and [M. O.] Crooks, *Sketch Book of St. Louis* (St. Louis, 1858), 277. Also see *Overland to California: The Gold Rush Diary of Bernard J. Reid*, ed. Mary McDougall Gordon (Stanford, Calif., 1983), 25.

35 Older, eastern cities grew by drawing from their hinterlands. Thus, most migrants traveled only short distances, and most were manual workers. Eastern merchants more often either inherited their status or experienced intergenerational mobility. See Stephan Thernstrom, *The Other Bostonians* (Cambridge, Mass., 1973); Thernstrom and Knights, "Men in Motion," 17–47; Knights, *The Plain People of Boston*, 70–77; Modell, "The Peopling of a Working-Class Ward," 72, 91. Also see David Paul Davenport, "Migration to Albany, New York, 1850–1855, " *Social Science History* 13 (Summer 1989): 159–85.

36 According to the ledger books of R. G. Dun and Company, nearly 80 percent of the city's merchants appear to have migrated directly to St. Louis. The proportion of direct migrants was particularly high during the 1840s. During the 1850s, however, an increasing percentage of travelers spent time in midwestern cities after leaving the Northeast and before arriving in St. Louis. See Missouri Vols. 36–38, RGD.

37 Missouri Vol. 38, p. 47, RGD; Missouri Vol. 36, p. 157, RGD.

38 Missouri Vol. 36, p. 171, RGD. Also see Gordon, ed., *Overland to California*, 22.

39 *Missouri Republican*, January 23, 1850.

40 See Lee, "A Theory of Migration," 294–96.

41 See Thernstrom and Knights, "Men in Motion," 17–47; Knights, *The Plain*

People of Boston, 70–77; Modell, "The Peopling of a Working-Class Ward," 72, 91; Davenport, "Migration to Albany."

42 For Phillips, see the manuscript schedules of the Seventh Census (1850), St. Louis County. Local editors and municipal officials often referred to the "floating population" of rivermen in the city. This label was simultaneously descriptive and derisive. For example, see *Missouri Democrat*, December 18, 1856.

43 On chain migration, see Robert Bieder, "Kinship as a Factor in Migration," *Journal of Marriage and the Family* 35 (August 1973): 429–39; James Allen, "Migration Fields of French Canadians to Southern Maine," *Geographical Review* 62 (July 1972): 366–83.

44 A number of manuscript sources indicate that most of Eliot's congregants were Bostonians. For example, see the records of the Church of the Messiah, First Congregational Church of St. Louis, St. Louis, Missouri; William Greenleaf Eliot Papers, Missouri Historical Society, St. Louis, Missouri; Day-Book of Reverend Carlton A. Staples, 1858, Records of the Church of the Messiah, First Congregational Church of St. Louis, St. Louis, Missouri. Also, see Walter Samuel Swisher, *A History of the Church of the Messiah, 1834–1934* (St. Louis, 1934).

45 Day-book of Reverend Carlton A. Staples, Church of the Messiah, First Congregational Church of St. Louis, St. Louis, Missouri; *Missouri Democrat*, April 14, 1856; Missouri Vol. 38, p. 112, RGD; J. Thomas Scharf, *The History of St. Louis City and County* (Philadelphia, 1883), 1:600, 1:692.

46 See the manuscript schedules of the Seventh Census (1850), St. Louis County.

47 Frederick Graff to Charles Graff, June 29, 1838, St. Louis History Collection, Missouri Historical Society, St. Louis, Missouri; John Seaton to Father, January 30, 1844, St. Louis History Collection, Missouri Historical Society, St. Louis, Missouri.

48 J. Davis to Lewis Sawyer, September 25, 1837, St. Louis History Collection, Missouri Historical Society, St. Louis, Missouri.

49 James S. Cowan to John W. Ellis, July 25, 1847, typescript, James S. Cowan Papers, Joint Collection, University of Missouri Western Historical Manuscript Collection–Columbia and State Historical Society of Missouri Manuscripts, Columbia, Missouri. Also see Charles D. Drake, "Autobiography," typescript, 469, 510, Charles D. Drake Papers, Joint Collection, University of Missouri Western Historical Manuscript Collection–Columbia and State Historical Society of Missouri Manuscripts, Columbia, Missouri; Thomas L. Karnes, *William Gilpin, Nationalist* (Austin, 1970), 48, 50.

50 Reavis, *St. Louis*, 532.

51 J. Davis to Lewis Bristol, July 22, 1838, St. Louis History Collection, Missouri Historical Society, St. Louis, Missouri.

52 Frederick Graff to Charles Graff, June 29, 1838, St. Louis History Collection, Missouri Historical Society, St. Louis, Missouri.

53 For example, see "Indictments," June 8, 1848, Criminal Court Records for the St. Louis District, Federal Courthouse, St. Louis, Missouri.

54 Reverend George Lewis, *Impressions of America and American Churches* (Edinburgh, 1848), 257.

55 Bremer, *The Homes of the New World*, 2:88.

56 Frederick Graff to Charles Graff, June 29, 1838, St. Louis History Collection, Missouri Historical Society, St. Louis, Missouri.

57 John Seaton to Father, January 30, 1844, St. Louis History Collection, Missouri Historical Society, St. Louis, Missouri.

58 Frederick Graff to Charles Graff, June 29, 1838, St. Louis History Collection, Missouri Historical Society, St. Louis, Missouri.

59 *New York Daily Tribune*, March 12, 1856.

60 Missouri Vol. 36, RGD, passim. Most of the commercial data discussed in this chapter was drawn from the Dun records. Every firm for which investigators compiled complete information was included in this data base. Thus, a broad range of information was accumulated for 2,086 firms that operated in St. Louis between the early 1840s and 1860. For a sample of other work using the Dun records, see Harriet A. Amos, *Cotton City* (University, Ala., 1985); Peter R. Decker, *Fortunes and Failures* (Cambridge, Mass., 1978); Don H. Doyle, *New Men, New Cities, New South* (Chapel Hill, N.C., 1990); David A. Gerber, "Cutting Out Shylock," *Journal of American History* 69 (December 1982): 615–37; Clyde Griffen and Sally Griffen, *Natives and Newcomers* (Cambridge, Mass., 1978); Michael B. Katz, *The People of Hamilton, Canada West* (Cambridge, Mass., 1975); Roger L. Ransom and Richard Sutch, *One Kind of Freedom* (New York, 1977). For a discussion of the disproportionate influence that Yankee entrepreneurs exerted in the urban West, see Carl Abbott, *Boosters and Businessmen* (Westport, Conn., 1981), 160; Haeger, "Capital Mobilization and the Urban Center," 75–93; id., "Eastern Money and the Urban Frontier," 267–84.

61 Bremer, *The Homes of the New World*, 2:95.

62 Robert Greenhalgh Albion, *The Rise of New York Port* (1939; reprint, Boston, 1984), 381; Johnson and Supple, *Boston Capitalists and Western Railroads*, 80.

63 *Hunt's Merchants' Magazine* 12 (April 1845): 470; Albion, *The Rise of New York Port*, 64, 79; Johnson and Supple, *Boston Capitalists and Western Railroads*, 79; Edward K. Spann, *The New Metropolis* (New York, 1981), 5, 6, 15; Harold D. Woodman, *King Cotton and His Retainers, 1800–1925* (Lexington, Ky., 1968), 171–73; Glenn Porter and Harold C. Livesay, *Merchants and Manufacturers* (Baltimore, 1971), 70.

64 Diane Lindstrom, *Economic Development in the Philadelphia Region, 1810–1850* (New York, 1978), 24.

65 Ibid.

66 Ibid., 9, 14, 53; Thomas C. Cochran, *Frontiers of Change* (New York, 1981), 40–43.

67 Allan Pred, *Urban Growth and City-Systems in the United States, 1840–1860* (Cambridge, Mass., 1980), 69; Alan Dawley, *Class and Community* (Cambridge, Mass., 1976), 30; Paul G. Faler, *Mechanics and Manufacturers in the Early Industrial Revolution* (Albany, N.Y., 1981), 70.

68 Johnson and Supple, *Boston Capitalists and Western Railroads*, 21, 103; Allan R. Pred, "The American Mercantile City: 1800–1840: Manufacturing, Growth, and Structure," in *The Spatial Dynamics of U.S. Urban-Industrial Growth, 1800–1914* (Cambridge, Mass., 1966), 157; Oscar Handlin, *Boston's Immigrants* (Cambridge, Mass., 1941), 9.

69 Johnson and Supple, *Boston Capitalists and Western Railroads*, 19–23.

70 Ibid., 21.

71 Ibid., 21, 80. Also see Younger, *John A. Kasson*, 59.

72 Ibid., 103; Albion, *The Rise of New York Port*, 354; Decker, *Fortunes and Failures*, 9. Also, see William B. Gates, *Michigan Copper and Boston Dollars* (Cambridge, Mass., 1951); John Lauritz Larson, *Bonds of Enterprise* (Cambridge, Mass., 1981); Irene D. Neu, *Erastus Corning* (Ithaca, N.Y., 1960).

73 Pred, *Urban Growth and City-Systems in the United States*, 69; Albion, *The Rise of New York Port*, 91, 119. Also see Lewis E. Atherton, *The Southern Country Store* (Baton Rouge, La., 1949).

74 Albion, *The Rise of New York Port*, 119; Glen E. Holt, "The Shaping of St. Louis, 1763–1860" (Ph.D. dissertation, University of Chicago, 1975), 273; Stuart Bruchey, *The Roots of American Economic Growth, 1607–1861* (London, 1965), 156.

75 For example, see Horace Smith to Abiel Leonard, November 3, 1852, Abiel Leonard Papers, Joint Collection, University of Missouri Western Historical Manuscript Collection–Columbia and State Historical Society of Missouri Manuscripts, Columbia, Missouri.

76 Porter and Livesay, *Merchants and Manufacturers*, 33, 64–65. Also, see James Neal Primm, *Economic Policy in the Development of a Western State* (Cambridge, Mass., 1954), 41; John Ray Cable, *The Bank of the State of Missouri* (New York, 1923), 227, 242; William G. Shade, *Banks or No Banks* (Detroit, 1971); George R. Taylor, *The Transportation Revolution* (New York, 1951), 324–51.

77 Samuel Troth to Eugene Massie, September 7, 1846, quoted in Porter and Livesay, *Merchants and Manufacturers*, 33.

78 Bankruptcy File of Bernard Manheimer, Bankruptcy Records, 1867, Federal Archives and Records Center, Kansas City, Missouri.

79 *A Review of the Commerce of St. Louis for the Year 1849*, 15.

80 Missouri Vols. 36–38, RGD. Also, see Porter and Livesay, *Merchants and Manufacturers*, 33; Pred, *Urban Growth and City-Systems in the United States*, 64.

81 Missouri Vols. 36–38, RGD.

82 For a discussion of branch arrangements, see Albion, *The Rise of New York Port*, 282; Decker, *Fortunes and Failures*, 68–69; Pred, *Urban Growth and City-Systems in the United States*, 74 ; Johnson and Supple, *Boston Capitalists and Western Railroads*, 23; Bernard Farber, *Guardians of Virtue* (New York, 1972), 75. Also see David Ralph Meyer, "A Dynamic Model of the Integration of Frontier Urban Places into the United States System of Cities," *Economic Geography* 56 (April 1980): 136.

83 Missouri Vol. 38, p. 81, RGD.

84 For example, Aaron Weld sent an experienced clerk to manage his
    western boot outlet. See Missouri Vol. 36, p. 120, RGD. Also see
    Coffin-Weld Company Papers, Joint Collection, University of Missouri
    Western Historical Manuscript Collection–Columbia and State Histori-
    cal Society of Missouri Manuscripts, Columbia, Missouri; Johnson and
    Supple, *Boston Capitalists and Western Railroads*, 23.

85 Dawley, *Class and Community*, 30; *First Annual Report of the St. Louis
    Young Men's Christian Association* (St. Louis, 1854), 36.

86 Over 40 percent of the merchants who operated in antebellum St. Louis
    received financial support from relatives. For additional information on
    kinship networks and nineteenth-century commerce, see Decker, *For-
    tunes and Failures*, 68–69; Farber, *Guardians of Virtue*, 75–110; Johnson
    and Supple, *Boston Capitalists and Western Railroads*, 23.

87 Missouri Vol. 36, p. 88, RGD; John C. Rand, *One of a Thousand* (Boston,
    1890), 117.

88 Missouri Vol. 36, p. 171, RGD. Also see J. M. D. Burrows, *Fifty Years in
    Iowa* (Davenport, Iowa, 1888), 186.

89 Missouri Vol. 36, p. 162, RGD. For a similar arrangement, see Missouri
    Vol. 37, p. 341, RGD.

90 Missouri Vol. 36, p. 296, RGD.

91 For example, see Missouri Vol. 36, p. 37, RGD; Johnson and Supple,
    Boston Capitalists and Western Railroads, 23; Farber, *Guardians of Virtue*, 97.

92 Reavis, *St. Louis*, 667; Missouri Vol. 38, p. 144, RGD.

93 Missouri Vol. 37, p. 557, RGD. Also, see Luke Shortfield, *The Western
    Merchant* (Philadelphia, 1849), 19.

94 See *Missouri Republican*, January 24, 1853; ibid., August 20, 1853.

95 Missouri Vol. 36, p. 64, RGD.

96 For example, see F. R. Roueche to John W. Ellis, March 11, 1848, in
    "Business and Life in St. Louis, Missouri, 1847–1848," ed. Lewis E.
    Atherton, *Missouri Historical Review* 37 (July 1943): 436–37.

97 Missouri Circuit Court Archives, Federal Courthouse, St. Louis, Missouri.

98 Missouri Vol. 36, p. 249, RGD.

99 Missouri Vol. 36, p. 98, RGD.

100 *Annual Review of the Commerce of St. Louis for the Year 1852* (St. Louis,
    1853), 23. Also see *Missouri Democrat*, January 6, 1855.

101 Missouri Vol. 36, p. 37, RGD. Also, see Johnson and Supple, *Boston
    Capitalists and Western Railroads*, 23; Farber, *Guardians of Virtue*, 97.

102 Missouri Vol. 36, p. 120, RGD; the manuscript schedules of the Seventh
    Census (1850), St. Louis County.

103 Rand, *One of a Thousand*, 117; Charles Henry Wight, *Geneology of the
    Claflin Family* (New York, 1903), 309.

104 For example, see Henry Thomas Mudd Papers, Joint Collection, Univer-
    sity of Missouri Western Historical Manuscript Collection–Columbia
    and State Historical Society of Missouri Manuscripts, Columbia, Mis-
    souri.

105 Doris Ann Phelan, "Boosterism in St. Louis, 1810–1860" (Ph.D. disser-
    tation, St. Louis University, 1970), 113, 122.

106 See the manuscript schedules of the Seventh Census (1850), St. Louis County.

107 Missouri Vol. 36, p. 30, RGD. For other discussions of merchants and real estate, see Haeger, "The Abandoned Townsite on the Midwestern Frontier," *Journal of the Early Republic* 3 (Summer 1983): 169; Clyde Griffen, "Workers Divided," in *Nineteenth-Century Cities*, edited by Stephan Thernstrom and Richard Sennett (New Haven, 1969), 59; Frederic Cople Jaher, *The Urban Establishment* (Urbana, Ill., 1982); Stuart M. Blumin, *The Emergence of the Middle Class* (New York, 1989). For an interesting comparison with Cincinnati, see Abbott, *Boosters and Businessmen*, 160.

108 See Clyde Griffen and Sally Griffen, *Natives and Newcomers* (Cambridge, Mass., 1978); Jaher, *The Urban Establishment*; Blumin, *The Emergence of the Middle Class*.

109 The Dun records, church letters of transfer, and literary sources indicate that unsuccessful merchants most often returned to their premigration homes. For example, see "Letters of Dismission," records of Second Baptist Church, Missouri Historical Society, St. Louis, Missouri (microfilm); Elizabeth Sargent to Friends, January 20, 1846, St. Louis History Collection, Missouri Historical Society, St. Louis, Missouri.

110 Missouri Vol. 36, p. 234, RGD.

111 Missouri Vol. 36, p. 263, RGD.

112 Elizabeth Sargent to Friends, January 20, 1846, St. Louis History Collection, Missouri Historical Society, St. Louis, Missouri.

113 Elizabeth Sargent to Mother, September 5, 1846, St. Louis History Collection, Missouri Historical Society, St. Louis, Missouri.

114 See Eliot, *Lectures to Young Men*; Reverend T. M. Cunningham, *Address Before the St. Louis Young Men's Christian Association* (St. Louis, 1853).

115 Kinship networks provided the principal backing for firms during this period – both branches and nonbranches. Also, see Farber, *Guardians of Virtue*, 108–10; Johnson and Supple, *Boston Capitalists and Western Railroads*, 23. Also see Haeger, "Eastern Money and the Urban Frontier," 284.

116 Missouri Vol. 37, p. 352, RGD. Also, see Missouri Vol. 36, p. 284, RGD.

117 Missouri Vol. 37, p. 326, RGD.

118 *Annual Review of the Trade and Commerce of St. Louis for the Year 1848*, 4.

119 *Missouri Democrat*, April 16, 1856. Also *Annual Review*, (St. Louis, 1854), 13.

120 *Missouri Democrat*, April 16, 1856.

121 Missouri Vol. 36, p. 171 , RGD.

122 Missouri Vol. 36, p. 297, RGD.

123 Missouri Vol. 36, p. 68, RGD.

124 *St. Louis Business Directory for 1847*, 50; *Missouri Republican*, August 20, 1853.

125 Lewis E. Atherton, *The Pioneer Merchant in Mid-America* (1939; reprint, New York, 1969), 98. Also see Missouri Vol. 36, p. 171, RGD.

126 Franklin and Perry to Coffin and Weld, January 19, 1846, Coffin-Weld

Company Papers, Joint Collection, University of Missouri Western Historical Manuscript Collection–Columbia and State Historical Society of Missouri Manuscripts, Columbia, Missouri.

127 *Missouri Democrat*, April 16, 1856.

128 *Missouri Republican*, January 24, 1853. Also see ibid., August 20, 1853.

129 *St. Louis Business Directory for 1847*, 50. Also, see ibid., 100, 130; [James] *Green's St. Louis Directory for 1847* (St. Louis, 1847), 222.

130 Jacob N. Taylor, comp., *The St. Louis Business Directory for 1850* (St. Louis, 1850), 111. For a similar message, see *St. Louis Business Directory for 1847*, 50.

131 Cable, *The Bank of the State of Missouri*, 246; *Annual Review of the Trade and Commerce of St. Louis for the Year 1848* (St. Louis, 1849), 8. In their retail businesses, however, Yankee merchants encountered problems with discounted currency.

132 J. F. Franklin to J. G. Weld, June 8, 1848, Coffin-Weld Company Papers, Joint Collection, University of Missouri Western Historical Manuscript Collection–Columbia and State Historical Society of Missouri Manuscripts, Columbia, Missouri.

133 I defined the "largest" firms as those termed "very large" or "enormous" by Dun credit investigators. See Missouri Vols. 36–38, RGD.

134 Missouri Vol. 37, p. 527, RGD.

135 Missouri Vol. 37, p. 588, RGD.

136 Missouri Vol. 36, p. 51, RGD. Similarly, credit reporters termed Joseph Neil and his brother "Israelites . . . uncouth but responsible." See Missouri Vol. 37, p. 497, RGD. Although David Gerber argued that anti-Semitism hurt Jews at the marketplace, he, too, found that most Jewish merchants were given strong credit ratings. See Gerber, "Cutting Out Shylock," 633.

137 For examples of successful local merchants, particularly before the boom, see Atherton, *The Pioneer Merchant in Mid-America*; James Neal Primm, *Lion of the Valley* (Boulder, Colo., 1981), 209–10. Also see the credit reports of local businessmen, such as members of the Chouteau family. Missouri Vol. 36, p. 27, RGD.

138 James S. Cowan to John W. Ellis, July 25, 1847, typescript, James S. Cowan Papers, Joint Collection, University of Missouri Western Historical Manuscript Collection–Columbia and State Historical Society of Missouri Manuscripts, Columbia, Missouri; John Seaton to Father, January 30, 1844, St. Louis History Collection, Missouri Historical Society, St. Louis, Missouri.

139 Frederick Dent, quoted in *Personal Memoirs of Julia Dent Grant*, ed. John Y. Simon (New York, 1975), 43.

140 John Hogan, *Thoughts About the City of St. Louis* (St. Louis, 1854), 13.

141 *Annual Review of the Commerce of St. Louis for the Year 1852*, 23; Pred, *Urban Growth and City-Systems in the United States*, 220.

142 Hogan, *Thoughts About the City of St. Louis*, 19.

143 Albion, *The Rise of New York Port*, 60; *Hunt's Merchants' Magazine* 12 (March 1845): 278.

144 For example, see *Missouri Republican*, January 6, 1843; Shortfield, *The Western Merchant*, 151. For a detailed discussion of these problems, see Timothy R. Mahoney, *River Towns in the Great West* (New York, 1990), 167–69.

145 Albion, *The Rise of New York Port*, 60; *Hunt's Merchants' Magazine* 12 (March 1845): 278. Import duties for the port of New York reached their highest levels in August and September. These revenues hit their lowest point in March, just as western traders arrived. In addition, eastern capital markets seemed to have followed similar rhythms. New York vaults were fullest in the late summer and most empty in the winter. Thus, both goods and capital were dearest – and most expensive – when St. Louis merchants purchased their stocks.

146 Cable, *The Bank of the State of Missouri*, 246. Also, see the Missouri Circuit Court Archives, Federal Courthouse, St. Louis, Missouri. These files indicate that 10 percent interest on thirty- and sixty-day notes was the standard fee. Also see Gustavus Wulfing to Julia Wulfing, September 20, 1850, *The Letters of Gustavus Wulfing*, trans. and ed. Carl Hirsch (Fitch, Mo., 1941), 309.

147 Cable, *The Bank of the State of Missouri*, 246; *Annual Review of the Trade and Commerce of St. Louis for the Year 1848* (St. Louis, 1849), 8.

148 Shortfield, *The Western Merchant*, 130. Also, see Albion, *The Rise of New York Port*, 282; Porter and Livesay, *Merchants and Manufacturers*, 27–28.

149 See Griffen and Griffen, *Natives and Newcomers*.

150 Missouri Vol. 36, p. 44, RGD. Among firms that began entirely without capital, none survived more than six years – while 25 percent of all firms remained in operation for seven years or more. In addition, only 6 percent of the ventures that started with less than five hundred dollars survived longer than fifteen years – compared to 15 percent of all businesses. Similarly, 25 percent of tiny firms experienced significant growth, compared to 40 percent of small firms, 77 percent of large businesses, and 90 percent of enormous enterprises. Although a few poor merchants achieved considerable commercial success, rags-to-riches tales were rare in antebellum St. Louis.

151 Missouri Vol. 36, p. 303, RGD; Missouri Vol. 37, p. 497, RGD; *Hunt's Merchants' Magazine* 25 (October 1851): 476.

152 *Hunt's Merchants' Magazine* 25 (October 1851): 476.

153 Missouri Vols. 36–38, RGD. Also see James E. Vance, Jr., *The Merchants' World* (Englewood Cliffs, N.J., 1970), chap. 5; Fred Mitchell Jones, *Middlemen in the Domestic Trade of the United States, 1800–1860* (Urbana, Ill., 1937).

154 Pred, *Urban Growth and City-Systems in the United States*, 231.

155 Ibid., 229, 231.

156 Henry Ames, "Address to the Chamber of Commerce," June 8, 1857, quoted in Scharf, *History of St. Louis City and County*, 2:1347. For a very different relationship between distant investors and indigenous traders, see Leila Tarazi Fawaz, *Merchants and Migrants in Nineteenth-Century Beirut* (Cambridge, Mass., 1983), 86–87.

157 *Missouri Republican*, February 25, 1845.

158 *Annual Review of the Trade and Commerce of St. Louis for the Year 1848*, 10. According to the *Missouri Democrat*, it was "men from the East [who] made St. Louis great, rich and prosperous." See *Missouri Democrat*, October 20, 1858.

159 *Annual Review of the Trade and Commerce of St. Louis for the Year 1848*, 1.

160 For example, see *Hunt's Merchants' Magazine* 28 (April 1853): 437; *De Bow's Review* 17 (October 1854): 39.

161 Holt, "The Shaping of St. Louis," 272, 507.

162 R. and William Scott to Children, October 15, 1849, St. Louis History Collection, Missouri Historical Society, St. Louis, Missouri; *A Review of the Commerce of St. Louis for the Year 1849* (St. Louis, 1850), 3.

163 O. W. Jerome to Robert H. Miller, June 26, 1849, Robert H. Miller Papers, Missouri Historical Society, St. Louis, Missouri; Gustavus Wulfing to Julia Wulfing, July 30, 1849, *The Letters of Gustavus Wulfing*, 287. Also, see "Cholera Epidemics in St. Louis," *Missouri Historical Society: Glimpses of the Past* 3 (March 1936): 45–76; Patrick E. McLear, "The St. Louis Cholera Epidemic of 1849," *Missouri Historical Review* 63 (January 1969): 171–80.

164 *De Bow's Review* 5 (April 1848): 372.

165 Ibid. 16 (April 1854): 399; *Hunt's Merchants' Magazine* 15 (August 1846): 164; ibid. 24 (March 1851): 316.

166 *Annual Review* (St. Louis, 1854), 13.

167 [James] *Green's St. Louis Directory for 1845* (St. Louis, 1844), viii.

168 For the relationship between St. Louis and its hinterland trading partners, see Timothy R. Mahoney, "Urban History in a Regional Context: River Towns on the Upper Mississippi, 1840–1860," *Journal of American History* 72 (September 1985): 336, id., "River Towns in the Great West, 1835–1860" (Ph.D. dissertation, University of Chicago, 1982).

169 Hunter, *Steamboats on the Western Rivers*, 49 ; *Hunt's Merchants' Magazine* 26 (February 1852): 324–25; *De Bow's Review* 7 (August 1849): 179.

170 *Hunt's Merchants' Magazine* 26 (February 1852): 325.

171 See Mahoney, "Urban History in a Regional Context."

172 Allan R. Pred, "American Metropolitan Growth: 1860–1914, Industrialization, Initial Advantage," in *The Spatial Dynamics of U.S. Urban-Industrial Growth, 1800-1914*, 12–85; id., "The American Mercantile City: 1800–1840: Manufacturing, Growth, and Structure," in *The Spatial Dynamics of U.S. Urban-Industrial Growth, 1800–1914*, 143–215; Roberta Balstad Miller, *City and Hinterland* (Westport, Conn., 1979), 154; Diane Lindstrom and John Sharpless, "Urban Growth and Economic Structure in Antebellum America," in Paul Uselding, ed., *Research in Economic History* 3 (1978): 211.

173 For example, see Hunter, *Steamboats on the Western Rivers*, 49; Holt, "The Shaping of St. Louis," 274, 346; Holliday, *The World Rushed In*, 73.

174 Frederick Hawkins Piercy, *Route from Liverpool to Great Salt Lake Valley*, ed. Fawn M. Brodie (1855; reprint, Cambridge, Mass., 1962), 198–99; Moritz Busch, *Travels Between the Hudson and the Mississippi, 1851–1852*, trans. Norman H. Binger (1854; reprint, Lexington, Ky., 1971), 231.

175 *Missouri Republican*, April 1, 1853; ibid., April 24, 1844.

176   Cable, *The Bank of the State of Missouri*, 233; Holt, "The Shaping of St. Louis," 276.
177   Cable, *The Bank of the State of Missouri*, 233.
178   *A Review of the Commerce of St. Louis for the Year 1849*, 3.
179   *Missouri Republican*, March 30, 1852.
180   Ibid., April 9, 1849.
181   Ibid. Also see Perry McCandless, *A History of Missouri, 1820 to 1860*, volume 2 (Columbia, Mo., 1972), 130.
182   *A Review of the Commerce of St. Louis for the Year 1849*, 3.
183   Randall Hobart, May 1, 1849, quoted in Holliday, *The World Rushed In*, 73.
184   *Missouri Republican*, February 28, 1849.
185   Ibid.; *Annual Review of the Trade and Commerce of St. Louis for the Year 1848*, 4.
186   Missouri Vol. 36, p. 124, RGD.
187   *De Bow's Review* 16 (April 1854): 402.
188   *Hunt's Merchants' Magazine* 28 (April 1853): 436.
189   B. H. Kinney to General E. A. Hitchcock, April 4, 1859, Hitchcock Collection, Missouri Historical Society, St. Louis, Missouri.
190   Pred, *Urban Growth and City-Systems in the United States*, 220. Also, see Hogan, *Thoughts About the City of St. Louis*, 13; Cable, *The Bank of the State of Missouri*, 213; *Annual Review*, 23.
191   Porter and Livesay, *Merchants and Manufacturers*, 72.
192   Ibid., 64–65.
193   *Annual Review* (St. Louis, 1854), 12.
194   *Missouri Republican*, April 29, 1855.
195   Ibid., January 9, 1844.
196   Ibid.; Hogan, *Thoughts About the City of St. Louis*, 19.
197   *Missouri Republican*, September 6, 1845.
198   Primm, *Economic Policy*, 54.
199   Porter and Livesay, *Merchants and Manufacturers*, 78.
200   Rand, *One of a Thousand*, 117.
201   For perceptive treatments of cities that grew more rapidly than they developed, see Thomas M. Doerflinger, *A Vigorous Spirit of Enterprise* (Chapel Hill, N.C., 1986), 344–64; Harriet E. Amos, *Cotton City* (University, Ala., 1985); William H. Pease and Jane N. Pease, *The Web of Progress* (New York, 1985); Don H. Doyle, *New Men, New Cities, New South* (Chapel Hill, N.C., 1990). For an interesting discussion of New York merchants in the South, see Pred, *Urban Growth and the Circulation of Information*, 199.

Chapter 5: "The offspring of the east"

1   For an overview of the city's development during this period, see James Neal Primm, *Lion of the Valley* (Boulder, Colo, 1981), chaps. 4–6.
2   For San Francisco, see Roger W. Lotchin, *San Francisco, 1846–1856* (New

York, 1974); Peter R. Decker, *Fortunes and Failures* (Cambridge, Mass., 1978). Also see Richard C. Wade, *The Urban Frontier* (Cambridge, Mass., 1959); Lawrence H. Larsen, *The Urban West At the End of the Frontier* (Lawrence, Kans., 1978).

3   For studies that examine this general process, see Don Harrison Doyle, *The Social Order of a Frontier Community* (Urbana, 1978); Rush Welter, "The Frontier West as Image of American Society," *Mississippi Valley Historical Review* 46 (March 1960): 593–614; Paul E. Johnson, *A Shopkeeper's Millennium* (New York, 1978); Mary P. Ryan, *The Cradle of the Middle Class* (New York, 1981).

4   See Larson, *The Urban West at the End of the Frontier*; Welter, "The Frontier West As Image of American Society."

5   *New York Daily Tribune*, March 12, 1856; John D. Thompson to Amos A. Lawrence, July 22, 1857, Missouri History Collection, Missouri Historical Society, St. Louis, Missouri.

6   For population figures, see *Missouri Democrat*, November 13, 1855; Glen E. Holt, "The Shaping of St. Louis, 1763–1869" (Ph.D. dissertation, University of Chicago, 1975), 296, 417; George Helmuth Kellner, "The German Element on the Urban Frontier" (Ph.D. dissertation, University of Missouri–Columbia, 1973), 316.

7   For example, see William Greenleaf Eliot, *Lectures to Young Men* (Boston, 1856), 47.

8   See Reverend T. M. Cunningham, *Address Before the St. Louis Young Men's Christian Association* (St. Louis, 1853), 20.

9   Eliot, *Lectures to Young Men*.

10   "The Evangelization of the West," *New Englander* 4 (1846): 31.

11   Frank Blackwell Mayer, *With Pen and Pencil on the Frontier in 1851*, ed. Bertha Heilbron (St. Paul, Minn., 1932), 74.

12   Richard Lord to Jeremiah Lord, June, 1849, St. Louis History Collection, Missouri Historical Society, St. Louis, Missouri.

13   Lieutenant-Colonel Arthur Cunyghame, *A Glimpse at the Great Western Republic* (London, 1851), 1860.

14   *Missouri Republican*, September 24, 1848.

15   Ibid., March 15, 1851. Also see ibid., October 17, 1848.

16   Elizabeth Sargent to Friends, January 20, 1846, St. Louis History Collection, Missouri Historical Society, St. Louis, Missouri.

17   Minute Books, St. Louis Board of Aldermen, November 16, 1849, City Hall Archival Library, St. Louis, Missouri, microfilm.

18   See Primm, *Lion of the Valley*, chap. 5. For law enforcement in the city, see Maximilian Ivan Reichard, "The Origins of Urban Police" (Ph.D. dissertation, Washington University, 1975).

19   See Kellner, "The German Element on the Urban Frontier." Also see Walter D. Kamphoefner, *The Westfalians* (Princeton, 1987), 94.

20   *Missouri Democrat*, November 13, 1855.

21   Ibid.

22   Charles O. Gerrish to Stephanus, July 30, 1858, St. Louis History Collection, Missouri Historical Society, St. Louis, Missouri.

23 For example, see *Missouri Republican*, November 2, 1851; *Missouri Democrat*, October 15, 1853; ibid., April 13, 1855; Holt, "The Shaping of St. Louis," 296.

24 For Donahue, see the manuscript schedules of the Seventh Census (1850), St. Louis County.

25 *Missouri Democrat*, June 27, 1854. Also see ibid., March 23, 1854; ibid., April 14, 1854.

26 Randall Hobart, May 1, 1849, quoted in J. S. Holliday, *The World Rushed In* (New York, 1981), 72.

27 J. W. McClure, June 19, 1846, quoted in "From Virginia to Missouri in 1846: The Journal of Elizabeth Ann Cooley," eds. Edward D. Jervey and James E. Moss, *Missouri Historical Review* 60 (January 1966): 190.

28 Elizabeth Sargent to Friends, January 20, 1846, St. Louis History Collection, Missouri Historical Society, St. Louis, Missouri. Also see Elizabeth Sargent to Family, June 21, 1846, St. Louis History Collection, Missouri Historical Society, St. Louis, Missouri.

29 Elizabeth Sargent to Family, August 9, 1846, St. Louis History Collection, Missouri Historical Society, St. Louis, Missouri.

30 Charles O. Gerrish to Stephanus, July 30, 1858, St. Louis History Collection, Missouri Historical Society, St. Louis, Missouri.

31 Luke Shortfield, *The Western Merchant* (Philadelphia, 1849), 206.

32 *Missouri Republican*, January 14, 1860.

33 Shortfield, *The Western Merchant*, 206.

34 *Missouri Democrat*, October 5, 1853.

35 Eliot, *Lectures to Young Men*, 12.

36 See the manuscript schedules of the Seventh Census (1850), St. Louis County. Also see Kamphoefner, *The Westfalians*, 84.

37 For example, see Eliot, *Lectures to Young Men*, 12; Cunningham, *Address Before the St. Louis Young Men's Christian Association*, 19.

38 For Fitzgerdon, see the manuscript schedules of the Seventh Census (1850), St. Louis County.

39 For Baum, see the manuscript schedules of the Seventh Census (1850), St. Louis County.

40 *Missouri Republican*, March 10, 1848.

41 For Blatchford, see the manuscript schedules of the Seventh Census (1850), St. Louis County.

42 Records of the Second Baptist Church, Missouri Historical Society, St. Louis, Missouri, microfilm.

43 Records of the Bonhomme Presbyterian Church, Missouri Historical Society, St. Louis, Missouri.

44 For a different discussion of prosperity and migration, see Michael B. Katz, Michael J. Doucet, and Mark J. Stern, *The Social Organization of Early Industrial Capitalism* (Cambridge, Mass., 1982), 127.

45 Elizabeth Sargent to Mother, September 5, 1846, St. Louis History Collection, Missouri Historical Society, St. Louis, Missouri.

46 For a fascinating study of target earners, see Michael J. Piore, *Birds of Passage* (New York, 1979).

47 Lucius Salisbury to Harriet Hutchinson, October 23, 1844, Lucius Salisbury Papers, Joint Collection, University of Missouri Western Historical Manuscript Collection–Columbia and State Historical Society of Missouri Manuscripts, Columbia, Missouri.

48 See Kellner, "The German Element on the Urban Frontier."

49 *Missouri Republican*, December 19, 1848.

50 William Kelly, *Across the Rocky Mountains* (London, 1852), 36.

51 See Missouri Vol. 36, p. 68, R. G. Dun and Company Collection, Baker Library, Harvard University Graduate School of Business Administration, Boston, Massachusetts (hereafter cited as RGD).

52 Logan U. Reavis, *St. Louis* (St. Louis, 1875), xxvi.

53 John F. Darby, *Personal Recollections* (St. Louis, 1880), 318, 467.

54 Sylvia Simons to Simeon Lelands, April 15, 1850, St. Louis History Collection, Missouri Historical Society, St. Louis, Missouri. Also see J. H. Joiner to Reverend H. I. Brown, January 10, 1849, Missouri History Collection, Missouri Historical Society, St. Louis, Missouri.

55 See Meeting of the St. Louis City Council, October 11, 1843, Missouri Historical Society, St. Louis, Missouri; *Missouri Democrat*, October 28, 1853.

56 *Missouri Democrat*, April 9, 1853.

57 *Missouri Republican*, February 16, 1849. Also see ibid., April 8, 1845.

58 *Missouri Democrat*, August 13, 1853.

59 Robert Moore, "The Vital Statistics of St. Louis Since 1840," *Journal of the Association of Engineering Societies* 33 (November 1904): 299–324.

60 E. G. Simmons to Simeon Lelands, May 9, 1849, St. Louis History Collection, Missouri Historical Society, St. Louis, Missouri.

61 United States Census Bureau, *St. Louis Statistics for 1851–54* (Washington, D.C., 1855), 150.

62 For example, see *Missouri Republican*, July 26, 1843.

63 F. R. Roueche to John W. Ellis, February 16, 1848, in "Business and Life in St. Louis, Missouri, 1847–1848," ed. Lewis E. Atherton, *Missouri Historical Review* 37 (July 1943): 435.

64 Reverend George Lewis, *Impressions of America and American Churches* (Edinburgh, 1848), 256.

65 Elizabeth Sargent to Mother, December, 1846, St. Louis History Collection, Missouri Historical Society, St. Louis, Missouri.

66 *Missouri Democrat*, June 29, 1854.

67 *Missouri Republican*, June 22, 1849.

68 For the attitudes of residents during the epidemic, see Lady Emmeline Stuart-Wortley, *Travels in the United States* (New York, 1851), 111.

69 James S. Cowan to John W. Ellis, July 25, 1847, typescript, James S. Cowan Papers, Joint Collection, University of Missouri Western Historical Manuscript Collection–Columbia and State Historical Society of Missouri Manuscripts, Columbia, Missouri.

70 Robert Moore, "The Vital Statistics of St. Louis Since 1840," 306.

71 Eliot, *Lectures to Young Men*, 12.

72 William Greenleaf Eliot, "The Neglected Juvenile Population of Our City," *Missouri Republican*, November 12, 1854.

73 Cunningham, *Address Before the St. Louis Young Men's Christian Association*, 19.
74 For example, see J. Davis to Lewis Bristol, July 22, 1838, St. Louis History Collection, Missouri Historical Society, St. Louis, Missouri.
75 Moritz Busch, *Travels Between the Hudson and the Mississippi, 1851–1852*, trans. Norman H. Binger (1854; reprint, Lexington, Ky., 1971), 235.
76 *Missouri Republican*, March 24, 1852.
77 *Missouri Democrat*, August 5, 1853.
78 Local editors were more concerned with prosperity than with the evil influence of prostitutions. "If the evils be a necessity in our population let it at least be deprived of its objectionable features, so far as may be found practicable, and above all let it flourish in some remote district, where it will not constantly be thrust upon the community." *Missouri Republican*, October 16, 1851. For a similar interpretation, see John C. Schneider, *Detroit and the Problem of Order, 1830–1930* (Lincoln, 1980), 25–28, 42–44. For an interesting treatment of prostitutes in a western boomtown, see Paula Petrik, "Capitalists With Rooms," *Montana* 31 (April 1981): 28–41.
79 *Missouri Republican*, March 10, 1845. Also see *Missouri Democrat*, November 2, 1853; ibid, September 8, 1853.
80 Randall Hobart, May 1, 1849, quoted in Holliday, *The World Rushed In*, 73.
81 Ibid.
82 A Victim to the Speculator's Art, *The Speculators of St. Louis* (St. Louis, 1851), 10.
83 *Missouri Republican*, January 3, 1849.
84 Gordon, ed., *Overland to California*, 26.
85 *Home Missionary* 26 (September 1853): 119; Scotch Jack, *A New Year's Address to the Sovereign People, For the Jubilee Year of Our Lord 1850*, 4. Also see *Missouri Republican*, March 26, 1845; *Missouri Democrat*, December 23, 1854.
86 *Missouri Republican*, March 27, 1852; ibid., February 9, 1852.
87 *Missouri Democrat*, May 7, 1853. Also see ibid., May 9, 1853.
88 Ibid., January 4, 1854.
89 Local editors, for example, devoted considerable attention to such "outrageous" events. See *Missouri Democrat*, May 19, 1853; *Missouri Republican*, July 26, 1845.
90 See *Missouri Republican*, March 23, 1852; ibid., July 8, 1851; ibid., July 16, 1849; ibid., August 5, 1853.
91 Ibid., June 7, 1844.
92 Ibid., August 5, 1853.
93 Ibid., October 15, 1848.
94 Ibid., August 8, 1854; ibid., August 9, 1854; ibid., August 10, 1854; G. Inglimann to Soulard, Soulard Papers, Missouri Historical Society, St. Louis, Missouri.
95 *Missouri Republican*, June 7, 1844.
96 William Swain to George Swain, April 25, 1849, quoted in Holiday, *The World Rushed In*, 74.
97 Cunningham, *Address Before the St. Louis Young Men's Christian Association*, 20.

98 *Presbyterian Casket* 3 (March 1852): 67. Also see Cunningham, *Address Before the St. Louis Young Men's Christian Association;* Eliot, *Lectures to Young Men.*

99 Eliot, *Lectures to Young Men,* 47.

100 *The Teacher and Western Educational Magazine* 11 (February 1853): 33.

101 Holt, "The Shaping of St. Louis, 1763–1860," 465.

102 *Missouri Democrat,* March 9, 1855.

103 *Annual Review of the Trade and Commerce of St. Louis For the Year 1848* (St. Louis, 1849), 3.

104 *Missouri Republican,* October 14, 1853.

105 Truman Marcellus Post, "The New Settlements of the West," May, 1854, quoted in T. A. Post, *Truman Marcellus Post, D. D.* (Boston, 1891), 216.

106 Holt, "The Shaping of St. Louis," 453.

107 *Missouri Republican,* April 16, 1855; *Missouri Democrat,* April 21, 1855.

108 *Missouri Republican,* May 15, 1855.

109 Ibid., February 15, 1854; Ibid., April 13, 1855; Holt, "The Shaping of St. Louis," 232. Also see *Missouri Republican,* July 9, 1855. Also see George A. Ketcham, "Municipal Police Reform: A Comparative Study of Law Enforcement in Cincinnati, Chicago, New Orleans, New York, and St. Louis, 1844–1877" (Ph.D. dissertation, University of Missouri-Columbia, 1967), 73–74.

110 Holt, "The Shaping of St. Louis," 465.

111 Marie George Windell, "Reform in the Roaring Forties and Fifties," *Missouri Historical Review* 39 (April 1945): 295.

112 *Missouri Republican,* November 12, 1854; Thomas L. Karnes, *William Gilpin* (Austin, 1970), 225.

113 *Missouri Republican,* June 25, 1855.

114 Ibid., June 13, 1855.

115 Ibid., September 15, 1854.

116 *Mayor's Message, with Accompanying Documents, Submitted to the City Council, of the City of St. Louis, At the Opening of the First Stated Session, May 14, 1855* (St. Louis, 1855), 5.

117 *Full and Accurate Report of the Trial of William P. Darnes,* ed. Thomas S. Nelson (Boston, 1841), 135; *The Western Journal* 4 (July 1850): 218.

118 *Missouri Republican,* January 22, 1854; ibid., March 29, 1855.

119 *Missouri Democrat,* April 6, 1855.

120 Ibid.

121 Walter Samuel Swisher, *A History of the Church of the Messiah, 1834–1934* (St. Louis, 1934), 31.

122 Ibid., 29–32.

123 *Missouri Republican,* January 26, 1855; *First Annual Report of the St. Louis Young Men's Christian Association* (St. Louis, 1854), 16.

124 *First Annual Report of the St. Louis Young Men's Christian Association* (St. Louis, 1854).

125 Cunningham, *Address Before the St. Louis Young Men's Christian Association,* 8.

126 *First Annual Report of the St. Louis Young Men's Christian Association* (St. Louis, 1854), 24.

127 Cunningham, *Address Before the St. Louis Young Men's Christian Association*, 6; Eliot, "The Neglected Juvenile Population of Our City," *Missouri Republican*, November 12, 1854; *First Annual Report of the St. Louis Young Men's Christian Association* (St. Louis, 1854), 10; *Missouri Republican*, December 13, 1853.

128 See *First Annual Report of the St. Louis Young Men's Christian Association* (St. Louis, 1854), 35–40; Swisher, *A History of the Church of the Messiah*.

129 John D. Thompson to Amos A. Lawrence, July 22, 1857, Missouri History Collection, Missouri Historical Society, St. Louis, Missouri.

130 Kellner, "The German Element on the Urban Frontier," 168–97.

131 Busch, *Travels Between the Hudson and the Mississippi, 1851–1852*, 247.

132 Ibid., 237.

133 Shortfield, *The Western Merchant*, 116; [James] *Green's St. Louis Directory for 1847* (St. Louis, 1847), 254.

134 *Missouri Republican*, January 19, 1849; ibid., May 3, 1854.

135 For example, see Missouri Vol. 36, p. 142, RGD; Missouri Vol. 36, p. 287, RGD.

136 For example, see [James] *Green's St. Louis Directory for 1847*, 254; [James] *Green's St. Louis Directory for 1851* (St. Louis, 1850), 429.

137 See Dale K. Doepke, "St. Louis Magazines Before the Civil War, 1832–1860" (Ph.D. dissertation, Washington University, 1963), 59, 249.

138 *Missouri Republican*, August 19, 1848.

139 Hiram Fuller, *Belle Briton On A Tour* (New York, 1858), 76. Also see Doepke, "St. Louis Magazines Before the Civil War," 140.

140 Truman Marcellus Post, quoted in T. A. Post, *Truman Marcellus Post*, 239.

141 Doepke, "St. Louis Magazines Before the Civil War," 184.

142 For example, see A. F. Burghardt, "A Hypothesis About Gateway Cities," *Annals of the Association of American Geographers* 61 (June 1971): 277.

143 In St. Louis prosperity did not produce both a high rate of persistence and an influx of migrants. Rather, the boom attracted newcomers, but they did not remain in the city. For a discussion of the relationship among persistence, migration, and prosperity in older and better-established cities, see Katz et al., *The Social Organization of Early Industrial Capitalism*, 127.

Chapter 6: A border city in an age of sectionalism

1 *Hunt's Merchants' Magazine and Commercial Review* 28 (March 1853): 436.

2 *Missouri Democrat*, August 6, 1860.

3 Ibid., November 9, 1855.

4 Ibid., November 18, 1859.

5 Ibid., December 24, 1856.

6 *Annual Review: The History of St. Louis, Commercial Statistics, Improvements of the Year and Account of Leading Manufactories* (St. Louis, 1854), 37. Also see *Missouri Republican*, February 3, 1853; ibid., March 8, 1853; Glen E. Holt, "The Shaping of St. Louis, 1763–1860" (Ph.D. dissertation, University of Chicago, 1975), 297; Alice Lida Cochran, "The Saga of an Irish Immigrant Family" (Ph.D. dissertation, St. Louis University, 1958), 103.

7 *Missouri Democrat*, November 13, 1855; Gustavus Wulfing to Mother and Sister, April 10, 1842, *The Letters of Gustavus Wulfing*, trans. and ed. Carl Hirsch (Fitch, Mo., 1941), 178.

8 Gustavus Wulfing to Julia, May 4, 1849, in "The Followers of Duden," trans. and ed. William G. Bek, *Missouri Historical Review* 17 (July 1923): 493. Also see George Helmuth Kellner, "The German Element on the Urban Frontier: St. Louis, 1830–1860" (Ph.D. dissertation, University of Missouri–Columbia, 1973), 75; *Missouri Republican*, February 19, 1852; *Missouri Democrat*, April 17, 1854; ibid., November 13, 1855; "The German Society of St. Louis," *Western Journal and Civilian* 5 (1851): 342.

9 *The Speculators of St. Louis* (St. Louis, 1851), 18.

10 Anson F. Ashley to Father, November 24, 1855, St. Louis History Collection, Missouri Historical Society, St. Louis, Missouri.

11 Kellner, "The German Element on the Urban Frontier," 274.

12 Missouri Vol. 36, p. 204, R. G. Dun and Company Collection, Baker Library, Harvard University Graduate School of Business Administration, Boston, Massachusetts (hereafter cited as RGD).

13 Missouri Vol. 38, p. 56, RGD; Missouri Vol. 37, p. 461, RGD.

14 John Hogan, *Thoughts About the City of St. Louis* (St. Louis, 1854), 14; *Annual Review of the Commerce of St. Louis for the Year 1854* (St. Louis, 1855), 30. The proportion of businesses operated by German immigrants increased by 121 percent during this period. See Missouri Vols. 36–38, RGD. For a fuller explanation of this kind of entrepreneurial enterprise, see Clyde Griffen and Sally Griffen, *Natives and Newcomers* (Cambridge, Mass., 1978), 139–92.

15 Missouri Vol. 38, p. 120, RGD. For a similar experience, see Missouri Vol. 37, p. 483, RGD.

16 See Griffen and Griffen, *Natives and Newcomers*, 139–92.

17 Kellner, "The German Element on the Urban Frontier," 272.

18 See J. M. D. Burrows, *Fifty Years in Iowa* (Davenport, Iowa, 1888); Timothy R. Mahoney, "Urban History in a Regional Context," *Journal of American History* 72 (September 1985): 318-39; id., "River Towns in the Great West, 1835–1860" (Ph.D. dissertation, University of Chicago, 1982); id., *River Towns in the Great West* (New York, 1990), 209–42.

19 Ibid. Also see *Annual Review: The History of St. Louis, Commercial Statistics, Improvements of the Year and Account of Leading Manufactories*, 7; *Missouri Democrat*, March 6, 1855.

20 *Missouri Democrat*, March 6, 1855. Also see Luke Shortfield, *The Western Merchant* (Philadelphia, 1849); Louis E. Atherton, *The Southern Country Store* (Baton Rouge, La., 1949).

21 Each spring St. Louis newspapers announced the "arrival of the country

merchants." For example, see *Missouri Democrat*, March 6, 1855; ibid., March 9, 1855. Also see Mahoney, *River Towns in the Great West*, 216; *Annual Review of the Commerce of St. Louis together with a List of Steamboat Disasters, for the Year 1856* (St. Louis, 1857), 4.

22 Allan Pred, *Urban Growth and City-Systems in the United States, 1840–1860* (Cambridge, Mass., 1980), 104.

23 Victor S. Clark, *History of Manufactures in the United States* (1929; reprint, New York, 1949), 1:474.

24 Mahoney, "Urban History in a Regional Context," 328, 336.

25 Clark, *History of Manufactures in the United States*, 1:474.

26 Pred, *Urban Growth and City-Systems in the United States*, 104. For example, see Missouri Vol. 37, p. 605, RGD. According to local credit investigators, Lyon and Shorb of Pittsburgh operated "one of the largest [iron] houses in the United States," and their St. Louis agent, George Hall, conducted a thriving outlet in the city. For other examples, see Missouri Vol. 37, p. 606, RGD; Missouri Vol. 37, p. 569, RGD.

27 Missouri Vol. 37, p. 458, RGD. For similar examples, see Missouri Vol. 36, p. 265, RGD; Missouri Vol. 38, p. 58, RGD; *Missouri Republican*, February 20, 1854. Also see [Jacob N.] Taylor and [M. O.] Crooks, *Sketch Book of St. Louis* (St. Louis, 1858), 298.

28 For example, see "deeds of assignment" in the Missouri Circuit Court Archives, Federal Courthouse, St. Louis, Missouri. Most of the debts contracted during this period were owed to midwestern creditors. See Ward and Doggett, Missouri Circuit Court Archives, Federal Courthouse, St. Louis, Missouri; Missouri Vol. 38, p. 14, RGD.

29 The proportion of businesses started by Yankee migrants fell by nearly 20 percent during this period, while the proportion of firms begun by midwesterners rose by almost 40 percent. Similarly, steamboat arrivals from the Mississippi valley skyrocketed during the early 1850s. See Louis C. Hunter, *Steamboats on the Western Rivers* (Cambridge, Mass., 1949), 49.

30 See Missouri Vols. 36–38, RGD.

31 Arthur M. Johnson and Barry E. Supple, *Boston Capitalists and Western Railroads* (Cambridge, Mass., 1967), 103.

32 Ibid.

33 Pred, *Urban Growth and City-Systems in the United States*, 181.

34 During the mid-1840s New Yorkers established nearly 40 percent of local businesses. By comparison, during the late 1840s they established one-third of St. Louis firms; during the mid-1850s New York migrants started fewer than one-quarter of local businesses, and less than one new firm in six was a New York venture during the late 1850s.

35 Robert Greenhalgh Albion, *The Rise of New York Port* (1939; reprint, Boston, 1984), 285.

36 For general discussions of trade, see Fred Mitchell Jones, *Middlemen in the Domestic Trade of the United States 1800–1860* (Urbana, Ill., 1937), 14–23; James E. Vance, Jr., *The Merchant's World* (Englewood Cliffs, N.J., 1970), chap. 5.

37 Scotch Jack, *A New Year's Address to the Sovereign People, For the Jubilee Year of Our Lord, 1850* (St. Louis, 1850), 6.

38 For example, see *Missouri Democrat*, January 4, 1854; Kellner, "The German Element on the Urban Frontier," 295.

39 For a discussion of the relationship between growth and opportunity, see John N. Ingham, "Rags to Riches Revisited," *Journal of American History* 63 (December 1976): 615–37.

40 Elizabeth Sargent to Family, August 17, 1847, St. Louis History Collection, Missouri Historical Society, St. Louis, Missouri.

41 Later travel accounts and journals devoted far less attention to the city than had earlier books on the West.

42 For examples of this kind of "boredom," see John A. Nicholls, Letter of October 11, 1857, *A Selection From the Letters of the Late J. Ashton Nicholls*, ed. Sarah Nicholls (Manchester, England, 1862), 206; *Hunt's Merchants' Magazine* 28 (May 1853): 557; ibid. 34 (June 1856): 706.

43 *Hunt's Merchants' Magazine* 28 (May 1853): 557; ibid. 36 (March 1857): 374.

44 Chicago and San Francisco captured the lion's share of eastern attention, though some smaller western towns received additional attention as well.

45 Nicholls, Letter of October 11, 1857, *A Selection From the Letters of the Late J. Ashton Nicholls*, 206.

46 Major Henry Smith Turner, quoted in Dwight L. Clarke, *William Tecumseh Sherman* (San Francisco, 1969), 19.

47 *Hunt's Merchants' Magazine* 36 (March 1857): 374. Also see Abbott, *Boosters and Businessmen*, 126–42.

48 Kalikst Wolski, *American Impressions*, trans. Marion Moore Coleman (1876; reprint, Cheshire, Conn., 1968), 65; *Hunt's Merchants' Magazine* 26 (April 1852): 424.

49 For example, see Cunyghame, *A Glimpse at the Great Western Republic*, 49; *Hunt's Merchants' Magazine* 32 (June 1855): 694. For a more general discussion of this type of boosterism, see Abbott, *Boosters and Businessmen*, 126–42; Wyatt Winton Belcher, *The Economic Rivalry Between St. Louis and Chicago 1850–1880* (New York, 1947), 125.

50 *Hunt's Merchants' Magazine* 34 (June 1856): 705.

51 Mrs. Isabella Lucy Bishop, *The Englishwoman in America* (London, 1856), 154. Also see Cunyghame, *A Glimpse at the Great Western Republic*, 49.

52 *Missouri Democrat*, September 10, 1857.

53 Truman Marcellus Post, quoted in T. A. Post, *Truman Marcellus Post* (Boston, 1891), 218.

54 For example, see *Home Missionary* 18 (January 1846): 104–5.

55 *Hunt's Merchants' Magazine* 36 (May 1857): 569.

56 *Missouri Democrat*, August 24, 1855. Also see Belcher, *The Economic Rivalry Between St. Louis and Chicago*, 125; Abbott, *Boosters and Businessmen*, 126–42.

57 *Hunt's Merchants' Magazine* 32 (June 1855): 684. Also see *Missouri Republican*, January 17, 1855; William Ferguson, *America By River and Rail* (London, 1856), 368.

58 *Missouri Republican*, January 17, 1855.
59 For an introduction to this literature, see Belcher, *The Economic Rivalry Between St. Louis and Chicago*; J. Christopher Schnell, "Chicago Versus St. Louis," *Missouri Historical Review* 71 (April 1977): 245–65. Overlooking the institutional problems and capital shortages that plagued Missouri railroad builders, Wyatt Belcher argues that local boosters and municipal officials expressed little interest in railroads. Instead, he suggests that the "Southern character" of St. Louis merchants produced an "innate conservatism." Despite numerous railroad conventions, bond sales, and tax plans, Belcher maintained that local officials were blind to the benefits of railroads and shunned construction efforts. See Belcher, *The Economic Rivalry Between St. Louis and Chicago*, 15. Belcher's portrayal of St. Louis merchants is incorrect, as is his analysis of local attitudes toward railroad construction. For an important corrective, see James Neal Primm, *Lion of the Valley* (Boulder, 1981), 234–38.
60 John Lauritz Larson, *Bonds of Enterprise* (Cambridge, Mass., 1984), 45. Also see *Hunt's Merchants' Magazine* 28 (May 1853): 557.
61 *Hunt's Merchants' Magazine* 28 (May 1853): 557.
62 Abbott, *Boosters and Businessmen*, 132–33; *Missouri Republican*, January 17, 1855. Also see Ferguson, *America By River and Rail*, 191.
63 Bishop, *The Englishwoman in America*, 157.
64 See *Missouri Republican*, August 24, 1855; ibid., October 30, 1854; *Missouri Democrat*, November 18, 1859. San Francisco's capital came from the same sources. See Peter R. Decker, *Fortunes and Failures* (Cambridge, Mass., 1978), 9.
65 See James A. Ward, *Railroads and the Character of America, 1820–1887* (Knoxville, 1986).
66 See *Hunt's Merchants' Magazine* 34 (June 1856): 706. Also see Belcher, *The Economic Rivalry Between St. Louis and Chicago*, 55; Abbott, *Boosters and Businessmen*, 136–38, 161–65; *Missouri Republican*, June 18, 1855; *Missouri Democrat*, July 26, 1855; Ward, *Railroads and the Character of America, 1820–1887*.
67 See Schnell, "Chicago Versus St. Louis."
68 Ibid. Also see *Missouri Republican*, April 28, 1835; ibid., February 25, 1836; James Neal Primm, *Economic Policy in the Development of a Western State* (Cambridge, Mass., 1954), 105; id., *Lion of the Valley*, 210–35.
69 *A Review of the Commerce of St. Louis for the Year 1849* (St. Louis, 1850), 2.
70 Ibid.
71 *Missouri Republican*, September 21, 1853. Also see *Missouri Democrat*, July 9, 1855; *Missouri Republican*, August 24, 1855.
72 Schnell, "Chicago Versus St. Louis," 255.
73 Ibid.
74 Thomas S. Barclay, *The Movement for Municipal Home Rule in St. Louis* (Columbia, Mo., 1943), 22.
75 *Missouri Democrat*, November 23, 1854. For a fuller discussion of St. Louis residents and Missouri railroads, see John W. Million, *State Aid to Railways in Missouri* (Chicago, 1896); Paul W. Gates, "The Railroads of

Missouri, 1850–1870," *Missouri Historical Review* 26 (January 1932): 126–41; Homer Clevenger, "The Building of the Hannibal and St. Joseph Railroad," *Missouri Historical Review* 36 (October 1941): 32–48; Primm, *Economic Policy*, 78–80, 100; id., *Lion of the Valley*, 197–238; John Ray Cable, *The Bank of the State of Missouri* (New York, 1923), 234; Schnell, "Chicago Versus St. Louis," 246–59; Robert E. Riegel, *The Story of the Western Railroads* (New York, 1926), 51–52; Belcher, *The Economic Rivalry Between St. Louis and Chicago*, 72–95.

76 *Missouri Democrat*, October 28, 1854.

77 See Schnell, "Chicago Versus St. Louis," 254–57; Belcher, *The Economic Rivalry Between St. Louis and Chicago*, 78.

78 *Missouri Democrat*, November 30, 1854.

79 *Western Journal and Civilian* 14 (October 1855): 298.

80 Governor Sterling Price, "Inaugural Address," January 3, 1853, in *Messages and Proclamations of the Governors of the State of Missouri*, eds. Buel Leopard and Floyd C. Shoemaker (Columbia, Mo., 1922), 2:408. Also see Governor Austin A. King, "Second Biennial Address," December 28, 1852, in *Messages and Proclamations*, 2:330.

81 Governor John C. Edwards, "Second Biennial Address," December 26, 1848, in *Messages and Proclamations*, 2:97. Also see Governor John C. Edwards, "Speech to the House of Representatives," February 16, 1847, in *Messages and Proclamations*, 2:236.

82 *Western Journal and Civilian* 11 (October 1853): 2; Primm, *Lion of the Valley*, 211; Belcher, *The Economic Rivalry Between St. Louis and Chicago*, 78.

83 Governor Austin A. King, "Second Biennial Address," December 28, 1852, in *Messages and Proclamations*, 2:352.

84 Governor Sterling Price, "Inaugural Address," January 3, 1853, in *Messages and Proclamations*, 2:408. Also see Governor Austin A. King, "Second Biennial Address," December 28, 1852, in *Messages and Proclamations*, 2:329; Primm, *Economic Policy*, 96–97; Gates, "The Railroads of Missouri," 129.

85 Governor Sterling Price, "Inaugural Address," January 3, 1853, in *Messages and Proclamations*, 2:408.

86 Governor Sterling Price, "Second Biennial Message," December 28, 1856, in *Messages and Proclamations*, 2:440. Also see Schnell, "Chicago Versus St. Louis," 247–48.

87 See Governor Austin A. King, "First Biennial Address," December 30, 1850, in *Messages and Proclamations*, 2:307; Governor Austin A. King, "Second Biennial Address," December 28, 1852, in *Messages and Proclamations*, 2:330; Million, *State Aid to Railways in Missouri*, 90, 94; Primm, *Economic Policy*, 112–13.

88 See Illinois Vols. 27–29, RGD.

89 *Western Journal and Civilian* 11 (March 1854): 442.

90 *Senate Journal*, Adjourned Session, 1855, Appendix, 114, quoted in Million, *State Aid to Railways in Missouri*, 94. Also see *Western Journal and Civilian* 11 (March 1854): 442 ; Riegel, *The Story of the Western Railroads*, 6, 21, 51.

91 *Western Journal and Civilian* 11 (March 1854): 442.

92 Local editors noted that "Missouri has but 50 miles in railroad in operation – the lowest in the list of states, but little Delaware." See *Missouri Democrat*, January 18, 1855.

93 See Governor Austin A. King, "First Biennial Address," December 30, 1850, in *Messages and Proclamations*, 2:307.

94 *Missouri Republican*, April 3, 1853. Also see Primm, *Economic Policy*, 112–13; Belcher, *The Economic Rivalry Between St. Louis and Chicago*, 80.

95 For example, see *New York Evening Post*, February 14, 1856.

96 See James A. Rawley, *Race and Politics* (Philadelphia, 1969), 60–62; Robert W. Johannsen, *Stephen A. Douglas* (New York, 1973).

97 Ibid.

98 *Missouri Republican*, June 18, 1855; *Missouri Democrat*, July 11, 1855; ibid., September 27, 1856.

99 See David M. Potter, *The Impending Crisis*, compl. and ed. Don E. Fehrenbacher (New York, 1976), 199. Also see Eli Thayer, *A History of the Kansas Crusade* (1889; reprint, Freeport, N.Y., 1971), 11.

100 Eli Thayer, *The New England Emigrant Aid Company* (Worcester, 1887); Johannsen, *Stephen A. Douglas*, 472; Larson, *Bonds of Enterprise*, 86; Rawley, *Race and Politics*, 84; James Brewer Stewart, *Holy Warriors* (New York, 1976), 164; Louis Filler, *The Crusade Against Slavery* (New York, 1960), 238.

101 Rawley, *Race and Politics*, 84–85; Edward Everett Hale, *Kanzas and Nebraska* (1854; reprint, Freeport, N.Y., 1972), 223. Thayer's "plan" enjoyed little success. Financial problems plagued the venture, and fewer than fifteen hundred "emigrants" migrated to Kansas under the auspices of the New England Emigrant Aid Company. Nonetheless, this scheme transformed the settlement process. According to Robert Johannsen, "the impact on Missourians was profound." Johannsen, *Stephen A. Douglas*, 473.

102 Rawley, *Race and Politics*, 84; Johannsen, *Stephen A. Douglas*, 316.

103 For example, see Governor Sterling Price, "Inaugural Address," January 3, 1853, in *Messages and Proclamations*, 2:408; Governor Austin A. King, "Second Biennial Address," December 28, 1852, in *Messages and Proclamations*, 2:329. Also see Johannsen, *Stephen A. Douglas*, 473.

104 See David Rice Atchison, *Address of Senator Atchison to the People of Missouri* (Washington, D.C., 1854).

105 See Maximilian Ivan Reichard, "The Origins of Urban Police: Freedom and Order in Antebellum St. Louis" (Ph.D. dissertation, Washington University, 1975), 29; James Shortridge, "The Expansion of the Settlement Frontier in Missouri," *Missouri Historical Review* 75 (October 1980): 70; William O. Lynch, "The Influence of Population Movements on Missouri Before 1861," *Missouri Historical Review* 16 (July 1922): 506–16; Russel L. Gerlach, *Settlement Patterns in Missouri* (Columbia, 1986), chap. 3.

106 Clairborne F. Jackson, January 15, 1849, quoted in Charles M. Harvey, "Missouri From 1849 to 1861," *Missouri Historical Review* 2 (October

1907): 23. Also see Norma L. Peterson, *Freedom and Franchise* (Columbia, Mo., 1965), 20–21; Don E. Fehrenbacher, *Slavery, Law, and Politics* (New York, 1981), 133.

107 Testimony of H. Miles Moore, May 30, 1856, *Report of the Special Committee Appointed to Investigate the Troubles in Kansas*, 34th Congress, 1st session, Report 22, William A. Howard, chairman (Washington, D.C., 1856), 421 (hereafter cited as Howard Report). Also see Governor Sterling Price, "Second Biennial Message," December 29, 1856, in *Messages and Proclamations*, 2:426.

108 In view of the climate of Missouri, many visitors to the region were surprised to find any slaves in the state. Frederika Bremer, for example, concluded that Missourians "maintain the institution of slavery rather out of bravado than any belief in its necessity. It has no products which might not be cultivated by white laborers, as its climate does not belong to the hot south." See Frederika Bremer, *The Homes of the New World* (New York, 1853), 2:93. Also see *Hunt's Merchants' Magazine* 38 (April 1858): 439; Harrison A. Trexler, *Slavery in Missouri, 1804–1865* (Baltimore, 1914), 225–26.

109 For example, see *Missouri Democrat*, September 27, 1856; ibid., October 11, 1856; ibid., March 31, 1858.

110 Rawley, *Race and Politics*, 80; Trexler, *Slavery in Missouri*, 173. Some antislavery writers expected the "peculiar institution" to wither and die in Missouri. Thus, they hoped that the state would eventually become a free-soil stronghold in the South. See Richard H. Sewell, *Ballots For Freedom* (New York, 1976), 318–20.

111 *Hannibal Tri-Weekly Messenger*, July 21, 1855; *New York Daily Tribune*, March 11, 1856; Perry McCandless, *A History of Missouri, 1820–1860* (Columbia, 1972), 270; Gerlach, *Settlement Patterns*, 23; Rawley, *Race and Politics*, 80; Trexler, *Slavery in Missouri*, 173.

112 According to William Kingsford, "slavery is not in request in the city, for owing to its proximity to Illinois, a slave could cross the river any night and be free. For there is in Illinois a strong anti-slavery party, ever ready to assist the slave." William Kingsford, *Impressions of the West and South* (Toronto, 1858), 34. Also see S. R. Shrader to Colby Shrader, January 12, 1846, St. Louis History Collection, Missouri Historical Society, St. Louis, Missouri; *Hannibal Tri-Weekly Messenger*, June 23, 1855; *Missouri Democrat*, August 23, 1856; *De Bow's Review* 23 (November 1857): 521; James Thomas, *From Slave to St. Louis Entrepreneur*, ed. Loren Schweninger (Columbia, Mo., 1984), 153; Trexler, *Slavery in Missouri*, 173, 185–87.

113 Trexler, *Slavery in Missouri*, 173, 187.

114 For example, see testimony of H. Miles Moore, May 30, 1856, *Howard Report*, 421; testimony of John Scott, May 26, 1856, *Howard Report*, 894; testimony of T. H. Day, May 31, 1856, *Howard Report*, 526.

115 Testimony of H. Miles Moore, May 30, 1856, *Howard Report*, 421; *Liberty Weekly Tribune*, April 27, 1855; Sara T. L. Robinson, *Kansas* (Boston, 1856), 85. Robinson's reports had a special importance because she was

married to Dr. Charles Robinson, Eli Thayer's agent in Kansas.

116 Testimony of Charles E. Kearney, June 2, 1856, *Howard Report*, 853. Also see Testimony of John Scott, May 26, 1856, *Howard Report*, 894.

117 For example, see [Columbia] *Dollar Missouri Journal*, May 24, 1855; *Liberty Weekly Tribune*, April 27, 1855; ibid., November 6, 1855; Newspaper Clipping, September, 1854, Frederick Starr, Jr., Papers, Joint Collection, University of Missouri Western Historical Manuscript Collection–Columbia and State Historical Society of Missouri Manuscripts, Columbia, Missouri.

118 David Atchison, quoted in Frederick Starr, Jr., to Father, August 14, 1854, Frederick Starr, Jr., Papers, Joint Collection, University of Missouri Western Historical Manuscript Collection–Columbia and State Historical Society of Missouri Manuscripts, Columbia, Missouri. Also see Frederick Starr, Jr., to Father, September 19, 1854, Frederick Starr, Jr., Papers, Joint Collection, University of Missouri Western Historical Manuscript Collection–Columbia and State Historical Society of Missouri Manuscripts, Columbia, Missouri; Rawley, *Race and Politics*, 81; William E. Parrish, *David Rice Atchison of Missouri* (Columbia, Mo., 1961).

119 "Platte County Self-Defense Association," Newspaper Clipping, Frederick Starr, Jr., Papers, Joint Collection, University of Missouri Western Historical Manuscript Collection–Columbia and State Historical Society of Missouri Manuscripts, Columbia, Missouri; Johannsen, *Stephen A. Douglas*, 473; Charles Sumner "The Crime Against Kansas. The Apologies For The Crime. The True Remedy," in *The Last Three Speeches on Kansas and Freedom* (Boston, 1856), 609; John H. Gihon, *Geary and Kansas* (Philadelphia, 1857), 30; Roy F. Nichols and Eugene H. Berwanger, *The Stakes of Power* (New York, 1982), 54; Trexler, *Slavery in Missouri*, 195.

120 Quoted in Trexler, *Slavery in Missouri*, 194–95.

121 Ibid.

122 [Columbia] *Dollar Missouri Journal*, May 24, 1855. Also see Trexler, *Slavery in Missouri*, 194.

123 *Liberty Weekly Tribune*, quoted in Trexler, *Slavery in Missouri*, 194.

124 David Atchison, quoted in Charles Robinson, *The Kansas Conflict* (Lawrence, Kans., 1908), 93–94.

125 For example, see Charles Robinson, *The Kansas Conflict*, 132.

126 Ibid., 88.

127 Testimony of Dr. George A. Cutler, May 6, 1856, *Howard Report*, 357.

128 Sara T. L. Robinson, *The Kansas Conflict*, 135. Also see *Liberty Weekly Tribune*, March 23, 1855.

129 For example, see testimony of Dr. George A. Cutler, May 6, 1856, *Howard Report*, 357; testimony of Erastus D. Ladd, April 25, 1856, *Howard Report*, 118; *Howard Report*, 18, 653–54; Sara T. L. Robinson, *Kansas*, 17; William Phillips, *The Conquest of Kansas by Missouri and Her Allies* (1856; reprint, Freeport, N. Y., 1971), 75. Phillips was a "special correspondent" for the *New York Daily Tribune*. Also see Rawley, *Race*

and Politics, 88; Gihon, *Geary and Kansas*, 38; McCandless, *A History of Missouri*, 273.

130 Phillips, *The Conquest of Kansas*, 104. Also see Rawley, *Race and Politics*, 91.

131 Sara T. L. Robinson, *Kansas*, 249; Potter, *The Impending Crisis*, 218.

132 For example, see *New York Evening Post*, March 20, 1856; ibid., March 25, 1856; *New York Times*, February 25, 1856; Thayer, *A History of the Kansas Crusade*, 218; Thayer, *The New England Emigrant Aid Company*, 24. Also see Samuel A. Johnson, *The Battle Cry of Freedom* (Lawrence, Kans., 1954), 102; Alice Nichols, *Bleeding Kansas* (New York, 1954); David Herbert Donald, *Charles Sumner and the Coming of the Civil War* (Chicago, 1960), 279.

133 For example, see Sara T. L. Robinson, *Kansas*, 19, 65, 249; Sumner, *The Last Three Speeches on Kansas and Freedom*, 617, 623, 635.

134 Sara T. L. Robinson, *Kansas*, 249.

135 For example, see *Howard Report*, 65; Sumner, *The Last Three Speeches on Kansas and Freedom*, 587.

136 Sara T. L. Robinson, *Kansas*, 65, 183, 654; Phillips, *The Conquest of Kansas*, 81. Also see testimony of Edmund R. Zimmerman, May 7, 1856, *Howard Report*, 364; *New York Times*, February 25, 1856.

137 Sara T. L. Robinson, *Kansas*, 220–21; Phillips, *The Conquest of Kansas*, 172; testimony of J. N. Mace, April 28, 1856, *Howard Report*, 174–75; *New York Daily Tribune*, January 19, 1856.

138 *New York Times*, August 1, 1857.

139 Sara T. L. Robinson, *Kansas*, 249; Phillips, *The Conquest of Kansas*, 157; Rawley, *Race and Politics*, 89.

140 Sara T. L. Robinson, *Kansas*, 14, 65.

141 Thayer, *The New England Emigrant Aid Company*, 24. Also see William Lawrence, *The Life of Amos A. Lawrence* (Boston, 1899), 85; Rawley, *Race and Politics*, 84–85.

142 See *Missouri Republican*, February 8, 1856; ibid., February 11, 1856. Also see Potter, *The Impending Crisis*, 206.

143 For example, *New Orleans Daily Picayune*, May 14, 1856; Charles Robinson, *The Kansas Conflict*, 133.

144 Phillips, *The Conquest of Kansas*, 250, 286, 296; Sara T. L. Robinson, *Kansas*, 254; "Kansas Aid Societies," in *Miscellaneous Pamphlets, Kansas-Nebraska, 1854–1856*, 12.

145 Phillips, *The Conquest of Kansas*, 296.

146 Ibid., 286.

147 Sara T. L. Robinson, *Kansas*, 220–21. Also see Sumner, *The Last Three Speeches on Kansas and Freedom*, 633.

148 See Potter, *The Impending Crisis*, 220.

149 *Missouri Republican*, August 25, 1856. Also see *Missouri Democrat*, August 23, 1856; ibid., April 12, 1856.

150 Thomas Hart Benton, February 2, 1857, quoted in Dale K. Doepke, "St. Louis Magazines Before the Civil War, 1832–1860" (Ph.D. dissertation, Washington University, 1963), 120. Also see William Nisbet Chambers,

Old Bullion Benton (Boston, 1956), 427; Trexler, *Slavery in Missouri*, 144, 163; Peterson, *Freedom and Franchise*, 34–55; Erasmus Manford, *Twenty-Five Years in the West* (Chicago, 1867), 241.

151 Edward Bates, quoted in Reinhard H. Luthin, "Organizing the Republican Party in the Border-Slave Regions," *Missouri Historical Review* 38 (January 1944): 144.

152 James Rollins, quoted in Trexler, *Slavery in Missouri*, 163–64. Also see John Vollmer Mering, *The Whig Party in Missouri* (Columbia, 1967), 66.

153 *Missouri Democrat*, August 23, 1856. Also see ibid., March 15, 1855; *Missouri Republican*, March 8, 1856; ibid., May 11, 1857.

154 Nathan L. Rice, quoted in Trexler, *Slavery in Missouri*, 230; Montgomery Schuyler, "Thanksgiving," 1856, quoted in William Schuyler, *Ambassador of Christ* (New York, 1901), 114–15.

155 Schuyler, *Ambassador of Christ*, 114–15.

156 *Missouri Republican*, December 19, 1853.

157 *Missouri Democrat*, May 23, 1857.

158 Ibid., March 24, 1856.

159 *Missouri Republican*, October 30, 1856.

160 *Missouri Democrat*, August 23, 1856.

161 See Doepke, "St. Louis Magazines Before the Civil War," 120; Peterson, *Freedom and Franchise*, 39; Trexler, *Slavery in Missouri*, 144; Luthin, "Organizing the Republican Party," 144; Mering, *The Whig Party in Missouri*, 167; Elmer LeRoy Craik, "Southern Interest in Territorial Kansas, 1854–1858," *Kansas State Historical Society Collections* 15 (1919–22): 354. Also see Chambers, *Old Bullion Benton*, 407–9.

162 *The Brown-Reynolds Duel*, ed. Walter B. Stevens (St. Louis, 1911).

163 Peterson, *Freedom and Franchise*, 34–68; Primm, *Lion of the Valley*, 239–46; Walter D. Kamphoefner, "St. Louis Germans and the Republican Party, 1848–1860," *Mid-America* 57 (April 1975): 69–88.

164 B. Gratz Brown, April 6, 1855, quoted in Peterson, *Freedom and Franchise*, 34.

165 *Missouri Democrat*, September 1, 1855.

166 Ibid., December 24, 1857. Also see Charles Robinson, *The Kansas Conflict*, 132.

167 *Missouri Democrat*, September 1, 1855. Also see ibid., June 2, 1856; ibid., April 14, 1856; ibid., August 25, 1856.

168 Ibid., April 20, 1857; ibid., April 16, 1857.

169 Ibid., April 13, 1857. Also see *New York Times*, August 30, 1855.

170 For example, see *New York Daily Tribune*, April 8, 1857; *Missouri Democrat*, August 23, 1858; Thomas, *From Slave to St. Louis Entrepreneur*, 157.

171 *Missouri Republican*, April 5, 1857; *New York Daily Tribune*, April 8, 1857.

172 *Missouri Republican*, February 24, 1857. Also see Governor Robert Marcellus Stewart, "Second Biennial Address," January 3, 1861, in *Messages and Proclamations*, 3:143.

173 *Missouri Republican*, July 19, 1856.

174 Ibid., November 27, 1856. Also see ibid., April 5, 1857; *Missouri Democrat*, August 25, 1855.

175 For example, see *New York Times,* August 30, 1855; *New York Evening Post,* March 20, 1856; *New York Journal of Commerce,* August 12, 1856.

176 Mrs. Isabella Trotter, *First Impressions of the New World* (London, 1859), 228.

177 Ibid. Also see *Missouri Democrat,* December 31, 1859; *Cincinnati Daily Gazette,* November 9, 1859.

178 *Missouri Republican,* February 24, 1857; *De Bow's Review* 23 (November 1857): 521; *New York Daily Tribune,* March 12, 1856; *New York Journal of Commerce,* February 14, 1857.

179 Anthony Trollope, *North America,* eds. Donald Smalley and Bradford Allen Booth (1861; reprint, New York, 1951), 385.

180 Charles Mackay, *Life and Liberty in America* (New York, 1859), 151.

181 Trotter, *First Impressions of the New World,* 218.

182 See Don E. Fehrenbacher, *The Dred Scott Case* (New York, 1978).

183 For example, see *New York Evening Post,* March 25, 1856; *New York Times,* quoted in *Missouri Democrat,* August 20, 1857; *New York Independent,* quoted in *Missouri Republican,* January 31, 1857; *Newburyport Herald,* quoted in *Missouri Democrat,* August 18, 1857; *Buffalo Republic,* quoted in *Missouri Democrat,* April 14, 1857; *Dover Enquirer,* August 21, 1858, quoted in *Missouri Democrat,* October 10, 1858; *Missouri Democrat,* February 22, 1856.

184 Eli Thayer to E. E. Hale, February 15, 1856, New England Emigrant Aid Company Correspondence, 1854–1858, New England Emigrant Aid Company Papers, microfilm, reel 1.

185 R. A. Chapman to the New England Emigrant Aid Company, October 20, 1855, New England Emigrant Aid Company Correspondence, 1854–1858, New England Emigrant Aid Company Papers, microfilm, reel 1.

186 Thayer, *A History of the Kansas Crusade,* 207.

187 Thayer, *The New England Emigrant Aid Company,* 24. Also see *New York Times,* September 1, 1856; Craik, "Southern Interest in Territorial Kansas, 1854–1858," 366.

188 Thayer, *The New England Emigrant Aid Company,* 24; Lawrence, *The Life of Amos A. Lawrence,* 85; Rawley, *Race and Politics,* 62. For a more general discussion of eastern merchants and the slavery issue, see Philip S. Foner, *Business and Slavery* (Chapel Hill, 1941). For a discussion of the later period, see Paul Renard Migliore, "The Business of Union: The New York Business Community and the Civil War" (Ph.D. dissertation, Columbia University, 1975). Yankee merchants in St. Louis, however, seem to have been most concerned with maintaining the smooth flow of commerce. Slavery was palatable; commercial disruption was not.

189 Thayer, *The New England Emigrant Aid Company,* 24.

190 Ibid.

191 Ibid.; id., *A History of the Kansas Crusade,* 208.

192 *New York Evening Post,* February 14, 1856. Also see *New York Daily Tribune,* April 7, 1856.

193 *New York Evening Post,* March 20, 1856; ibid., February 14, 1856.

194 Ibid., March 3, 1856.

195 Ibid.; ibid., March 20, 1856; ibid., March 25, 1856.

196 *New York Independent*, quoted in *Missouri Republican*, January 31, 1857.

197 *Erie Constitution*, quoted in *Missouri Democrat*, June 23, 1858.

198 *New York Times*, October 1, 1855.

199 *New York Daily Tribune*, September 1, 1856.

200 *Missouri Democrat*, June 25, 1856.

201 Ibid., March 12, 1857. Also see *Missouri Republican*, November 19, 1859; Phillips, *The Conquest of Kansas*, 81; testimony of Lewis O. Wilmarth, May 6, 1856, *Howard Report*, 206; Sara T. L. Robinson, *Kansas*, 85, 282; W. H. Isley, "The Sharp's Rifle Episode in Kansas History," *American Historical Review* 12 (April 1907): 559.

202 For example, Timothy Hill, writing from St. Louis, summarized the problems that missionaries faced in Missouri. "A fierce excitement has prevailed," he noted, "in consequence of the National Legislation, in reference to slavery." Hill's reports never noted the political and cultural differences between "interior farmers" and St. Louis residents. See *Home Missionary* 28 (June 1855): 43.

203 *Home Missionary* 30 (July 1857): 75.

204 Ibid. 28 (July 1855): 77. Also see Frederick Starr, Jr., Papers, Joint Collection, University of Missouri Western Historical Manuscript Collection–Columbia and State Historical Society of Missouri Manuscripts, Columbia, Missouri.

205 Gihon, *Geary and Kansas*, 36.

206 *Home Missionary* 28 (November 1856): 172.

207 Ibid. 28 (June 1855): 43. Also see ibid. 28 (October 1855): 249; ibid. 29 (April 1857): 287.

208 Ibid. 29 (April 1857): 287.

209 For example, see ibid. 28 (June 1855): 43; ibid. 28 (July 1855): 76–77; ibid. 28 (October 1855): 249; ibid. 30 (June 1857): 47.

210 Ibid. 15 (September 1842): 104–5; ibid. 30 (June 1857):47.

211 For example, see ibid. 28 (October 1855): 249; ibid. 29 (July 1856): 73; ibid. 29 (April 1857): 287; ibid. 29 (June 1856): 43.

212 One missionary concluded that "it would be useless for me to stay longer. . . . It is, in reality, a forcible expulsion." See ibid. 28 (July 1855): 76–77. The *Home Missionary* was filled with accounts of such "expulsions" from Missouri.

213 Ibid. 27 (April 1855): 277.

214 Kingsford, *Impressions of the West and South*, 37. Also see *New York Daily Tribune*, March 12, 1856.

215 *Missouri Democrat*, March 22, 1856.

216 Reverend W. M. Leftwich, *Martyrdom in Missouri* (St. Louis, 1870), 118. Also see *Missouri Democrat*, August 25, 1855; Sara T. L. Robinson, *Kansas*, 282; testimony of Richard R. Rees, May 19, 1856, *Howard Report*, 397; testimony of C. R. Mobley, May 28, 1856, *Howard Report*, 275; testimony of A. B. Wade, June 9, 1856, *Howard Report*, 160; *Missouri Republican*, December 16, 1860.

217 For eastern capitalists, see [Columbia] *Dollar Missouri Journal*, May 24, 1855. For a more general assessment of the relationship between St. Louis and the abolitionist cause, see testimony of B. F. Nicholson, May 20, 1856, *Howard Report*, 1144. Also see testimony of C. R. Mobley, May 28, 1856, *Howard Report*, 275; testimony of Richard R. Rees, May 19, 1856, *Howard Report*, 397. Also see Atchison, *Address of Senator Atchison to the People of Missouri*, 7.

218 Testimony of A. B. Wade, June 6, 1856, *Howard Report*, 160. Also Sara T. L. Robinson, *Kansas*, 282; *Missouri Democrat*, March 22, 1856; Missouri Vol. 37, p. 430, RGD. Also see *Weekly St. Louis Pilot*, March 29, 1856; *Liberty Weekly Tribune*, March 14, 1856.

219 Testimony of F. A. Hunt, June 12, 1856, *Howard Report*, 832–35; Sara T. L. Robinson, *Kansas*, 282; *Missouri Democrat*, March 22, 1856; Missouri Vol. 37, p. 430, RGD. The New England Emigrant Aid Company sold tickets for passage from Boston to Kansas for twenty-five dollars – ten dollars below "regular" fare. See Samuel A. Johnson, *The Battle Cry For Freedom*, 35.

220 Records of the Board of Trustees, August 7, 1854, New England Emigrant Aid Company Papers, microfilm, reel 7.

221 Missouri Vol. 37, p. 332, RGD.

222 Testimony of F. A. Hunt, June 12, 1856, *Howard Report*, 832–35; Sara T. L. Robinson, *Kansas*, 282; *Missouri Democrat*, March 22, 1856; Missouri Vol. 37, p. 430, RGD.

223 Benjamin Slater, quoted in Sara T. L. Robinson, *Kansas*, 282.

224 *Missouri Democrat*, March 22, 1856.

225 For example, see *Liberty Weekly Tribune*, March 14, 1856; *Weekly St. Louis Pilot*, March 29, 1856.

226 Sara T. L. Robinson, *Kansas*, 282.

227 *Missouri Democrat*, July 8, 1857.

228 Ibid., March 22, 1856. Forwarding merchants experienced increasing difficulty finding steamboat captains willing to transport goods from St. Louis to Kansas. Boat operators feared "anti-abolitionist" sentiment in the region. See Samuel A. Johnson, *The Battle Cry for Freedom*, 175.

229 *New York Evening Post*, March 25, 1856. Also see *New York Daily Tribune*, August 15, 1857.

230 *New York Evening Post*, March 25, 1856; testimony of F. A. Hunt, June 12, 1856, *Howard Report*, 835; *Missouri Democrat*, March 22, 1856.

231 Ibid.

232 Thomas Webb to George Hopkins, July 10, 1856, New England Emigrant Aid Company Correspondence, 1854-1858, New England Emigrant Aid Company Papers, microfilm, reel 3.

233 Testimony of F. A. Hunt, June 12, 1856, *Howard Report*, 835; *Missouri Democrat*, March 22, 1856; Missouri Vol. 37, p. 430, RGD.

234 Hunt failed to note that charges of mismanagement levelled by his principal customer – the New England Emigrant Aid Company – and the questionable business practices of his partner weakened his commission firm, though the efforts of Missouri radicals probably contri-

buted significantly to Hunt's problems. See Thomas Webb to S. C. Pomeroy, April 28, 1856, New England Emigrant Aid Company Correspondence, 1854–1858, New England Emigrant Aid Company Papers, microfilm, reel 1.

235 *Liberty Weekly Tribune,* April 13, 1855. Also see *Hannibal Tri-Weekly Messenger,* June 23, 1855; Robert William Duffner, "Slavery in Missouri River Counties, 1820–1865" (Ph.D. dissertation, University of Missouri-Columbia, 1974), 157; Newspaper Clipping, Frederick Starr, Jr., Papers, Joint Collection, University of Missouri Western Historical Manuscript Collection–Columbia and State Historical Society of Missouri Manuscripts, Columbia, Missouri.

236 *Missouri Democrat,* December 24, 1856.

237 Ibid., December 15, 1858.

238 *Missouri Republican,* July 18, 1858; Missouri Vol. 37, p. 445, RGD.

239 *Boston Journal,* quoted in *Missouri Democrat,* April 16, 1857.

240 *Missouri Democrat,* December 15, 1858.

241 *The Autobiography of Carl Schurz* (New York, 1961), 121.

242 William Rey, quoted in Holt, "The Shaping of St. Louis," 357.

243 *New York Daily Tribune,* April 15, 1857; *New York Independent,* quoted in *Missouri Republican,* January 31, 1857. Also see Foner, *Business and Slavery,* 102.

244 For example, see *Missouri Democrat,* September 21, 1854; ibid., February 6, 1855; ibid., December 28, 1855; ibid., October 22, 1856; ibid., December 3, 1856; ibid., April 20, 1857; ibid., November 28, 1857; *New York Daily Tribune,* April 15, 1857; *New York Evening Post,* February 12, 1856; ibid., February 23, 1856; *Dover Enquirer,* August 21, 1858, quoted in *Missouri Democrat,* October 20, 1858; *New York Times,* quoted in *Missouri Democrat,* August 20, 1857; *Buffalo Republic,* quoted in *Missouri Democrat,* April 14, 1857; George Williams, *Oregon Statesman,* July 28, 1857, quoted in Eugene H. Berwanger, *The Frontier Against Slavery* (Urbana, Ill., 1967), 92; William H. Seward, *Memoir,* (Boston, 1886), 106–7. Also see Peterson, *Freedom and Franchise,* 56–68; Foner, *Business and Slavery,* 139–68; Larson, *Bonds of Enterprise,* 85. For a more general discussion of this issue, see Eric Foner, *Free Soil, Free Labor, Free Men* (New York, 1970); Berwanger, *The Frontier Against Slavery.*

245 *Missouri Democrat,* December 15, 1858.

246 Ibid., November 18, 1859.

247 *Missouri Democrat,* November 9, 1855.

248 For the notion that Yankees "created" St. Louis, see *Missouri Democrat,* October 20, 1858.

249 Yankees started fewer than one-third of the businesses that opened during this period; Yankees had started nearly two-thirds of the firms that opened during the late 1840s. Although many of the Yankee ventures established before midcentury remained in operation, Yankee domination of the St. Louis marketplace disappeared during this period. See Table 6.1.

250 Few local entrepreneurs possessed adequate financial resources. Thus,

when Yankees left St. Louis, poorer merchants and weaker firms increasingly dominated the local marketplace.

251 St. Louis's role as a "regional node" changed. For a discussion of regional nodes, see David Ralph Meyer, "A Dynamic Model of the Integration of Frontier Urban Places into the United States System of Cities," *Economic Geography* 56 (April 1980): 132–36.

252 *Missouri Democrat*, February 20, 1856.

253 For increasing local capital shortages, see ibid., December 28, 1855; ibid., July 18, 1857; ibid., November 18, 1859; *Missouri Republican*, June 18, 1855; ibid., August 24, 1855; ibid., November 21, 1855. Also see Riegel, *The Story of the Western Railroads*, 21; Belcher, *The Economic Rivalry Between St. Louis and Chicago*, 80.

254 See *Missouri Democrat*, August 15, 1859.

255 For example, see *Missouri Republican*, June 15, 1856; *Missouri Democrat*, March 16, 1857.

256 *De Bow's Review* 18 (March 1855): 384. Also see *Annual Review of the Commerce of St. Louis for the Year 1855* (St. Louis, 1856), 3; *New York Daily Tribune*, March 11, 1856; Belcher, *The Economic Rivalry Between St. Louis and Chicago*, 107. Changes in the regional economy reinforced these shifts. See Mahoney, *River Towns in the Great West*.

257 Cable, *The Bank of the State of Missouri*, 234; Primm, *Lion of the Valley*, 197. In 1853 there were seven major real estate subdivisions in the city. Eight subdivisions occurred during 1854 and an additional eight subdivisions during 1855. The following year, however, only three subdivisions were dedicated in the city. See Holt, "The Shaping of St. Louis," 370.

258 *New York Times*, quoted in *Missouri Republican*, June 15, 1856.

259 During the years following the Kansas war the proportion of businesses that failed rose by more than 74 percent. In part, this reflects the "blighting" influence of the border turmoil. Structural changes in the local marketplace – the growing proportion of small and locally oriented firms – also produced an increase in the failure rate. At the very least, these changes exaggerated one another.

260 Only the southern hinterland and small Missouri and southern Illinois markets remained tied to the St. Louis marketplace. Chicago increasingly claimed the city's larger and more prosperous northern hinterland.

261 Kellner, "The German Element on the Urban Frontier," 316.

262 *Missouri Democrat*, July 11, 1855.

263 Ibid., July 18, 1857.

264 See ibid., June 25, 1856; ibid., July 21, 1856; *New York Evening Post*, February 14, 1856.

265 *New York Evening Post*, February 14, 1856; *Missouri Democrat*, February 22, 1856; ibid., December 28, 1855; Primm, *Economic Policy*, 112.

266 *New York Evening Post*, March 20, 1856; ibid., March 25, 1856.

267 Ibid., February 14, 1856.

268 Eli Thayer to E. E. Hale, February 15, 1856, New England Emigrant Aid Company Correspondence, 1854–1858, New England Emigrant Aid

Company Papers, microfilm, reel 1. Also see *Missouri Democrat*, July 29, 1856; Belcher, *The Economic Rivalry Between St. Louis and Chicago*, 80; Charles N. Glaab, *Kansas City and the Railroads* (Madison, 1962), 39.

269 For example, see *Missouri Democrat*, June 18, 1855; ibid., December 28, 1855; ibid., June 25, 1856; ibid., July 21, 1856; ibid., November 18, 1859.

270 *Missouri Republican*, October 30, 1854. Also see Belcher, *The Economic Rivalry Between St. Louis and Chicago*, 80.

271 *Missouri Democrat*, June 25, 1856.

272 *Missouri Democrat*, July 29, 1856. For the efforts of one St. Louis resident to stimulate investment, see Belcher, *The Economic Rivalry Between St. Louis and Chicago*, 121; Cable, *The Bank of the State of Missouri*, 234; Taylor and Crooks, *Sketch Book of St. Louis*, 128; James Neal Primm, "Yankee Merchants in a Border City," *Missouri Historical Review* 78 (July 1984): 377–78; id., *Lion of the Valley*, 217–22.

273 *Missouri Democrat*, August 1, 1860.

274 For example, see ibid., January 15, 1857; Taylor and Crooks, *Sketch Book of St. Louis*, 359; Missouri Vol. 36, p. 294, RGD.

275 Credit records reveal this shift. See Illinois Vols. 27–29, RGD. Also see Abbott, *Boosters and Businessmen*, 136.

276 Belcher, *The Economic Rivalry Between St. Louis and Chicago*, 38–39. The economy of Chicago, however, grew rapidly during this period. See Mahoney, *River Towns in the Great West*, 51.

277 See Constance McLaughlin Green, *American Cities* (New York, 1957), 105; Abbott, *Boosters and Businessmen*, 135. As long as St. Louis preserved its role as a regional node, migration and investment would continue. See Meyer, "A Dynamic Model of the Integration of Frontier Urban Places into the United States System of Cities," 132–36.

278 *Missouri Republican*, October 30, 1854. Also see ibid., February 18, 1856; Abbott, *Boosters and Businessmen*, 136; Frederic Cople Jaher, *The Urban Establishment* (Urbana, Ill., 1982), 458–60.

279 Eli Thayer to E. E. Hale, February 15, 1856, New England Emigrant Aid Company Correspondence, 1854–1858, New England Emigrant Aid Company Papers, microfilm, reel 1.

280 *Missouri Republican*, June 18, 1855.

281 For Laflin, see Missouri Vol. 38, p. 144, RGD; Illinois Vol. 28, p. 41, RGD. Also see *Missouri Democrat*, April 14, 1856; Abbott, *Boosters and Businessmen*, 132–33. Also see id., "Civic Pride in Chicago, 1844–1860," *Journal of the Illinois State Historical Society* 63 (Winter 1970): 415.

282 For a few examples of Boston men operating branches of shoe firms in Chicago, see Illinois Vol. 27, p. 208, RGD; Illinois Vol. 28, p. 58, RGD; *A Review of the Commerce of Chicago* (Chicago, 1857), 23. Also see Lawrence A. Brown, John Odland, and Reginald G. Gelledge, "Migration, Functional Distance, and the Urban Hierarchy," *Economic Geography* 66 (July 1970): 477.

283 *Chicago Magazine* 1 (April 15, 1857): 151.

284 Belcher, *The Economic Rivalry Between St. Louis and Chicago*, 50, 67, 70, 80. Also see *Hunt's Merchants' Magazine* 33 (November 1855): 637.

285 *Missouri Republican*, February 24, 1855.

286 Agricultural receipts for the decade peaked in 1855 and fell sharply thereafter. For example, oats, beef, pork, corn, lead, and hemp receipts plummeted after 1855. See *Hunt's Merchants' Magazine* 38 (February 1858): 223–24; *Annual Review of the Commerce of St. Louis together with a Very Full List of Steamboat Disasters and Complete River Statistics for the Year 1859* (St. Louis, 1860), 20. Also see *De Bow's Review* 24 (March 1858): 212; Belcher, *The Economic Rivalry Between St. Louis and Chicago*, 48, 124. By late in 1855 the decline had begun. See Mahoney, "Urban History in a Regional Context," 329; John G. Clark, *The Grain Trade of the Old Northwest* (1966; reprint, Westport, 1980), 85.

287 *Hunt's Merchants' Magazine* 35 (August 1856): 170. Also see *New York Journal of Commerce*, September 2, 1856.

288 For Chicago, see *Chicago Magazine* 1 (April 15, 1857): 151; *The Rail-Roads and Commerce of Chicago* (Chicago, 1854), 10–16. For San Francisco, see Decker, *Fortunes and Failures*, 9–19.

289 For example, see Decker, *Fortunes and Failures*, 130–40, 164; Abbott, *Boosters and Businessmen*, 132. A few transplanted Yankee merchants, most often those who had migrated to St. Louis before the mid-1840s boom, formed deeper ties to the Missouri city. See Primm, "Yankee Merchants in a Border City," 375–86.

290 For example, see *New York Evening Post*, February 23, 1856; *Missouri Democrat*, February 18, 1858; ibid., November 18, 1859.

291 John Kasson, for example, chose to abandon his St. Louis law practice and leave the city. Instead, he resolved to migrate to another rapidly growing western city – Des Moines. See Edward Younger, *John A. Kasson* (Iowa City, Iowa, 1955), 72.

292 Miscellaneous Financial Papers, Subscriptions, June 29, 1855, New England Emigrant Aid Company Papers, microfilm, reel 9.

293 For the view that St. Louis was a Southern city, see *New York Daily Tribune*, quoted in *Missouri Democrat*, April 20, 1857. For similar assessments of St. Louis, see *Boston Journal*, quoted in *Missouri Democrat*, April 16, 1857; *Rock Island Advertiser*, quoted in *Missouri Democrat*, April 16, 1857. For Yankee merchants and Southern cities, see Harriet E. Amos, *Cotton City* (University, Ala., 1985); David R. Goldfield, *Urban Growth in the Age of Sectionalism* (Baton Rouge, La., 1977).

Chapter 7: Rebirth

1 See Timothy R. Mahoney, *River Towns in the Great West* (New York, 1990), 51; John G. Clark, *The Grain Trade in the Old Northwest* (1966; reprint, Westport, 1980).

2 See John Lauritz Larson, *Bonds of Enterprise* (Cambridge, Mass., 1984).

3 The cities fought to control the exchange of goods between the region and the "national metropolis." See David Ralph Meyer, "A Dynamic Model of the Integration of Frontier Urban Places into the United States

System of Cities," *Economic Geography* 56 (April 1980): 132–34.

4 The larger and more important process was the shift in New York investment strategies. Capitalists no longer invested in St. Louis. Moreover, merchants looking to the West during the late 1850s increasingly chose Chicago ventures. See Illinois Vols. 27–29, R. G. Dun and Company Collection, Baker Library, Harvard University Graduate School of Business Administration (hereafter cited as RGD). For a thoughtful analysis of the rivalry and the ways in which "Chicago and St. Louis also needed one another," see Eric H. Monkkonen, *America Becomes Urban* (Berkeley, 1988), 45.

5 *Missouri Democrat*, April 1, 1857.

6 Ibid., February 26, 1858.

7 Ibid., September 27, 1856.

8 Ibid., November 18, 1859.

9 Ibid., March 31, 1858.

10 Ibid., July 8, 1858.

11 For example, see ibid., July 8, 1858; ibid., March 31, 1858; ibid., February 18, 1858.

12 Ibid., April 1, 1857.

13 Ibid., April 14, 1857.

14 W. A. Scay, "Missouri Safe For The South, " *De Bow's Review* 24 (April 1858): 336.

15 *Missouri Democrat*, February 13, 1857.

16 For example, see ibid., April 5, 1857; ibid., February 5, 1858; ibid., March 30, 1858; ibid., March 31, 1858.

17 Ibid., March 10, 1857.

18 Ibid., February 13, 1857.

19 Ibid., April 27, 1857.

20 Ibid., October 11, 1856; ibid., September 30, 1856.

21 Ibid., September 30, 1856.

22 Ibid., March 10, 1857.

23 Ibid., November 25, 1857; ibid., December 19, 1859.

24 Ibid., March 10, 1857.

25 Ibid., August 1, 1860.

26 See Eric Foner, *Free Soil, Free Labor, Free Men* (New York, 1970), 27. For a very different discussion of western politics, see Eugene H. Berwanger, *The Frontier Against Slavery* (Urbana, 1967).

27 *Missouri Democrat*, April 14, 1857; ibid., April 5, 1857.

28 Ibid., February 18, 1858; ibid., November 9, 1859.

29 Ibid., February 26, 1858; ibid., April 5, 1857.

30 Ibid., August 1, 1860. Also see ibid., March 30, 1858.

31 Ibid., April 5, 1857.

32 *New York Daily Tribune*, April 13, 1857; *Missouri Democrat*, April 8, 1857.

33 See *Missouri Democrat*, April 15, 1857.

34 Ibid.

35 Ironically, Wimer joined the Confederate army and died in battle. See Charles W. Cornwell, *St. Louis Mayors* (St. Louis, 1965), 7.

36 *New York Daily Tribune*, April 15, 1857.

37 Ibid.

38 *Rock Island Advertiser*, quoted in *Missouri Democrat*, April 16, 1857.

39 *New York Daily Tribune*, April 20, 1857.

40 *Missouri Democrat*, August 1, 1858.

41 *Philadelphia North American and United States Gazette*, April 6, 1859.

42 *Chicago Press and Tribune*, April 6, 1859.

43 *Boston Journal*, quoted in *Missouri Democrat*, April 16, 1857.

44 *Missouri Republican*, December 30, 1858.

45 *Weekly St. Louis Pilot*, August 23, 1856. For the role of Germans, see
    Walter D. Kamphoefner, "St. Louis Germans and the Republican Party,
    1848–1860," *Mid-America* 57 (April 1975): 69–88; George Helmuth Kellner,
    "The German Element on the Urban Frontier" (Ph.D. dissertation, Uni-
    versity of Missouri–Columbia, 1973), chaps. 5–6.

46 W. A. Scay, "Missouri Safe For The South," 335–36.

47 John A. Kasson, quoted in Edward Younger, *John A. Kasson* (Iowa City,
    Iowa, 1955), 72–73.

48 Illinois Vol. 28, p. 19, RGD.

49 For example, see Missouri Vol. 37, p. 467, RGD; Illinois Vol. 29, p. 60,
    RGD.

50 Missouri Vol. 37, p. 387, RGD; Illinois Vol. 28, p. 218, RGD.

51 [Jacob N.] Taylor and [M. O.] Crooks, *Sketch Book of St. Louis* (St. Louis,
    1858), 359; Missouri Vol. 36, p. 294, RGD; Logan U. Reavis, *St. Louis*
    (St. Louis, 1875), 546. Also see Reavis, *St. Louis*, 571.

52 *Missouri Democrat*, March 2, 1859; Missouri Vol. 36, p. 294, RGD; Illinois
    Vol. 28, p. 257, RGD.

53 *Missouri Republican*, June 16, 1856.

54 Truman Marcellus Post, quoted in T. A. Post, *Truman Marcellus Post,
    D.D.* (Boston, 1891), 218.

55 *Missouri Republican*, July 27, 1857; *Missouri Democrat*, September 10, 1857.

56 Mahoney, *River Towns in the Great West*, 235–38.

57 Missouri Vol. 37, p. 569, RGD; *Missouri Democrat*, October 5, 1857; *New
    York Journal of Commerce*, October 5, 1857.

58 For example, see Missouri Vol. 37, p. 356, RGD; Missouri Vol. 36, p. 175,
    RGD; Missouri Vol. 38, p. 107, RGD; Missouri Vol. 38, p. 30, RGD.

59 Missouri Vol. 37, p. 475, RGD.

60 Missouri Vol. 37, p. 606, RGD.

61 Montgomery Schuyler, *An Ambassador of Christ* (New York, 1901), 138.

62 Edward Miller to Samuel Reeves, October 6, 1857, St. Louis History
    Collection, Missouri Historical Society, St. Louis, Missouri.

63 Governor Robert Marcellus Stewart, "Speech to the Senate and House of
    Representatives," October 29, 1857, in *The Messages and Proclamations of
    the Governors of the State of Missouri*, eds. Buel Leopard and Floyd C.
    Shoemaker (Columbia, Mo., 1922), 3:226. Also see Governor Robert
    Marcellus Stewart, "Inaugural Address," October 22, 1857, in *Messages
    and Proclamations*, 3:68; *Missouri Republican*, October 15, 1857.

64 *Missouri Democrat*, October 7, 1859.

65 Ibid.
66 Governor Sterling Price, "Second Biennial Message," December 29, 1856, in *Messages and Proclamations*, 2:441.
67 Judge N. Holmes, quoted in Reavis, *St. Louis*, 112.
68 Paul W. Gates, "The Railroads of Missouri, 1850–1870," *Missouri Historical Review* 26 (January 1932): 130–31; James Neal Primm, *Lion of the Valley* (Boulder, Colo., 1981), 218.
69 Homer Clevenger, "The Building of the Hannibal and St. Joseph Railroad," *Missouri Historical Review* 36 (October 1941): 40.
70 *Missouri Democrat*, October 23, 1859; Wyatt Winton Belcher, *The Economic Rivalry Between St. Louis and Chicago 1850–1880* (New York, 1947), 89–90.
71 *Missouri Republican*, September 4, 1859. Also see *Missouri Democrat*, April 11, 1857; *Weekly St. Louis Pilot*, November 17, 1855.
72 *Missouri Republican*, September 11, 1859. Also see ibid., December 14, 1860; *Missouri Democrat*, June 26, 1857.
73 Gates, "The Railroads of Missouri," 134–41; Belcher, *The Economic Rivalry Between St. Louis and Chicago*, 68.
74 Judge N. Holmes, quoted in Reavis, *St. Louis*, xv.
75 Agricultural receipts for the decade peaked in 1855 and fell sharply thereafter. For example, oats, beef, pork, corn, and hemp receipts plummeted after 1855. See *Hunt's Merchants' Magazine and Commercial Review* 38 (February 1858): 223; *Annual Review of the Commerce of St. Louis, Together with a Very Full List of Steamboat Disasters and Complete River Statistics for the Year 1859* (St. Louis, 1860), 20; *De Bow's Review* 24 (March 1858): 212; Belcher, *The Economic Rivalry Between St. Louis and Chicago*, 48, 124.
76 *Annual Review of the Commerce of St. Louis, Together with a Very Full List of Steamboat Disasters and Complete River Statistics for the Year 1859*, 16, 33; *Hunt's Merchants' Magazine* 42 (March 1860): 331; *De Bow's Review* 28 (February 1860): 220.
77 *Weekly St. Louis Pilot*, November 17, 1855.
78 *Missouri Democrat*, October 7, 1859.
79 *Missouri Republican*, November 11, 1859.
80 William Kingsford, *Impressions of the West and South* (Toronto, 1858), 14.
81 Every spring local newspapers announced the arrival of country merchants and listed these newcomers in a daily "Hotel Arrival" column. These figures were drawn from local newspapers, the *Missouri Republican* and the *Missouri Democrat*, during the spring of 1850 and the spring of 1859. Also see Mahoney, *River Towns in the Great West*, 209–42.
82 Changes in the regional economy reflected and exaggerated this process.
83 See *Missouri Democrat*, September 21, 1855; Belcher, *The Economic Rivalry Between St. Louis and Chicago*, 124; Timothy R. Mahoney, "Urban History in a Regional Context," *Journal of American History* 72 (September 1985): 329; Clark, *The Grain Trade in the Old Northwest*.
84 *Missouri Democrat*, October 7, 1859.
85 See the "Hotel Arrival" columns of the *Missouri Republican* and the *Missouri Democrat*.

86 For Eddy, see Missouri Vol. 36, p. 78, RGD; Missouri Vol. 36, p. 134, RGD; Missouri Vol. 37, p. 436, RGD; Missouri Vol. 36, p. 126, RGD.

87 Missouri Vol. 37, p. 527, RGD.

88 *Annual Review of the Commerce of St. Louis, Together with a List of Steamboat Disasters, for the Year 1856* (St. Louis, 1857), 4. Also see *Annual Review of the Commerce of St. Louis, Together with a Very Full List of Steamboat Disasters and Complete River Statistics for the Year 1859*, 4.

89 *Annual Review of the Commerce of St. Louis, Together with a List of Steamboat Disasters, for the Year 1856* (St. Louis, 1857), 4.

90 *Annual Review of the Commerce of St. Louis, Together with a List of Steamboat Disasters, for the Year 1856*, 4; *Missouri Democrat*, February 26, 1858.

91 For population figures, see Holt, "The Shaping of St. Louis," 507.

92 Reavis, *St. Louis*, 498. Also see Missouri Vol. 37, p. 464, RGD.

93 Missouri Vol. 38, p. 189, RGD.

94 Missouri Vol. 36, p. 96, RGD; Missouri Vol. 38, p. 106, RGD.

95 Missouri Vol. 38, p. 171, RGD.

96 Missouri Vol. 38, p. 59, RGD.

97 Only 40 percent of these migrants traveled from the principal commercial center in the lower Ohio valley, Cincinnati. The remaining 60 percent migrated from smaller towns in the region.

98 Bankruptcy File of William Sheppard, Bankruptcy Records, 1867, Federal Archives and Records Center, Kansas City, Missouri.

99 Missouri Vol. 37, p. 576, RGD.

100 For example, see Luke Shortfield, *The Western Merchant* (Philadelphia, 1849), 119.

101 For example, see *Missouri Democrat*, May 22, 1859.

102 Mark Twain, *Life on the Mississippi* (1883; reprint, New York, 1961), 39.

103 Richard K. Vedder and Lowell E. Gallaway, "Migration and the Old Northwest," in *Essays in Nineteenth Century Economic History*, eds. David C. Klingaman and Richard Vedder (Athens, Ohio, 1975), 161.

104 See Carl Abbott, *Boosters and Businessmen* (Westport, 1981), 157.

105 Louis C. Hunter, *Steamboats on the Western Rivers* (Cambridge, Mass., 1949), 381.

106 *Missouri Republican*, November 15, 1857.

107 *Missouri Democrat*, May 22, 1859.

108 Ibid.

109 *Missouri Republican*, November 15, 1857.

110 Ibid., December 3, 1857.

111 This pattern is similar to the eastern model of internal migration. See John Modell, "The Peopling of a Working-Class Ward," *Journal of Social History* 5 (Fall 1971): 82.

112 For a similar process, see Priscilla Ferguson Clement, "The Transformation of the Wandering Poor in Nineteenth-Century Philadelphia," in *Walking to Work*, ed. Eric H. Monkkonen (Lincoln, 1984), 56–84.

113 *Missouri Democrat*, August 8, 1858. Also see Norma L. Peterson, *Freedom and Franchise* (Columbia, Mo., 1965), 85.

114 *Missouri Democrat*, September 5, 1859.

115 Kellner, "The German Element on the Urban Frontier," 316.
116 For Willei, see the manuscript schedules of the Eighth Census (1860), St. Louis County.
117 For Sauter, see the manuscript schedules of the Eighth Census (1860), St. Louis County.
118 See Russel L. Gerlach, *Settlement Patterns in Missouri* (Columbia, Mo., 1986), 31.
119 For Bentz, see the manuscript schedules of the Eighth Census (1860), St. Louis County.
120 Kellner, "The German Element on the Urban Frontier," 168–207.
121 Ibid., 251; *Mrs. Hill's Journal*, ed. Mark M. Krug (Chicago, 1980), xxxi. Also see Kamphoefner, "St. Louis Germans and the Republican Party."
122 James Parton, "The City of St. Louis," *Atlantic Monthly* 19 (June 1867): 658.
123 William H. Seward, October 2, 1860, *The Complete Works of William H. Seward* (Boston, 1884), 4:107. Also see Kamphoefner, "St. Louis Germans and the Republican Party."
124 Missouri Vol. 37, p. 588, RGD.
125 For example, see *Missouri Republican*, June 24, 1859; *Missouri Democrat*, June 24, 1859.
126 *Missouri Republican*, January 25, 1859.
127 Taylor and Crooks, *Sketch Book of St. Louis*, 6.
128 *Missouri Democrat*, May 28, 1857. Cincinnati boosters responded in a similar manner. See Abbott, *Boosters and Businessmen*, 155.
129 *Missouri Democrat*, May 28, 1857. Also see ibid., October 20, 1856. Also see James Thomas, *From Tennessee Slave to St. Louis Entrepreneur*, ed. Loren Schweninger (Columbia, Mo., 1984), 145.
130 *Missouri Democrat*, December 15, 1858.
131 Ibid.
132 Ibid., May 28, 1857.
133 *Annual Review of the Commerce of St. Louis, Together with a List of Steamboat Disasters, for the Year 1856*, 4. Also see *Missouri Democrat*, October 23, 1859; *Missouri Republican*, October 15, 1856.
134 *Missouri Republican*, October 15, 1856. Also see Parton, "The City of St. Louis," 663, 667.
135 Robert V. Kennedy, comp., *Kennedy's St. Louis Directory for the Year 1857* (St. Louis, 1857), 6.
136 *Missouri Democrat*, May 28, 1857.
137 Lillian Foster, *Way-Side Glimpses* (New York, 1859), 126. Also see *Missouri Republican*, November 17, 1859.
138 Thomas, *From Tennessee Slave to St. Louis Entrepreneur*, 145.
139 *Annual Review of the Commerce of St. Louis, Together with a List of Steamboat Disasters, for the Year 1856*, 4. Also see Belcher, *The Economic Rivalry Between St. Louis and Chicago*, 15.
140 For example, see *Missouri Democrat*, April 7, 1859; ibid., October 20, 1856; ibid., June 15, 1857. For a similar brand of boosterism, see Don Harrison Doyle, *The Social Order of a Frontier Community* (Urbana, Ill., 1978), 255–59.

141 *Missouri Democrat*, April 7, 1859. Also see *Annual Review of the Commerce of St. Louis, Together with a List of Steamboat Disasters, for the Year 1856*, 5; Thomas, *From Tennessee Slave to St. Louis Entrepreneur*, 145

142 Taylor and Crooks, *Sketch Book of St. Louis*, 6.

143 *Annual Review of the Commerce of St. Louis, Together with a List of Steamboat Disasters, for the Year 1856*, 4.

144 *Missouri Democrat*, April 7, 1859.

145 See Doyle, *The Social Order of a Frontier Community*, 255–59; id., *New Men, New Cities, New South* (Chapel Hill, N.C., 1990), 20–21; Thomas M. Doerflinger, *A Vigorous Spirit of Enterprise* (Chapel Hill, N.C., 1986), chap. 8.

146 Parton, "The City of St. Louis," 667.

147 *Missouri Democrat*, December 15, 1858; ibid., June 15, 1857.

148 Ibid., May 28, 1857; *Hunt's Merchants' Magazine* 39 (August 1858): 216.

149 *Missouri Republican*, January 24, 1855; *Missouri Democrat*, April 2, 1857.

150 *Western Journal and Civilian* 25 (January 1856): 138, quoted in Dale K. Doepke, "St. Louis Magazines Before the Civil War" (Ph.D. dissertation, Washington University, 1963), 175. Also see *Missouri Republican*, October 17, 1858.

151 See *Missouri Democrat*, December 23, 1859; *Missouri Republican*, February 3, 1861.

152 *Missouri Democrat*, June 15, 1857. Also see ibid., October 23, 1859; *Missouri Republican*, November 17, 1859.

153 See *Missouri Republican*, November 17, 1859; ibid., November 19, 1859; *Missouri Democrat*, April 7, 1859; ibid., February 27, 1860.

154 See Jeffrey S. Adler, "Vagging the Demons and Scoundrels," *Journal of Urban History* 13 (November 1986): 3–30.

155 *Missouri Republican*, May 14, 1845; Maximilian Ivan Reichard, "The Origins of Urban Police," (Ph.D. dissertation, Washington University, 1975), 84–86; City of St. Louis v. Bentz, 11 Mo. 62 (1847).

156 Adler, "Vagging the Demons and Scoundrels," 8–11.

157 See Roberts, alias Ward v. State, 14 Mo. 138, 146 (1851); State v. Roberts, 15 Mo. 28, 41 (1851); City of St. Louis v. Bentz, 11 Mo. 62 (1847).

158 See *The Revised Ordinances of the City of St. Louis, Revised and Digested By the City Council, in the Year 1850* (St. Louis, 1850), 407; *Missouri Republican*, October 13, 1857.

159 Adler, "Vagging the Demons and Scoundrels," 8–11.

160 *Missouri Democrat*, February 13, 1857. For prostitution and thievery, see ibid., August 23, 1859; ibid., October 12, 1859.

161 See *Missouri Republican*, November 19, 1859; *Missouri Democrat*, February 27, 1860; ibid., March 6, 1860; *The Ordinances of the City of St. Louis, State of Missouri, Digested and Revised By the Common Council of Said City, in the Years 1860 and 1861* (St. Louis, 1861), 614–17.

162 *Missouri Republican*, February 9, 1861; *Missouri Democrat*, October 26, 1859.

163 *Missouri Democrat*, October 26, 1859.

164 Ibid., April 10, 1858.

165   *The Ordinances of the City of St. Louis, State of Missouri, Digested and Revised By the Common Council of Said City, in the Years 1860 and 1861*, 502; *Missouri Republican*, January 20, 1861.

166   Report of the Joint Committee of the General Assembly Appointed to Investigate the Police Department of St. Louis (1868; reprint, New York, 1971), 347.

167   *Missouri Republican*, November 5, 1859. Also see *Annual Review of the Commerce of St. Louis, Together with a Very Full List of Steamboat Disasters and Complete River Statistics for the Year 1859*, 4.

168   *Missouri Republican*, November 11, 1859. Also see ibid., December 9, 1860; Governor Claiborne Fox Jackson, "Inaugural Address," January 3, 1861, in *Messages and Proclamations*, 3:334; *De Bow's Review* 24 (March 1858): 214; *Missouri Republican*, June 1, 1859; *Annual Review of the Commerce of St. Louis, Together with a Very Full List of Steamboat Disasters and Complete River Statistics for the Year 1859*, 4.

169   *Annual Review of the Commerce of St. Louis, Together with a Very Full List of Steamboat Disasters and Complete River Statistics for the Year 1859*, 4; *Missouri Democrat*, February 14, 1858.

170   *Memphis Bulletin*, quoted in *Missouri Republican*, June 1, 1859.

171   *Missouri Republican*, January 7, 1859. Also see ibid., January 1, 1856.

172   *Western Journal and Civilian* 14 (August 1855): 153.

173   *Annual Statement of the Trade and Commerce of Saint Louis for the Year 1857* (St. Louis, 1858), 2.

174   For example, see *Annual Review of the Commerce of St. Louis, Together with a List of Steamboat Disasters, for the Year 1856*, 3; *Fifth Annual Report of the St. Louis Chamber of Commerce* (St. Louis, 1860), 11, 17, 24; *Annual Statement of the Trade and Commerce of Saint Louis for the Year 1857*, 4, 11; *Annual Statement of the Trade and Commerce of St. Louis for the Year 1858* (St. Louis, 1859), 3, 10, 13, 18; St. Louis Board of Trade, *Fourth Annual Report of the St. Louis Chamber of Commerce* (St. Louis, 1860), 25; St. Louis Board of Trade, *Fourth Annual Report of the St. Louis Chamber of Commerce* (St. Louis, 1860), 48.

175   Ibid.

176   St. Louis Board of Trade, *Fourth Annual Report of the St. Louis Chamber of Commerce* (St. Louis, 1860), 31.

177   *Hunt's Merchants' Magazine* 42 (March 1860): 325.

178   *Missouri Republican*, October 13, 1860.

179   Parton, "The City of St. Louis," 662.

180   *Cincinnati Daily Gazette*, February 2, 1860.

181   *Missouri Republican*, February 7, 1861.

182   Ibid., November 11, 1860. Also see William Greenleaf Eliot, "Annual Report of the Western Sanitary Commission for the Years Ending July, 1862, and July 1863," *North American Review* 98 (April 1864): 519–20.

183   Ibid., October 26, 1860. Also see ibid., January 6, 1861; James Neal Primm, "Yankee Merchants in a Border City, " *Missouri Historical Review* 78 (July 1984): 380.

184   Although most Missourians supported the Southern cause, the state

did not secede. Instead, Missourians feared that their state would become a battlefield if Southern radicals triumphed. Thus, Missourians remained ideologically committed to the Confederacy, though they eschewed radical action. See *Missouri Republican*, October 30, 1860; ibid., November 17, 1860; *Missouri Democrat*, November 19, 1860; *Annual Review of the Commerce of St. Louis, Together with a Very Full List of Steamboat Disasters and Complete River Statistics for the Year 1859*, 3; Reverend W. M. Leftwich, *Martyrdom in Missouri* (St. Louis, 1870), 119; Montgomery Schuyler, quoted in William Schuyler, *An Ambassador of Christ*, 174, 177; *Mrs. Hill's Journal*, 4; Parton, "The City of St. Louis," 659; Truman Marcellus Post, quoted in T. A. Post, *Truman Marcellus Post*, 263; William E. Parrish, *Turbulent Partnership* (Columbia, Mo., 1963), 1–14.

185 Giles Filley, quoted in Reichard, "The Origins of Urban Police," 305.
186 Hunter, *Steamboats on the Western Waters*, 548; Parton, "The City of St. Louis," 662.
187 Parton, "The City of St. Louis," 655–72.
188 Ibid., 662. Also see *Appletons' Journal* 8 (November 16, 1872): 535.
189 Parton, "The City of St. Louis," 667.
190 Ibid., 655.
191 Ibid.
192 Ibid., 667.
193 Ibid.
194 Ibid., 667, 659.
195 Ibid., 667.
196 Ibid., 658.
197 Ibid., 657.
198 Ibid., 656.

Bibliography

Primary Sources

Manuscripts

Bankruptcy Files, 1867–1868. Federal Archives and Records Center, Kansas City, Missouri.

Records of Interments in the Bellefontaine Cemetery, 1850–1852. Bellefontaine Cemetery, St. Louis, Missouri.

Records of the Bonhomme Presbyterian Church. Missouri Historical Society, St. Louis, Missouri.

Records of the Church of the Messiah. First Congregational Church of St. Louis, St. Louis, Missouri.

Coffin-Weld Company Papers. Joint Collection, University of Missouri Western Historical Manuscript Collection–Columbia and State Historical Society of Missouri Manuscripts, Columbia, Missouri.

James S. Cowan Papers. Joint Collection, University of Missouri Western Historical Manuscript Collection–Columbia and State Historical Society of Missouri Manuscripts, Columbia, Missouri.

Charles D. Drake Papers. Joint Collection, University of Missouri Western Historical Manuscript Collection–Columbia and State Historical Society of Missouri Manuscripts, Columbia, Missouri.

Nathan Dresser Papers. Joint Collection, University of Missouri Western Historical Manuscript Collection–Columbia and State Historical Society of Missouri Manuscripts, Columbia, Missouri.

R. G. Dun and Company Collection. Baker Library, Harvard University Graduate School of Business Administration, Boston, Massachusetts.

William Greenleaf Eliot Papers. Missouri Historical Society, St. Louis, Missouri.

J. E. Hawley Papers. Joint Collection, University of Missouri Western Historical Manuscript Collection–Columbia and State Historical Society of Missouri Manuscripts, Columbia, Missouri.

General E. A. Hitchcock Papers. Missouri Historical Society, St. Louis, Missouri.

Archy Kasson Papers. Joint Collection, University of Missouri Western Historical Manuscript Collection–Columbia and State Historical Society of Missouri Manuscripts, Columbia, Missouri.

Abiel Leonard Papers. Joint Collection, University of Missouri Western Historical Manuscript Collection–Columbia and State Historical Society of Missouri Manuscripts, Columbia, Missouri.

William Carr Lane Papers. Missouri Historical Society, St. Louis, Missouri.

John D. McKown Papers. Joint Collection, University of Missouri Western Historical Manuscript Collection–Columbia and State Historical Society of Missouri Manuscripts, Columbia, Missouri.

Missouri History Collection. Missouri Historical Society, St. Louis, Missouri.

Henry Thomas Mudd Papers. Joint Collection, University of Missouri Western Historical Manuscript Collection–Columbia and State Historical Society of Missouri Manuscripts, Columbia, Missouri.

New England Emigrant Aid Company Papers. Microfilm.

Moses Payne Papers. Joint Collection, University of Missouri Western Historical Manuscript Collection–Columbia and State Historical Society of Missouri Manuscripts, Columbia, Missouri.

Justus Post Papers. Joint Collection, University of Missouri Western Historical Manuscript Collection–Columbia and State Historical Society of Missouri Manuscripts, Columbia, Missouri.

William Robyn Papers. Missouri Historical Society, St. Louis, Missouri.

St. Louis History Collection. Missouri Historical Society, St. Louis, Missouri.

Lucius Salisbury Papers. Joint Collection, University of Missouri Western Historical Manuscript Collection–Columbia and State Historical Society of Missouri Manuscripts, Columbia, Missouri.

Records of the Second Baptist Church, 1827–1884. Missouri Historical Society, St. Louis, Missouri. Microfilm.

General George Smith Papers. Missouri Historical Society, St. Louis, Missouri.

Soulard Family Papers. Missouri Historical Society, St. Louis, Missouri.

Frederick Starr, Jr., Papers. Joint Collection, University of Missouri Western Historical Manuscript Collection–Columbia and State Historical Society of Missouri Manuscripts, Columbia, Missouri.

William L. Sublette Papers. Missouri Historical Society, St. Louis, Missouri.

George R. Taylor Papers. Missouri Historical Society, St. Louis, Missouri.

Dexter Tiffany Papers. Missouri Historical Society, St. Louis, Missouri.

U.S. Government. Manuscript schedules of the Seventh Census of the United States (1850), St. Louis County. Federal Archives and Records Centers, Waltham, Massachusetts.

U.S. Government. Manuscript schedules of the Eighth Census of the United States (1860), St. Louis County. Federal Archives and Records Centers, Waltham, Massachusetts.

Periodicals and Newspapers

Boston Daily Evening Transcript (1856).
Chicago Magazine (1857).
Cincinnati Daily Gazette (1859–1860).
Chicago Press and Tribune (1859–1860).
De Bow's Review 1–28 (January 1846–May 1860).
[Columbia] *Dollar Missouri Journal* (1855).
Hannibal Tri-Weekly Messenger (1855).
Home Missionary 1–30 (January 1828–July 1857).

Hunt's Merchants' Magazine and Commercial Review 8–42 (January
    1843–March 1860).
Jefferson Enquirer (1840–1843).
Liberty Weekly Tribune (1856).
The Merchant's and Banker's Almanac (1850–1860).
Merchants and Manufacturers Magazine (1858).
[St. Louis] *Missouri Argus* (1835–1839).
[St. Louis] *Missouri Democrat* (1852–1861).
[St. Louis] *Missouri Gazette* (1820).
[Franklin] *Missouri Intelligencer* (1821).
[St. Louis] *Missouri Republican* (1835–1861).
New Orleans Daily Picayune (1856).
New York Daily Tribune (1856–1858).
New York Evening Post (1856).
New York Journal of Commerce (1856–1859).
Philadelphia North American and United States Gazette (1859).
The Presbyterian Casket (1852).
Weekly Platte Argus (1855).
Weekly St. Louis Pilot (1855–1856).
The Western Journal and Civilian (1848–1855).

Pamphlets

Annual Review of the Trade and Commerce of St. Louis for the Year 1848. St.
    Louis, 1849.
A Review of the Commerce of Chicago: Her Merchants and Manufacturers.
    Chicago, 1855.
A Review of the Commerce of Chicago: Her Merchants and Manufacturers.
    Chicago, 1856.
A Review of the Commerce of St. Louis for the Year 1849. St. Louis, 1850.
*Annual Review of the Commerce of St. Louis, for the Year 1852: Carefully
    Compiled From Daily Reports Published in the Missouri Republican, and
    Other Reliable Sources.* St. Louis, 1853.
*Annual Review: The History of St. Louis, Commercial Statistics, Improvements of
    the Year and Account of Leading Manufactories, etc., From the Missouri
    Republican, January 10, 1854.* St. Louis, 1854.
*Annual Review of the Commerce of St. Louis for the Year 1854, Published in the
    Missouri Republican, January 3, 1855.* St. Louis, 1855.
*Annual Review of the Commerce of St. Louis, for the Year 1855, Published in the
    Missouri Republican, January 10, 1856.* St. Louis, 1856.
*Annual Review of the Commerce of St. Louis, Together with a List of Steamboat
    Disasters, for the Year 1856, Published in the Missouri Republican, January
    31, 1857.* St. Louis, 1857.
*Annual Review of the Commerce of St. Louis, Together with a Very Full List of
    Steamboat Disasters and Complete River Statistics for the Year 1859,
    Published in the Missouri Republican, December 31, 1859.* St. Louis, 1860.

Annual Statement of the Trade and Commerce of St. Louis for the Year 1856. St. Louis, 1857.

Annual Statement of the Trade and Commerce of Saint Louis for the Year 1857. St. Louis, 1858.

Annual Statement of the Trade and Commerce of St. Louis for the Year 1858. St. Louis, 1859.

Atchison, David Rice. *Address of Senator Atchison to the People of Missouri.* Washington, 1854.

Cunningham, Reverend T. M. *Address Before The St. Louis Young Men's Christian Association, At Its First Public Meeting, November 20, 1853.* St. Louis, 1853.

Excursion Party of the Board of Trade of Philadelphia. Philadelphia, 1860.

First Annual Report of the St. Louis Young Men's Christian Association, Presented January 16, 1854, Including the Constitution, Names of Officers, etc. St. Louis, 1854.

Hogan, John. *Thoughts About the City of St. Louis, Her Commerce, Manufactures, Railroads, etc.* St. Louis, 1854.

Proceedings of the German Mission Society of the Mississippi Valley At Its First Annual Meeting. St. Louis, 1850.

The Speculators of St. Louis: A Tale Founded On Well Authenticated Facts, By A Victim to the Speculator's Art. St. Louis, 1851.

St. Louis Board of Trade, Fourth Annual Report of the St. Louis Chamber of Commerce for 1859. St. Louis, 1860.

St. Louis Board of Trade, Fifth Annual Report of the St. Louis Chamber of Commerce, for 1860. St. Louis, 1860.

Articles

Atherton, Lewis E., ed. "Business and Life in St. Louis, Missouri, 1847–1848." *Missouri Historical Review* 37 (July 1943): 430–37.

Beck, Lewis C. "A Gazetteer of the States of Illinois and Missouri, 1823." In *The Early Histories of St. Louis,* edited by John F. McDermott, 75–88. St. Louis, 1952.

"Cholera Epidemics in St. Louis." *Missouri Historical Society: Glimpses of the Past* 3 (March 1936): 45–76.

Cooley, Elizabeth Ann. "From Virginia to Missouri in 1846: The Journal of Elizabeth A. Cooley." *Missouri Historical Review* 60 (January 1966): 162–206.

Duden, Gottfried. "Duden's Reports, 1824–1827." Edited by William G. Bek. *Missouri Historical Review* 12 (October 1917): 1–21.

———, "Duden's Reports, 1824–1827." Edited by William G. Bek. *Missouri Historical Review* 12 (January 1918): 81–89.

———, "Duden's Reports, 1824–1827." Edited by William G. Bek. *Missouri Historical Review* 12 (April 1918): 163–79.

———, "Duden's Reports, 1824–1827." Edited by William G. Bek. *Missouri Historical Review* 12 (July 1918): 258–70.

————, "Duden's Reports, 1824–1827." Edited by William G. Bek. *Missouri Historical Review* 13 (October 1918): 44–56.

————, "Duden's Reports, 1824–1827." Edited by William G. Bek. *Missouri Historical Review* 13 (January 1919): 157–81.

————, "Duden's Reports, 1824–1827." Edited by William G. Bek. *Missouri Historical Review* 13 (April 1919): 251–81.

Eliot, William Greenleaf. "Address Before the Franklin Society of St. Louis." *North American Review* 43 (July 1836): 288–89.

————, "Gazetteer of the State of Missouri." *North American Review* 48 (April 1839): 514–26.

————, "The Religious and Moral Wants of the West." *American Unitarian Association Tracts* 10 (April 1837): 1–20.

"The Evangelization of the West. How Shall It Be Affected? And By Whom?: The Nineteenth Annual Report of the American Home Missionary Society." *New Englander* 4 (1846): 29–39.

Hesse, Nicholas. "Nicholas Hesse, German Visitor to Missouri, 1835–1837." Edited by William G. Bek. *Missouri Historical Review* 41 (October 1946): 19–44.

Miller, Henry B. "The Journal of Henry B. Miller." Edited by Thomas Maitland Marshall. *Missouri Historical Society Collections* 6 (June 1931): 213–87.

Nicollet, Joseph P. "Sketch of Early St. Louis, 1832." In *The Early Histories of St. Louis*, edited by John F. McDermott, 131–64. St. Louis, 1952.

Norstrom, Carl Edward. "A Swedish View of St. Louis: 1848." Edited by Mrs. Frederick Celsing. *Bulletin of the Missouri Historical Society* 27 (January 1971): 147–50.

"North Carolinians Comment on Missouri." *Missouri Historical Society: Glimpses of the Past* 1 (August 1934): 71–84.

Parton, James. "The City of St. Louis." *Atlantic Monthly* 19 (June 1867): 655–72.

"Popular Education in the West By Female Teachers From the East." *New Englander* 7 (1849): 593–609.

"A Walk in the Streets of St. Louis in 1845 by a Traveler." *Missouri Historical Society Collections* 6 (October 1928): 33–40.

Zimmerman, Eduard. "Travel into Missouri in October, 1838." *Missouri Historical Review* 9 (January 1914): 33–43.

Books

Audubon, John J. *Audubon and His Journals*. Edited by Maria R. Audubon. 2 vols. New York, 1897.

Baird, Robert. *A View of the Valley of the Mississippi or The Emigrant's and Traveller's Guide to the West*. Philadelphia, 1832.

Beecher, Lyman. *A Plea For the West*. Cincinnati, 1835.

————, *The Autobiography of Lyman Beecher*. Edited by Barbara Cross. 2 vols. Cambridge, Mass., 1961.

Berkeley, Grantley F. *The English Sportsman in the Western Prairies*. London, 1861.

Bishop, Mrs. Isabella Lucy. *The Englishwoman in America*. London, 1856.

Boomer, George Boardman. *Memoir of George Boardman Boomer*. Boston, 1864.

Brackenridge, Henry Marie. *Views of Louisiana: Together with a Journal of a Voyage Up the Mississippi River, in 1811*. Pittsburgh, 1814.

Bremer, Frederika. *The Homes of the New World: Impressions of America*. Translated by Mary Howitt. 2 vols. New York, 1853.

Brokmeyer, Henry C. *A Mechanic's Diary*. Washington, D.C., 1910.

Buckingham, J[ames]. S[ilk]. *The Eastern and Western States of America*. 3 vols. London, 1842.

Burrows, J. M. D. *Fifty Years in Iowa: Being the Personal Reminiscences of J. M. D. Burrows, Concerning the Men and Events, Social Life, Industrial Interests, Physical Development, and Commercial Progress of Davenport and Scott County, During the Period from 1838 to 1888*. Davenport, Iowa, 1888.

Busch, Moritz. *Travels Between the Hudson and the Mississippi, 1851–1852*. Translated by Norman H. Binger. 1854. Reprint. Lexington, Ky., 1971.

Catlin, George. *The Letters of George Catlin and His Family*. Edited by Marjorie Catlin Roehm. Berkeley, 1966.

Clark, Reverend John A. *Gleanings By the Way*. Philadelphia, 1842.

Cunyghame, Lieutenant-Colonel Arthur. *A Glimpse at the Great Western Republic*. London, 1851.

Dana, Charles A. *The Great West or The Garden of the World*. Boston, 1857.

Darby, John F. *Personal Recollections of Many Prominent Persons Whom I Have Known and Events – Especially of Those Relating to the History of St. Louis – During the First Half of the Present Century*. St. Louis, 1880.

Devol, George H. *Forty Years a Gambler on the Mississippi*. New York, 1926.

Dickens, Charles. *American Notes For General Circulation*. New York, 1842.

Douglas, Stephen A. *The Letters of Stephen A. Douglas*. Edited by Robert W. Johannsen. Urbana, Ill., 1961.

Drury Clifford, ed. *The First White Women Over the Rockies*. Glendale, Calif., 1963.

Duden, Gottfried. *Report on a Journey to the Western States of North America and a Stay of Several Years Along the Missouri During the Years 1824, '25, '26, and 1827*. Edited by James W. Goodrich, and translated by George Kellner, Elsa Nagel, Adolf E. Schroeder, and W. M. Senner. Columbia, 1980. Originally published as *Bericht uber eine Reise nach den westlichen Staaten Nordamerika's und einen mehrjahrigen Aufenthalt am Missouri (in den Jahren 1824, 25, 26, und 1827) in Bezug auf Auswanderung and Uebervolkerung* Elberfeld, Germany, 1829.

Eliot, William Greenleaf. *Lectures to Young Men*. Boston, 1856.

Lectures to Young Women. Boston, 1860.

Ellet, Mrs. [Elizabeth]. *Summer Rambles in the West*. New York, 1853.

Elliott, Richard Smith. *Notes Taken in Sixty Years*. St. Louis, 1883.

Featherstonhaugh G[eorge]. W[illiam]. *Excursion Through the Slave States, From Washington on the Potomac to the Frontier of Mexico: With Sketches of Popular Manners and Geological Notices*. New York, 1844.

Ferguson, William. *America By River and Rail or, Notes by the Way On The New World and Its People*. London, 1856.

Ferrall, S. A. *A Ramble of Six Thousand Miles Through the United States of America*. London, 1832.

Finley, Reverend James B. *Sketches of Western Methodism: Biographical, Historical, and Miscellaneous*. Edited by W. P. Strickland. Cincinnati, 1855.

Flagg, Edmund. *The Far West: or, A Tour Beyond the Mountains, in Two Volumes*. 2 vols. New York, 1838.

Flint, Timothy. *A Condensed Geography and History of the Western States or The Mississippi Valley*. 2 vols. Cincinnati, 1828.

———, *Recollections of the Last Ten Years in the Valley of the Mississippi*. Edited by George R. Brooks. 1826. Reprint. Carbondale, Ill., 1968.

Foster, Lillian. *Way-Side Glimpses, North and South*. New York, 1859.

Fuller, Hiram. *Belle Briton On A Tour, At Newport, and Here and There*. New York, 1858.

Gihon, John. *Geary and Kansas. Governor Geary's Administration in Kansas; with a Complete History of the Territory Until 1857; Embracing A Full Account of its Discovery, Soil, Rivers, Climate, Products; Its Organization as a Territory, Transactions and Events Under Governors Reeder and Shannon, Political Dissensions, Personal Rencountres, Election Frauds, Battles and Outrages. All Fully Authenticated*. Philadelphia, 1857.

Gilpin, William. *The Central Gold Region: The Grain, Pastoral, and Gold Regions of North America with Some New Views of Its Physical Geography; and Observations on the Pacific Railroad*. Philadelphia, 1860.

Goodrich, C[arter]. A. *The Family Tourist: A Visit to the Principal Cities of the Western Continent; Embracing an Account of Their Situation, Origin, Plan, Extent, Their Inhabitants, Manners, Customs, and Amusements, and Public Works, Institutions, Edifices, etc. Together with Sketches of Historical Events*. Hartford, Conn., 1848.

Grant, Julia Dent. *The Personal Memoirs of Julia Dent Grant*. Edited by John Y. Simon. New York, 1975.

Gustorf, Frederick Julius. *The Uncorrupted Heart: The Journal and Letters of Frederick Julius Gustorf, 1800–1845*. Edited by Fred Gustorf. Columbia, Mo., 1969.

Hale, Edward Everett. *Kanzas and Nebraska: The History, Geography and Political Characteristics and Political Position of Those Territories; An Account of the Emigrant Aid Companies and Directions to Emigrants*. 1854. Reprint. Freeport, N.Y., 1972.

Hall, James. *The West: Its Commerce and Navigation*. Cincinnati, 1848.

Hart, Adolphus M. *The History of the Valley of the Mississippi*. Cincinnati, 1853.

Hill, Sarah Jane Full. *Mrs. Hill's Journal: Civil War Reminiscences*. Edited by Mark M. Krug. Chicago, 1980.

Hoffman, Charles Fenno. *A Winter in the West by a New Yorker.* 2 vols. New York, 1835.

Holliday, J. S., ed. *The World Rushed In: The California Gold Rush Experience.* New York, 1981.

Hone, Philip. *The Diary of Philip Hone.* Edited by Bayard Tuckerman. Vol. 2. New York, 1889.

Jack, Scotch. *A New Year's Address To The Sovereign People, For The Jubilee Year of Our Lord 1850: or St. Louis and The World in Six Cantos.* St. Louis, 1850.

James. J. H. *Rambles in the United States and Canada During the Year 1845.* London, 1847.

Kelly, William. *Across the Rocky Mountains, From New York to California.* London, 1852.

Kennerly, William Clark, as told to Elizabeth Russell. *Persimmon Hill: A Narrative of Old St. Louis and the Far West.* Norman, Okla., 1948.

Kingsford, William. *Impressions of the West and South, During A Six Week's Holiday.* Toronto, 1858.

Koch, Dr. Albert C. *A Journey Through a Part of the United States of North America in the Years, 1844–1846.* Translated by Ernest A. Stadler. 1846. Reprint. Carbondale, Ill., 1972.

Larpenteur, Charles. *Forty Years A Fur Trader on the Upper Missouri: The Personal Narrative of Charles Larpenteur, 1833–1872.* Chicago, 1933.

Latrobe, Charles Joseph. *The Rambler in North America, 1832–1833.* London, 1835.

Leftwich, Reverend W. M. *Martyrdom in Missouri: A History of Religious Proscription, The Seizure of Churches, and The Persecution of Ministers of the Gospel, in the State of Missouri, During the Late Civil War and under the "Test Oath" of the New Constitution.* St. Louis, 1870.

Lewis, Reverend George. *Impressions of America and American Churches: From the Journal of The Reverend G. Lewis.* Edinburgh, 1848.

Lucas, J. B. C. *The Letters of Hon. J. B. C. Lucas From 1815 to 1832.* Compiled by John B. C. Lucas. St. Louis, 1905.

Leopard, Buel, and Floyd C. Shoemaker, eds. *The Messages and Proclamations of the Governors of the State of Missouri.* Vols. 1–3. Columbia, Mo., 1922.

Mackay, Alex. *The Western World; or, Travels in the United States in 1846–47: Exhibiting Them in their Latest Development, Social, Political, and Industrial; Including a Chapter on California.* Vol 1. Philadelphia, 1849.

Mackay, Charles. *Life and Liberty in America: or Sketches of a Tour in the United States and Canada in 1857–58.* New York, 1859.

Manford, Erasmus. *Twenty-Five Years in the West.* Chicago, 1867.

Marryat, Captain Frederick. *Diary in America.* Edited by Jules Zanger. 1839. Reprint. Bloomington, Ind., 1960.

Mayer, Frank Blackwell. *With Pen and Pencil on the Frontier in 1851: The Diary and Sketches of Frank Blackwell Mayer.* Edited by Bertha Heilbron. St. Paul, Minn., 1932.

Morris, John [John O'Connor]. *Wanderings of a Vagabond.* New York, 1873.

Murray, Charles Augustus. *Travels in North America During the Years 1834, 1835, and 1836.* Vol. 2. New York, 1839.

Murray, Henry A. *Lands of the Slave and the Free or, Cuba, the United States, and Canada.* London, 1857.

Nelson, Thomas S., ed. *A Full and Accurate Report of the Trial of William P. Darnes.* Boston, 1841.

Nicely, Wilson. *The Great Southwest or Plain Guide For Emigrants and Capitalists, Embracing A Description of the States of Missouri and Kansas.* St. Louis, 1867.

Nicholls, John Ashton. *A Selection From the Letters of the Late John Ashton Nicholls.* Edited by Sarah Nicholls. Manchester, England, 1862.

Olliffe, Charles. *American Scenes: Eighteen Months in the New World.* Translated by Ernest Falbo and Lawrence A. Wilson. 1852. Reprint. Painesville, Ohio, 1964.

Parker, Amos Andrew. *A Trip to the West and Texas: Comprising a Journey of Eight Thousand Miles, Through New-York, Michigan, Illinois, Missouri, Louisiana and Texas, in the Autumn and Winter of 1834–1835.* Concord, N. H., 1835.

Parker, Reverend Samuel. *Journal of an Exploring Tour Beyond the Rocky Mountains, Performed in the Years 1835, '36 and '37.* Ithaca, N.Y. 1838.

Parkman, Francis. *The Oregon Trail: Sketches of Prairie and Rocky Mountain Life.* Boston, 1880.

Pattie, James O. *The Personal Narrative of James O. Pattie of Kentucky.* Edited by M. M. Quaife. Chicago, 1930.

Peck, John Mason. *Forty Years of Pioneer Life: Memoir of John Mason Peck, D.D..* Edited by Rufus Babcock. 1864. Reprint. Carbondale, Ill., 1965.

————, *A New Guide for Emigrants to the West.* Boston, 1837.

Peyton, John Lewis. *Over the Alleghenies and Across the Prairies. Personal Recollections of the Far West One and Twenty Years Ago.* London, 1870.

Phelps, Humphrey. *Phelps' Hundred Cities and Large Towns of America.* New York, 1853.

Phillips, William. *The Conquest of Kansas By Missouri and Her Allies: A History of the Troubles in Kansas, From the Passage of the Organic Act Until the Close of July, 1856.* 1856. Reprint. Freeport, N.Y., 1971.

Piercy, Frederick Hawkins. *Route From Liverpool to Great Salt Lake Valley.* Edited by Fawn M. Brodie. Cambridge, Mass., 1962.

Pulszky, Francis, and Theresa Pulszky. *White, Red, and Black: Sketches of American Society.* New York, 1853.

Reid, Bernard J. *Overland to California with the Pioneer Line: The Gold Rush Diary of Bernard J. Reid.* Edited by Mary McDougall Gordon. Stanford, Calif., 1983.

Report of the Joint Committee of the Assembly Appointed to Investigate the Police Department of the City of St. Louis. 1868. Reprint. New York, 1971.

Robinson, Charles. *The Kansas Conflict.* Lawrence, Kans., 1898.

Robinson, Sara T. L. *Kansas: Its Interior and Exterior Life including A Full View of its Settlement, Political History, Social Life, Climate, Soil, Productions, Scenery, etc.* Boston, 1856.

Schurz, Carl. *Autobiography*. Edited by Wayne Andrews. New York, 1961.

Sears, Robert. *A Pictorial Description of the United States*. New York, 1852.

Seward, William H. *The Complete Works of William H. Seward*. Boston, 1884.

Sherman, William Tecumseh. *Memoirs of William T. Sherman*. Vol. 1. New York, 1875.

Shirreff, Patrick. *A Tour Through North America; Together With A Comprehensive View of the Canadas and United States, As Adapted For Agricultural Emigration*. Edinburgh, 1835.

Shortfield, Luke [John Beauchamp Jones]. *The Western Merchant: A Narrative Containing Useful Instructions For The Western Man of Business Who Makes His Purchases In The East; Also Information For The Eastern Man Whose Customs Are In The West*. Philadelphia, 1849.

Solitaire [John S. Robb]. *Streaks of Squatter Life and Far-West Scenes. A Series of Humorous Sketches Descriptive of Incidents and Characters in the Wild West*. Philadelphia, 1846.

Steele, Eliza R. *A Summer Journey in the West*. 1841. Reprint. New York, 1975.

Stone, Richard Cecil. *Life-Incidents of Home, School and Church*. St. Louis, 1874.

Stuart-Wortley, Lady Emmeline. *Travels in the United States etc., During 1849 and 1850*. New York, 1851.

Sumner, Charles. "The Crime Against Kansas. The Apologies For The Crime. The True Remedy." In *The Last Three Speeches on Kansas and Freedom*. Boston, 1856.

Taylor, [Jacob N.]., and [M. O.] Crooks. *Sketch Book of St. Louis: Containing A Series of Sketches of the Early Settlement, Public Buildings, Hotels, Railroads, Steamboats, Foundry and Machine Shops, Mercantile Houses, Grocers, Manufacturing Houses Etc.* St. Louis, 1858.

Thayer, Eli. *A History of the Kansas Crusade: Its Friends and Its Foes*. 1889. Reprint. Freeport, N.Y., 1971.

———, *The New England Emigrant Aid Company and Its Influence, Through the Kansas Contest, Upon National History*. Worcester, 1887.

Thomas James. *From Tennessee Slave to St. Louis Entrepreneur: The Autobiography of James Thomas*. Edited by Loren Schweninger. Columbia, Mo., 1984.

Trollope, Anthony. *North America*. Edited by Donald Smalley and Bradford Allen Booth. 1861. Reprint. New York, 1951.

Trotter, Mrs. Isabella. *First Impressions of the New World or Two Travellers From The Old in the Autumn of 1858*. London, 1859.

Twain, Mark [Samuel Clemens]. *Life on the Mississippi*. 1883. Reprint. New York, 1961.

Vessey, John Henry. *Mr. Vessey of England: Being The Incidents and Reminiscences of Travel in a Twelve Weeks' Tour Through the United States and Canada in the Year 1859*. Edited by Brian Waters. New York, 1956.

Wetmore, Alphonso. *Gazetteer of the State of Missouri*. St. Louis, 1837.

Williams, W. *Appleton's Southern and Western Traveller's Guide*. New York, 1849.

Wolskli, Kalikst. *American Impressions*. Translated by Marion Moore
    Coleman. 1876. Reprint. Cheshire, Conn., 1968.
Wulfing, Gustavus. *The Letters of Gustavus Wulfing*. Edited by Eugene
    Tavenner, and translated by Carl Hirsch. Fulton, Mo., 1941.
*A Young Traveller's Journal of a Tour in North and South America During the
    Year 1850*. London, 1852.

Directories

Green, James, comp. *Green's St. Louis Directory For 1845: Containing The
    Names of the Inhabitants, Their Occupations, Places of Business and Dwelling
    Houses; Also, A List of the Streets and Avenues; Together With Other Useful
    Information, And An Advertisement Directory*. St. Louis, 1844.
————, comp. *Green's St. Louis Directory, For 1847: Containing The Names of
    the Inhabitants, Their Occupations, Places of Business, and Dwelling Houses;
    Also, A List of the Streets and Alleys Together With Other Useful
    Information*. St. Louis, 1847.
————, comp. *The St. Louis Business Directory, For The Year of Our Lord
    1850*. St. Louis, 1850.
————, comp. *Green's St. Louis Directory, For 1851: Containing The Names of
    the Inhabitants, Their Occupations, Places of Business, and Dwelling Houses;
    Together With The Business Cards of A Large Portion of Citizens*. St. Louis,
    1851.
Keemle, Charles, comp. *The St. Louis Directory, For The Years 1840–41 The
    Names of the Inhabitants, Their Occupations, and the Numbers of Their
    Places of Business and Dwellings With A Sketch of the City of St. Louis,
    Also, The Names of the City, Township, County and State Officers, And the
    Names and Officers of the Various Literary, Scientific, Benevolent, Religious
    and Public Institutions With A Variety of Other Interesting Matter*. St.
    Louis, 1840.
Kennedy, Robert V., comp. *Kennedy's St. Louis Directory For The Year 1857;
    Containing A General Directory of Citizens, A Business Mirror of the City–
    An Advertising Department–A Street Guide–The Names of City Officers,
    Generally–A List of Post-Offices in Missouri, and Several Other States and
    Territories–Postal Census and Other Statistical Tables–Times of Holling
    Courts–Tables of Distance on Various Rail Road and River Routes–Dates of
    Discount at the City Banks With Much Other Useful Information*. St. Louis,
    1857.
Montague, William L., comp. *St. Louis Business Directory, For 1853–4*. St.
    Louis, 1853.
*Morrison's St. Louis Directory, For 1852, Containing The Names of the
    Inhabitants, Their Occupations, Places of Business and Residences; A Map of
    the City; Also Business Cards*. St. Louis, 1852.
Paxton, John A. "St Louis Directory and Register, 1821." In *The Early
    Histories of St. Louis*, edited by John F. McDermott, 61–74. St. Louis,
    1952.

The St. Louis Directory, For The Year 1842; Containing The Names of the Inhabitants, And the Numbers of Their Places of Business and Dwellings With A Sketch of the City of St. Louis. Also The Names of the City, Township, County and State Officers, And The Names and Officers of the Various Literary, Scientific, Benevolent, Religious and Public Institutions, With A Variety of Other Interesting Matter. St. Louis, 1842.

The St. Louis Directory, For 1847: Containing The History of St. Louis, From The Period of Its First Settlement, Down To The Present Time: Statistical, And Other Useful Information: Together With The Cards of a Large Majority of the Merchants and Business Men of St. Louis. St. Louis, 1847.

The St. Louis Directory, For The Years 1854–5, Containing A General Directory of the Citizens, and A Business Directory. With An Almanac, From July, 1854 to January, 1856. St. Louis, 1854.

St. Louis 1859: Containing A Directory of Citizens, Including, Also A Business Mirror, Appendix, Co-Partnership Directory etc. St. Louis, 1859.

Sloss, J. H., comp. *The St. Louis Directory, For 1848: Containing The Names of the Inhabitants, Their Occupations, Places of Business, and Dwelling Houses; Together With Other Useful Information.* St. Louis, 1848.

Taylor, [Jacob N.], comp. *The St. Louis Directory for 1850.* St. Louis, 1850.

Government Documents

City of St. Louis. *Minute Books of the St. Louis Board of Aldermen.* City Hall Archival Library, St. Louis, Missouri. Microfilm.

City of St. Louis. *Journal of the St. Louis Board of Delegates to the City Council, 1839–1841.* City Hall Archival Library, St. Louis, Missouri. Microfilm.

City of St. Louis. *The Ordinances of the City of St. Louis, State of Missouri, Digested and Revised by the Common Council of Said City, in the Years 1860 and 1861. With the Constitutions of the United States and the State of Missouri, And the Various Charters of the City of St. Louis.* St. Louis, 1861.

City of St. Louis. *The Revised Ordinances of the City of St. Louis, Revised and Digested By the Fifth City Council During the First Session, begun and held in the City of St. Louis, on the Second Monday of May, A.D. 1843. With the Constitutions of the United States and the State of Missouri, and the City Charter.* St. Louis, 1843.

City of St. Louis. *The Revised Ordinances of the City of St. Louis, Revised and Digested By the Eighth City Council, in the Year 1846; with the Constitutions of the United States and the State of Missouri; The Various Charters of, and Laws Applicable to, the Town and City of St. Louis; And A List of the Trustees of the Town, And of the Officers of the City, of St. Louis, From 1810 to 1846, Inclusive.* St. Louis, 1846.

City of St. Louis. *The Revised Ordinances of the City of St. Louis, Revised and Digested By the City Council, in the Year 1850, with the Constitutions of the United States and the State of Missouri; The Various Charters of, and Laws Applicable to the Town and City of St. Louis.* St. Louis, 1850.

State of Missouri. Missouri General Assembly. *Laws of the State of Missouri; Revised and Digested by Authority of the General Assembly*. 2 vols. St. Louis, 1825.

U.S. Congress. *Report of the Special Committee Appointed to Investigate the Troubles in Kansas; with The View of the Minority of Said Committee*. 34th Cong., 1st sess. 1856. Rept. 200.

SECONDARY SOURCES

Articles

Abbott, Carl. "Civic Pride in Chicago, 1844–1860." *Journal of the Illinois State Historical Society* 63 (Winter 1970): 399–421.

———, "Popular Economic Thought and Occupational Structure: Three Middle Western Cities in the Antebellum Decade." *Journal of Urban History* 1 (February 1975): 175–87.

Alcorn, Richard S. "Leadership and Stability in Mid-Nineteenth-Century America: A Case Study of an Illinois Town." *Journal of American History* 61 (December 1974): 685–702.

Allen, James, P. "Migration Fields of French Canadian Immigrants to Southern Maine. *Geographical Review* 62 (July 1972): 366–83.

Anderson, Hattie M. "Missouri, 1804–1828: Peopling a Frontier State." *Missouri Historical Review* 31 (January 1937): 150–80.

Atherton, Lewis E. "James and Robert Aull: A Frontier Missouri Mercantile Firm." *Missouri Historical Review* 30 (October 1935): 10–28

———, "The Problem of Credit in the Ante-Bellum South."*Journal of Southern History* 12 (1946): 534–56.

Baritz, Loren. "The Idea of the West. *American Historical Review* 66 (April 1961): 618–40.

Bieder, Robert. "Kinship as a Factor in Migration." *Journal of Marriage and the Family* 35 (August 1973): 429–39.

Billington, Ray. "Anti-Catholic Propaganda and the Home Missionary Movement, 1800–1860." *Mississippi Valley Historical Review* 22 (December 1935): 361–84.

Blumin, Stuart M. "When Villages Become Towns: The Historical Contexts of Town Formation." In *The Pursuit of Urban History*, edited by Derek Fraser and Anthony Sutcliffe, 54–68. London, 1983.

Brown, Lawrence A., John Odland, and Reginald G. Golledge. "Migration, Functional Distance, and the Urban Hierarchy." *Economic Geography* 46 (July 1970): 472–85.

Burghardt, A. F. "A Hypothesis About Gateway Cities." *Annals of the Association of American Geographers* 61 (June 1971): 269–85.

Clevenger, Homer. "The Building of the Hannibal and St. Joseph Railroad." *Missouri Historical Review* 36 (October 1941): 32–48.

Craik, Elmer LeRoy. "Southern Interest in Territorial Kansas, 1854–1858." *Kansas State Historical Society Collections* 15 (1919–1922): 334–448.

Crockett, Norman L. "A Study of Confusion: Missouri's Immigration Program, 1865–1916." *Missouri Historical Review* 57 (April 1963): 248–60.

Davenport, David Paul. "Migration to Albany, New York, 1850–1855." *Social Science History* 13 (Summer 1989): 159–85.

Davis, Ronald L. F. "Community and Conflict in Power: St. Louis, Missouri." *Western Historical Quarterly* 10 (July 1979): 337–55.

Dorsey, Dorothy B. "The Panic and Depression of 1837–1843 in Missouri." *Missouri Historical Review* 30 (October 1935): 132–61.

Easterlin, Richard A. Population Change and Farm Settlement in the Northern United States" *Journal of Economic History* 36 (March 1976): 45–75.

Foley, William E. "Justus Post: Portrait of a Frontier Land Speculator." *Bulletin of the Missouri Historical Society* 36 (October 1979): 19–26.

Gates, Paul W. "The Railroads of Missouri, 1850–1870." *Missouri Historical Review* 26 (January 1932): 126–41.

Gerber, David A. "Cutting Out Shylock: Elite Anti-Semitism and the Quest for Moral Order in the Mid-Nineteenth-Century American Marketplace." *Journal of American History* 69 (December 1982): 615–37.

Glaab, Charles N. "Jessup W. Scott and a West of Cities." *Ohio History* 73 (Winter 1964): 3–12.

———, "Visions of Metropolis: William Gilpin and Theories of City Growth in the American West." *Wisconsin Magazine of History* 45 (Autumn 1961): 21–31.

Gleick, Paul S. "Banking in Early Missouri." *Missouri Historical Review* 61 (July 1967): 427–43.

Gold, David M. "Public Aid to Private Enterprise Under the Ohio Constitution: Sections 4, 6, and 13 of Article VIII in Historical Perspective." *Toledo Law Review* 16 (Winter 1985): 405–505.

Goodrich, James W. "Gottfried Duden: A Nineteenth-Century Missouri Promoter." *Missouri Historical Review* 75 (January 1981): 131–46.

Haeger, John D. "The Abandoned Townsite on the Midwestern Frontier: A Case Study of Rockwell, Illinois." *Journal of the Early Republic* 3 (Summer 1983): 165–83.

———, "Capital Mobilization and the Urban Center: The Wisconsin Lakeports." *Mid-America* 60 (April–July 1978): 75–93.

———, "Eastern Money and the Urban Frontier: Chicago, 1833–1842." *Journal of the Illinois Historical Society* 64 (Autumn 1971): 267–84.

Harvey, Charles M. "Missouri from 1849 to 1861." *Missouri Historical Review* 2 (October 1907): 23–40.

Hollander, Stanley C. "Nineteenth Century Anti-Drummer Legislation in the United States." *Business History Review* 38 (Winter 1964): 479–500.

Holt, Glen E. "The Birth of Chicago: An Examination of Economic Parentage." *Journal of the Illinois Historical Society* 76 (Summer 1983): 82–94.

———, "St. Louis's Transition Decade, 1819–1830." *Missouri Historical Review* 76 (July 1982): 365–81.

262   Bibliography

Isley, W. H. "The Sharps Rifle Episode in Kansas History." *American Historical Review* 12 (April 1907): 546–66.
Kamphoefner, Walter D. "St. Louis Germans and the Republican Party, 1848–1860." *Mid-America* 57 (April 1975): 69–88.
Larson, Lawrence H. "Chicago's Midwest Rivals: Cincinnati, St. Louis, and Milwaukee." *Chicago History* 5 (Fall 1976): 141–51.
Lee, Everett S. "A Theory of Migration." In *Migration*, edited by J. A. Jackson, 282–97. Cambridge, 1969.
Lindstrom Diane and John Sharpless. "Urban Growth and Economic Structure in Antebellum America." In Paul Uselding, ed., *Research in Economic History* 3 (1978): 161–216.
Luthin, Reinhard H. "Organizing the Republican Party in the Border-Slave Region: Edward Bates's Presidential Candidacy in 1860." *Missouri Historical Review* 38 (January 1944): 138–61.
Lynch, William O. "The Influence of Population Movements in Missouri Before 1861." *Missouri Historical Review* 16 (July 1922): 506–16.
McDermott, John F. "Dr. Brown's St. Louis." *Missouri Historical Review* 54 (April 1960): 245–53.
McDonald, John S. and Leatrice McDonald. "Chain Migration, Ethnic Neighborhood Formation, and Social Networks." *Milbank Memorial Fund Quarterly* 42 (January 1964): 82–95."
McLear, Patrick E. "The St. Louis Cholera Epidemic of 1849." *Missouri Historical Review* 63 (January 1969): 171–80.
Mahoney, Timothy R. "Urban History in a Regional Context: River Towns on the Upper Mississippi, 1840–1860." *Journal of American History* 72 (September 1985): 318–39.
Meyer, David Ralph. "A Dynamic Model of the Integration of Frontier Urban Places into the United States System of Cities. *Economic Geography* 56 (April 1980): 120–40.
Modell, John. "The Peopling of a Working-Class Ward: Reading, Pennsylvania, 1850." *Journal of Social History* 5 (Fall 1971): 71–95.
Moore, Robert. "The Vital Statistics of St. Louis Since 1840." *Journal of the Association of Engineering Societies* 33 (November 1904): 299–324.
Pierce, Bessie Louise. "Changing Urban Patterns in the Mississippi Valley." *Journal of the Illinois Historical Society* 43 (Spring 1950): 46–57.
Pred, Allan. "Manufacturing in the American Mercantile City, 1800–1840." In *Cities in American History*, edited by Kenneth T. Jackson and Stanley K. Schultz, 110–42. New York, 1972.
Primm, James Neal. "Yankee Merchants in a Border City: A Look at St. Louis Businessmen in the 1850s." *Missouri Historical Review* 78 (July 1984): 375–86.
Reichard, Maximilian Ivan. "Urban Politics in Jacksonian St. Louis." *Missouri Historical Review* 70 (April 1976): 259–71.
Schneider, John C. "Riot and Reaction in St. Louis 1854–1856." *Missouri Historical Review* 68 (January 1974): 171–85.
Schnell, J. Christopher. "Chicago Versus St. Louis: A Reassessment of the Great Rivalry." *Missouri Historical Review* 71 (April 1977): 245–65.

Shortridge, James. "The Expansion of the Settlement Frontier in Missouri." *Missouri Historical Review* 75 (October 1980): 64–90.

Thernstrom, Stephan and Peter R. Knights. "Men in Motion: Some Data and Speculations about Urban Population Mobility in Nineteenth-Century America." In *Anonymous Americans: Explorations in Nineteenth-Century Social History*, edited by Tamara K. Hareven, 17–47. Englewood Cliffs, N.J., 1971.

Vedder, Richard K. and Lowell E. Gallaway. "Migration and the Old Northwest." In *Essays in Nineteenth-Century Economic History: The Old Northwest*, edited by David C. Klingaman and Richard K. Vedder, 159–76. Athens, Oh., 1975.

Welter, Rush. "The Frontier West as Image of American Society: Conservative Attitudes Before the Civil War." *Mississippi Valley Historical Review* 46 (March 1960): 593–614.

Windell, Marie George. "Reform in the Roaring Forties and Fifties." *Missouri Historical Review* 39 (April 1945): 291–319.

Books

Abbott, Carl. *Boosters and Businessmen: Popular Economic Thought and Urban Growth in the Antebellum Middle West*. Westport, Conn., 1981.

Albion, Robert Greenhalgh. *The Rise of New York Port*. 1939. Reprint. Boston, 1984.

Amos, Harriet E. *Cotton City: Urban Development in Antebellum Mobile*. University, Ala., 1985.

Atherton, Lewis E. *The Pioneer Merchant in Mid-America*. University of Missouri Studies, vol. 14, no. 2. Columbia, Mo., 1939.

———, *The Southern Country Store 1800–1860*. Baton Rouge, La., 1949.

Barclay, Thomas S. *The Movement for Municipal Home Rule in St. Louis*. University of Missouri Studies, vol. 18, no. 3. Columbia, Mo., 1943.

Belcher, Wyatt Winton. *The Economic Rivalry Between St. Louis and Chicago 1850–1880*. Columbia University Studies in History, Economics and Public Law, no. 529. New York, 1947.

Berwanger, Eugene R. *The Frontier Against Slavery: Western Anti-Negro Prejudice and the Slavery Extension Controversy*. Urbana, Ill., 1967.

Billington, Ray Allen. *Land of Savagery, Land of Promise: The European Image of the American Frontier in the Nineteenth Century*. New York, 1981.

———, *The Protestant Crusade, 1800–1860*. Chicago. 1938.

Blumin, Stuart M. *The Emergence of the Middle Class: Social Experience in the American City, 1760–1900*. New York, 1989.

Browne, Gary Lawson. *Baltimore in the Nation, 1789–1861*. Chapel Hill, N.C., 1980.

Cable, John Ray. *The Bank of the State of Missouri*. Columbia University Studies in History, Economics and Public Law, vol. 102, no. 2, New York, 1923.

Chambers, William Nisbet. *Old Bullion Benton: Senator from the New West.* Boston, 1956.

Chittenden, Hiram Martin. *The American Fur Trade of the Far West: A History of the Pioneer Trading Posts and Early Fur Companies of the Missouri Valley and the Rocky Mountains and of the Overland Commerce with Santa Fe.* 2 vols. New York, 1935.

Clark, John G. *The Grain Trade in the Old Northwest.* 1966. Reprint. Westport, Conn., 1980.

Clark, Victor S. *History of Manufactures in the United States.* Vol. 1. 1929. Reprint. New York, 1949.

Clarke, Dwight L. *William Tecumseh Sherman: Gold Rush Banker.* San Francisco, 1969.

Conzen, Kathleen Neils. *Immigrant Milwaukee, 1836–1860.* Cambridge, Mass., 1976.

Cornwell, Charles H. *St. Louis Mayors.* St. Louis, 1965.

Decker, Peter R. *Fortunes and Failures: White-Collar Mobility in Nineteenth-Century San Francisco.* Cambridge, Mass., 1978.

Dillon, Merton L. *Elijah P. Lovejoy, Abolitionist Editor.* Urbana, Ill., 1961.

Doerflinger, Thomas M. *A Vigorous Spirit of Enterprise: Merchants and Economic Development in Revolutionary Philadelphia.* Chapel Hill, N.C., 1986.

Doyle, Don H. *New Men, New Cities, New South: Atlanta, Nashville, Charleston, Mobile, 1860–1910.* Chapel Hill, N.C., 1990.

———, *The Social Order of a Frontier Community: Jacksonville, Illinois, 1825–70.* Urbana, Ill., 1978.

Edwards, Richard and M. Hopewell. *Edwards' Great West and Her Commercial Metropolis, Embracing A General View of the West and a Complete History of St. Louis, From the Landing of Liqueste, in 1764 to the Present Time.* St. Louis, 1860.

Folsom, Burton W. Jr. *Urban Capitalists: Entrepreneurs and City Growth in Pennsylvania's Lackawanna and Lehigh Regions, 1800–1920.* Baltimore, 1981.

Foner, Eric. *Free Soil, Free Labor, Free Men: The Ideology of the Republican Party Before the Civil War.* New York, 1970.

Foner, Philip S. *Business and Slavery: The New York Merchants and the Irrepressible Conflict.* Chapel Hill, N.C., 1941.

Forster, Walter O. *Zion on the Mississippi: The Settlement of the Saxon Lutherans in Missouri 1839–1841.* St. Louis, 1953.

Foster, Charles I. *An Errand of Mercy: The Evangelical United Front, 1790–1837.* Chapel Hill, N.C., 1960.

Fussell, Edwin. *Frontier: American Literature and the American West.* Princeton, 1965.

Gerlach, Russel L. *Immigrants in the Ozarks: A Study in Ethnic Geography.* University of Missouri Studies, vol. 64. Columbia, Mo., 1976.

———, *Settlement Patterns in Missouri: A Study of Population Origins, with a Wall Map.* Columbia, Mo., 1986.

Glaab, Charles N. *Kansas City and the Railroads: Community Policy in the Growth of a Regional Metropolis.* Madison, Wis., 1962.

Goldfield, David R. *Cotton Fields and Skycrapers: Southern City and Region, 1607–1982*. Baton Rouge, La., 1982.

———, *Urban Growth in the Age of Sectionalism: Virginia, 1847–1861*. Baton Rouge, La., 1977.

Green, Constance McLaughlin. *American Cities in the Growth of the Nation*. New York, 1957.

Green, George D. *Finance and Economic Development in the Old South: Louisiana Banking, 1804–1861*. Stanford, Calif., 1972.

Griffen, Clyde, and Sally Griffen. *Natives and Newcomers: The Ordering of Opportunity in Mid-Nineteenth-Century Poughkeepsie*. Cambridge, Mass., 1978.

Haeger, John Denis. *The Investment Frontier: New York Businessmen and the Economic Development of the Old Northwest*. Albany, N.Y., 1981.

Haites, Eric F., James Mak and Gary M. Walton. *Western River Transportation*. Baltimore, 1975.

Hansen, Marcus Lee. *The Atlantic Migration, 1607–1860*. New York, 1961.

Hine, Robert V. *The American West: An Interpretive History*. Boston, 1973.

Hunter, Louis C. *Steamboats on the Western Rivers: An Economic and Technological History*. Cambridge, Mass., 1949.

Jaher, Frederic Cople. *The Urban Establishment: Upper Strata in Boston, New York, Charleston, Chicago, and Los Angeles*. Urbana, Ill., 1982.

James, D. Clayton. *Antebellum Natchez*. Baton Rouge, La., 1968.

Jennings, Marietta. *A Pioneer Merchant of St. Louis, 1810–1820: The Business Career of Christian Wilt*. London, 1939.

Johannsen, Robert W. *Stephen A. Douglas*. New York, 1973.

Johnson, Arthur M., and Barry E. Supple. *Boston Capitalists and Western Railroads: A Study in the Nineteenth-Century Railroad Investment Process*. Cambridge, Mass., 1967.

Johnson, Samuel A. *The Battle Cry for Freedom: The New England Emigrant Aid Company in the Kansas Crusade*. Lawrence, Kans., 1954.

Jones, Fred Mitchell. *Middlemen in the Domestic Trade of the United States*. Illinois Studies in the Social Sciences, vol. 21. Urbana, Ill., 1937.

Kamphoefner, Walter D. *The Westfalians: From Germany to Missouri*. Princeton, 1987.

Karnes, Thomas L. *William Gilpin, Western Nationalist*. Austin, Tex., 1970.

Katz, Michael B. *The People of Hamilton, Canada West: Family and Class in a Mid-Nineteenth-Century City*. Cambridge, Mass., 1975.

———, Michael J. Doucet, and Mark J. Stern. *The Social Organization of Early Industrial Capitalism*. Cambridge, Mass., 1982.

Knights, Peter R. *The Plain People of Boston, 1830–1860: A Study in City Growth*. New York, 1971.

Lantz, Herman R. *A Community in Search of Itself: A Case History of Cairo, Illinois*. Carbondale, Ill., 1972.

Larson, John Lauritz. *Bonds of Enterprise: John Murray Forbes and Western Development in America's Railway Age*. Cambridge, Mass., 1984.

Larson, Lawrence H. *The Urban West at the End of the Frontier*. Lawrence, Kans., 1978.

Lawrence, William. *The Life of Amos A. Lawrence*. Boston, 1899.

Lindstrom, Diane. *Economic Development in the Philadelphia Region, 1810–1850*. New York, 1978.

Lotchin, Roger W. *San Francisco, 1846–1856: From Hamlet to City*. 1974. Reprint. Lincoln, Nebr., 1979.

McCandless, Perry. *A History of Missouri, 1820–1860*. Columbia, Mo., 1972.

McClelland, Peter D., and Richard J. Zeckhauser. *Demographic Dimensions of the New Republic: American Interregional Migration, Vital Statistics, and Manumissions, 1800–1860*. New York, 1982.

McCormick Richard P. *The Second American Party System: Party Formation in the Jacksonian Era*. Chapel Hill, N.C., 1966.

Mahoney, Timothy R. *River Towns in the Great West: The Structures of Provincial Urbanization in the American Midwest, 1820–1870*. New York, 1990.

Mering, John Vollmer. *The Whig Party in Missouri*. University of Missouri Studies, vol. 61. Columbia, Mo., 1967.

Million, John W. *State Aid to Railways in Missouri*. Economic Studies of the University of Chicago, vol. 4. Chicago, 1896.

Norris, James D. *R. G. Dun and Company, 1841–1900: The Development of Credit-Reporting in the Nineteenth Century*. Westport, Conn., 1978.

Oglesby, Richard E. *Manual Lisa and the Opening of the Missouri Fur Trade*. Norman, Okla., 1963.

Parrish, William E. *Turbulent Partnership: Missouri and the Union, 1861–1865*. Columbia, Mo., 1963.

Pease, William H. and Jane H. Pease. *The Web of Progress: Private Values and Public Styles in Boston and Charleston, 1828–1843*. New York, 1985.

Peterson, Norma L. *Freedom and Franchise: The Political Career of B. Gratz Brown*. Columbia, Mo., 1965.

Porter, Kenneth. *John Jacob Astor, Businessman*. 2 vols. Cambridge, Mass., 1931.

Post, T. A. *Truman Marcellus Post, D.D.: A Biography*. Boston, 1891.

Pred, Allan. *City-Systems in Advanced Economies: Past Growth, Present Processes and Future Development Options*. New York, 1977.

————, *The Spatial Dynamics of U.S. Urban-Industrial Growth, 1800-1914: Interpretive and Theoretical Essays*. Cambridge, Mass., 1966.

————, *Urban Growth and the Circulation of Information: The United States System of Cities, 1790–1840*. Cambridge, Mass., 1973.

————, *Urban Growth and City-Systems in the United States, 1840–1860*. Cambridge, Mass., 1980.

Primm, James Neal. *Economic Policy in the Development of a Western State: Missouri, 1820–1860*. Cambridge, Mass., 1954.

————, *Lion of the Valley, St. Louis, Missouri*. Boulder, Colo., 1981.

Rawley, James A. *Race and Politics: "Bleeding Kansas" and the Coming of the Civil War*. Philadelphia, 1969.

Reavis, Logan U. *St. Louis: The Future Great City of the World*. St. Louis, 1875.

Rombauer, Robert J. *The Union Cause in St. Louis in 1861*. St. Louis, 1909.

Russell, James Michael. *Atlanta, 1847–1890: City Building in the Old South and the New.* Baton Rouge, La., 1988.

Saum, Lewis O. *The Popular Mood of Pre-Civil War America.* Westport, Conn., 1980.

Scharf, J. Thomas. *History of St. Louis City and County, From the Earliest Periods to the Present Day: Including Biographical Sketches of Representative Men.* 2 vols. St. Louis, 1883.

Schuyler, William. *An Ambassador of Christ: Being A Biography of the Very Reverend Montgomery Schuyler, D. D.* New York, 1901.

Schweikart, Larry. *Banking in the American South from the Age of Jackson to Reconstruction.* Baton Rouge, La., 1987.

Seavoy, Ronald E. *The Origins of the American Business Corporation, 1784–1855: Broadening the Concept of Public Service During Industrialization.* Westport, Conn., 1982.

Sewell, Richard H. *Ballots for Freedom: Antislavery Politics in the United States, 1837–1860.* New York, 1976.

Shade, William G. *Banks or No Banks: The Money Issue in Western Politics, 1832–1865.* Detroit, 1972.

Sharp, James Roger. *The Jacksonians Versus the Banks: Politics in the States After the Panic of 1837.* New York, 1970.

Smith, Henry Nash. *Virgin Land: The American West as Symbol and Myth.* Cambridge, Mass., 1950.

Smith, William Ernest. *The Francis Preston Blair Family in Politics.* 2 vols. New York, 1933.

Swisher, Walter Samuel. *A History of the Church of the Messiah, 1834–1934.* St. Louis, 1934.

Taylor, George Rogers. *The Transportation Revolution, 1815–1860.* New York, 1951.

Thelen, David. *Paths of Resistance: Tradition and Dignity in Industrializing Missouri.* New York, 1986.

Thernstrom, Stephan. *The Other Bostonians: Poverty and Progress in the American Metropolis, 1880–1970.* Cambridge, Mass., 1973.

———, ed. *Harvard Encyclopedia of American Ethnic Groups.* Cambridge, Mass., 1980.

Trexler, Harrison A. *Slavery in Missouri, 1804–1865.* Johns Hopkins University Studies in Historical and Political Science, ser. 32, no. 2. Baltimore, 1914.

Troen, Selwyn K. *The Public and the Schools: Shaping the St. Louis System, 1838–1920.* Columbia, Mo., 1975.

Unruh, John D., Jr. *The Plains Across: The Overland Emigrants and the Trans-Mississippi West, 1840–1860.* Urbana, Ill., 1979.

Vance, James E., Jr. *The Merchant's World: The Geography of Wholesaling.* Englewood Cliffs, N.J., 1970.

Wade, Louise Carroll. *Chicago's Pride: The Stockyards, Packingtown, and Environs in the Nineteenth Century.* Urbana, Ill., 1987.

Wade, Richard C. *The Urban Frontier: Pioneer Life in Early Pittsburgh, Cincinnati, Lexington, Louisville, and St. Louis.* Cambridge, Mass., 1959.

Weber, Adna Ferrin. *The Growth of Cities in the Nineteenth Century: A Study in Statistics.* Columbia University Studies in History, Economics and Public Law, vol. 11. New York, 1899.

Younger, Edward. *John A. Kasson: Politics and Diplomacy From Lincoln to McKinley.* Iowa City, Iowa, 1955.

Theses

Cochran, Alice Loda. "The Saga of an Irish Immigrant Family: The Descendents of John Mullanphy." Ph.D. diss., St. Louis University, 1958.

Doepke, Dale K. "St. Louis Magazines Before the Civil War, 1832–1860." Ph.D. diss., Washington University, 1963.

Duffner, Robert William. "Slavery in Missouri River Counties, 1820–1865." Ph.D. diss., University of Missouri–Columbia, 1974.

Holt, Glen E. "The Shaping of St. Louis, 1763–1860." Ph.D. diss., University of Chicago, 1975.

Kellner, George Helmuth." The German Element on the Urban Frontier: St. Louis, 1830–1860. Ph.D. diss., University of Missouri–Columbia, 1973.

Ketcham, George A. "Municipal Police Reform: A Comparative Study of Law Enforcement in Cincinnati, Chicago, New Orleans, New York, and St. Louis, 1844–1877." Ph.D. diss., University of Missouri–Columbia, 1967.

Kropp, Simon F. "The Struggle for Limited Liability and General Incorporation Laws in Missouri to 1849." Master's thesis, University of Missouri–Columbia, 1939.

Mahoney, Timothy R. "River Towns in the Great West, 1835–1860." Ph.D. diss., University of Chicago, 1982.

Mayer, Herbert Theodore. "The History of St. Louis, 1837–1847." Master's thesis, Washington University, 1949.

Melom, Galvor Gordon. "The Economic Development of St. Louis, 1803-1846." Ph.D. diss., University of Missouri, Columbia, 1947.

Olson, Audrey Louise. "St. Louis Germans, 1850–1920: The Nature of an Immigrant Community and Its Relation to the Assimilation Process." Ph.D. diss., University of Kansas, 1970.

Parks, Thomas E. "The History of St . Louis, 1827–1836." Master's thesis, Washington University, 1948.

Phelan, Doris Ann." Boosterism in St. Louis, 1810–1860." Ph.D. diss., St. Louis University, 1970.

Reichard, Maximilian Ivan. "The Origins of Urban Police: Freedom and Order in Antebellum St. Louis." Ph.D. diss., Washington University, 1975.

Wells, Eugene T. "St. Louis and Cities West, 1820–1860." Ph.D. diss., University of Kansas, 1951.

Williams, Helen Devault. "Factors in the Growth of St. Louis From 1840 to 1860." Master's thesis, Washington University, 1934.

Index

Printed in the United States
21895LVS00004B/107